SAMS
PUBLISHING

M T W T F S S **24**

Using the *Teach Yourself in 24 Hours* Series

Welcome to the *Teach Yourself in 24 Hours* series. You're probably thinking to yourself, "What? They want me to stay up all night and learn this stuff?" Well, no, not exactly. This series introduces a new concept in teaching you about exciting new products: 24 one-hour lessons, designed to keep your interest and keep you learning. By breaking the learning process into smaller units, you will not be overwhelmed by the complexity of some of the new technologies being introduced in today's market. Each hourly lesson has a number of special items, some old, some new, to help you along.

10 Minutes

In the first 10 minutes of the hour, you will be given a complete list of all of the topics and skills you will have a solid knowledge of by the time you finish the hour. You will be able to know exactly what the hour will bring, with no hidden surprises.

20 Minutes

By the time you have delved into the lesson for 20 minutes, you will know what many of the newest features of the software application are. In the constantly evolving computer arena, knowing everything a program can do will aid you enormously, if not right now, then definitely in the near future.

30 Minutes

Before 30 minutes have passed, you should have learned at least one useful task, oftentimes more. Many of these tasks will take advantage of the newest features of the application. These tasks take the hands-on approach, and tell you exactly which menus and commands you need to step through to accomplish the goal. This approach is found through each lesson in the *24 Hours* series.

40 Minutes

As you will see after 40 minutes, many of the tools you have come to expect from the *Teach Yourself* series are still here. Notes and Tips offer you quick asides into the special tricks of the trade to make your work faster and more productive. Warnings give you the knowledge to avoid those nasty time-consuming errors.

50 Minutes

Along the way, you may run across terms that you haven't seen before. Never before has technology thrown so many new words and acronyms into the language, and the New Terms elements you will find in this series will carefully explain each and every one of them.

60 Minutes

At the end of the hour, you may still have questions that need to be answered. You know the kind—questions on skills or tasks that may come up every day for you, but weren't directly addressed during the hour. That's where the Q&A section can help. By asking and answering the most frequently asked questions about the topics discussed in the hour, Q&A will possibly not only get your specific question answered, it will definitely provide a succinct review of all that you have learned in the hour.

Teach Yourself

WINDOWS NT® 4 WORKSTATION

in 24 Hours

Teach Yourself
WINDOWS
NT® 4
WORKSTATION
in 24 Hours

Martin Kenley, et al.

SAMS
PUBLISHING

201 West 103rd Street
Indianapolis, Indiana 46290

This book is dedicated to my mother, Jean Kenley, who has helped me whenever needed with a gracious and generous heart. Her kindness and support have helped to make this book a reality. It is also for the memory of my father. These memories give me inspiration, happiness, and a deeper understanding of what maturity, discipline, and love are all about.

Copyright © 1997 by Sams Publishing

FIRST EDITION

International Standard Book Number: 0-672-31011-2

Library of Congress Catalog Card Number: 96-70720

2000   99   98   4   3

Interpretation of the printing code: the rightmost double-digit number is the year of the book's printing; the rightmost single-digit, the number of the book's printing. For example, a printing code of 97-1 shows that the first printing of the book occurred in 1997.

Composed in AGaramond and MCPdigital by Macmillan Computer Publishing

Printed in the United States of America

Trademarks

Publisher and President: Richard K. Swadley
Publishing Manager: Dean Miller
Director of Editorial Services: Cindy Morrow
Managing Editor: Jodi Jensen
Director of Marketing: Kelli S. Spencer
Assistant Marketing Managers: Kristina Perry, Rachel Wolfe

Acquisitions Editor
Kim Spilker

Development Editor
Brian-Kent Proffitt

Production Editor
Tonya R. Simpson

Copy Editors
Margaret Berson
Marilyn Stone

Indexer
Erika Millen

Technical Reviewer
Vince Averello

Editorial Coordinator
Katie Wise

Technical Edit Coordinator
Lynette Quinn

Resource Coordinator
Deborah Frisby

Editorial Assistants
Carol Ackerman
Andi Richter
Rhonda Tinch-Mize

Cover Designer
Tim Amrhein

Book Designer
Gary Adair

Copy Writer
David Reichwein

Production Team Supervisors
Brad Chinn
Charlotte Clapp

Production
Jeanne Clark
Cyndi Davis
Janet Seib
Mary Ellen Stephenson

Overview

Appendix

Contents

Appendix

Acknowledgments

I would like to say thanks to the hard-working people at Sams. Over the past few months, I have learned why other authors mention their editors' patience, and are so grateful for it. Thanks for everything Kim Spilker, Brian Proffitt, Robert Bogue, Jeff Koch, and others there. Your assistance was greatly appreciated.

A special thanks also to Gary Neely for the help and technical advice that helped to make this a better book.

About the Authors

Martin Kenley

Martin Kenley works as a computer consultant for Indiana University specializing in troubleshooting operating systems and communications software. He has worked for the university for five years. His interests include music, especially MIDI, hiking, traveling, and cooking different ethnic foods.

Robert L. Bogue

Robert L. Bogue owns Thor Projects, a consulting company located in Indianapolis, Indiana. Thor Projects specializes in solving the networking and integration needs of medium-sized organizations. Rob has been involved in over 50 book projects on topics ranging from Visual Basic to Windows NT to Novell to Microsoft Office. He can be reached at rbogue@iquest.net or (317) 844-5310.

Darren Schubert

Darren Schubert, a graduate of Indiana University's Business School, is an NT Systems Administrator and the acting Network Administrator at the Veterans Administration Medical Center in Indianapolis, Indiana. A former consultant, his client projects involved network design, database design, and PowerBuilder and Visual Basic programming. Darren's current topics of research include NT networking, Cisco router configuration, HP Openview, and Network General Sniffer Network Analyzer. And one of these days, he'll get around to taking those MCSE exams. Darren can be reached at `schubert.darren@indianapolis.va.gov`.

Gary Robert Neely

Gary Robert Neely, 36, lives in Bloomington, Indiana with a wolf and a variable number of ferrets. A graduate of Purdue engineering, he has worked as a contracted software engineer for both the Navy and the Air Force. His work has included database evaluation and design, technical writing, quality assurance, and instruction. He is now a partner in SCIgate Publishing, an Internet publishing and consulting firm. He is a caver, amateur astronomer, occasional rock-hound, and an avid fan of *Babylon 5*. Rob can be reached via e-mail at `grneely@scigate.net`.

Jeff Perkins

Jeff Perkins is a Senior Software Engineer with TYBRIN Corporation. He has been a Program Manager, Team Leader, Project Leader, Technical Leader, and Analyst. A graduate of the United States Air Force Academy, he is a veteran with over 2,500 hours of flying time as a Navigator and Bombardier in the B-52. He has co-authored three other books, *Teach Yourself SQL in 14 Days*, *Teach Yourself ODBC in 21 Days*, and *Teach Yourself ActiveX in 21 Days*.

Tell Us What You Think!

As a reader, you are the most important critic and commentator of our books. We value your opinion and want to know what we're doing right, what we could do better, what areas you'd like to see us publish in, and any other words of wisdom you're willing to pass our way. You can help us make strong books that meet your needs and give you the computer guidance you require.

Do you have access to CompuServe or the World Wide Web? Then check out our CompuServe forum by typing GO SAMS at any prompt. If you prefer the World Wide Web, check out our site at http://www.mcp.com.

JUST A MINUTE

> If you have a technical question about this book, call the technical support line at 317-581-3833.

As the publishing manager of the group that created this book, I welcome your comments. You can fax, e-mail, or write me directly to let me know what you did or didn't like about this book—as well as what we can do to make our books stronger. Here's the information:

Fax: (317) 817-7355

E-mail: Dean Miller
           opsys_mgr@sams.samspublishing.com

Mail: Dean Miller
           Sams Publishing
           201 W. 103rd Street
           Indianapolis, IN 46290

Introduction

Because this book is coming out several months after the release of NT 4 (while many books at the bookstore were written before the final release, using beta or unfinished releases of NT), it has the advantage of incorporating a lot of information about bugs, undiscovered power tips, conflicts with other software, and conflicts with hardware and installation problems. I have had the time to install it in my work environment more than 50 times on a variety of computers with different configurations. There is no shortcut for actual use and experimentation of the final product to actually determine how NT 4 Workstation performs under different conditions. I hope this experience assists the value of this book. I have also followed the online discussions of NT 4 Workstation that have taken place on the World Wide Web, in newsgroups, and in the computer magazines and have incorporated knowledge gathered from these sources.

Who Should Read This Book?

This book covers all of the essential elements of Windows NT 4 Workstation and is designed both for readers who have not used NT 4 before as well as readers who have had some experience but want to learn more. I have designed the book to be useful for those working either in an office environment or at home; both groups of readers will learn all of the useful components of NT 4.

How To Use This Book

This book is designed to teach you topics in one-hour sessions. All of the books in the Sams *Teach Yourself* series enable the reader to start working and become productive with the product as quickly as possible. This book will do that for you! In fact, the first several lessons are concerned with showing you how to use the basic, as well as power elements, of NT 4: it takes you through managing the desktop, file management, the Explorer, installing applications, and optimizing NT 4. It is designed to teach you all the navigational skills you need to be an effective user of NT. If you are not lucky enough to have NT 4 already installed, you can skip to the section dealing with installation issues.

JUST A MINUTE

Although most computer books use jargon that is not understood, this book does not. I have consciously avoided terms that would be unfamiliar to most readers. Only where necessary do I use technical wording, and at these points, I make sure that you can follow the discussion. I include glossaries of technical vocabulary at the end of each lesson.

Each hour, or session, starts with an overview of the topic to inform you of what to expect. The overviews help you determine the nature of the lesson and whether the lesson is relevant to your needs.

Main Section

Each lesson has a main section that discusses the lesson topic in a clear, concise manner by breaking the topic down into logical component parts and explaining each component clearly.

Embedded into each lesson are Tips, Cautions, and Notes inside gray boxes that provide additional information.

TIME SAVER

> A tip informs you of a trick or element that is easily missed by most computer users. You can skip them, but often the tip will show you an easier way to do a task.

CAUTION

> A caution deserves at least as much attention as a tip because cautions point out a problematic element of the operating system. Ignoring the information contained within the caution could have adverse effects on the stability of your computer. These are the most important informational bars in this book.

JUST A MINUTE

> A note is designed to clarify the concept that is being discussed. It elaborates on the subject, and if you are comfortable with your understanding of the subject, you can bypass them without danger.

Workshop

This section of each lesson provides exercises that reinforce concepts learned in the lesson and help you apply them in new situations. You can skip this section, but it is advised that you go through the exercises to see how the concepts can be applied to other common tasks.

Glossary

This portion of each lesson is a mini-dictionary, providing definitions for technical terms used in the lesson. All words are defined as they are used, so the glossary provides a way to review technical terms.

PART
I

The Morning Session: Getting Up and Running with Windows NT 4 Workstation

Hour

Hour 1

Introduction to Windows NT 4

by Martin Kenley

This lesson introduces you to the operating systems that preceded Windows NT and discusses how NT compares with these earlier systems. You will learn about some of the components that are new with Windows NT 4 and why they are important. In addition, the lesson presents a brief overview of the structure and architecture of NT.

The Early Years of Windows

Before 1985, computer operating systems used a command-line interface, which involves the computer user typing commands to interact with the computer. Most of these operating systems were vaguely similar to DOS (Disk Operating System). In 1985, Microsoft released version 1.0 of Windows, and it was not a big hit. In fact, moving PC users away from DOS didn't really happen until five years later, with the release of version 3.0. With this release, Microsoft incorporated much better memory management as well as a nicer user interface; because Windows is all about how the interface looks and feels, this was a critical advancement. (People in the computer industry refer to systems such as Windows as graphical user interfaces [GUIs]).

Windows 3.x

Microsoft later released a more stable version of Windows, the version many people are familiar with: 3.1. This version could run in protected mode and use virtual memory, thus enabling the operating system to access more of the user's computer memory than the earlier limitation of 1MB of RAM. Microsoft developed another version, Windows for Workgroups 3.11, which provided greater built-in networking functions. Although it is not sophisticated by today's standards, Windows for Workgroups did enable offices to share some resources and is more stable than version 3.1. The Program Manager is shown in Figure 1.1.

Figure 1.1.

Here is what the basic Windows 3.1 user interface looked like.

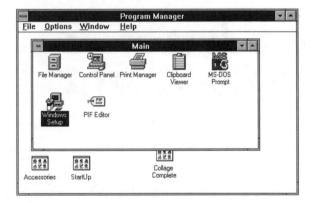

A Big Step Forward: Windows NT

The next big advancement from Microsoft came when it offered Windows NT, which predates Windows 95. Microsoft developers realized that there were computer users out there, especially in the corporate environment, who needed greater stability than that offered by Windows 3.x. The big move here was to discard the underlying DOS and build an operating system with a GUI that could stand on its own and run completely in protected mode, a state in which the microprocessor runs 32-bit protected mode instructions. This would make the computer capable of multitasking and addressing more memory than the previous limitation of 1MB, depending on the processor. *Protected mode* indicates that the processor runs memory protection routines in order to keep two programs running at the same time from crashing into each other.

1

The discarding of DOS enabled Microsoft to move away from the inherent built-in limitations of DOS and devices that use real-mode drivers. (*Real-mode drivers* directly address memory rather than making a call to the operating system and letting it do the work. See the "Glossary" section for more information on real mode.) Although the hardware requirements for NT 4 are greater than those for previous operating systems, so is the payoff in terms of stability and security. Because Windows NT is fully 32-bit (as opposed to Windows 3.1, which is 16-bit), it is capable of moving and processing information in blocks twice as big as those a 16-bit operating system is capable of moving and processing.

Windows 95

In the fall of 1995 Microsoft finally, after many delays, released Windows 95. To maintain backward compatibility, the developers included a fair amount of 16-bit code in the kernel of Windows 95, more than many would have liked. But because many parts of Windows 95 that are responsible for moving information around inside the computer and managing devices (the subsystems) are 32-bit code, the performance of Windows 95 is still fairly robust.

The overhauling of the user interface radically changed the look and feel of the operating system from earlier versions of Windows. Instead of the Program Manager, Windows 95 uses the Explorer. The Explorer is a much more flexible interface and can more easily be customized to suit different users' needs. The Windows 95 interface was so successful that Microsoft developers decided to use it for Windows NT 4 (see Figure 1.2).

Figure 1.2.

The Windows 95 Explorer program was first released with Windows 95 and was later used as the interface for Windows NT 4.

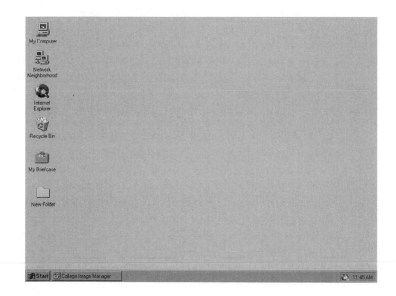

Another great advancement in Windows 95 is the support for third-party devices and multimedia products. With the control panel device you can add new hardware devices, and the operating system will automatically detect it and load drives for it. This feature, known as *plug-and-play*, has made life much easier for computer users who add devices to their computers. Windows NT does not support plug-and-play, and as of this writing, there is still debate over whether it will be incorporated into the next version. Windows 95 has a huge number of device drivers for a wide variety of hardware components; this is especially useful for those interested in doing multimedia. It is capable of supporting a wide variety of sound cards, CD-ROM drives, MIDI devices, and video input/output devices. If compatibility is your top concern and you have a lot of devices that are older, you are probably better off with Windows 95, especially if you don't plan on upgrading those devices anytime soon.

Microsoft also integrated the capability to use preemptive multitasking for 32-bit applications. This feature means that the operating system, rather than an application, determines what receives the control of system resources. Therefore, if you have several 32-bit applications running, Windows 95 will take control from one application and temporarily give it to another application.

Moreover, an application can also have several pieces of code, or *threads*, processed simultaneously. For example, you could send a document to the printer and spell check it at the same time. In this transaction, the word processor passes off the thread for the print job to the operating system, which handles this in the background while you run the spell checker, another thread. A thread is simply a portion of code that can get a share of the operating system's resources and can run concurrently with other threads. An application such as Microsoft Word 7.0 for Windows 95, which is 32-bit, is capable of spawning several threads simultaneously. This enables the operating system to process a thread, taking control away from the application and giving it to another thread. Similarly, if you have two 32-bit coded applications open, Windows 95 regulates the system resources and time to each application, instead of letting the application assign its own resources. This capability to process several threads together is called *multithreading*.

Under Windows 3.1, applications used cooperative multitasking, which is not as good at managing system resources. Using this scheme, an application is supposed to periodically check the operating system's message queue for other tasks that are pending and then relinquish control to the system. However, it is not uncommon for an application to be lazy about checking the queue and therefore hog the central processing unit (CPU). Even worse, if that application freezes, the operating system has no way to recover, because it is waiting for the application to return control back to it; and if the application crashes, it would not be able to pass control back to the system.

Advantages of Windows NT 4 Workstation

There are many advantages Windows NT 4 has over other Windows operating systems. Microsoft added a host of new features that make NT 4 superior on several levels, and many components that are not new have been enhanced to work better and faster. Some of the main features follow:

☐ One of the primary reasons why computer users will want to upgrade to Windows NT 4 is for the greater speed and stability it offers. Many of the subsystems have been upgraded from NT 3.51 for improved performance. As compared with the 16-bit way in which Windows 3.1 operates, the 32-bit kernel of NT is significantly faster. And the drivers are all 32-bit as well, so they can communicate more quickly. Even compared with Windows 95, which has a substantial amount of 32-bit code, NT is more robust.

☐ Moreover, the nature of the multitasking and multithreading is superior in NT 4. Every 32-bit application run under Windows NT can be handled by its preemptive multitasking capabilities. This means that no single program can dominate the CPU, unless of course it is an older 16-bit application. The end result is that you can perform more tasks without waiting. Windows NT gives each 16-bit application its own address space (memory) to run, whereas Windows 95 devotes one single block of address space for all of your older 16-bit applications to run in. So under the NT architecture, each 16-bit application can be multitasked with other 16-bit applications or any newer 32-bit applications you have running, allowing for a more efficient work environment because the older applications don't have to compete with each other for resource time (CPU cycles).

The multithreading capabilities enable a program to execute several threads at the same time. Windows 95 and NT 4 have similar multithreading capabilities.

☐ Unlike Windows 3.1 and Windows NT 3.51, the new version of NT has a new user interface, the Explorer, which was first released as the interface for Windows 95. The main elements include a desktop, enabling you to customize your workspace; a taskbar, giving you access to the Start menu and showing which applications are open; a Start menu, which gives you access to the applications and resources on your computer; an improved Task Manager, which enables you to see which applications are running and to terminate or switch among them, and also graphically displays the operating system's current memory usage, CPU usage, and processes.

☐ Microsoft has included an enhanced Windows NT 4 Diagnostics program (see Figure 1.3) for troubleshooting problems, collecting information about the resources devices are using, and checking build number. You can get a list of which IRQs (interrupt requests), DMAs (direct memory access), and I/O (input/output) addresses are used and what devices are using them. These are vital system resources used by components inside your computer.

Figure 1.3.

The Windows NT 4 Diagnostics program helps users configure their computers more easily.

For the corporate environment, there are several features that make it worthwhile to upgrade to the new version:

☐ Peer Web Services provide a way to publish both documents and interactive applications on your Web site. These services have a lot in common with the Internet Information Server, which comes with Windows NT 4 Server.

☐ Point-to-Point Tunneling Protocol (PPTP) is another component many corporate managers will find useful. This networking protocol is used with Remote Access Services (RAS) to enable local area network (LAN) traffic to cross a wide area network (WAN). It is very flexible because it works with any protocol; the connection also is encrypted and secure.

☐ An enhanced networking control panel (see Figure 1.4) makes network administration easier for LAN administrators because it now contains a single location where you can set the protocols, change or add adapters and bindings, and choose the computer name.

☐ The security features of Windows NT 3.51 and 4 Workstation are far superior to anything that either Windows 3.1 or Windows 95 can offer you. NT enables you to securely share local resources (files, directories, volumes, printers, and so on) by choosing groups and individual persons with whom you would like to share the item(s), as well as set the permissions those persons receive. Most of the account management you will need to do is in the User Manager (see Figure 1.5).

1

Figure 1.4.

A more useful networking manager lets you do more configuring in one location.

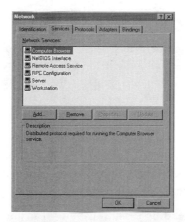

Figure 1.5.

The User Manager centralizes security and sharing management.

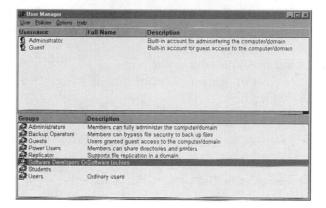

Summary

This hour presented a quick look at how Windows NT fits into the family of Microsoft operating systems and outlines some of the advantages that it offers. Although the concepts in this lesson will not make you more proficient at using NT directly, understanding its architecture will provide you with information needed to understand other concepts you learn in this book.

Workshop

The Workshop helps you solidify the skills you learned this hour.

Glossary

32-bit capable   This refers to applications that are programmed to use the computer's internal system architecture to a much greater extent than under DOS or Windows 3.1, which are 16-bit operating systems. Of course, for a 32-bit application to have this capability, the computer's operating system also must be coded for this functionality. A major part of this involves the capability to send data on the bus in 32-bit chunks.

cooperative multitasking   The capability of an operating system to launch and run several applications simultaneously, but giving control to the application in the foreground, which is supposed to check the task queue and relinquish control back to the operating system after a given time.

multithreading   The capability of an operating system to take threads from an application and direct them to be processed independently without interrupting other processes.

operating system   The most elemental and important piece of software on a computer. For example, the operating system controls the flow of information inside the computer to the different peripheral devices, is in charge of file management, and interacts with device drivers. Examples of operating systems include MS-DOS, Apple's System 7, Windows 3.l, and Windows NT.

plug-and-play   Plug-and-play is a standard that some newer devices support, meaning that if your system supports plug-and-play, you can install the device and your system will detect the device when you restart and configure its settings.

preemptive multitasking   The capability of an operating system to run several applications simultaneously and control the length of time each application receives for its processes. In effect, the operating system behaves as a traffic cop, providing a smooth flow of processing and regulating the flow of threads to the CPU.

protected mode   In this state, the microprocessor runs 32-bit protected mode instructions, capable of multitasking, and can address more memory than 1MB, depending on the processor. The term *protected mode* comes from the fact that the processor runs memory protection routines in order to keep two programs running at the same time from crashing into each other. Device drivers that use real-mode drivers throw the processor into real mode when the driver is used, causing the system to slow down and become less stable. Windows 95 attempts to use protected mode drivers completely but can run real-mode drivers if no protected-mode drivers exist. Windows NT can use only protected-mode drivers, so if you have an older CD-ROM drive that does not have protected-mode drivers, NT will not recognize it.

1

real mode   An operating mode of which 80286 and higher x86 processors are capable that enables an application to write and read directly to memory addresses; this is the conventional way DOS works. Developers at Intel created two modes to maintain backward compatibility with previous hardware components. A processor operating in real mode behaves as though it were an 8086 Intel processor (the original PC processor), thus limiting its capability to address a maximum of 1MB of memory. Of course, real-mode processors cannot multitask, either. The reason for moving away from this scheme to protected mode is because applications could crash into each other's memory space and corrupt the application or data.

thread   A segment of an application's code that can be processed as a unit or item. For example, when a spreadsheet recalculates the figures in it, this recalculation can be a thread that the application could "spawn" or pass off to the processor, while the user continues to add data to the spreadsheet.

Exercises

1. Which version of Windows introduced protected mode?
2. Does Windows NT need DOS to run?
3. Does Windows 95 use 16-bit code in the kernel?
4. Is Windows 3.1 capable of doing preemptive multitasking?
5. What is the difference between preemptive and cooperative multitasking?
6. Name two benefits to upgrading to Windows NT.

I

Hour **2**

The Desktop and the Explorer

by Martin Kenley

The Explorer interface is a dramatic break from the past. It enables you to see your resources—files, folders, applications, drives, and printers—from new and exciting perspectives. It also enables you to control and manipulate these resources in more creative ways, and certainly in ways more intuitive than either Windows 3.*x* or DOS does. The shift Microsoft has been promoting since moving from DOS has been an increasingly graphics- and icon-driven operating system. With the release of Windows 95, another big advancement occurred. Microsoft developers conducted studies on the user interface, and because the results were positive, they decided to use this interface with NT. As you learn today, the Explorer interface gives you many options to explore your computer's resources.

The best way to view the Explorer desktop interface is to ask, "How does it make my work easier?" That is what today's lesson is all about: how to use the Explorer to access programs and files, do searches, view your files and applications, create shortcuts, and manage your files. Users who are familiar with Windows 3.*x* and

Windows NT 3.*x* will find a great deal more flexibility built into NT 4. If you are familiar with Windows 95, you might learn some tips you had not previously discovered.

The Explorer interface offers more ways to arrange your workspace, which is now called the *desktop*, than previous Windows versions. You can put practically any kind of resource you need on the desktop—a printer, a shortcut to a drive or volume, a shortcut to a folder or document, or a shortcut to an application. Having these resources on the desktop lets you access them more easily and quickly. Rather than navigating through your hard drive and locating the file or application you need, you can have it at your fingertips on the desktop. Start by looking at the resources that NT 4 puts on the desktop by default.

The Windows NT Desktop

Figure 2.1 shows how the desktop looks. By default, NT will put several icons (visual representations of resources) on the desktop:

- ☐ My Computer
- ☐ Network Neighborhood
- ☐ Inbox
- ☐ Briefcase
- ☐ Recycle Bin
- ☐ Taskbar
- ☐ Start menu

Figure 2.1.

All the elements of the Microsoft Explorer desktop can be modified and configured to suit your own personal look and feel.

2

The first icon, My Computer, represents your computer and all of the resources in it. Whether you want to double-click it to access resources is a matter of preference, but I will show you more convenient ways to access items you frequently use.

The Briefcase is a handy way to coordinate files and folders between a desktop and a laptop.

The Network Neighborhood icon represents all the resources available on the network to which your computer is attached. If you are not connected directly to a network and do not use PPP or SLIP to dial into an Internet service provider, you will have no use for this icon and might want to remove it.

The Recycle Bin is a trash can in which you can drag items no longer needed. NT's taskbar shows you which resources are open; you can quickly change to any open resource by clicking it in the taskbar. The Start menu is another very important resource, similar to My Computer, in that it gives you access to most of the resources on your computer.

The Inbox enables you to connect to your mail account, whether you have a network connection or use a modem, and download (transfer to your local machine) and send mail messages, as well as manage mail in other ways.

Each of the items just mentioned can be configured to be set up exactly as you would like. In the following sections you will take a detailed look at a few of these resources and learn how to customize them before you look at the Explorer program.

My Computer

You either have been or will be using the My Computer icon quite frequently. Figure 2.2 shows an example of the resources found in My Computer. Note that inside the My Computer icon you can see two categories of items:

☐ You can access the contents of the drives—floppy disk drives (A: and B: if you have them), hard disk drives (C:, D:, E:, J:, and L:), CD-ROM drives (G:), and any removable drives (the F: drive is a removable drive), as well as any mapped network (remote) drives.

☐ You can also access and configure resources such as printers, the Control Panel, and dial-up networks by using the corresponding folders.

Now look at how to open My Computer:

1. Move your mouse pointer until its arrow is resting on top of the My Computer icon.

2. Now, hold the mouse firm and steady so it does not move, and click the left mouse button two times quickly.

Figure 2.2.

*My Computer contains
all of the computer's
resources.*

When you do this, the My Computer icon will open and present a window, as shown in
Figure 2.2. You will use this same technique to open folders and hard drive icons.

Within My Computer you also have menus at the top, which will vary depending on which
item is selected. If you click an item one time, the item is selected and you can then perform
actions on the item, as you will see in the section "The Toolbar." If, on the other hand, you
double-click an item in My Computer, you will open it and another window appears that
displays the contents of the item you clicked.

Display the contents of My Computer by double-clicking the icon. As with most of the
resources NT provides, there are a variety of ways to display your computer's files, folders,
and applications.

The Toolbar

The toolbar is a row of icons that appear under the menus at the top of the window. Follow
these steps to learn more about it:

1. Go to the View menu and click Toolbar; a check mark will appear next to it. This
   causes the toolbar to be displayed, enabling you to quickly perform different
   actions on files and folders.
2. To determine what the different tools do, move the mouse pointer on top of the
   first icon on the toolbar. Don't click the mouse button; a small information
   window appears stating what that icon does if you click it. Try the others.

Now try selecting other options under View. NT provides the option of viewing the contents
of your computer as icons (small and large), names, or names with details (sizes and free
space).

☐ Go to the View menu and choose Large Icons. Notice how this affects the icons in
   the window.

☐ Go to the View menu and choose Small Icons.

☐ Go to the View menu and choose Details. This is a useful default option because it
   will display information about each resource.

2

☐ Finally, go to the View menu and choose Arrange Icons | by Free Space. This will reorder the drives with the hard drive or partition with the most free space at the top of the list.

Selecting the Status Bar under View and clicking the C: disk drive displays the size of the drive and how much free space remains on the drive on the status bar at the bottom of the window. If you then double-click the C: drive to display its contents, the status bar displays the number of objects inside the drive as well as the total size of the "loose" files inside of it. (The loose files consist of all the files that are not inside directories or folders. So, the status bar does not calculate the folder sizes and add them into the total.)

TIME SAVER

> If you find your desktop cluttered with folders and you want to shut them all with a single keystroke, try the following: Before clicking the X box in the upper-right corner of the window, hold down the Shift key. Doing so will cause all open folders to close.

You might want to experiment with the settings in the View menu offered under Options. NT gives you the ability to view folders in different ways when you open a new one.

You can set NT to open a new window to display the contents of the folder, or you can have the current window modify itself and display the contents. Try both and see which way is most suitable to you. If you want to move files around by opening different windows and then dragging your file to different locations, you might want to have NT open a new window after you double-click a folder. However, you can use the Explorer to handle your file management (see the section "The Explorer," later in this lesson).

TIME SAVER

> If you choose to keep the default setting of having a new window pop up each time a folder is opened but on occasion prefer to have the current window replaced by the new folder you are opening, you can do so by holding down the Ctrl key while clicking the folder. Conversely, if you have NT set so that a new window replaces the existing window, holding the Ctrl key down while double-clicking will open a separate window rather than replace the current window.

Options has two other tabs: View and File Types. Clicking the View tab presents several important options. NT gives you the option of viewing all the files on your computer or automatically hiding system files and shared program files. If the computer you are configuring will have multiple users and you want to avoid the possibility of one user accidentally deleting system files, this is a good option to choose. Of course, NT provides more powerful ways of guarding against such accidents, and that is by setting privileges for different resources (discussed in Hour 11, "Security: Planning a Secure System"). You are also given the option of viewing the entire path for the location of the resource you have selected. The path will appear in the title bar if you have this option selected. I recommend doing so because it is easy to become lost if you are like me and have a tendency to open up many windows at the same time. Regardless of the number of windows you open, you can always see where the folder resides by looking at its path in the title bar.

Finally, you can manually associate applications with files if you need to. Under normal circumstances, NT will automatically associate files with the proper applications, but there might be times when you want to change the application used to open a particular type of file. To do this, go to View | Options, and then select the File Types tab at the top of the window. Choose the type of file for which you want to change the association, and click Edit. This brings up a new dialog box showing the properties for the specific file. Click Open and then choose Edit; NT will display the application (and its path) in a new window. You can now edit the associated application by typing in a new application. Be sure to include its path.

Dealing with Floppy Disks: Formatting and Copying

If you click one time on the floppy disk icon and go to the File menu, you will find that one of the options is to copy the disk. When a floppy disk is selected, you also have the option of formatting the disk under the File menu.

JUST A MINUTE

You can also use the File Manager to perform actions on a floppy disk as well as for any other file management task. To launch the File Manager, click the Start menu, or, if you have an Explorer-enhanced keyboard (the key between the Alt key and the Ctrl key will have the Windows 95 logo on it; this is the Start key), press the Start button, which pulls up the Start menu, and go to Run. On a regular keyboard, press Ctrl and Esc at the same time. This activates the Start menu; again, go to Run. At the Run window, type WINFILE to launch File Manager. After File Manager has opened, go to the Disk menu and select either Format or Copy.

Copying the Disk to a Hard Drive

To copy the contents of a floppy disk to your computer's hard drive, follow these instructions:

1. Double-click My Computer to open it.

2. Double-click the drive to which you want to copy the disk.

3. Create a folder for the contents of the floppy disk by positioning the mouse inside the window that represents the drive you are copying the floppy disk to (but make sure the mouse is not touching a folder or file).

4. Right-click the mouse button. When the pop-up menu appears, go to New | Folder, and NT will automatically create a new folder on the hard drive.

5. When the folder is created, its name is highlighted. You can just begin typing the new name, and it will replace the default name (New Folder) with what you type.

JUST A MINUTE

When you right-click inside a hard drive (make sure your mouse isn't on a folder or document icon) you see the pop-up menu as shown in Figure 2.3. If you right-click a document icon, you will get a slightly different menu. Try right-clicking various objects and explore the properties of different objects. Right-clicking a floppy disk icon gives you several options, one of which is to format the disk (see Figure 2.4).

Figure 2.3.
Right-clicking a hard disk provides a pop-up menu to let you quickly access various functions you can perform on the hard drive.

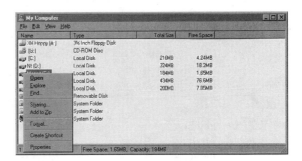

Figure 2.4.
The pop-up menu NT provides when you right-click a floppy disk has different options.

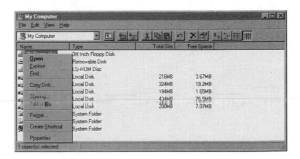

Now you can drag the floppy disk icon on top of the new folder and release the mouse button, and the contents of the disk will be copied into the folder. Or, you could double-click the floppy disk icon to display its contents and select specific items to copy into the new folder. To select items that are not next to each other, hold down the Ctrl key while you click items. To select a list of consecutive items, hold down the Shift key. First, click the item at the top of your list, and then hold the Shift key down and click the last item you want to select. All items in between are automatically selected as well.

Copying Files: The "Send To" Option

When you right-click a file, NT gives you a new option of sending it to a specific location (see Figure 2.5). NT provides two default locations: the floppy drive and the Briefcase. Fortunately, you can add choices to the Send To menu option as follows:

1. Locate the Send To folder in the WINNT/Profiles/X directory (substitute your login name for X) and double-click it. After it opens, you will see the two default locations: floppy disk and Briefcase.

2. To add more locations, such as a printer (to be able to send jobs directly to the printer) or other folders, just drag a shortcut of the desired resource to this folder, and it will appear in the Send To menu. To drag a shortcut, hold the mouse button down while the arrow is touching the Shortcut icon, and then move the mouse so the shortcut moves. To create a shortcut, right-click the object and choose Create Shortcut from the pop-up menu.

3. Each user on your computer can thus modify the Send To folder by adding to the Send To folder in his or her profile. Changes made by one user will not affect other users as long as they have different login names.

Figure 2.5.

When you right-click a file, NT provides a special option, Send To, which lets you directly copy the file to any location in the Send To folder.

2

The Explorer

Microsoft developers put a lot of thought into the Explorer interface. You will find its flexibility and power amazing. If you are used to using the Windows 3.*x* File Manager or DOS to manage files, you will see that all the capabilities that you are used to having are present, plus quite a bit more.

Just like My Computer, the Explorer shows you all of your computer's resources, with the addition of one new one: the desktop. If you have shortcuts on your desktop, the Explorer will show them if you click the desktop icon on the left side of the Explorer window. You have a choice of views, as you do whenever you are viewing a folder that has files or folders in it. (Review the "My Computer" section to refresh your memory on what options the View menu provides.)

Go to the View menu and make sure that the toolbar has a check next to it (if not, select it with the mouse) and look at some of the tools it offers. Figure 2.6 shows the Explorer along with the toolbar at the top of the window.

Figure 2.6.

The Explorer provides you with different ways for viewing your resources.

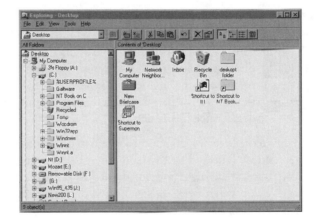

 Starting at the left, the Up One Level Button will take you up one level in the hierarchy. If you are inside a directory, it will take you to the folder's parent directory. If there is no parent directory, then this icon will be gray, and you cannot select it.

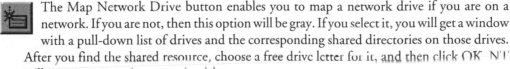 The Map Network Drive button enables you to map a network drive if you are on a network. If you are not, then this option will be gray. If you select it, you will get a window with a pull-down list of drives and the corresponding shared directories on those drives. After you find the shared resource, choose a free drive letter for it, and then click OK. NT will prompt you to log onto the drive.

The Disconnect Network Drive button will be gray if you have not connected to any drives.

 The scissors button represents the Cut option. Select an icon that represents any type of file, and click the scissors. Then, select a new folder and click Paste. The entire file is moved to the new location, not copied.

 The Copy icon enables you to select a document icon and place a copy in the Explorer's clipboard. You can then navigate to another folder and click the Paste icon to copy a clone to the new location.

 The picture of the clipboard is the Paste button. Choose it to paste an item from the clipboard to the desired location.

 With the Undo button, you can reverse your previous action.

 The Delete button is for deleting items. Click an item you no longer need and then click here.

 The Properties button is useful because it enables you to display the properties of any item you have selected. Click once on an object, and then click the Properties button.

 These four icons (Large icons, Small icons, List, and Details) let you view the directories and files in different ways. Clicking the first button displays the resources using large icons; the next button displays the resources using small icons; the third displays a list, and the last button displays the resources by name with details such as size and type.

The Explorer uses a hierarchical scheme to display the items. At the top of the hierarchy is the desktop, followed by My Computer; below it are the disk drives, Network Neighborhood, Recycle Bin, Briefcase, and the desktop folder. Your disk drives and printer and control panel folders will have a plus sign next to them indicating that you can click them to display their contents.

The other menu items here are similar to those given when you double-click My Computer; the one important difference is that you have a Tools menu with new options (see Figure 2.7).

Finding Files and Folders

The Find option under Tools is very useful. Whenever you are unable to find a folder or file—or even a computer on your network—use the Find option. Even if you are unsure of the exact name, you can use a wildcard, the asterisk (*). For example, suppose you are looking for a file that begins with the word ANNUAL, but you are not sure what is after that. Type ANNUAL*, which tells the computer to find all documents beginning with that word. The NT Explorer enables you to use the same trick to find computers on your network. Again, go to Tools | Find, but this time choose Computer rather than File or Folders.

Figure 2.7.

The Tools menu in Explorer provides a quick way to find resources.

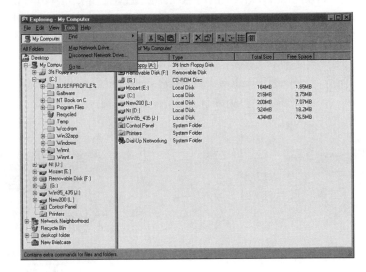

The Recycle Bin

The Recycle Bin is your desktop trash can. You can drag items into it, although it is usually more convenient to simply select the items and press Delete. The difference between deleting items under NT and deleting them under Windows 3.*x* or DOS is that under NT 4, recovering an item you accidentally deleted is easier.

You can open the Recycle Bin by directly double-clicking it, or by using the Explorer application (see Figure 2.8). To empty it, go to the File menu and choose Empty. The advantage of saving the items moved to the Recycle Bin is that if you delete something by mistake and have not emptied the Recycle Bin, you can simply drag the item out of the Bin.

Figure 2.8.

NT's Recycle Bin stores items that have been deleted until you empty it.

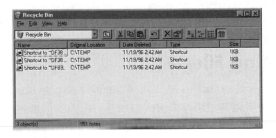

Forcing the Recycle Bin to Remain Empty

If you don't want items saved in the Recycle Bin, but rather prefer to have them immediately removed, you can change the default setting by following these steps:

1. Right-click the Recycle Bin from the desktop.
2. Choose Properties in the pop-up menu.
3. A new window appears, as shown in Figure 2.9. Choose Global.
4. Choose "Do not move files to the Recycle Bin. Remove files immediately on delete."

Figure 2.9.

Customizing the settings for the Recycle Bin.

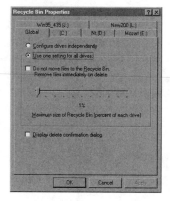

Alternatively, NT lets you set the amount of space that the Recycle Bin can occupy before it needs to empty some items.

The Taskbar

The taskbar at the bottom of the screen displays which programs and file folders you have open. It is a handy navigational tool: Simply click any of the items listed on the taskbar, and it automatically pops up. You can still use the old Windows 3.*x* method of holding down the Alt key and pressing Tab to cycle through the open documents. Notice that as you open more items, the space that holds each item on the taskbar shrinks to accommodate more items. If you have too many items to comfortably display them, then you might want to increase the size of the taskbar. Move the mouse down to it until the pointer has two arrows, hold the mouse button down, and drag the bar up. It will increase in size and be easier to read.

JUST A MINUTE

You will also see that on the right side of the taskbar is a clock and a space to display controls. If you have a sound card, a volume control will appear here. Some programs put additional controls here. Norton Utilities for NT locates several icons here for quick access. You can click any item in this space to launch the associated application (see Figure 2.10). If you click the clock, it gives you the current date.

Figure 2.10.

The NT taskbar is a handy navigational tool for switching to open folders or applications.

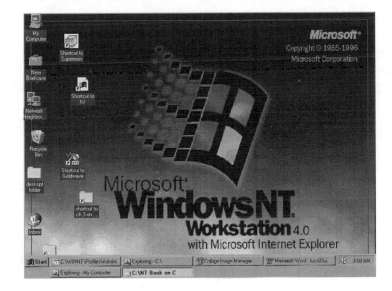

Summary

In this hour, you have learned tasks that you will be using every day with Windows NT. If much of the material was unfamiliar to you, I urge you to review it and try different options as suggested. A good understanding of the material here is crucial to becoming efficient and productive.

Workshop

The Workshop helps you solidify the skills you learned this hour.

Glossary

desktop When you first launch Windows NT and log onto the computer, the first thing you see is a desktop, which shows you the basic resources of your computer (refer to Figure 2.1).

Explorer   A built-in navigational tool that Windows 95 and Windows NT use for a variety of purposes, such as file management and searching for files.

File Manager   If you are used to the File Manager of Windows 3.*x*, you can still use it under NT. You need to type WINFILE in the Run box (Start | Run).

folders   When you open your hard drive, you will see many directories or folders. They are a way of organizing your work. You can create a folder to store your personal letters, for example. Within it, you might have a folder for letters 1996 and another for letters 1997.

formatting   To use a floppy disk, it must be formatted first. This prepares the surface of the disk for use.

Start menu   The Start menu allows you to access all the resources your computer has and is also a convenient way to access your applications and documents; it is possible to customize it, as it is many of the features of NT.

taskbar   Located at the bottom of your computer screen, the Explorer taskbar shows you which applications and folders are open.

Exercise 3.1: Practicing File Management

1. Create a small file using a word processor and save it. Exit the word processor. Move the file from its current location to a floppy disk. When you move a file rather than copy it, you should be moving only *one* file. When you copy a file, you essentially create a second file that appears in the new location, while the original file stays in its original location.

2. Now, instead of moving the file from its original location to a floppy, copy the file to the floppy disk.

3. Create a temporary folder on your C: drive and label it TEMP. Copy the file to this location.

Exercise 3.2: General Navigational Practice

1. Go to the Start menu to Settings to Task bar. Following the instructions in this lesson, practice using the settings for the taskbar. Add a new program to the Start menu.

2. Create a shortcut to one of your most frequently used applications and put it on the desktop. To create a shortcut, first find the application, for example WordPerfect.EXE, and right-click it. Choose Shortcut from the pop-up menu.

3. Open the Explorer and practice copying a file from your hard drive to the floppy drive and vice versa.

2

Hour 3

Getting Started: Running NT for the First Time and Configuring the Desktop

by Martin Kenley

The first part of this hour is devoted to the process of booting NT. It is designed to give you a stronger understanding of NT, particularly how NT boots up, which files are needed, how to control the process, and how to troubleshoot the startup process. The information presented here will be useful for information managers, technical support personnel, and home users willing to troubleshoot their own problems, which I encourage end users to try. If you work in an environment in which support is provided and you don't have an interest in the "behind-the-scenes" working of NT, feel free to skip ahead to the "Configuring the Desktop" section.

The second part of the hour involves desktop and file management and backups. Most users should look at this section because it provides essential information on using NT. You are likely to find important information in the discussion of the items inside the Control Panel folder, because when it comes to customizing and configuring your computer, the Control Panel is at the heart of the process.

Booting Your NT Workstation

When you press the power button on your computer, many things happen. In this section you'll go through the process, beginning with the Power-On Self-Test, and end with a lesson on the NT boot process and how to troubleshoot it.

Your computer goes through the following steps to power all the way up:

1. The Power-On Self-Test (POST) runs.
2. The boot search process begins.
3. The NT boot loader (NTLDR) scans the boot.ini.
4. The user makes a selection from the Boot menu.
5. The loader runs NTDETECT.
6. The blue screen stage: basic components of NT are loaded.
7. NT makes calls to the Registry for driver information.
8. NT loads the basic services.
9. NT loads the higher-level components.
10. The NT welcome box appears, prompting the user to log on.
11. After the user logs on, NT loads information from his or her user profile.

Let's start at the beginning and take a closer look at these steps.

The Power-On Self-Test (POST)

The first few seconds after you have turned the power on, it might seem as though nothing is happening, but in reality, your computer is sending signals throughout various components to ensure that they are in proper working order.

First, the CPU sends a signal to the ROM chips on the motherboard, prompting them to begin their boot program. During their booting process, electrical signals are sent to verify the working order of components. First, the central processing unit (CPU), which is your 486 or Pentium chip, tests itself and the integrity of the POST.

3

Next, the CPU tests the system bus, the electrical circuits that connect all the components to one another. If all has gone well, the boot process will display the adapter's memory. At this point, the BIOS code for the video adapter is integrated into the system's BIOS.

The computer's random access memory (RAM) is tested. RAM actually is controlled to a certain extent by the user (more can be added to the computer, and the user determines what is written to RAM; read-only memory [ROM] is not controlled by the user). Data is written to each of the chips, and the accuracy of the data is then checked.

The boot process next checks for a keyboard and queries whether the user has pressed any keys. Disk drives are then tested, and the data is checked against the information held in the Complementary Metal Oxide Semiconductor (CMOS, an area of memory that holds information about your computer when it is turned off). Finally, any controller cards (such as a SCSI hard drive/peripheral controller) that have their own BIOS are tested, and the BIOS is incorporated into the main system BIOS.

If the computer encounters any problems during the POST, the user is alerted by a specific type of beep through the computer's speaker. The most common types of errors are listed in Table 3.1.

Table 3.1. Error beep messages during the POST.

Number and type of beeps	What monitor displays	Most likely problem
1 short beep	No problem, normal	
1 short, 1 long beep	Nothing on the monitor	Monitor problem
2 short beeps	Anything	Either memory or monitor
1 long, 1 short beep	Anything	Motherboard
1 long, two short beeps	Anything	Monitor
1 long, three short beeps	Anything	Monitor

Now that your PC has tested its hardware, it is ready to actually begin to load the operating system. There is one more brief step to outline that is common to Intel machines before we get into the NT-specific boot process.

Boot Search

After running the POST, the bootstrap (code which is stored in the ROM) will search the hard drives for an operating system. Most computers are set to check the floppy drive first for a disk with an operating system before checking the hard drives. This enables you to boot from a floppy if your operating system on the hard drive has crashed. If no floppy is available, it searches the hard drive, specifically its Master Boot Record (MBR), which is loaded into memory. A program from it is run that examines a table known as the Partition Boot Record; here, information about the active partition is stored. The active partition is where the operating system is stored. Up to this point, the process outlined here occurs on all Intel-based computers, regardless of the operating system.

NT-Specific Stages of the Boot Process

Now the boot sector from the active partition is loaded into memory, in this case NTLDR.BIN. Several files are necessary for the loading process to continue: BOOT.INI, BOOTSECT.DOS (if you have two operating systems on your computer), and NTDETECT.COM. NT expects to find these files in the root folder of the C: drive, if it is your boot disk. If you are booting off a SCSI hard drive, you will have one more file, Ntbootdd.sys, which should be in the root folder.

The NTLDR.BIN file sends code to the processor (CPU), which forces it to operate according to the 32-bit flat memory model. The computer can now support up to 4GB of memory. NTLDR.BIN then determines the type of file system NT is using (FAT, NTFS, or HPFS) and then reads the BOOT.INI. Your computer can now list your operating systems so you can select which one you want to load. By default, NT will wait a specified period of time before making the choice for you.

NTLDR.BIN makes a call to NTDETECT.COM, which checks your hardware and passes the list to NTLDR so the items can be put into the Registry later. After this, four stages remain: loading the kernel, initializing the kernel, loading services, and starting the subsystems.

First, while the kernel is being loaded, two specific modules are loaded: the Hardware Abstraction and information from the system involving drives and services. While this happens you will see dots or periods appear across the top of the screen.

Next, the kernel is initialized, and NT searches the system for specific drives to load. The computer screen is blue during this phase of the boot process.

The third step is the services load phase. All programs in the HKEY_LOCAL_MACHINE\SYSTEM\CurrentControlSet\control\Session Manager:BootExecute directory are loaded and run. NT also performs a disk check on all partitions, and then sets up a *pagefile*, a portion of hard drive space used only by NT that enables it to swap code out of RAM to the pagefile. (You learn more about this in Hour 5, "Optimizing Windows NT Memory.")

The last step is the subsystem start phase. Now the WINLOGON.EXE file starts the Local Security Authority application, and the user is prompted to log on.

3

Troubleshooting and Controlling the Booting Process

Fortunately, the developers of NT built in several methods that let you have some control over the boot-up process. There are two general ways to do this: Select "Last Good Known Configuration" when NT switches to the black screen and lists this option, or edit the contents of the boot.ini file.

Regarding the first option, you must be ready to invoke the Last Good Known Configuration when you see it during the start-up process. You will be prompted to press the spacebar. If you do so, NT will use the configuration information from the Registry that was used the last time you successfully logged onto the computer. For example, if you just installed a device and NT will not properly boot, you can reboot and choose this option.

Editing boot.ini

The boot.ini file controls the operating system menu that NT provides during boot-up. You can change the two items inside it by either editing the file or choosing the System control panel. The control panel device is easier and less likely to introduce errors into the file, making it the preferred method. Therefore, use it now to modify the boot process:

1. Go to Start | Settings | Control Panel.
2. When the Control Panel window is open, double-click the System icon.
3. After you have opened the System control panel device, choose the Startup/Shutdown tab at the top of the window (see Figure 3.1).

Figure 3.1.

The System control panel device enables you to modify the boot process for NT.

4. The first choice you can make lets you select the default operating system to boot up. Clicking the arrow in the System Startup window brings up the list of installed systems that NT has detected; you can click any operating system in the list, thereby setting it as the default choice, which NT will boot after a certain period of time (see step 5).

5. The second configurable item is the amount of time you have to choose from the list that NT will present during boot-up before it launches the default selection. Click either the up or down arrow to change the amount of time.

6. You also can set other defaults. In the box below the two items involving the operating selection, there are five options to configure, all involving what you want NT to do when a critical or stop error occurs. The first option is "Write an event to the system log." This is a good item to check.

7. The next option, "Send an administrative alert," will cause a message to appear when the administrator logs into the computer.

8. The next options are important. Use "Write debugging information to:" to type a location for the file. Below this is a checkbox that says "Overwrite any existing file," which you want to check; otherwise, these files could accumulate and waste space (although this probably would not happen except possibly over a long period of time, because NT is so stable).

9. Finally, the last option is "Automatically reboot." It is best to leave this option unchecked so you can see any error messages NT might report.

CAUTION

Be very careful if you decide to go into `boot.ini` manually and make changes. If you accidentally make a typographical error, NT might not boot. You might want to make a backup copy before editing it; that way, you can replace it with the original if necessary. The `boot.ini` file resides in the root directory of the C: drive.

Configuring the Desktop

You can configure the NT desktop environment in a variety of ways. The trick is finding out what works for you. In this section, you'll look at the following:

- ☐ Managing windows
- ☐ Handling icons, folders, and files
- ☐ Modifying the desktop with the Display control panel

3

After you have finished this section you should have the skills necessary to customize your computer work environment in a way that makes it more enjoyable and makes you more efficient.

Managing Windows

The Explorer interface gives you more ways to handle windows than before, and here I am speaking of the actual windows that the operating system draws on your computer screen. Regardless of the type of window you are looking at, whether it is a window of an opened folder, disk drive, My Computer, or an open application, all can be managed by the methods described here. Look at one and note the different ways you can handle it.

Hour 2, "The Desktop and the Explorer," covers the different views the Explorer provides you. Figure 3.2 shows the files and folders on a hard drive. Note that below the menu bar (File, Edit, View, and Help) are more functions: Name, Size, Type, Modified, and Attributes. Clicking these enables you to quickly change the view and find what you are looking for.

Figure 3.2.

A typical Explorer window.

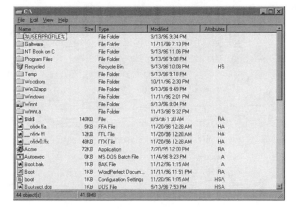

Viewing Files By Name: A–Z, Z–A

If you click Name, the Explorer will list the files in alphabetical order. However, what a lot of people don't know is that if you click a second time, it will list the items in reverse alphabetical order.

Viewing Files By Size

Similarly, if you click the rectangular box that has Size in it, the Explorer will display the files by size, from smallest to largest. And if you click a second time…? Try clicking Modified and Attributes; by now you have probably guessed what will happen. If you click Modified, it will rearrange the files based on their modification dates, and if you click Attributes, it will rearrange them based on their attributes.

Minimizing, Maximizing, and Closing Windows

Look at Figure 3.2, or better yet, sit in front of your computer as you learn how to manage windows on your desktop. Open your C: drive and go through some techniques. First, look at the simple, most common methods NT provides. Look at the upper-right corner of the window, and you'll see three small boxes.

The first box will minimize the window or application and place its icon on the taskbar. If you have several windows you want access to but do not want them cluttering the desktop, keep them minimized on the taskbar; when you need to see one, simply click its icon. The one problem with having multiple windows and applications open is that the space devoted to each window gets smaller to make room for each new window that is minimized. Open several folders on your C: drive and click the first of the three boxes in the upper-right corner of one of the windows (it has a horizontal line; the second box has two overlapping boxes; and the third box has an X in it).

After you minimize each one, watch what happens to the taskbar. To enlarge the taskbar, drag the mouse down to it, and when the pointer changes so that it has two arrows (position the pointer on the top edge of the taskbar), hold down the mouse button and drag the bar up one-fourth of an inch. Now the taskbar will have two rows of items. If you drag the taskbar even higher, more rows appear.

The second box enables you to change the size of the current window. After you click this box, the window will become smaller. The amount by which it shrinks is determined by what size the window was the last time you clicked this box. Therefore, if you resize the window and then click this button, it will remember the previous size to which you had adjusted the window. It is also important to note that when you click this box, NT will let you use other items on the desktop that you can see. If you are unable to see the item, you simply resize the window until you can see the desired items (see the "Resizing Windows" section).

To close a window, click in the box on the far right (it has an X in it). Some applications have two rows of boxes for minimizing, maximizing, and closing windows. One row is for handling the document window, and the second is for handling the application itself.

Resizing Windows

In addition to the three boxes in the upper-right corner, you can resize windows using the mouse. To do this, first determine whether the window is maximized. If it is, click the maximize button, and it will reduce the size of the window. Now that you can see the edge of the window, move the mouse pointer to the edge of the window; when the pointer changes its shape and has two arrows, you can hold down the mouse button and resize the window. Note that some windows have special places for resizing them, usually in the lower-right corner of the window. Position the mouse pointer there (notice it changes shape), and then press the mouse button and drag the window until it is the size you want.

You can also resize a window by double-clicking the title bar of the item. The first double-click will reduce the size of the window; the second will maximize the window.

Dragging Windows

To drag a window, you must move the mouse pointer to the title bar of the window. The title bar is at the top of the window and contains the name of the resource—whether it is an application, folder, or drive. Then, hold down the mouse button and drag the window to its desired location. It usually helps to resize the window first, and then move it.

Finally, be aware of the fact that if you have several windows open at the same time and need to see all or several of the windows, you have several options. You can either reposition the windows by resizing them and then dragging them so they do not cover each other up (see Figure 3.3), or use a quicker method, described next.

Figure 3.3.

By carefully resizing the windows, you can see many resources at the same time.

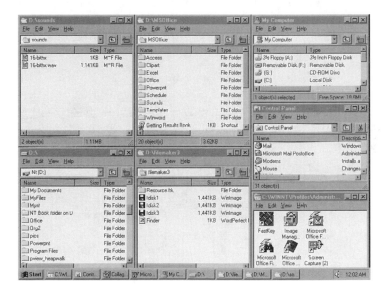

Right-click a blank spot on the taskbar, and a pop-up menu appears, giving you a selection of how to arrange all the open windows—to cascade the windows or tile them horizontally or vertically. By using the options on this pop-up menu, you let NT do the work of resizing the windows. Further, you can copy a file or folder from one window to another if you have the appropriate resources open. In Figure 3.3, several windows are open. You could copy a folder from the window in the upper-left corner to the window in the lower-right corner.

Also, it is still possible, after you have tiled the windows, to resize the windows or move them, or close one or more selected windows.

Handling Icons, Files, and Folders

Each of these items (an icon representing a drive or computer, or an icon representing a file or folder) can be customized. You can change the icon that represents that item, and you can create a shortcut to it as well.

To change the icon of a file or folder, position the mouse over the item and right-click it. A pop-up menu appears. Select Properties, which will open a properties window on the item. Generally, you can change only the icon of shortcut items, not the target file or folder. If you have right-clicked a shortcut, there will be two tabs at the top of the properties window; click the Shortcut tab. In this window is a button you can click to change the icon.

You can change both the icons and the names of the default items on the desktop—My Computer, Network Neighborhood, and Recycle Bin. Position the mouse on the desktop so it is not touching any item and right-click to bring up the pop-up menu. Select Properties. When the properties dialog box comes up, select Plus; now you can see which items you can change. If you have more icons in addition to the default icons, you can select one of your own.

To change the name of an icon, simply click the name of the item, wait about one second, and click a second time. If you click too quickly, NT will try to open the file or folder, so you must wait between clicks so NT understands that you just want to change the name and not open the resource.

Modifying the Desktop

Windows NT 4 lets you configure the desktop by using the Display Properties control panel. The control panel device appears in Figure 3.4. You can configure the background to the desktop, the screen saver, the appearance of windows (for example, the color of the window border, menus, message boxes), desktop icon appearance, and the number of colors for the display, as well as other settings.

Desktop Background

You can add your own pictures and use them as backgrounds relatively easily. Either scan your favorite pictures onto a disk, or find pictures on the Web and download them into your computer. Then follow these steps:

1. Open the pictures with the Accessories item Imaging, which you can access through Start | Programs | Accessories.

3

Figure 3.4.

The Display Properties dialog box.

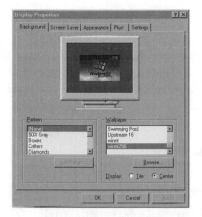

2. Save the document as a bitmap (.bmp) file so the Display control panel can read it.

3. Save it inside the WINNT directory.

4. Go to the Display control panel, and click the Background tab.

5. Scroll through the list until you find the picture you want to select.

6. You might want to either center it or tile it by using the buttons. Centering it will force the picture to the center of the screen and Tile will put several copies of the picture on the screen and place them side by side.

7. Click it and then click Apply. Click OK.

Screen Saver

Setting up a screen saver is a simple procedure, as seen in the following steps:

1. Go into the Display Properties control panel, and choose the Screen Saver tab at the top of the window.

2. Click the Screen Saver drop-down menu and choose a screen saver.

JUST A MINUTE

You can check for freeware and shareware versions of screen savers on the Internet. Freeware is free, whereas shareware lets you try the software for free and then buy it if you like it. Shareware fees are quite inexpensive when compared with commercial software. Use your favorite Web browser and do a search for screen saver and NT—you'll be sure to find something.

3. Click Settings, which will change for the different screen savers. Modify the settings in the desired fashion. Click OK.

4. Click Preview to see what the screen saver looks like. If you need to adjust the settings more, do so.

5. Select the amount of time you want to wait until the screen saver runs. The amount of time that NT is referring to is how much time after the last keyboard or mouse response NT should wait until running the screen saver.

6. Choose Apply, and you are finished.

Appearance

You can customize the Appearance of your windows to suit your own personal tastes. To do so, follow these instructions:

1. Go to the Display control panel.

2. Choose the Appearance tab in the Display control panel. You will see the different color schemes you can apply to windows.

3. Try different color schemes and find the ones you like. You can also set the spacing of desktop icons, the color of the desktop, and other features as well by using the Item function in the Appearance tab of this control panel.

4. You can set the size of objects by choosing the Size option listed next to the Item option. First, select the item you want to resize. Then change the size by clicking in the up or down arrow next to Size.

5. Finally, notice that you can change the default font for your windows and other objects such as icons. Click Fonts at the bottom of the Appearance tab, and select the desired font.

6. Click Apply, and you are finished. Look at some windows and see how it looks.

Settings

In the final tab, Settings, you are able to set the screen resolution, number of colors, refresh rate, and choose the driver for your video adapter card. The larger the numbers on the resolution, the smaller (and crisper) are the images on your screen. It is a good idea to find a compromise between the number of colors displayed and the resolution. As a general rule, you will probably want to display the maximum number of colors that your adapter can handle, although if you have a slow processor, it will take more time to display items on your monitor. Thus, be aware that you may need to adjust the number of colors to increase your speed.

1. To change the screen resolution in the Desktop Area of the Settings tab window, grab the slider bar with the mouse, hold down the button, slide it to the right, and watch the numbers at the bottom of the slider bar change. Go as far to the right as possible, noticing the different settings in between.

2. After you have made your change, click the Test button at the bottom of the window.

3. Now try changing the fonts by using the Fonts box. Make your changes, but keep in mind that you will not be able to see the difference until you have restarted NT.

4. Be careful when you change the Refresh Frequency or Display Type because these settings can cause your system to malfunction. Make changes only after you know what refresh rates your monitor can handle. Change the display type only if you make a hardware change to your computer by installing a new video card.

Summary

Experienced computer users should have learned the most in the first half of this hour, which discusses the boot-up process and the files needed to boot NT. Inexperienced users should make sure that everything in the lesson makes sense and be especially familiar with the second half, because these skills are necessary for becoming proficient in using your computer. Pay special attention to managing windows, viewing files, and changing settings with different control panel utilities.

Workshop

The Workshop helps you solidify the skills you learned this hour.

Glossary

boot.ini   This file is used by the NTLDR to display the operating systems from which you can select during the boot process.

BOOTSECT.DOS   This file contains information on any other operating systems on your computer.

NTDETECT.COM   This file is used to check your hardware upon booting.

NTLDR.COM   This file performs two basic functions: first, it handles the process of enabling you to choose an operating system during boot-up, and second, it performs some hardware detection. When the NTLDR is running you will see OS Loader V4.0.

RAM (random access memory)   Memory chips inside your computer that are used to hold portions of the operating system and applications while the computer is on.

ROM (read-only memory)   Chips that permanently hold boot-up information. You cannot modify the information on these chips.

system bus   An electrical pathway on your computer's main board (motherboard) that connects the components.

Exercises

1. Which files are necessary for NT to boot correctly?
2. What is the role of the NTLDR file?
3. Can you change the My Computer icon? If so, how?
4. If you wanted a picture of your grandmother as the background picture on your desktop, how would you do this?

Hour 4

Installing Applications

by Martin Kenley

You probably have several applications you are familiar with and want to run on Windows NT 4. There is a good chance that most, if not all, of your applications will run under NT 4 as well as they did under Windows 3.*x* or Windows 95. However, as you move to NT 4, now is a good time to evaluate which software packages you want to use. The move to a new operating system is a big transition, and you should be making it in the belief that it will make your work more efficient and provide a more stable environment.

All indications are that NT will provide these benefits to you; but the applications you use on a daily basis are important as well. Most important, newer 32-bit applications provide new features and enhancements that will probably make your work easier. Also, these applications are designed to operate smoothly with Windows NT; specifically, they are designed to take advantage of the multitasking capabilities, enabling you to work better with several programs open at the same time. Multithreading capabilities enable the programs to pass off different jobs to the operating system at the request of the user. Therefore, for example, when you are using Microsoft Excel, you can have the program do calculations on the spreadsheet at the same time you enter new data. Finally, all programs will take advantage of the flat memory model used by NT 4, as well as the fact that all programs under NT run in protected mode.

Before Installation

If you have owned or used a computer for any length of time, you know that there are several fundamental rules to follow. One of these regards what to do before you undertake any fundamental changes to your computer: Back up your data files as well as important system files. If something should go wrong while you are making the change, you will be able to recover from it. Important changes include installing software, adding new hardware, and editing system files. In particular, the files you should back up include the following:

- [ ] NT Registry
- [ ] `autoexec.nt`
- [ ] `config.nt`
- [ ] `win.ini`
- [ ] `system.ini`

Again, you should back up any personal data files on your hard drive. The vast majority of the time, things will proceed smoothly and you will not need these backups, but the one time you do need them, you'll be glad you took the precaution.

Creating an Updated Emergency Repair Disk

This is also a good time to create an updated emergency repair disk (ERD), which you need to use if NT somehow becomes corrupted. This disk also contains some system files and configuration information. The information on this disk is duplicated on your hard drive in the `\WINNT\REPAIR` subdirectory. The ERD is not a bootable disk but rather is designed to be used with the three NT installation disks created at installation time.

To update your ERD, go to the Start menu on the taskbar, go to Run, and type the following:

`RDISK`

This starts the Emergency Repair Disk utility. First choose Update, which will update the files in `%SystemRoot%\Repair` subdirectory. After these files are updated, you are asked whether you want to create a new ERD. Choose Yes, and insert a blank high-density disk or one that has data you are sure you no longer need. The program will automatically format the disk and then copy the files to it.

4

Checking Hard Drive Space for Your Applications

Finally, make sure your computer has the free hard drive space to install the application as well as the necessary random access memory (RAM). (The manual that came with the application should indicate how much disk space and RAM is needed.) Follow these steps to find out whether you have enough hard drive space:

1. Go to the My Computer icon and double-click it to open it. This is the icon on the desktop that contains more icons inside it representing your hard drive and any other drives (network drives, for example) as well as icons representing your Control Panel folder, Printer folder, Dial-Up Networking folder, and CD-ROM drive (if you have one). Of course, you can change the name, just as with any other icon.

2. Now use the right button on the mouse, which in the Windows 3.*x* days was usually ignored because it had very little function. In the new worlds of NT 4 and Windows 95, the right mouse button becomes very useful. Position the mouse so the tip of the arrow on the pointer is touching the drive designated as C: (if this is where you want to install the application). Then click the right mouse button; this causes a pull-down menu to appear. On your screen, you should see a menu similar to that shown in Figure 4.1.

Figure 4.1.

The right button on the mouse finally has a useful function in Windows.

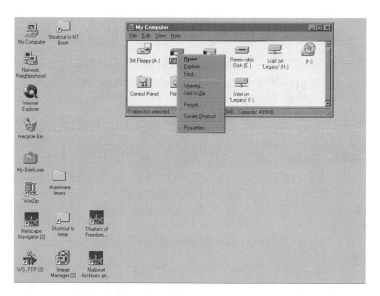

Although there are several useful items in the pull-down menu, we're now interested in hard drive space. Drag the mouse down to the bottom choice, Properties, and release the right mouse button. Now you have a useful pie chart showing how much space on your drive is already taken up, and how much is still free (see Figure 4.2).

Figure 4.2.

The properties of your hard drive are displayed after right-clicking the drive and choosing Properties. Now you can quickly see how soon you'll need to buy a second hard drive.

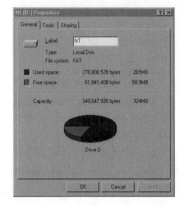

If you have partitioned your drive so that you have several drive letters (C:, D:, and so on), then the Properties dialog box will only show you information about the partition you selected. NT 4 treats each drive letter as a separate hard drive; therefore, you might have to get properties on multiple partitions to find the amount of space you need.

Checking RAM for Your Applications

One of the main determinants of your application's performance is the amount of RAM you have installed on your system. In the early 1990s, many computers shipped with only 4MB of RAM. Now it is common for most computers to come with 16MB, and 32MB is preferable.

JUST A MINUTE

When you are considering how much RAM you need for the application you are about to install, keep in mind that occasionally the recommended minimum is unrealistic, and it really takes more RAM to run the application smoothly. Vendors set a low amount in order to sell more software. They are aware that most computer owners have 8 to 16MB of RAM, and they want to sell the majority of PC users.

Look on the box that the software came in or check the manual to see what the recommended minimum amount of RAM is for that application. To check for the amount of RAM you have installed on your computer, follow these steps:

4

1. Go to My Computer and double-click to open it.

2. Find the Control Panel folder and double-click it. Now you see all the useful items that enable you to customize your computer—from the action of the keyboard to the wallpaper (in the Display icon). Find the System icon and double-click it.

3. You will notice six tabs at the top: Startup/Shutdown, Hardware Profiles, User Profiles, General, Performance, and Environment. When the System control panel opens, it should be at the General tab, and inside this tab is information about your computer: which version of the operating system you are running, to whom it is registered, the type of computer you have, and how much RAM you have on your computer.

If you notice that you have only 12 or 16MB of RAM, you should increase this to meet the needs of the application you are installing. Prices on RAM fell tremendously in 1996, so if you need more, it is worth checking on the current prices, because RAM has such a tremendous impact on the performance of your computer.

Types of Applications NT Can Run

The following three sections are intended to help you set up your DOS, Windows 3.*x* (16-bit), and Windows 95 (32-bit) applications under Windows NT. You probably will not need to read all the sections, so skip to the section that addresses the types of applications you intend to install.

DOS Applications

Windows NT 4 is capable of running most of your DOS applications, Windows 3.*x* applications, and most Windows 95 applications. However, I hope you don't have to run many DOS applications on NT because they don't take advantage of the power of the operating system. Running DOS applications on NT 4 is like buying a high-performance British sports car to drive to the grocery store. You should ask yourself what you want your computer to do for you and search for the best applications available to do the job. With the exception of games and a few other applications, most DOS applications have been replaced with software that is far superior. DOS applications are written with 16-bit code, as are the Windows 3.*x* applications.

If you plan on running many DOS applications, Windows 95 might be a better choice. It is written to be capable of running a substantial number of DOS applications, and it does a good job at it. For game enthusiasts, it is worth noting that Windows 95 has a good reputation for handling DOS games, as well as being particularly good at multimedia. Fortunately, many 32-bit protected-mode games are being developed, so holding on to DOS will become less important as time goes on.

Under Windows NT, if the DOS application tries to communicate directly with the hardware, NT will generally not run the application. Many games do just this (they are designed to have their own drivers for the sound card and video). Drivers that try to talk directly to the hardware are called *real-mode drivers*, and NT will not run any real-mode driver. Therefore, if you have an older piece of hardware that uses only real-mode drivers, it probably will not work with NT. All applications under NT run in protected mode—that is, a state in which the processor can use all of the computer's extended memory. Refer to Hour 1, "Introduction to Windows NT 4," for more information on real-mode drivers and protected mode.

Windows 3.x Applications

Generally speaking, 16-bit Windows applications are newer and have more sophisticated capabilities than do the DOS applications. They are developed using the Win16 software development kit and generally will run under Windows 95 and NT. The Win16 kit specifies the guidelines programmers should follow as they write the code for a software application. Each application is generally coded to work for a specific operating system. Because newer operating systems are usually backward compatible, applications coded for older operating systems generally run on newer ones.

Windows 95 Applications

The Windows 95 applications are known as 32-bit applications because they are written using the Win32 Application Program Interface (API), which, like its 16-bit counterpart, provides guidelines for programmers to follow when writing applications for Windows 95. These guidelines assist the programmer in figuring out how the application will interact with the operating system. For example, a programmer needs to know how the software should address memory (that is, write information into RAM) and how the program should send a message to a hardware device (for example, how it should interact with the operating system when saving a file to the hard drive). Early on, when Microsoft developers drew up the requirements for programmers, one stated that all 32-bit applications written for Windows 95 must also be capable of being run on NT as well. However, this requirement was later changed: The application does not have to run under NT, but if it cannot, it must be coded to terminate cleanly and not cause a system freeze.

Types of Applications That You Cannot Install

You probably have some utilities you were fond of using either in DOS, Windows 3.x, or Windows 95. These utilities might have helped you manage your hard drive by keeping it

4

from becoming fragmented. *Fragmentation* occurs over a period of time and happens when data on the hard drive is written to different spots.

For example, you can copy a large file to your hard drive, but if there is not a large enough contiguous block free, then it will copy part of the file in different blocks in several parts of the drive until the entire file has been saved. As this happens to more files and applications, it takes more time to access information on the drive, because it has been broken up and scattered all over the drive. NT 4 does not have a built-in defragmenting tool, so you should buy a third-party utility written specifically for NT. However, keep in mind that NT will not let applications make direct requests to the hardware, and this is what a defragmenting utility must do—make calls to the hard drive.

Fortunately, the utilities you have used in the past to manage your computer's memory cannot be used with NT. I say "fortunately" because memory management has become more simplified than in the old days of 640KB limits. With DOS and Windows 3.*x*, your computer's performance in part was determined by how you used the first 640KB of your computer's RAM. A large part of the trick involved loading device drivers high, so you could keep more of the 640KB region free for loading Windows, or if you only ran DOS, for loading applications.

Installing Applications

Most people are used to locating the `setup.exe` or `install.exe` files using the File Manager under Windows 3.1 when installing applications. NT 4 has a new method, in which NT will track what files are installed and where they go.

Installing Applications the Old Way

When you install your applications onto NT, you'll have two methods from which to choose. As under Windows 3.*x*, you can put the first disk of the application into the disk drive or load the CD into the CD-ROM drive, open the File Manager, go to File | Run, and type in the name of the install program, which is usually `INSTALL` or `SETUP`.

In the NT environment, you still have the option of installing applications from within File Manager or DOS, or you can use the NT Explorer. Installing an application using the Explorer is similar to installing with the File Manager: The Explorer gives you a window divided into two screens, and in the screen on the right you navigate to the subdirectory in which the installer is located. When you open this subdirectory by double-clicking it, its contents are displayed on the right side of the window. Find the installer and double-click it to start it. If you prefer the File Manager, go to the Start menu and choose Run; in the dialog box, type `winfile`, thereby launching the File Manager. Now you can proceed as usual: Go to File | Run, and type in the path and the name of the application setup utility.

You can also go directly to the Start menu, go to Run, and type in the path and the name of the setup program (for example, A:\SETUP).

Installing Applications the New Way: The Add/Remove Programs Utility

The preferred way to install your applications is to use a new utility located in the Control Panel folder called Add/Remove Programs. Keep in mind that Windows 95 and Windows NT applications will take full advantage of the features of this utility, whereas 3.1 and DOS applications will not. Specifically, Windows NT 4 and 95 applications have the capability of properly registering the files that the application installs into the computer; some of the installation files typically will go into the operating system subdirectory (in the case of NT, the WINNT subdirectory) as well as an application subdirectory created during the installation process.

Fortunately for those of you who install Windows 95 and NT applications, all of this record keeping is done by the NT Registry, the master database that stores all the information about your software and hardware setup. (You learn more about the Registry in Hour 21, "The Windows NT Registry.") Because NT tracks all this information about the files placed on your computer, it is easy to remove applications at a later date, when the application is no longer needed or replaced by a new program. The Add/Remove utility registers not only the files, but the Uninstaller utility that comes with the application.

Setting Up Windows NT and Windows 95 Applications

For applications that have the official Windows 95 logo, testing must be done to ensure the following:

☐ They are developed with the Win32 Software Developer's Kit, which ensures that the applications can run under either Windows 95 or NT, can handle multithreading capabilities, and can multitask with other 32-bit applications.

☐ They can support plug and play.

☐ They are developed to use the Explorer interface and support long filenames.

Therefore, if a software package does not have the 95 logo, it might have been only minimally tested for its compatibility with Windows 95. Unless it explicitly states that it can run under NT, you are taking a risk purchasing the product.

To remove applications, you must know what files were installed and which subdirectories they went into.

4

Setting Up DOS Applications

The first thing you should be aware of is that some of your DOS applications will not install because they attempt to "talk" to the hardware inside the computer. For example, the application might try to send information directly to the video card that controls your monitor, rather than using the software driver that the video card uses. Windows NT 4 normally will not allow a direct call to the hardware by a piece of software. The usual procedure is for the software to make a call that NT receives and then "mediate" the conversation between the application and the hardware. NT uses a layer of virtual device drivers (VDDs) that intervene and handle the request the application is sending to the hardware. However, a VDD does not exist for every device or component inside your computer, so the only way to find out if an application will work is to install it.

Several factors will determine how DOS applications run under NT:

☐ Settings in the configuration files: the autoexec.bat, autoexec.nt, config.sys, and config.nt files

☐ Device drivers

☐ Property sheet settings

You look at each of these variables after you examine how NT handles DOS applications.

Virtual DOS Machines

Each DOS application that you run on Windows NT operates in a 32-bit environment known as a Virtual DOS Machine (VDM). A new VDM is created for each DOS application and runs in user mode, an operational state in which applications and subsystems run; therefore, the following is true for user mode components:

☐ They do not have the capability to communicate directly with the hardware.

☐ They have a lower priority in accessing central processing unit (microprocessor) cycles.

☐ They must operate in a specific memory address space.

☐ They might be forced to use hard drive space as RAM (also known as virtual memory).

It might be easier to understand user mode by contrasting it to privileged processor mode. The most important components of NT—such as the kernel and the hardware abstraction layer—operate in *privileged processor mode*, which protects them from applications and subsystems and also gives them a higher priority when CPU cycles are allocated. The parts of the operating system code that run in privileged mode also have direct access to hardware and system memory.

Although the application thinks it is running in a DOS environment, it is actually operating in a VDM, which simulates a DOS environment. When the DOS application sends requests to NT, it does so by the VDDs, which send the request to the appropriate NT 32-bit device driver. The importance of this for the user is that the hardware is buffered or protected from applications; and because NT only allows its own 32-bit drivers to interact directly with hardware, the system is more stable.

`autoexec.bat` **and** `config.sys` **Files**

The `autoexec.bat` file still can be used with NT to load special path and environment variables to the system environment during startup. You will not be able to load any drivers this way because NT cannot use real-mode drivers; any such commands in the configuration files would be ignored by NT. However, under Windows 95, these files can still play an important role if necessary.

`autoexec.nt` **and** `config.nt` **Files**

`autoexec.nt` and `config.nt`, which by default are located in the SYSTEM32 subdirectory inside the WINNT directory, behave much like the `autoexec.bat` and `config.sys` files: They enable you to customize the DOS environment in which the application will run. Therefore, for example, this is where you would set path information if the application needs it. The settings in these files will affect all applications that you run from the command prompt, with the exception of the `.nt` files, which are executed only when applications are run from `.PIF` files.

Device Drivers

Applications must be capable of communicating with hardware or making requests through the operating system. For example, when you want to save a file you have created with an application, you save it either to the hard drive or to a floppy disk. The application must send a save request through the operating system to the drive. Although this is fairly routine and the application relies on drivers for the hard drive supplied by the operating system, there are other cases in which it needs its own device drivers. If a DOS application needs to send information to the sound card of the computer, then the information must be mapped for it using either the `config.sys` or `autoexec.bat` file. If NT is unable to permit the application to address the hardware, it will shut down the application rather than crash the system.

4

Using Property Sheets for DOS Applications

A property sheet is created for each shortcut to an application. To create a shortcut, first locate the executable application using Windows, not DOS. Then, using the right mouse button, click the icon that represents the executable file. From the menu that appears, choose Create shortcut, which creates another icon called Shortcut to *application name*, where *application name* is replaced by the name of the current application with which you are working. Now, right-click the Shortcut icon, and another drop-down menu appears; move the mouse down to Properties and release the button to see the property sheet for that application. See Figure 4.3 for an example of a property sheet.

Figure 4.3.

A property sheet for an application named Software Bridge. Notice the tabs at the top of the property sheet.

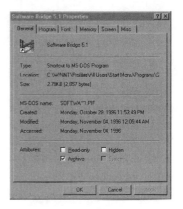

The property sheet replaces the program information file (PIF) editor used in Windows 3.*x*, which sets the properties of DOS programs. However, under NT using the property sheet, you have more ways to adjust DOS applications than under 3.*x* or Windows 95.

The General Sheet

All DOS applications will have a property sheet labeled General, as shown in Figure 4.3. On this page, you will find the application's full name, the location of the application, its size, the dates it was created and modified, and its attributes. You can make a few modifications on this page but will practically never need to do so. On most sheets, you will see only a check mark in the archive attribute, indicating that this is an important file to back up if you are making fundamental changes to your system.

The Version Sheet

Not all applications will show a tab for Version, but if one does, it will give you information on the precise version of the software, copyright information, product name, and the name of the corporation that developed or owns the software copyright (see Figure 4.4).

Figure 4.4.

The Properties dialog box sometimes gives you a Version sheet, which shows which company developed the product, which version you own, and other information.

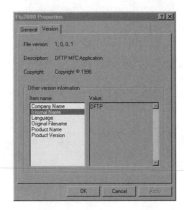

The Program Sheet

The Program sheet (see Figure 4.5) lets you modify how NT runs the DOS program. The top line next to the icon provides a space so you can type the name of the application, and the Cmd line provides a space for you to type the path and application to be run. The space next to Working is where you put the directory information of where the application is located and where files should be saved.

Figure 4.5.

The Program property sheet enables you to specify special configuration files, if necessary.

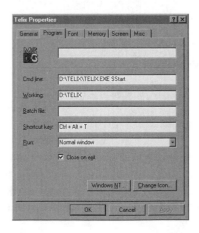

4

The following line, Batch file, which is new with Windows 95, enables you to specify a batch file to run when the application is run. The Shortcut key space is useful—it enables you to specify a keystroke to launch the application rather than clicking the icon or typing the application name and path at the command prompt. (Note that one of the shortcut keys must be either Ctrl or Alt.) Below that (in the Run box), you can specify in what kind of window you want the application launched: normal, maximized, or minimized.

The Windows NT button enables you to specify which configuration files you will use to set any environment variables for the application, or you can rely on the default selection and ignore this option if no special variables need to be set. The Change Icon button is self-explanatory: Use it to change the icon for the application.

The Font Sheet

The Font page (shown in Figure 4.6) offers several ways to customize how fonts appear and which fonts the application will use. In the upper-left corner of the dialog box, you can choose which type of fonts you have available in the window to the right, the Font Size box. Unless the display cannot handle both bitmap and TrueType, select both types of fonts. In the Font Size box you can select, in pixels, the font size the application will use. The Window preview and Font preview windows let you preview the window size as well as the font.

4

Figure 4.6.
The Font property sheet enables you to customize how text appears in the application.

The Memory Sheet

Windows NT provides the applications with simulated expanded and extended memory. Most of the time, NT will be the best judge of choosing the appropriate options, but occasionally, you might need to adjust the settings.

Under conventional memory, you can choose how much of the 640KB of conventional memory the application has access to (see Figure 4.7). NT also lets you choose the amount of memory set aside for the command interpreter environment. Therefore, if you have many environment variables, you can allocate 2–4 MB of memory. In this section, you can also choose to run the application in protected mode to keep Windows protected from possibly bad DOS applications. This is good to have checked, but if you notice performance is suffering, try running it in unprotected mode.

Figure 4.7.

The property sheet for Telix, a DOS applica-tion, lets you choose the environment in which it will run.

NT has the capability to simulate expanded memory for applications that require this older standard. If you leave it set to Auto, keep in mind that some applications might use too much memory and leave very little for other applications, thereby requiring you to set it manually. Do some trial-and-error experimenting here to find an optimum amount for applications that use expanded memory.

Most applications will use extended memory, which is the memory after the 1MB limit imposed by DOS. This setting is important to many DOS applications. Try to set it manually, giving the application as much extended memory as possible without negatively affecting other tasks or applications that will run simultaneously. Leave the Use HMA (High Memory Area) box unchecked if you load DOS into this area; if not, check it.

The Screen Sheet

The Screen page (see Figure 4.8) enables you to modify screen settings. Most important, in the Usage area you can set the number of lines as well as the mode. It is wise to set the number of lines before you make adjustments to the Font page. Under the Window section, you can select whether you want to display a toolbar and whether NT should revise the PIF after you make changes using the toolbar. To preserve new settings made with the toolbar, check the "Restore settings on startup" box.

4

Figure 4.8.
*With the Screen proper-
ties sheet you can control
how NT displays your
DOS application.*

The Misc Sheet

Although most of the settings in the Miscellaneous sheet are obvious (see Figure 4.9), a few require some explanation. The Always Suspend setting will idle the application when it is in the background so the foreground applications get all of the system resources. The QuickEdit option in the Mouse section enables you to select text in a DOS application to copy to another location. If the Exclusive Mode box is checked, the mouse will work only with the foreground DOS application. Setting the Idle sensitivity to High tells NT to quickly allocate CPU cycles to other applications if there is no keyboard activity in the foreground DOS application. If it is set to Low, NT will wait longer before reallocating CPU cycles.

Figure 4.9.
*The Miscellaneous
property sheet contains
options to set the screen
saver, mouse settings, and
Windows shortcut keys.*

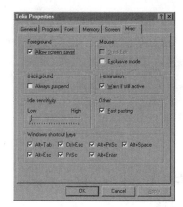

Using Property Sheets for Windows 3.x Applications

As with DOS applications, you must first make a shortcut to the application before you can modify its property sheet. To make changes to it, go to the shortcut icon, or create one, and right-click it. A pop-up menu appears; drag the mouse down to Properties and release the mouse button. (The General tab is identical to that in DOS applications, so refer to the "Using Property Sheets for DOS Applications" section for information on it.)

The Shortcut Properties sheet has several useful options. The Target line provides a space in which you can specify which file is run when the shortcut is double-clicked. You can also choose whether you want to run applications in a separate memory space. Because all Win16 applications run in the same memory space or a single virtual DOS machine, you might need to protect other applications from a poorly written application that causes other programs to crash. If you notice crashes and freezes with a Win16 application, try checking the separate memory area box.

The Start In line enables you to set the working directory. The directory you set here will become the default directory when the application is launched. On this property sheet, you can set the shortcut key for quickly launching the application, such as Ctrl + Alt + F8.

TIME SAVER

If you want to start a Win16 application in its own memory space and launch it from the command line, type start /separate *application name*, where *application name* is replaced by the program's name. For example, if you wanted to run WordPerfect, you would type start /separate WP. If you need to, you can type the path before the name of the executable. Now the application will run in its separate memory space, preventing it from taking all the processor cycles away from other applications.

Running Windows 95 and NT Applications

Windows 95 and NT applications are the easiest to deal with. They make the most efficient use of system resources, they are the easiest to install and uninstall, and they are coded to work with NT.

The property sheets for Windows 95 and NT applications are similar to that of Win16 applications, so I will not cover the same ground again. (Refer to the "Using Property Sheets

4

for Windows 3.x Applications" section for more information.) The one exception you will notice is that the option to run the application in a separate memory space is grayed out because all 32-bit applications are always run in a separate memory space.

Although you might notice that some of the new Windows 95 and NT applications, also known as 32-bit applications, seem slower upon startup, don't be alarmed. These newer applications are indeed larger, because it now takes 32 bits for all operations rather than 16 bits of code. Therefore, it can take longer to process 32 bits depending on the operation. However, the advantage is that these applications are capable of real multitasking and multithreading, whereas the 16-bit applications are not.

Optimizing is discussed in Hour 5, "Optimizing Windows NT Memory." Fortunately, you don't have to make any adjustments to the property sheets of Windows 95 and NT applications.

Summary

In this hour, you have learned how to install different types of applications and the precautions to take when doing so. It is especially important to create an emergency repair disk before you change your system by installing new applications. If your repair disk is old, it is a good idea to update it so it has your current system information on it. It is also important to avoid installing older utilities applications that worked under Windows 95 or Windows 3.x because they might break some of your NT components.

Workshop

The Workshop helps you solidify the skills you learned this hour.

Glossary

hard disk   This physical device holds all the items you install on your computer and remains there whether or not the computer is turned on.

RAM (random access memory)   The physical memory that holds portions of the operating system and applications when your computer is turned on.

Virtual Device Drivers (VDDs)   Windows NT has a sublayer called the Virtual Device Drivers that handles hardware requests from your DOS applications. NT will not enable any of your applications to directly make calls to the hardware, so it intercepts the call and sends its own request to the hardware.

Virtual DOS Machine (VDM)   A condition in which NT creates an environment for your DOS application to run in.

Exercises

1. Using the method shown in this lesson, determine the amount of hard drive space that is free on your system. If you have several partitions or more than one hard drive, check all partitions and drives. Determine a strategy for installing applications.

2. Determine the amount of RAM on your system by following the instructions in this lesson. Before installing any application, look at the box the software came in and look for system requirements.

3. Find the Add/Remove Program utility in the Control Panel folder. Open it and click the Install/Uninstall tab. Take a look at which programs are listed here.

Hour 5

Optimizing Windows NT Memory

by Martin Kenley

Memory and Windows NT 4

The amount of memory you have is a crucial element in how well NT will run. In fact, with any operating system, the more memory you have, the better the performance will be (although there is an upper limit at which the performance will no longer be noticeable). Because of the architecture of NT and its new interface, the Explorer, random access memory (RAM) is even more important. It is safe to say that the amount of memory is one of the central factors, if not the most important factor, affecting performance.

RAM and How It Works

Let's look at how RAM works, and then you can see why it is so important. When your computer starts up, the system needs to transfer certain data from the hard drive to the RAM, where the data can be accessed quickly. Specifically, the computer will take portions of the operating system and load it into RAM (see Figure 5.1). And when you launch an application, parts of the code or program are copied from the hard disk to memory.

Figure 5.1.

Your computer needs to move vital parts of the operating system into RAM in order to access the information quickly.

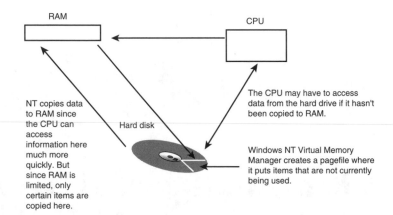

RAM speed is measured by nanoseconds (NS), whereas hard drive speeds are measured in milliseconds. The difference in speed is dramatic: A nanosecond is one-billionth of a second, and a millisecond is one-thousandth of a second. By comparison, you can see how quickly your CPU is able to get information it needs from RAM. But to access it from the hard drive, the speed is slowed by the fact that a motor must spin the drive around until the data is found and read.

Therefore, speed is a crucial issue when you are looking at the performance of a computer. It is worth noting here that RAM is sold in varying speeds. Currently, 60 and 70 NS are the standards, with 60 being faster and more preferable. You need to make sure your motherboard (the electronic circuit board inside your computer) can handle faster RAM if you want to upgrade. Just as important as speed is the amount of RAM in your system.

NT 4 Workstation has demanding system requirements, and when it comes to RAM, there is no exception. If you have a fast processor—a Pentium 100 or faster—you might be able to get by with 16MB of RAM; however, even under these circumstances more memory is desirable. Certainly with slower processors, a minimum of 24MB of RAM is necessary. Without the necessary RAM, your computer will be slow, and you will hear your hard drive constantly being read to and written to as NT saves data to the pagefile (space on the hard drive that the Virtual Memory Manager [VMM] uses to swap data that applications need in RAM but that are not currently being used).

5

Overview of Virtual Memory

Virtual memory is handled by the operating system, and applications don't need to be involved with moving the data from RAM to the hard drive and vice versa. Virtual memory gets around one central problem: not having enough RAM in the system. When data is moved from RAM to the hard disk, a map of the locations must be maintained so the data can be found when it is again needed. And NT is smart about what it swaps to disk: an algorithm is used to determine the least-used data and swap it out. The data is swapped to disk in pages (blocks of equal size), and the RAM is divided into page frames to hold the pages. NT uses a page size of 4KB (kilobytes). This enables a lot of data to be moved quickly.

The pagefile that NT creates is a real file you can find on your hard drive in the root directory of all partitions and drives where one has been created. NT enables the user to set a minimum and maximum pagefile by following these steps:

1. Go to the Start menu, up to Settings, to Control Panel, and click Control Panel.

2. Locate the System icon at the bottom of the Control Panel window and double-click.

3. You will see several tabs at the top of the window. Click Performance (see Figure 5.2).

Figure 5.2.

The System control panel shows the total pagefile for all drives and partitions.

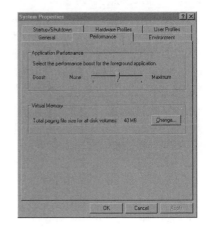

4. When you get to the System control panel, you must click the Performance tab at the top of the screen.

5. To make changes to the pagefile, click the Change box. Another window appears that looks like Figure 5.3.

Figure 5.3.

You can use the Virtual
Memory dialog box to
customize the pagefile.

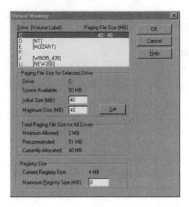

Inside the Virtual Memory dialog box, several areas are important and deserve attention.

The Drive window shows you the hard drives in your computer as well as any partitions (because partitions get a drive letter, as does a real drive).

Pagefile Size: To the right of the drive's letters you will see the size of the pagefile on each drive. You can also see how much free space is available in the selected drive if you look below the drive window.

Initial Size: Below Space Available, you will see Initial Size, which shows the size of the pagefile when NT starts. NT will automatically set the pagefile to the size of the RAM you have in your computer, plus 12MB (for the kernel). Therefore, if your system has 24MB of RAM, the initial pagefile size will be 36MB.

Maximum Size and Minimum Allowed: The next item shows the maximum size that the pagefile will become after the VMM adds data to it; the minimum allowed is the smallest size the pagefile can be.

Recommended: The recommended initial size is the recommendation for all drives and partitions you have. NT calculates this number by adding 11 to the total amount of RAM in your system.

Currently Allocated: NT also displays the currently allocated pagefile size, which is the sum of all the pagefiles on all drives and partitions.

Current Registry Size: Finally, you are shown the amount of RAM devoted to the Registry, as well as the maximum amount of RAM that the Registry can use (in megabytes).

Changing Virtual Memory Settings

After installing NT 4, you will have an initial pagefile of 16MB, but this size will be changed as NT makes adjustments to it. You should to try to optimize the setting for your own computer. To do this, follow these procedures:

5

1. Go to My Computer, and open the Control Panel folder.

2. Double click on the System icon.

3. The System window has tabs at the top. Choose the Performance tab at the top of the window.

4. Carefully note the current settings, and write them down. When you make adjustments, try to be systematic; that is, note the performance of your applications and the current settings, and make an adjustment to only one performance tuner (in this case, the pagefile size). Run your frequently used applications, note the performance, and see if you have made the situation better. It is important to make only incremental changes and monitor the performance of your system.

5. Click the Set button in the Virtual Memory window. The selected drive or partition at the top of this window will be the drive that you are about to change or establish a pagefile for.

6. Next, enter an initial size; if you have 8 to 16MB of RAM, then choose a pagefile size equal to the amount of RAM. If you have more than 32MB of RAM, set the pagefile size to half the amount of RAM.

7. Again, the maximum amount of pagefile size depends on how much RAM is on your system, the types of applications you are running, the number of applications you open at the same time, and the number of pagefiles you will have. As a general rule, the maximum size of the pagefile should be in the neighborhood of twice the amount of real RAM on your system. However, if you have an unusually large amount of RAM—64MB or more—then you can safely reduce this number. Also, if you plan on having a swap file on several drives, then each file can be smaller. You have two choices if you have several drives (actual hard drives, not partitions) in your system:

    a. Set a swap file on both drives that are one-half to three-quarters the size of the total pagefile size; the goal with two swap files is to enable the computer to be able to read to one while it writes to the other. If the files are on separate drives, then the drive head that reads and writes to the drives will be able to read one swap file while writing to the other.

    b. Set one pagefile on the drive that does not contain the system folder (usually the C: drive). The idea is that your system can read the drive that has the system on it at the same time that your system can read and write to the swap file on a separate drive. The heads that read the data will not have to jump around the drive reading and writing to both the system files and the swap file if they are on separate drives.

It is debatable which is most efficient. I have experimented with both, but the results were uncertain. There are several variables to consider: speed of the drives, amount of RAM on the system, speed of the process, and so on. You should try both methods and see which way gives you the best performance.

5

8. Finally, click Set to establish the new settings, which will be implemented after the machine is rebooted.

RAM Versus Virtual Memory

You might wonder why you should purchase RAM when your computer has the capability to simulate RAM. Consider a few of the points made previously, such as the speed performance of RAM versus hard disk. You pay quite a penalty here if you plan to rely on virtual memory. Second, given the price of RAM, you will be much better off spending the money to increase your RAM to at least 24MB if you run normal business applications. The general guidelines for the amount of RAM you will need are as follows:

☐ If you normally work on really large files and have more than one application open, then you could very well benefit by increasing your RAM to 32MB or more.

☐ If you work much with multimedia or graphics, then you will want as much RAM as you can reasonably afford.

☐ Network services consume a fair amount of RAM, and you should plan on adding another 2 to 4MB for each type of service: Novell NetWare, Windows Networks, Dial-up services, and so on.

☐ If you plan on doing computer programming on the system, you will want to add another 12 to 16MB of RAM.

☐ If you have a small hard drive and do not plan to add a second drive or replace the first drive, you will not have much room on the drive for the pagefile. Therefore, you should provide more room in RAM for the system and applications.

☐ Finally, if you will be implementing disk mirroring or disk striping, add another 4 to 16MB, depending on the size of the drives.

Examining Your Memory Usage

NT provides several tools for monitoring the way your system is using its memory; they will help you to find the places that cause performance decreases. Using several of these monitors will give you a fairly complete picture of your system performance.

Performance Monitor

The Performance Monitor utility is the best little application built into NT 4 for checking how your system is using its resources. It can be accessed clicking Start | Programs | Administrative Tools | Performance Monitor. Fortunately, this utility has the capability to track memory-related systems over time, which enables you to start the Performance Monitor and then begin to use the computer as you normally would. That way, you can watch to see how the resources are used and look for bottlenecks. Figure 5.4 shows the Performance Monitor; the utility lets you choose colors for each element you want to measure.

Figure 5.4.

The Performance Monitor is the most complete utility NT 4 offers for measuring resource usage.

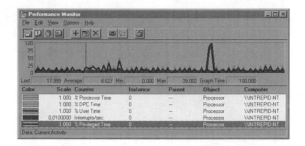

To use the utility, you will need to add the elements you want to monitor by following these steps:

1. Choose Edit | Add to Chart. Now the dialog box enables you to choose which objects you want to monitor; in this case, choose Memory. After this, you can select the color, style, and width for the band.

2. Next, choose the Add button.

When monitoring memory performance you will have different choices for monitoring:

Page Faults | sec: This shows how often the information is not found in a process's working set. This measurement shows both hard page faults, in which the information must be retrieved from the pagefile, and soft page faults, in which the system finds the pages elsewhere in memory.

Pages Input | sec: This shows how many pages are being pulled from the hard disk to correct page faults.

Pages Output | sec: This shows the volume of pages written to disk in order to create space for faulted pages.

Page Reads | sec: This shows how frequently the system must read from the hard disk because of page faults. This is a key way of determining whether your system does not have enough memory.

General Physical Memory

To get a bird's eye view of the amount of physical RAM on your system, follow these steps:

1. Open the Explorer.

2. Go to the Help menu, and choose About Windows NT (see Figure 5.5). This window will show you the physical memory on your system as expressed in kilobytes. (Keep in mind that 1024KB is equal to 1MB.)

5

Figure 5.5.

To quickly determine the amount of RAM on a machine, use About Windows NT.

Task Manager

Finally, you can use the Task Manager to see information on all the processes running on your computer as well as different information on each process. For example, you can see the amount of memory each process is using or how long the process has been running. To display the Task Manager, right-click the mouse after you have moved the pointer to a blank spot inside the taskbar at the bottom of your screen. Next, choose Task Manager from the pop-up list.

The Task Manager also enables you to display the percentage of power the CPU is using, the amount of memory your system is using, as well as the number of threads, handles, and processes (see Figure 5.6). You can leave this window open while you perform various tasks and see how your resources are used. Don't be surprised to see the CPU usage jump to 100% as you do various tasks. This does not indicate that you need a faster processor, it simply indicates that some tasks will take up the entire power of the CPU for a short while. If you notice your CPU usage is always hovering near 100%, however, then you probably need more CPU power.

Figure 5.6.

The Task Manager gives you an overall view of how system resources are used.

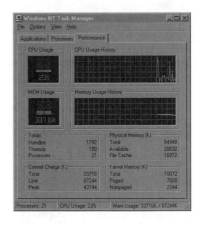

Summary

This lesson should have taught you more about how NT manages and uses your system memory. Many computer users can get along fine without such information, but if you enjoy experimenting and adjusting your computer's configuration settings, this lesson will help you maximize the performance of your NT computer. I must emphasize that any adjustments you make should be small and incremental, and make adjustments only after you have made careful note of the current settings. Then, begin to make adjustments and determine if they have increased your system's speed.

Workshop

The Workshop helps you solidify the skills you learned this hour.

Glossary

CPU (central processing unit)   The brain of the computer. It processes the code or lines of instruction of which applications are composed. Most of today's computers have Intel Pentium CPUs.

page   Your computer's RAM holds program code and data in units that are referred to as pages, each of which is 4096 bytes.

page frame   Where pages in memory are stored.

pagefile   As it applies to virtual memory, a pagefile is an area on the hard disk that is reserved for backing up data and code from RAM.

Performance Monitor   A good utility built into Windows NT that enables you to track the performance of various system components such as the CPU, hard drive, and memory.

process(es)   A part of code from an application. NT identifies a process as an address space and group of threads.

RAM (random access memory)   Your computer's main system memory, which is used by the system to hold portions of your data and running applications.

swap file   A file on the hard disk used to temporarily hold a program or a part of a program that is running in memory.

Task Manager   A utility built into Windows NT that enables you to access information about the different processes running on your computer. For example, you can see how different tasks affect the CPU.

5

virtual memory   How your computer uses hard drive space to imitate system memory. It will enable you to "trick" your computer so that it thinks it has more memory than it really has and will open more applications simultaneously.

Virtual Memory Manager (VMM)   Designed to move pages between memory and your hard disk.

Exercises

1. Which utility provides the most detail of your system resources?

2. Is it possible to have more than one pagefile (swap file)?

3. What is the default size of the pagefile (initially)?

4. What is the recommended amount of RAM to run Windows NT 4?

5. Is real physical RAM better than virtual memory? Why or why not?

6. Explore the Performance Monitor, specifically looking at the different objects you can monitor. Note what counters you can use to monitor memory usage and determine how your typical computer activities use memory resources.

    a. Do you have any memory bottlenecks?

    b. Do you have any processor bottlenecks?

Hour 6

Monitoring Performance

by Martin Kenley

This hour looks at more ways to optimize your system. Hour 5, "Optimizing Windows NT Memory," was concerned solely with getting the most out of your computer's memory and using different tools to help you do so. This lesson is concerned with other performance issues, such as finding bottlenecks or points inside your computer that slow down the entire system, examining the performance of your CPU and hard disk, and maintaining your hard drive. You look at some of the same tools that you used to investigate your computer's memory.

The primary focus of this lesson is on the Performance Monitor, which is the major utility that is included with NT. You'll see how to use its different features. However, there are some caveats to be aware of while using any utility that helps monitor performance. Because these utilities are applications that consume part of your computer's resources, the measurements they give aren't entirely accurate. The measurements include the resources that the utility is using as well as the resources that your operating system is using plus any additional applications you happen to be running. So, the trick is to try to determine how much RAM, how many processor cycles, and so on that the utility uses and subtract this from the total. Furthermore, be aware that network activity can alter the results you get from performance utilities. In addition, boot-up activity also will affect results. It is therefore best to wait until the computer is fully booted before starting your utilities and run them at a time when no network activity is occurring.

Performance Monitor

The Performance Monitor is a great item for tracking the performance of nearly all the important aspects pertaining to your computer's resources. If there are any shortcomings in this tool, it's that its measures are sometimes too complex to understand; it should have come with better online documentation to help users understand the significance of its measures. It can also be a bit overwhelming attempting to choose which values to monitor. You'll see as you use the tool that there are many values to choose from, and unless you are very familiar with how PCs work, you might not even know what a certain measure is.

The Performance Monitor will let you export data that it collects to a spreadsheet. This is very useful, because you can compare different activities. One spreadsheet can contain the performance data of a specific set of operations (running your word processor and spreadsheet applications at the same time) while another spreadsheet can show performance while you used your graphics applications. Additionally, different spreadsheets can show the measurement and use of different computer resources. I would find this utility far less useful if it didn't have a way to easily export the data. I tend to start the Performance Monitor, begin to perform typical tasks, and then export the results. After I have a representative sample of my computer's behavior, I fine tune the virtual memory and other settings and print out more reports using the Performance Monitor to see how the changes I made affected the speed and performance.

The Performance Monitor also lets you save different chart settings so that each time you run the utility you don't have to again select all the objects you want to measure.

Performance Monitor will enable you to collect information about trends over a period of time. This can be especially useful if you need to track the affect different users have on a computer's resources or have other needs for collecting information over time.

If you need to, you can have multiple copies of Performance Monitor running using different resource measures in each window. When it is first started, Performance Monitor will look in the `%SystemRoot%_Default.pmc` directory for default chart settings. Another way of having it automatically open a settings file is to save the chart settings and put a shortcut to this file in the Startup folder; after doing this, the utility will be launched each time NT boots up.

If you are on a network and need to monitor other computers, you can. If you launch Performance Monitor from the command line or from a batch file, the command would look as follows:

```
C:\perfmon \\computer_name
```

You would replace *computer_name* with the real name of the computer you want to monitor. If you would like to choose a computer or a specific settings file then you need to list the settings file before the computer name, as in the following:

```
C:\perfmon settings_file_name \\computer_name
```

Understanding Units of Measure in Performance Monitor

One of the most difficult aspects of using this utility is understanding what all the different units you can measure represent. We don't have space to cover all the different items you can measure but let's look at the more important ones. After you have started the Performance Monitor by either going to Start | Programs | Administrative Tools | Performance Monitor, or going to Start | Run and typing perfmon, you are then ready to choose elements that you want to monitor. To see the options NT gives you, go to Edit | Add to Chart. This will bring up the screen in Figure 6.1.

Figure 6.1.

Adding objects to the Performance Monitor brings up the Add to Chart window.

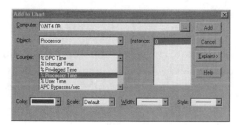

The Performance Monitor now gives you the option of adding various objects if you go to the Object window and click on the pull-down window. Let's examine some of these.

Performance Monitor and Its Components

If you look at Figure 6.2, the window of this utility, you'll see that it offers several ways to view the information that it can track. First, notice the toolbar, which is directly under the menus and contains small icons.

Figure 6.2.

The Performance Monitor window has several useful features and different ways to view the information it collects.

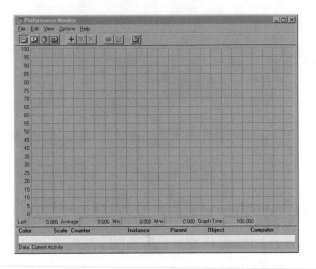

The Chart View

The first icon in the toolbar (on the far left in Figure 6.2) is a small picture of a graph. By default, the Performance Monitor will use this choice to display objects after you have added them from the Edit menu. It will display a chart with lines that show how resources are being used in real time. That is, it shows you how different components of your computer behave while the application is running. To use the chart view, follow these steps:

1. Choose the Edit menu item, and choose Add to Chart.
2. In the window that pops up, you can choose which computer to monitor, what objects to view, which counters to use, and which instance for the counter to use. Each of these items are defined in the glossary at the end of the chapter. Chart View files are automatically given the extension of .PMC.

The Alert View

The second icon on the toolbar presents a different view: an Alert View. It lets you configure it so that any time the performance measures you have set are not met, the computer will record it and enable you to look at the log. For example, you might want to know when your memory usage is getting low and be notified when it hits a certain level. You would use the Alert View to do this.

1. Click on the Alert icon in the toolbar.
2. Go to the File menu, down to New Alert Settings.

6

3. In the new window that appears, select Add Counter, which brings up the Add to Alert window. Now, you can add items as you would normally.

4. In the Add to Alert window you need to establish the point at which you want it to log data. Be careful to use a percentage number if that is how the counter measures or whole numbers if it is not a percentage. You will see a percentage before the measure if it uses percentages.

5. Finally, you can prompt the Performance Monitor to run a batch file or program when an alert is recognized. In the Run Program on Alert box, type in the name of the batch file or application to be launched.

You can set a wide variety of conditions that you want to be logged as alerts. Alert View files are automatically given an extension of .PMA.

The Log View

The Log view enables you to keep continuous records of your choice that you can look at to understand your computer or use to learn about resource usage. Because this is meant to give you an overall view of your computer over time, choose lengthy gaps or intervals.

1. Click on the Log View icon.

2. Go to the Edit menu and select Add to Log item.

3. Select which items you would like to log and the intervals at which you want each item measured.

4. Go to the File, save log settings. Give the file a name and click Save.

You have selected objects that you want to track, but now you need to create the log file. To do this, go to the Options menu and select Log; this displays the Log Options window. You now need to enter a name for the file. You also need to set an update time, which tells the program how often you want the file to be updated.

The intervals that are used are in seconds, so you probably want to set a very large number so the file is not constantly updated. However, you can turn off automatic updating and select manual updating. If you are ready to begin logging, click on Start Log. However, if you don't want to start logging now, simply click Save and return to the Log window later when you are ready to start logging. To do this, open the Log Window, select Options, and then select start to log. The start log button changes to stop log. To stop logging, simply click the stop button if you want to stop the logging process. Log View files are automatically given an extension of .PML.

The Report View

The Report view enables you to save information about objects and other elements you have selected. Report view formats the information and columns, making it easy to read. To create a report, follow these steps:

1. Click the fourth icon from the left in the toolbar. Next, select Options | Data From, and make the appropriate selections. The Performance Monitor will ask you if you want to create a new report based on the computer's current activity or if you want to use a log file that you might have already created.

2. Go to the Edit menu and choose Add to Report. The Add to Report dialog box appears, and you can select your objects, counters, and instances.

3. When you finish making your selections, click Done.

Performance Monitor will create Report and a Report window which you can view at any time by clicking on the Report view icon and the toolbar. For your convenience you can export reports to a spreadsheet application. By exporting multiple reports to a spreadsheet you can make comparisons. Report view files are automatically assigned the extension .PMR.

Monitoring the Processor: Counters

The Performance Monitor provides you with several ways to see how your processor handles applications. The way performance Monitor measures processor usage is by sampling threads. It does not time the duration it takes to complete a task. Let's look at some of the counters you can use to measure the processor activity.

System: % Total Processor Time: This measures the duration during which the processor was busy. The measurement is a percentage of the sample intervals.

System: % Processor Queue Length: This measures the number of threads that need to wait in order to be processed. Be aware that this measurement is not an average but rather a snapshot of a given moment.

Processor: % Processor Time: This measures the percentage of time that the processor was busy. If you are lucky enough to have several processors, it will inform you of the percentage of time that each processor was busy.

Processor: % User Time: This measures the percentage of time that the processor was executing threads running in user mode. Applications are run in user mode while the operating system runs in kernel mode. Kernel mode is a special or privileged mode of operation in which the code has access to all the memory, even memory used by applications. Kernel mode also provides the code with direct access to the hardware and access to special CPU features involving memory management.

Processor: % Privileged Time: This measures the percentage of time that the processor was executing threads running in privileged mode.

Process: % Processor Time: This measures the percentage of time that the processor was executing the threads sent through the CPU.

Process: % Processor Time(_Total): This measures the percentage of time that the processor was executing threads.

Process: % User Time: This measures the percentage of time that the process executes in user mode. (This means it is executing application code.)

Process: % Privileged Time: This measures the percentage of time that the process executes in privileged mode. (This means it is executing operating system code.)

Interpreting Counters

Now that you have looked at some of the primary processor counters, look at how to interpret the results they will give you. You might want to assume that a high amount of processor activity might indicate that you need a more powerful processor. However, this is not the case. If you notice that a lot of threads need to wait in the queue, then perhaps it is time to upgrade your processor, because this indicates that the processor cannot execute threads quickly enough. However, before you jump to this conclusion, make sure that a lack of memory is not causing the problem. (Consult Hour 5 for memory problems.) Try to determine which processes are causing the bottleneck. When you have determined which application is responsible, you might be able to fine-tune this application.

Measuring Disk Performance

Disk performance is another crucial element to measure. When taken in conjunction with the other elements you have learned to monitor, it will give you a complete picture of your system's performance. Again, use the Performance Monitor to help you analyze efficiency.

% Disk Time: This measures how busy the disk is. This measurement will be shown as a percentage.

Current Disk Queue Length: This measures the extent to which disk requests have to wait. If you noticed that two or more requests are waiting, the disk might be the bottleneck.

Avg. Disk sec/Transfer: This measures the speed at which data is transferred.

Disk Bytes/sec: This measures the speed at which data is transferred; the measurement is in bytes.

6

According to the Microsoft Windows NT Workstation Resource Kit, you might have a disk bottleneck if you have continuous disk activity above 85% and a continuous queue of more than 2 for each disk. Be careful not to assume mistakenly that these problems are caused by a disk bottleneck when, in fact, it could be from a lack of memory. If you don't have much RAM in your system, NT will begin to write items from memory to the hard disk, and as a general rule, disk activity is higher the less memory you have. To determine if it is a memory bottleneck, use the Performance Monitor to measure the following counters: Memory: Page reads/sec, memory: Page writes/sec, memory: Pages input/sec, memory: Pages output/sec.

It is possible to measure the throughput of your hard disk by using the Performance Monitor to chart several elements. By looking at the speed at which your hard disk can read, write, and transfer data, you can measure throughput. In the Performance Monitor, choose logical and physical disk as your object and then select the following counters: Avg. disk bytes/read, Avg. disk sec/read, disk read bytes/sec, disk reads/sec, Avg. disk bytes/write, Avg. disk sec/write, disk write bytes/sec, and disk writes/sec.

Cache Memory

There is one more area that you will want to consider when you are determining the performance of your computer system. Windows NT file system cache is created by the operating system as an area used by the I/O which maps recently used data to a special area in RAM. Because file system cache is part of your RAM, if you are low in memory NT might not be able to set aside enough cache, forcing your system to access data from the hard disk.

The Performance Monitor provides several important counters for measuring the effectiveness of your cache. Particularly you will want to use the following counters: Cache: Copy Reads/sec, Cache: Copy Read Hits %, Cache: Read Aheads/sec, Memory: Cache Bytes, and Memory: Cache Faults/sec.

Summary

This hour explained various ways in which you can gather more information on your computer and how it uses its resources. In this regard NT is more sophisticated because it offers much better built-in tools than Microsoft has offered in the past. You should be aware that adjusting how your computer uses its resources can have important effects—both good and bad. Therefore, it is a good idea to use the Performance Monitor first to simply see how resources are used, and then make minor adjustments to improve on how the system uses resources. NT's default settings will often work fine, but the only way of being sure of this is to use utilities to check.

Workshop

The Workshop helps you solidify the skills you learned this hour.

Glossary

cache   Memory space that holds information that the computer has recently used from data storage. Cache RAM can pass information to the processor faster than data storage.

counters   The Performance Monitor uses units called counters to display activity. Different objects have their own particular sets of counters.

instance   In the Performance Monitor, an instance represents a tracking of an object. You are able to track multiple instances of some objects.

logical disk   Partitions on a drive. A single hard disk may be broken up by partitioning using FDISK to create several distinct areas known as logical disks, each of which will be assigned its own drive letter. While we normally assume each drive letter designation refers to a separate hard disk, it does not always.

object   When you initially launch the Performance Monitor, you get a blank chart, and need to add objects; an object can be a thread or process, an allocated section of memory, or a physical device in your computer. Performance Monitor can track the way the different objects use resources. You may want to check your Control Panel | Services to see which services you have running. Some objects will not appear in the utility unless they are running, while other objects are always listed.

Paging File   Paging File is used by the Virtual Memory Manager to swap information from RAM to the hard drive, in affect allowing your computer's hard drive to simulate RAM.

process   Representation of an application being executed by the computer. Therefore, a process represents something such as a task or application that is running.

processor   The physical device or central processing unit that executes code.

thread   As a process has several parts, a thread is the part that the processor executes. Threads, more specifically, are parts of computer code that are responsible for making things happen. For example, when you send a print job to the printer, a thread is spawned or passed to the processor to get the job down.

Exercises

1. Launch the Performance Monitor and add the processor as your object. Now, select several counters that will give you an overall picture of your processor's performance. Are you able to detect whether or not you have a bottleneck here?

2. Launch the Performance Monitor and add Logical disk as your object. Now, select several counters that will help you determine the performance of your hard disk.

3. Perform similar tasks for the cache and memory objects. Now, after you have collected data for each of these objects, export the data to a spreadsheet and compare the charts. Try to determine the weakest components of your system.

PART

II

The Afternoon

Hour

Hour 7

Setting Up Printers with NT Workstation

by Martin Kenley

This hour looks at setting printers up under Windows NT 4 and troubleshooting them when a problem occurs. We can be thankful that the programmers at Microsoft have done a much better job at creating a truly easy interface in the operating system, which makes installing printers a simple task. With the decrease in prices, most people now own some type of printer directly connected to their computer. But this hour also shows you how to install a printer connected by a local area network (LAN).

Generally, today you have the option of buying three types of printers: dot matrix, ink jet, and laser jet. Dot matrix printers are the oldest and have the lowest quality output, and laser jets are the most expensive.

Dot matrix printers work in a simple way: as the name implies, they produce an image by printing a series of small dots that connect together to form either a graphical image or a letter.

Ink jet printers, on the other hand, spray ink onto the page. By controlling how the ink sprays, the printer can form images and characters. Fortunately, this technology has allowed the price of good-quality printing to fall, and you can now get good print output for under $300.

Laser jet printers use the most expensive technology of the three type of printers discussed here (there is more expensive print technology, but it is beyond the scope of this book). They work by using a laser to burn ink images on the paper.

Setting Up Printers

The Explorer interface makes setting up printers a relatively easy task. To set up a printer, use the Add Printer wizard and follow these steps:

1. Go to the Start menu and select Settings.
2. Click the Printers folder.
3. Click Add Printer.
4. A window will appear asking if you are connecting the printer directly to your computer or are connecting remotely (see Figure 7.1).

Figure 7.1.

NT makes the installation of remote and local printers easy.

5. If you are installing a local printer, you'll see a window similar to that shown in Figure 7.2. You will usually choose LPT1. If you scroll down the list of ports, you will find an option called FILE. This is the option you would use if you did not want to send the file to a printer, but rather wanted to send it to a dump file on the hard drive.

6. If you are installing a network printer on your computer, you will see a window similar to that shown in Figure 7.3; navigate to the remote printer and click it.

Figure 7.2.

The Add Printer wizard prompts you to select a port if it is a local printer.

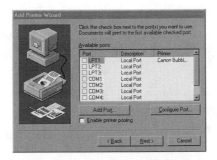

Figure 7.3.

If you are installing a network printer on your computer, you must use this window to locate the network printer.

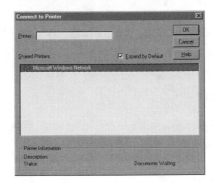

7. Next, choose the type of printer you are installing. You are presented with a list of printers from which to select. If your printer isn't in the list, install the driver from a disk or from the network (if you have it on your network). If the file is on your network, use the Browse button to navigate to where the driver is.

TIME SAVER

You can navigate through the list of manufacturers more quickly if you type the first letter of the company. For example, if you are installing a printer made by Hewlett Packard, you can simply type h, and the Add Printer wizard will take you down to the manufacturers whose names begin with the letter h. The same rule applies to the list of printers.

8. You are then given the option of whether you want this new printer to be the default printer. If it is, then all of your Windows applications will automatically print to it, unless told to do otherwise. Click Next.

9. If you are installing a local printer, the next window queries whether you want to share this printer on your network. If you decide to share it, you must give it a name and then select which operating systems the computers that will print to the new printer use.

7

10. You are asked if you want to print a test page. I recommend doing so immediately so you can see if the printer is correctly set up.

11. After you click Finish, Windows NT will prompt you for the driver, which could be in the i386 directory of the NT CD or on your network.

When you complete these steps, your printer should be successfully connected, but there is still more to configure. The next thing that happens is the Add Printer wizard opens the Printer properties sheet so you can complete the setup. If it did not do so, go to the printer folder, right-click on the new printer, and select Properties.

Printer Properties Sheet

After you have added your printer, you should go through the Printer properties sheet to complete the installation of your printer. Figure 7.4 shows how the properties sheet window looks.

Figure 7.4.

The Printer properties sheet provides you with a handful of options. Take time to check out the options under each tab.

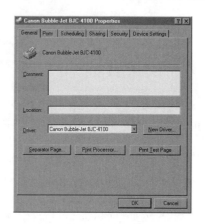

The General Tab

The first page you see when you go to the properties sheet is the General tab. Most of the items on this page don't need an explanation, but look at the three buttons near the bottom of the page:

☐ Separator Page: This button enables you to modify what appears on the separator page that is printed between each document sent to the printer. If this page has not been modified, the name of the user who is logged on will appear. If your printer is not being shared, then you will probably not want a separator page. Because the separator pages are also used to switch a printer between different printer languages, you might need one if you use more than one language with your printer.

☐ Print Processor: Click this button to configure a different print processor that handles the rasterizing (conversion of images or fonts to bitmap images for printing) of the print job. Try clicking each of the processors and you'll see that each has different datatypes. By default, NT chooses Winprint as the print processor because it is capable of handling numerous datatypes.

☐ New Driver: This is an important option. If the driver you have chosen is not working or your print jobs are getting garbled characters, try using another printer driver. Many print devices (what most people refer to as printers) are compatible with a Hewlett Packard (HP) print driver. Try several of them if you do not have the driver for your print device. NT also supplies a generic text-only driver, which works with many printers. Note that NT also provides a Print Test Page option here. After changing the driver, try printing a test page.

The Ports Tab

The next tab at the top of the Printer properties sheet is Ports (see Figure 7.5). This page lets you select the port to which you want to print. This page is similar to the page you get when you are initially adding a printer using the Print Setup wizard. This page does give you one option not available before: you can now enable bidirectional support. Generally, you should select this option, unless it is grayed out (meaning your port does not support bidirectional communication, or it already is using this capability as fully as it can).

Figure 7.5.

The Ports page enables you to configure ports for printing.

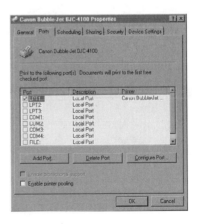

It is also possible to reconfigure the port that your computer is using. You can delete or add a port here as well.

7

The Scheduling Tab

The Scheduling page enables you to establish the priorities for your print jobs and configure the spooling options (see Figure 7.6). In addition, you can set the times for which the print device is available. This is useful if the print device is on the network and you want to restrict the times that it is available. Otherwise, you should choose Always so there is no limit. Other items on this page include the following:

☐ Priority: NT will rank the print jobs it sends on the basis of the order it sends them as well as by the priority that you have used for that print job or that computer. If jobs coming from a certain computer should have a higher priority than other print jobs, then move the slider bar over to Highest on that particular computer.

Figure 7.6.

To set spool features of the print job priority, use the Scheduling page.

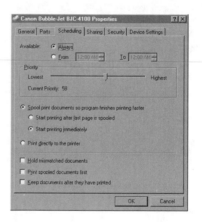

☐ Spool print documents so program finishes printing faster: The Scheduling page also gives you the option to spool the print job so the application finishes printing faster. If you select this option, you regain control of your application faster than choosing Print directly to the printer. By spooling, NT will take the entire print job from your application all at once and feed it to the print device in the background. It is best to let NT worry about this rather than the application, because NT does it in a less obtrusive manner.

☐ Print directly to the printer: If you select this option, NT will not spool the job, and it lets your application direct the output to the print device. A practical time to select this option is when you use applications that have their own spooling capabilities.

☐ Hold mismatched documents: Select this option if you want NT to be able to delay a print job if it is interrupted during the print process. It may be interrupted for several reasons: for example, if the print job does not match the current printer setup, then the job could be held for you.

7

   ☐ Print spooled documents first: When you have selected this option, print jobs that are sent directly to the print device will print after those jobs that have been spooled.

   ☐ Keep documents after they have printed: If you need a record of what has been printed, then you will want to use this option. Make sure the box next to this line is checked. If you do so, you will have to manually delete the jobs from the queue after they have printed.

The Sharing Tab

If you are connected to a network and would like to share your printer to other computers, you must use the options presented on the Sharing tab (see Figure 7.7).

Figure 7.7.

Sharing your printer over the network requires you to configure the options presented in the Sharing page.

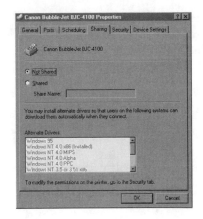

Click the white circle next to Shared and type in a name for the printer; make sure the name is not being used. If other computers will be running other versions of NT, you should install drivers for them so that when they attempt to print, the driver will automatically be transferred to their computer.

The Security Tab

The Security tab, shown in Figure 7.8, enables you to configure the security of shared printers on your network: permissions, auditing, and ownership. To have full use of these options, log on to NT with administrative privileges.

7

Figure 7.8.

The Security page enables you to grant individual persons and groups access to the print device, audit its use, and take ownership.

Permissions

The Permissions section of the Security page enables you to set which users can use the printer (see Figure 7.9). Clicking the Permissions button shows you who has permission; you can then add or remove them. It is possible to assign different levels of access:

1. Full control gives a person or group the ability to print, halt a job, change priorities, and so on.
2. Manage documents enables users to send and delete jobs, but they cannot configure the settings in any way.
3. Print permission enables users to print but does not give them permission to cancel a job.
4. No access permission will not enable users to use the printer in any way.

Figure 7.9.

To add or remove access to the print device for users or groups, use the Printer Permissions dialog box.

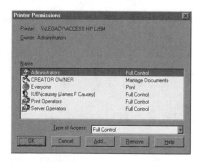

Auditing

The Auditing feature of the Security page enables you to monitor the print device. You can audit print jobs, change control, delete, change permissions, and change ownership. To use these features, make sure you have first enabled Auditing for each person or group you want to audit (see Figure 7.10).

7

Figure 7.10.

The Printer Permission box enables you to grant users or groups the right to print to a specific printer.

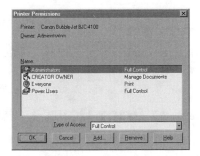

Ownership

Finally, use the Ownership button of the Security page to take ownership of the printer. Be aware that you will need to be an administrator in order to have ownership of a printer. In fact, nothing administratively changes when you take ownership of a printer—administrative matters are handled in ways already discussed. This button is useful for assigning responsibility, however.

Device Settings

Each printer will list its own set of options according to its capabilities. For example, color printers will offer options on setting up color balance options and other settings (see the example shown in Figure 7.11).

Figure 7.11.

The property sheet shown here indicates the device settings for a Cannon Bubble-Jet printer.

Halftone Setup enables you to configure how the printer maps dots using shades of gray or color. It is possible to adjust the size of the dots, place colored dots close to each other to produce other colors, and adjust the color intensity.

7

Troubleshooting Printer Problems

When you are troubleshooting printers, there are several ways to solve the problem. Make sure to write down any error messages NT gives you. These may help to correct the problem.

Problem 1: Print Device Outputs Junk

If your print device outputs junk, the most common problem is that you have a bad or corrupt print driver or you have installed the wrong driver. Follow the steps to reinstall the driver, and when NT prompts you to keep the existing driver, select No.

If your print device is printing the incorrect fonts, the font table of your printer (assuming it has one) might be incorrect. Look at this table to determine what font the printer chooses if the screen font is not available.

Problem 2: Printing Speed Is Too Slow

There are several ways you can speed up print jobs. Look at the following list and see which items might apply to your current situation:

1. Use color only when absolutely necessary. If you can get by with black ink, choose it, because it is much faster.
2. If you are preparing a presentation, try to use primary colors (black, cyan, yellow, magenta, green, red, and blue). Less information is needed to print these colors.
3. If your printer allows diffusion, turn it off. Go the printer folder, right-click your printer, select Device Settings, and choose Halftones. Generally, you will want to turn on Diffusion only when you are ready to print final works in high-quality or photographic images.
4. If your printer has the option of Match as the Color Adjustment, turn it off and your printer device will print more quickly. This process requires additional information that slows down the printing process.
5. Try to free up some of your computer's RAM. To do this, try closing other open applications and unloading wallpaper and screen savers to reduce the memory used by them.
6. Choose Draft quality for your print job, unless it is a final draft and you need high-quality output.
7. Add RAM to your computer. Print jobs will be handled more quickly, and your applications will run faster.

7

Problem 3: Printer Is Not Responding

If your printer is not responding, try using a different cable, especially if you get a message saying the printer is off. A bad cable can make the computer think your printer is not turned on.

Try substituting a known good printer for the printer that is malfunctioning. If the good printer works on that computer, then you can narrow it down to the printer and eliminate the computer as a source of problems.

Conversely, try using the existing printer that is having troubles on another computer. If it works on another computer, it is likely a problem with the original computer.

Test the parallel port with a loop-back plug and a diagnostics application such as AmiDiag.

Summary

This hour provided information on how to set up both network and local printers. It also gave you information on how to troubleshoot a printer that isn't working. In addition, you have learned how to set up the printer so it is shared on your LAN. After you have set up sharing, make sure you have limited access to the necessary groups and individual persons so you don't receive print jobs from unauthorized parties.

Workshop

The Workshop helps you solidify the skills you learned this hour.

Glossary

EMF   Enhanced is the format that the NT graphical device interface uses when it sends data to the printer driver.

print client   Any computer that sends a job to an NT print server is a print client. This concept can be confusing; as NT defines the client, it can be either a machine on a LAN or simply the computer that is directly connected to the print device.

print device   As defined by NT, a print device is the actual piece of hardware that is generally referred to as a printer. You load it with paper and it outputs your documents.

print job   In NT, a print job is the computer program language that holds the data being sent to the printer as well as the code that tells the printer what to do.

7

print server   A computer used to manage the printer or printers and the print jobs. All the computers on the network can send their jobs to the print server, which then handles the rest of the job.

print spooler   The spooler is a set of dynamic-link libraries (DLLs) responsible for handling print jobs. The DLLs handle the processing, scheduling, and routing of the jobs. The spooler also spools or writes the print file to disk; the file then becomes a spool file.

printer driver   Software that is specific to the print device and allows applications to successfully talk to a print device.

printer (Logical printer)   The printer is a software interface that enables the operating system (NT) to successfully send signals and data to the print device. Normally, you can configure various settings in the printer—for example, specify a port. You can have more than one printer installed; conversely, you can have one logical printer controlling several physical printers.

PSCRIPT1   A data format that tells the spooler that the data is coming from a Macintosh computer using PostScript, and the printer is not PostScript-capable. The spooler will create a bitmap to print the document correctly.

queue   A group of documents that are in line to be printed.

RAW   This is a data type, like EMF. Whereas Windows NT uses EMF, most other clients use the RAW format. RAW format is not altered by the spooler, because the RAW format itself is printable.

rendering   The process of rendering a document involves actually processing the document. For example, when your word processor sends a print job, it is intercepted by a graphical device interface, which then talks to the printer (not the print device), and a print job is created. When the print job reaches the print device, it is interpreted and translated into a bitmap.

TEXT   The TEXT data format sends ANSI (American National Standards Institute; the ANSI character set defines 256 characters) text to the spooler, which uses the printer driver to handle print elements such as default font. A TEXT file uses numbers ranging from 0 to 255, where each number correlates to a specific character or symbol. When printing from an application that does not use the ANSI character set, some characters may be incorrectly printed. Another character set, PC-437, is often used in MS-DOS applications.

7

Exercises

1. Go to the Printer property sheet on your system and look at how your printer is being shared. Note the current settings. Is the printer being shared by the appropriate individual persons and groups?

2. Go to the Printer property sheet and look at the options under Device settings. Note the current settings. Are all the settings configured according to your preference?

3. Go to the Printer property sheet and look at the options under Security settings. Look at the current settings. Are all the settings configured according to your preference?

7

Hour 8

Remote Access to Your Work and Setting Up Laptops

by Martin Kenley

The question of how to coordinate files between your work at the office and at home has become more important in recent times. These days work requires us to use computers for so much that we now take files home or on the road with us, not to mention having needs such as checking electronic mail and getting the latest information from the company database. The need to access such resources has been recognized by software developers, who have provided a variety of solutions. This hour focuses solely on what is built into Windows NT—specifically, the Briefcase and dial-up networking. These two products help alleviate the problem of having to transport files away from your office computer (and coordinating the files), as well as being able to access files on the company network or your workstation.

To understand the Briefcase and dial-up networking, it makes sense to view these two products in two ways, depending on your needs: both can accomplish a similar task, or one can complement the other. They both involve remote computing. The Briefcase enables you to coordinate files you take from your desktop computer.

Understanding the Briefcase

The Briefcase, which was first introduced in the Windows 95 Explorer interface, is a powerful tool for synchronizing the files between two or more computers. It was especially developed with laptop computers in mind, so that users with portables could take the Briefcase with them and not have to worry about where the most recently updated files are (in the Briefcase or on the desktop computer). In fact, the name of this utility is very appropriate, because the Briefcase folder does indeed behave like a briefcase: You copy the Briefcase itself to the floppy disk or another computer on the network. In essence, you take it with you, as you would a real briefcase.

Using the Briefcase

Using the Briefcase is easy. The first thing is to decide which files you would like to coordinate between the two computers. Keep in mind you have several limitations to work within. Unfortunately, the Briefcase will work only on computers that are running Windows NT 4 or Windows 95; it is not compatible with Windows 3.1 or Windows NT 3.51 or earlier. Also, if you will be transferring the files by floppy disk, the files cannot exceed the memory of one high-density floppy; the Briefcase is unable to break files up across multiple disks.

After you have selected your files, open the destination (either your floppy disk or the network computer to which you are transferring it). Make sure you can see both the Briefcase and the destination.

Verifying the Status of Files in the Briefcase

If you are uncertain about a file in the Briefcase—for example, where the original file that it is attached to is located—you can easily find out by following these steps:

1. Go to the Briefcase and double-click it to open it.
2. Find the file you want to check the status of, and click it one time to select it.
3. Right-click the file and scroll down the pop-up menu; go to Properties.
4. Choose the Update Status tab, as shown in Figure 8.1. You will now see two files shown in the middle of the property sheet: one file, generally the one on the left, represents the file inside the Briefcase; and the other, the file to which it is attached.

If you hold the mouse over either file, a tiny window appears indicating the path to the file. If the option to Update the files is grayed out, this means that the files have been synchronized and you don't need to update them now.

Figure 8.1.

The properties sheet of items inside the Briefcase shows detailed information on the files, including which file they are attached to, as displayed here.

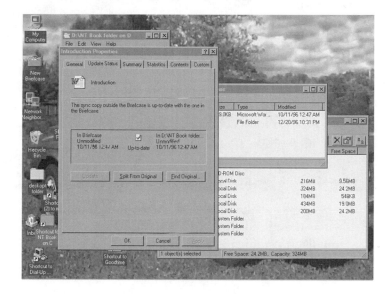

Remote Access Services: Using a Modem to Dial into Your NT Workstation

Remote Access Services (RAS) enables you to access all your files on your office workstation from a remote location with another computer. NT has RAS built into it; to use this service, you only need to configure it properly. If your office machine has a connection to the Internet, it is possible to configure RAS to access it remotely as well as the files on your office computer.

Preparation for Setting Up RAS

Before you begin, you will need two pieces of information: what type of modem you have and to which communications port it is connected. If you are unsure which port it is attached to, continue on and you can have Windows NT or 95 automatically detect the port.

In addition, if you are planning to dial into your office computer and want to see the entire network of your office, you will need to know another IP number not in use that your office computer can assign to your home computer. In most cases, you can get this IP number from the person in charge of your computers.

JUST A MINUTE

> Keep in mind that setting up RAS will not enable you to run applications from your office computer while at home. The connection is far too slow to make this practical. However, to access files and transfer files from the office to home and vice versa, RAS is a fine solution. Other valid reasons for using RAS are for IP applications such as Telnet and FTP and for browsing the Web with Netscape or other Web browsers.

First, you learn how to set up RAS services on the server that will be holding documents you want to access remotely. In most cases, your office computer will be the server to which you will want to connect from home. Then you learn how to set up the computer that is dialing into the server.

Setting Up RAS on NT 4 Workstation

Follow these steps to set up RAS services on the computer you want to be able to access remotely. After you have done this, you only need to configure the remote computer to dial into the RAS station to access your files or the Internet.

1. A user must be logged on as an administrator or as a user with administrative privileges to set up RAS.

2. To install RAS, go to the Control Panel and select the Network icon.

3. Choose Services and click Add. Next, scroll down to Remote Access Service (RAS) and click it. NT will now need to know the location of the install files. In most cases, this will be the I386 file on the NT CD-ROM (D:\I386). Click OK.

4. NT will then ask you if you want to start the Modem installer, if you have not yet installed a modem. Answer yes to this. Allow NT to autodetect your modem and com port. If it does not find it from the list, choose Standard Modem and then select the appropriate speed. Click Finish.

5. Next, NT will ask you to choose a RAS device to preselect your modem. Choose OK. This takes you to the RAS setup dialog box. Here, choose Network, and in the new dialog box, select TCP/IP (and IPX if you need to connect to any NetWare servers). De-select NetBEUI, and click OK.

6. This takes you back to the RAS setup box again. Choose Configure | Dial Out only. Click OK. Next in the RAS setup, click continue.

Granting Dial-In Permissions

You have set up RAS, and now you must grant permissions for yourself (and perhaps others) to dial into this server. Permissions provide security so that only those who are authorized may dial into your computer. Follow these steps:

1. Go to the Start menu | Programs | Administrative Tools, and click the User Manager.
2. Select the users to whom you would like to grant access.
3. Open the User Menu, choose properties, and click the Dial-In button.
4. Choose No Call Back if you want a user to make only one call to this computer (the computer that is being dialed into).
5. Select Set by Caller to let the caller indicate a telephone number for a return call.

Starting RAS Services for the First Time

The first time you start RAS services, you need to do so manually by following these steps. As you follow through these steps, notice that you can set RAS to automatically start itself when you turn your computer on.

1. Go to the Control Panel, and click Services.
2. Select RAS.
3. On the right side of the dialog box, click Start.
4. Click Close; you have now started the RAS Server to accept calls. Or click Startup, select Automatic, and now RAS will be started automatically whenever the computer is booted. However, if you do this, RAS will attempt to answer the phone if it rings. If your office phone shares this same phone number, you will probably want to start RAS manually when you leave in the evening.

Now you can set up a dial-up configuration on your home machine. (See the "Setting Up Your Home Computer to Dial into Your Office Computer" section for instructions on accomplishing this.)

Setting Up RAS on an NT 4 Server

If you have an NT server installed on your computer at work rather than Workstation, follow these instructions to set up the RAS services. Again, these steps are for setting up RAS on the computer you will want to access remotely.

1. A user must be logged on as an administrator to set up RAS.
2. To install RAS, double-click Dial-Up Networking.

3. Click Install in the new dialog box that appears.

4. Next, a new dialog box appears prompting you to choose the type of modem and the com port to which it is connected. If you know the com port and type of modem, you can select the "Don't detect my modem, I will select it from a list" item. Click Next and choose your modem. If you don't know the type of modem, deselect the "Don't detect my modem, I will select it from a list" and click Next. NT will find which com port your modem is attached to.

5. After it detects a modem, click Next to choose the type of modem that you have. If your specific brand of modem is not in the list, then choose the Standard modem in the list that matches the speed of your modem. For example, if you have a 28.8 that is an unusual brand not in the list, choose Standard 28.8.

6. Click Next after you have chosen your modem type, click Finish, and then click OK. The computer will add the RAS services.

7. To configure network settings, in the Remote Access Setup Box, click Network, select TCP/IP, and click Configure. You need to decide whether your office uses DHCP (which allows a server to automatically assign your IP number). If so, select DHCP. If not, you must select Use Static Address pool and type in a range of valid IP numbers so the server can assign a number to the computer that is dialing into it (commonly, your home computer). The IP numbers can be obtained from your local computer support provider. If you need to connect to NetWare servers, make sure you have the IPX box checked, in addition to TCP/IP. Next to IPX, click Configure, and keep the default settings, making sure that Allocate network numbers automatically is selected.

8. Click OK until you get back to the Remote Access Setup window. Then click Configure, and choose Receive Calls. This will let your computer accept calls. If it prompts you to install NetBIOS, click No and then Finish. You have now success-fully set up RAS services on your computer.

Granting Dial-In Permissions

There are still a few more steps. You must grant a person or group access to dial into your computer; otherwise, when prompted for a username and password, the party dialing into your computer will not be authenticated (granted permission) to access the computer. Follow these steps:

1. Go to Start | Programs | Administrative Tools, and click the User Manager.

2. Select the users to whom you would like to grant access.

3. Open the User Menu, choose properties, and click the Dial-In button.

8

4. Choose No Call Back if you want a user to make only one call to this computer (the computer that is being dialed into).

5. Select Set by Caller to let the caller indicate a telephone number for a return call.

6. Choose Preset to tell the computer to call a computer at a particular number.

7. Click OK.

Starting RAS Services

Now that you have given permission to a person or group to dial in, you must actually start the RAS services so the computer is ready to accept the signal when the phone rings. To do this, follow these steps:

1. Go to the Control Panel, and click Services.

2. Select RAS.

3. On the right side of the dialog box, click Start.

4. Click Close; you have now started the RAS Server to accept calls. Or click Startup | Automatic, and now RAS will be started automatically whenever the computer is booted. However, if you do this, RAS will attempt to answer the phone if it rings. If your office phone shares this same phone number, you will probably want to start RAS manually when you leave in the evening.

You have now successfully set up RAS on the server. Now go to the "Setting Up Your Home Computer to Dial into Your Office Computer" section.

Configuring Windows 95 to Act as a Dial-Up Server

Finally, if your office computer is running Windows 95, follow these steps to set it up to accept dial-in calls from a remote computer—your home computer, a laptop you use while traveling, or for a colleague. The following information assumes that you have installed the Microsoft Plus! Pack, which provides the Dial-Up server capability.

1. Select the connections menu in Dial-Up Networking, and then select Dial-Up Server. A dialog box appears in which you can choose Allow Caller Access.

2. Click the Server Type button; this enables you to select a server type. Selecting the Default server type causes the computer to start in PPP mode for incoming calls but change to RAS for NT 3.1 and Windows for Workgroups if the PPP fails. Click the OK box, and the server is ready for calls.

Setting Up Your Home Computer to Dial into Your Office Computer

To use NT 4 Workstation at home, follow these instructions:

1. A user must be logged on as an administrator or as a user with administrative privileges to set up RAS.

2. To install RAS, go to the Control Panel, and select the network icon.

3. Choose Modem, and then select how you want to use the modem: dial out, receive calls, or both. In this case, you will want to dial out (to your office computer).

4. Choose TCP/IP as the protocol. TCP/IP must be the protocol on both your home computer and your office computer that you are dialing. Do not select NetBEUI, and use IPX only if your workstation has IPX and you need NetWare access.

Dial-Up Network Phonebook

Before you make a connection to your office computer for the first time, you must create a phonebook entry for the connection.

1. Choose the Accessories icon group, and select Dial-Up Networking. You will get a message indicating that the phonebook is empty; click OK. This will take you to a New Phonebook wizard.

2. Enter a name for the entry.

3. In the server box, make an appropriate selection and click Next.

4. Select Use Telephony.

5. Put in the area code, number, and country, and click Next. Then click OK.

Making a Connection

Now that you have set up the dial-up networking, you are ready to actually dial into your office computer. To do so, follow these steps:

1. Click Dial-Up Networking.

2. Click Dial.

8

8

Setting Up RAS Under Windows NT 3.51

If you are using NT 3.51 at home rather than NT 4 or Windows 95, then you will need to follow these instructions to set up your home computer to dial your office computer:

1. Go to the Main icon group.
2. Double-click the Control Panel icon.
3. Double-click the Network icon.
4. Click Add Software.
5. Choose RAS.
6. NT then will want to know where the files are so it can install the RAS services. Usually, this will be the CD-ROM, which is the D: drive, so you would type D:\I386. (I386 is the directory on the CD-ROM where the NT setup files are stored.)
7. NT will then install the software and ask you to choose a modem and com port to which it is attached.
8. Select the Network button and choose TCP/IP, and deselect NetBEUI and IPX.

Using the Remote Access Program

Now that you have set up your 3.51 workstation at home, you are ready to use it. Follow these steps to add the proper telephone number and dial it:

1. Log onto the computer. Start the Remote Access program, which is in the RAS icon group. If there are no entries in the phonebook, you'll get a message informing you of this.
2. Choose OK, which pops open another box to which you can add a name and number.
3. After adding the name and number, choose OK. In the Remote Access program, choose the Dial button at the top of the Remote Access window. The computer will now dial the RAS server, and you can connect and do your work.

Configuring Windows 95 to Dial a RAS Server

Follow these steps if you are running Windows 95 and want to dial into your office computer:

1. Go into My Computer, double-click Dial-Up Networking, and then double-click on Make New Connection. Type a phone number, and click Finish. Now right-click the connection icon that you just created. Scroll down the pop-up menu and choose Properties.

2. A dialog box appears that will let you select the server type. The server type is a pull-down menu; choose PPP; Windows 95, Windows NT 3.5, Internet.

3. Below the Server type are more options. You should be concerned with the Log on to Network option, which by default is selected. This will enable the dial-up user to connect to the server and see other machines on the network to which the server is attached (in this case, the IU network and the Internet). If you will not need to see the network and simply want to connect to the computer (to retrieve files and upload files), deselect Log on to Network.

4. The other option to be concerned with is TCP/IP and IPX/SPX. If you only need to access files from the local machine, you don't need to select any protocols other than NetBEUI. However, if you want to see the IU network or use Netscape, you will want to enable TCP/IP by checking the box next to it.

Summary

In this hour, you have learned how to configure the remote access services of Windows NT. The RAS services have filled an important gap in networking because many people now must access their office files from the road or at home. If you followed the instructions in this lesson and are still having trouble making a connection, review the steps and try them again. If you still have troubles, see Hour 24, "Using the Internet to Maintain Your System," which describes getting information from the World Wide Web. Also try Microsoft's Web site, as well as the site of the company that manufactured your modem.

Workshop

The Workshop helps you solidify the skills you learned this hour.

Glossary

Dial-Up Networking   A utility built into Windows NT and Windows 95 that enables you to dial into a remote access server or Internet service provider and run TCP/IP applications such as Telnet, FTP, and Netscape or Internet Explorer.

IP address (Internet protocol address)   A number assigned to every computer on the Internet. It is configured by the network administrator of your LAN.

permissions   Windows NT enables you to establish different levels of access to the resources on your computer, whether it be a drive, file, directory, or printer. Users who connect to your computer can be assigned read privileges, read and write privileges, and so on.

remote access services (RAS) A service in Windows NT that enables other computers to dial into it and access services on that machine, or if it is on a network, access Internet resources.

TCP/IP (Transmission Control Protocol/Internet Protocol) A stack of protocols most commonly used on the Internet. Telnet and Netscape are two applications that use TCP/IP.

Exercises

1. Using the directions in this lesson, set up the RAS services on your computer (assuming you have a modem) and attach to it from a remote machine with a modem using dial-up networking.

2. Select two or three documents you are presently working on and, following the directions in this chapter, use the Briefcase to take those files with you. You can either put them on a floppy or use the network to transfer them to another machine. After revising the files in the Briefcase, use the Update feature to see how it works.

Hour 9

Working with Hard Disks

by Martin Kenley

This lesson and Hour 10, "Volumes and the Disk Administrator," involve hard drives; this lesson covers basic considerations of setting up one or more hard drives, and Hour 10 goes into detail on more complex elements of hard drives. This lesson examines fundamental issues of hard drives, how they work, upgrading and installing a hard drive, volumes, labels, and how to handle partitions. Hour 10 examines RAID levels.

Understanding Hard Disks

Hard drives are one of the most important components inside your computer. They are where your precious data is stored (unless you are storing it on a remote server—then it is on someone else's hard drive), along with your applications. Understanding how to manage this space is critical, and Windows NT offers ways of managing volumes that are different from Windows 3.1 or Windows 95.

First, you look at how hard drives work, and then you'll learn how information is stored on the disk. In the early 1980s, when hard drives started appearing in PCs, their capacity was 10 to 20MB, and they often had access times that were greater than 80 milliseconds. Moreover, these drives were very expensive—a 5MB drive would have cost nearly $2,000. Today's fast drives have access times under 10 milliseconds, are normally more than 1,000MB (1GB, or 1 gigabyte), and cost around $200. In addition, most of the drives use sophisticated techniques for transferring data, such as direct memory access (DMA), which enables them to transfer data directly to RAM without interrupting the CPU.

Components of a Hard Disk

Today's hard drives consist of several metal platters that spin around, with a read/write head for each side of each platter. Each platter is coated with a magnetic material that enables the read and write heads to read and write data to and from the drive. Each platter is divided into concentric circles called *tracks* (similar to the tracks on an album), which are further subdivided into *clusters*. A cylinder consists of the corresponding tracks of the different drives (see Figure 9.1). As the platter moves in a circle below the read/write head, the passing of one full revolution defines a track. The head can move, or "jump," across the surface of the disk to reach different tracks, enabling it to access data quickly. When it gets to the right track, it has to let the disk spin around until the right clusters are under it. Then the head can change the bit below it to what would be the magnetic equivalent to on or off (1 or 0). Other devices such as tape systems are truly sequential in that all the data must be read in a linear fashion, from beginning to end, whereas a hard disk can jump around in a nonlinear fashion and is therefore called *random access media*.

9

Figure 9.1.

Cylinders on each track correspond to the same track on other platters.

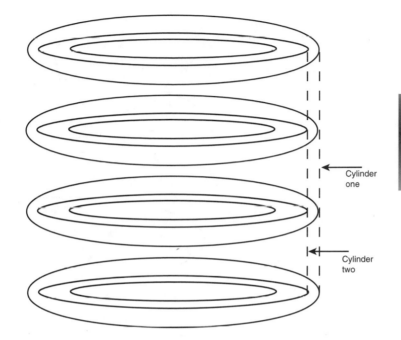

Cylinder
one

Cylinder
two

9

A cluster is the smallest unit to which a file can be allocated. Each cluster is composed of an even smaller unit called *sectors*, created when the disk is formatted (see Figure 9.2). The size of each cluster is dependent on the size of the drive, the way it is formatted, and the operating system your computer is using. (See Hour 13, "File Systems and Windows NT 4," for more general information on cluster sizes on different sized drives.)

Clusters consist of a group of sectors created when you format the hard disk (or floppy disk). The read/write head can find the beginning of sectors because they are marked by a gap followed by a numerical value, indicating either the beginning or end of a sector. Newer hard drives usually have 51 or more sectors per track, with each sector capable of holding 512 bytes.

Figure 9.2.

Hard disks are composed of several platters; each platter is divided into tracks, clusters, and sectors.

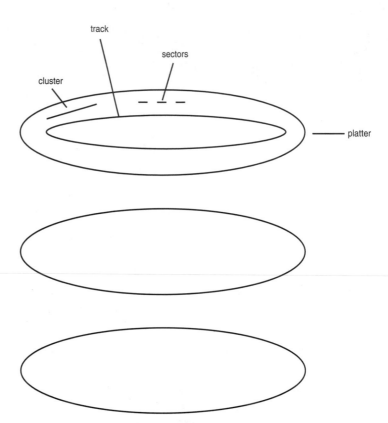

Preparing a New Hard Disk for Use

The necessity for larger hard drives has existed since the first PCs were introduced. The very first computers had no hard drives at all, and the operating system was loaded off a 5¼-inch floppy disk (with a capacity of 360KB). Today's current operating systems are as large as the entire hard drives that shipped with computers only several years ago. With NT, you will want at least 125MB of free space. The new applications that vendors are releasing take up more space than ever. If you install Microsoft Office 95, for example, a typical install requires 55MB, whereas a full install takes up about 90MB. Microsoft Word Version 7 (the Office 95 version) requires nearly 25MB (this includes the helper applications). Therefore, if you don't have a relatively new computer, you should consider upgrading to a larger hard drive.

Upgrading Your Hard Drive: A Few Considerations

Upgrading your hard drive assumes that you have enough power in the rest of the computer to warrant upgrading. In 1997, I wouldn't recommend upgrading anything older than a very powerful 486DX computer. If you are still running a computer slower than 486DX2/66, your money would probably be better spent on replacing the computer rather than on upgrading the components. The reason I say this is that even after you have upgraded the RAM, the hard drive, and perhaps your video card or processor, you still are limited by the bus speed at which your computer can operate. On the other hand, if you have a Pentium and your demands are not excessive—you are not programming, using it as a server, or doing high-end graphic editing—it is probably worth upgrading the hard drive to a larger, faster drive.

Choosing a Hard Drive

If you are replacing the old drive rather than leaving it in as a second drive, when you have everything backed up, you can then take out the old drive and swap in the new drive. When doing so, keep in mind you must replace it with a drive of the same type (Integrated Drive Electronics [IDE], EIDE [Enhanced IDE], or Small Computer System Interface [SCSI]), unless you want to add an adapter card. For example, if your computer uses IDE technology and you decide you want to replace it with a SCSI drive, then you must put a SCSI adapter card in your computer (unless you already have one installed). A possible exception is that if you have a computer that uses IDE and you want to replace it with an EIDE drive, you must make sure your ROM BIOS (basic input/output system) on the motherboard is capable of being upgraded. Most of the time, you will need to use an EIDE interface card that the new drive will plug into, instead of using the existing IDE connector. Another way to get around the problem of an old ROM BIOS is to use a software driver that will enable NT to see the whole drive. The driver must be written for NT 4, of course. Without an EIDE interface card or BIOS upgrade, the EIDE drive might work, but only by compromising performance.

Measuring the Speed of Hard Drives

When you go shopping for a hard drive, you will be bombarded with different specifications about drive performance. The most important factors are MTBF (mean time between failures—measured by the amount of time between failures) and speed. Measuring speed is a bit more complicated. The question about speed is how quickly the drive can provide the information to the CPU. Several components are involved in such measuring. One is the average access time, which is a combination of the time data buffer size (size of the cache on the drive itself), latency (the time between when the data request occurred and the data transfer began), and seek (the amount of time taken to move the read/write heads of the disk to the proper location). Therefore, when you see a drive manufacturer's access time, this figure is based on the amount of time it takes the drive to find the proper sector holding the data, in addition to the time necessary for the read/write head to stabilize over the sector and the time it takes for the drive to spin below the head so all the necessary clusters can be read.

Another element is the transfer rate of the drive, which amounts to how quickly the drive can feed information to the computer's bus. Regardless of the access time, if the drive cannot transfer the data quickly, you will have a bottleneck that in effect degrades the performance of the whole system.

Now, take a quick look at the three types of drives common today: IDE, EIDE, and SCSI.

IDE

Integrated drive electronics hard drives are by far the most common hard disk interfaces currently available. These drives are known as integrated drives because the hardware that talks to the computer and manipulates the data—the controller—is part of the hard drive itself. So, there is no need for a separate controller card. An IDE drive specification does not support drives larger than 504MB. Keep in mind that IDE can support two drives (both must be hard drives—not, for example, one hard drive and a CD-ROM drive). One of the drives is designated, through jumper settings, as the master drive; the other, again through jumpers, is designated as the slave. The master drive really doesn't control the other as the terminology implies; it is only the first to run its diagnostic tests and in most circumstances is called the C: drive. The slave drive usually receives the D: designation. If you don't set these jumpers or switches correctly, your computer will most likely fail to boot. Be sure to check your manuals or the drives themselves for instructions on how to set the jumpers or switches.

CAUTION

> You cannot run a CD-ROM drive from the IDE connector; this is possible only with EIDE and SCSI. It is possible, however, to use an IDE host adapter that will enable your PC to use four drives, by placing two chains on a single adapter.

IDE is also commonly referred to as ATA or AT attachment drives, because it was first introduced in the mid-1980s to work with the IBM AT computers.

The performance of most IDE drives is approximately 3 to 8MB per second. However, the specifications have been upgraded by Seagate Technology to allow for better performance in Fast ATA drives capable of throughputs approaching 13MB per second.

EIDE

Enhanced IDE is another approach to get around the slow transfer speeds of standard IDE. The hard drive manufacturer Western Digital's implementation of the new specification provided that drives could be larger than 504MB; speed and transfers were increased, allowing a maximum of four drives rather than two; and finally, users could connect CD-ROM devices as well as hard drives. EIDE, similar to Fast ATA, doesn't use the CPU to control the data transfer; instead, the controller on the drive controls the expansion bus using a form of programmed I/O (PIO) known as I/O channel Ready. Moreover, improvements have been made in direct memory access (DMA), allowing transfers directly to the computer's RAM without interrupting the CPU; these have contributed to performance gains.

EIDE can get around the limited drive size of IDE by changing the cylinder, sector, and head data into virtual elements; that is, assigning them new values that don't correspond to the actual number of cylinders, sectors, and heads. The drive is actually fooling the computer into thinking it has a smaller number of elements (that are within the old limits).

Because EIDE must be supported by your computer's BIOS, you must check it for certain parameters (most BIOSs that came out after 1994 are able to use EIDE drives) to ensure that it will work properly. If you see such parameters as CHS, ECHS, and LBA, your computer's BIOS might support EIDE. If not, check with your manufacturer to see if you can get a BIOS update.

With these changes, EIDE or ATA-2 can achieve throughputs of more than 11MB per second.

SCSI

Small Computer System Interface (SCSI) also embeds the controller technology directly on the drive and can support up to seven devices on an external SCSI chain, where the first item in the chain is connected directly to a SCSI adapter card, the second item is connected to a port on the first item, the third item is connected to the second item, and so on. Each item in the chain—whether it be a hard drive, scanner, CD-ROM drive, Iomega Zip, or Jazz drives, or other devices such as a tape back-up unit—operates independently of the others. Furthermore, you do not need a separate interface card for each device; one adapter card lets you control a variety of peripheral devices, thereby keeping other expansion slots open for other uses. Internally, SCSI devices would use the same cable, like IDE, but the cable would have more connectors.

Windows NT 4 has a large number of drivers for most of the common SCSI adapter cards. If you or your office has several platforms (for example, PC, Macintosh, Alpha, PowerPC) the advantage of SCSI is that the same SCSI device can work on all platforms.

As far as performance goes, SCSI and newer SCSI standards are quite fast. SCSI-1 specification, which was approved in 1986, has a transfer rate of 5MB per second. In 1994, SCSI-2 standard was approved; its transfer rate is up to 10MB per second on an 8-bit bus. SCSI-2 fast and wide has a transfer rate of 20MB per second on 16- and 32-bit buses. SCSI-3 is capable of rates approaching 40MB per second on 16- and 32-bit buses, 20MB on an 8-bit bus.

Connecting Hard Drive Cables

When you are connecting hard drive cables, there are a few considerations to remember. There are two cables to worry about when connecting hard drives: an electric power cable and a flat, wide cable for data. All hard drive data cables are marked with a red stripe on one edge of the cable, indicating that the connectors at this edge of the cable have pin 1 located here. On the hard drive itself, pin 1 usually is located at the end closest to the connector for the power cable (the four-pin cable that supplies the drive with electricity). To find the other end of the cable that connects to either the motherboard or adapter card, you must search the area around the connector for the number 1 and match this end with the cable pin 1. The cable that provides electricity to the drive is a small four-wire cable, with each of the wires a different color. The connector will attach to your hard drive only if the proper side is facing up, so it is hard to connect it the wrong way. Always make sure you are using the proper cable for the job (see Figure 9.3), and never force a cable if it does not seem to fit properly.

Using Alternative Drives: Removable Drives

For some people, adding another drive is not the best solution. If you want to be able to back up data files, then I urge you to consider tape backup devices for most traditional backup needs. In other situations, again, another hard drive might not be the answer. If you must make permanent archives of data, then you might want to consider either a tape, CD writer, or an optical drive.

If, on the other hand, you don't need permanent archives, but must back up and share large files, then a removable medium might be the answer. Iomega makes two products that have introduced midsize removable storage at a very competitive price. Iomega's Jazz drive holds 1 gigabyte (1,000 MB) of data and sells for under $500. Iomega also makes a scaled-down version, the Zip drive; each disk holds 100MB of data. Iomega makes SCSI and parallel port versions. With the parallel port device, you connect the Zip drive to your computer's parallel port. Iomega's SCSI version needs a SCSI adapter card, which is put inside your computer into one of the ISA/VESA/or PCI expansion slots. After installing it and putting your case

9

back on the computer, you then have a new port on the back of the computer (from the SCSI card) that enables you to connect SCSI devices (hard drives, scanners, CD-ROM drives, tape drives, and so on). SCSI cards come in a wide variety of choices, so pick a card carefully depending on the speed and the types of features you need. Other companies that make removable media include Syquest, MicroSolutions, Toray, and Pinnacle Micro.

Figure 9.3.

This diagram shows the common cable types for hard drives.

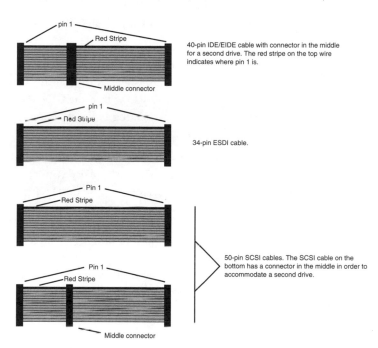

40-pin IDE/EIDE cable with connector in the middle for a second drive. The red stripe on the top wire indicates where pin 1 is.

34-pin ESDI cable.

50-pin SCSI cables. The SCSI cable on the bottom has a connector in the middle in order to accommodate a second drive.

Upgrading Your Hard Drive: Installation

Installing a new hard drive is not difficult, but it does require some planning. Take time to consider the following points.

Replacing Your Existing Drive

Make sure to take all data files and drivers off the disk before you reformat it. For example, if you have drivers for your CD-ROM drive, SCSI adapter, or sound card, save those to a floppy disk.

Next, decide whether you want a single operating system setup or a multi-boot computer. If it is going to be a one-operating system computer and you already have an operating system on it, then you must check the hardware compatibility list (HCL) from Microsoft's Web site to ensure that all the hardware on your PC is supported. The issue here is whether there are NT drivers for each of the devices you have.

If you don't find the devices listed on the HCL, you might want to check with the manufacturer of the device to see if it has NT 4 drivers. You cannot use NT 3.51 or earlier drivers. They simply will not work. However, you might be able to use compatible drivers for your device. For example, I purchased a Soundblaster32 sound card from Creative Labs, and although there was not a driver specifically for this card, another Soundblaster driver worked. After checking the Creative Labs' Web site, I found that NT 4 drivers for nearly all of their sound cards are due out in spring 1997.

Now you have determined you want only NT on your computer and the hardware is supported under NT. Consult Hour 14, "Pre-Installation Concerns with NT 4 Worksta-tion," for other pre-installation considerations. Boot up your computer using the current operating system, put the NT CD-ROM into the CD-ROM drive, and begin the installa-tion. Complete instructions for installing NT can be found in Hour 15, "Installation and Setup of NT 4 Workstation."

When you have finished the installation, reboot your computer and make sure NT is working properly, testing all the devices. After you have had your computer turned on for a while and launched the software that controls the different devices inside your computer (software that manages your SCSI devices, sound card, and so on) check the Event Viewer to see if NT has problems with any of the subsystems. To get to the Event Viewer, go to Start | Programs | Administrative Tools | Event Viewer. A final check would be to look at the Services Control Panel: Go to the Control Panel folder, open it, and click Services. Scroll down the list to make sure no services failed to load. Now after ensuring that your new installation of NT works properly and all your devices work, you can delete the other operating system that is on your computer if you want only NT.

Adding a Second Drive

If you will be keeping your current hard drive and adding a second one, the procedure is a little different. Adding a second drive makes sense, but how you do it is important. Normally, the new drive is going to be the fastest drive, and this is where you want your operating system, but you face a catch-22: When you add a second drive, you must set each drive to be either a slave or a master. The drive you are installing must be the slave, and the drive already in your computer should be set to be the master. The master will be assigned as the C: drive, and the slave will be assigned as the D: drive. The exception to this is that if the first drive has an extended partition, then DOS will label the first drive C:, the partition D:, and the second drive E:. NT will not do it this way. With NT, the two drives are labeled C: and D:, respectively, and the extended partition on the first drive would be labeled E:. With NT, you can change these assignments in the Disk Administrator; you will look at this utility in the next hour.

It doesn't matter which drive is first or second on the chain; many books will tell you otherwise, but they are wrong. Some people are confused about this because with floppy disk cables, it does matter where the floppy drive is located on the cable. With hard drives, it is best to think of the cable as a bus (in a crude way similar to a SCSI bus) in which data is passed through it—that is all the cable does.

Formatting and Partitioning a New Hard Drive

If you have a computer manufactured before 1994, your BIOS probably won't automatically recognize the new drive; therefore, you need to go into the CMOS or Setup program. If you are not sure, go ahead and reboot and check to see whether your computer found the drive. If it did not find it, after the hard drive is installed, reboot the computer and go into the CMOS or Setup program by pressing the appropriate keys during the initial stages of the boot process. At this point, you should locate the parameter settings for the second drive. You will have to consult the literature that came with the drive to type in parameters such as loading zone, cylinders, heads, pre-comp, and sectors. If your BIOS is capable of autoconfiguring, then you won't have to type these settings in yourself.

You must format a new hard drive so that your computer recognizes it and assigns it a drive letter. Use your operating system to format the drive. However, before formatting your hard drive you will need to partition it with FDISK (refer to the section "Formatting with DOS"). If you will have a dual boot computer (a computer with two or more operating systems such as DOS or Windows 95) use the File Allocation Table (FAT) as the file system; with NT, you can use FAT or NTFS (New Technology File System). (The advantages and disadvantages of NTFS are explored in Hour 13, "File Systems and Windows NT 4.") If you choose FAT, the disk will be divided into four areas, although to you it appears it is one area. Here I am not referring to partitions; suppose you use NT to format a 1GB drive and you don't partition it. FAT will still create four areas for special use as follows:

☐ The first area is a reserve area consisting of one or more sectors. The first sector is the boot sector, which contains the partition table and the bootstrap program. The partition table provides FAT with information about the number of partitions (if there are any), what type each partition is (primary partition, extended logical, and so on), where the beginning and end of each partition is (beginning and ending sector), which partition is active, and other information. The bootstrap program handles the loading of the operating system, so when you start your computer, this application is executed as it loads the operating system.

☐ The second area of the drive is the File Allocation Table, which contains a reference table showing each cluster on the hard drive. For example, an O by a cluster means that the cluster is available; BAD means the cluster has one or more bad sectors and is marked as unavailable; Reserved means the cluster is to be used by the operating

9

system and not other applications; and EOF (end of file) tells the operating system that this is the last cluster of a file. DOS actually stores a second copy of the File Allocation Table in case the original becomes corrupt.

☐ The third area that FAT creates is a Root Directory Table; this area is used in conjunction with the FAT. The Directory Table stores the names of files in the root directory, as well as in subdirectories. It also notes the locations of the first cluster of all the files.

☐ The fourth area is largest; it is the area you actually see and where you can store applications and data.

Formatting with Windows NT

If you are using NT to format the disk, follow these steps. If you are using DOS to format the disk, skip these steps and go to the next section, "Formatting with DOS." If it is a new drive, and your only drive, you will have to boot with a DOS disk and format it with DOS. If you are installing a second drive and NT is on the first drive, you can use either DOS or NT; NT is quicker.

1. Go to Start | Programs | Administrative Tools | Disk Administrator (see Figure 9.4).

Figure 9.4.

To perform an operation on any disk with Disk Administrator, click the disk first.

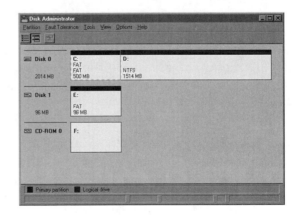

2. Select the disk you want to format by clicking it. Make sure you are in the Disk Configuration view (go to View, and choose Disk Configuration; see Figure 9.5).

9

Figure 9.5.

You have two different options in Disk Administrator for viewing your volumes.

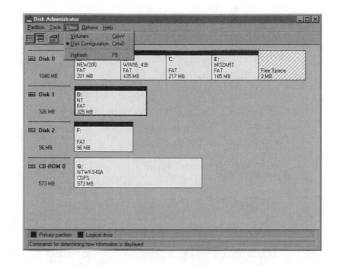

3. Go to the Tools menu and click Format (see Figure 9.6). Be sure you have selected the appropriate drive, because formatting destroys all data on the drive.

Figure 9.6.

The Disk Administrator formatting utility is under the Tools menu.

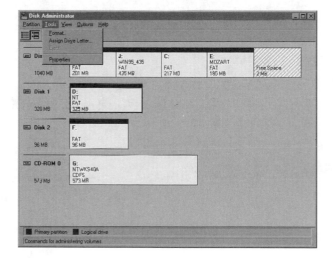

Formatting with DOS

If you install a new hard drive and need to boot from a floppy to format the new drive, follow these steps:

1. Prepare a DOS disk from which to boot the computer. Go to another computer that has DOS installed and type SYS a:. This will transfer the files necessary to boot the computer.

2. Copy onto the disk FDISK and format from the DOS directory.

3. Put the disk into the computer that has a new hard drive, and turn the computer on.

4. After the computer boots up, type FDISK at the prompt. FDISK is used to prepare one or more DOS partitions by establishing the logical drive information that DOS uses. You will have to decide how you want the drive partitioned (divided). This is not always an easy decision. (See Hour 10 for volumes to help you make this decision.) FDISK will give you the following options:

   ☐ Create DOS partition or Logical DOS Drive

   ☐ Set active partition

   ☐ Delete partition or Logical DOS drive

   ☐ Display partition information

   If you have two hard drives, you must select which drive to work with.

5. To prepare the disk, choose option 1 and create a primary DOS partition. Choose the maximum size.

6. Create an extended DOS partition by again choosing option 1, and then option 2: Create Extended DOS partition.

Summary

This hour explains how the mechanics of drives work and how to set up a drive in your computer and prepare it for use. Installing a drive can be tricky business, so read the steps carefully and follow the instructions that come with the drive.

Workshop

The Workshop helps you solidify the skills you learned this hour.

Glossary

BIOS (basic input/output system)   The program that controls various fundamental elements of how your computer operates. The code in the BIOS activates peripheral devices on your PC and tests the system on startup. The OS will at times make calls to the BIOS while at other times it will bypass it and make the calls directly to the hardware.

cluster   Hard drives using the File Allocation Table (FAT) such as DOS, Windows 3.*x*, and Windows 95 break up the hard drive into units called clusters. FAT uses a small unit called

9

sectors, but the smallest unit that FAT can use for storage is a cluster. Here is where you could be wasting space because a small file might use only a small percentage of the cluster. How you format the drive and how you partition will determine how large each cluster is.

expansion slots   Inside your computer, on the motherboard (the main system board that holds the chips that run your computer) are expansion slots that enable you to expand the capability of your PC. Expansion cards that go in the slots include modems, sound cards, video cards, TV cards, SCSI adapter cards, and so on. Depending on the type of motherboard you have, you might have ISA, VESA, or PCI expansion slots. The cards you plan to use must match your slots. Nearly all new motherboards use a combination of ISA and PCI slots.

gigabyte   An amount of storage space equal to 1000 MB.

hard drives   There are different interface standards for connecting hard drives to the computer. IDE drives are an older and slower standard; EIDE is a newer version of IDE that transcends some of the limitations of IDE. SCSI, pronounced "scuzzy," is a different technology that requires a SCSI interface card. The newer SCSI drives are the fastest drives available.

megabyte   A unit of storage space equal to 1000KB, or one million bytes. One KB is equal to 1000 bytes. If we were discussing RAM MBs, then one MB would be equal to 1024 bytes or 1 kilobyte.

millisecond   A measure of speed equal to one thousandth of a second.

platter   Inside a hard drive, the metal disks that spin around and hold the data; each are called platters. Each platter is coated with a magnetically sensitive material.

remote server   If your computer is connected to a network server via a remote connection such as a modem, then the server is called a remote server. For example, if your office computer is running NT 4 Workstation, it can be set up as a remote access server so you can dial into it from home.

removable media   Hardware devices such as floppy drives and specific types of "hard drives" are removable in that the storage media can be removed and replaced by another disk. The Iomega Zip drive is an example.

sector   When a hard drive is formatted, the smallest unit that the computer can read is a sector. A group of sectors composes a cluster.

track   Hard drives, when formatted, contain a unit known as a track, which is a concentric ring around the drive consisting of several clusters (exactly how many depends on the size of the drive and how it is formatted and partitioned). Each platter is divided into many concentric circles or tracks.

Exercises

1. Boot your computer, go into the BIOS, and look at the parameters of your hard drive. How many cylinders, tracks, and sectors does it have?

2. Using the information in this hour and Hour 13, determine the size of the clusters on your drive. Can you calculate what the potential amount of wasted space on the drive is?

3. In attempting to calculate potential bottlenecks, determine the access and transfer speeds of your hard drive.

Hour 10

Volumes and the Disk Administrator

by Martin Kenley

Whereas Hour 9, "Working with Hard Disks," taught you some of the more fundamental aspects of hard drives, this hour covers more advanced material. For example, many users might never create a volume set, but those who need to know how will find this information here. Everyone will benefit from the section on volumes and partitions and using the Disk Administrator.

Understanding Volumes: Strategies for Partitioning Your Hard Drive

Begin by looking at the differences between partitions and volumes. To many people, they are the same thing, but technically, there are important differences. A *partition* is a portion of the hard drive that, if formatted, may become a volume. In fact, the entire hard drive can be considered a partition that uses all the available space on the drive. For example, if you have a 500MB hard disk, you can create one primary partition that is 500MB large.

This primary partition can hold NT and your data and applications (see Figure 10.1). Let's take another example, this time with a 1 gigabyte (1000 megabytes) drive (see Figure 10.2). Rather than just a single partition, you can choose to create one primary partition of 200MB for NT and an extended partition that contains two logical drives of 400MB each.

Figure 10.1.

People usually do not create more than one partition.

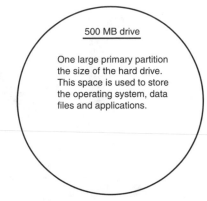

Figure 10.2.

Another strategy for partitioning a drive is to create separate partitions for data, the operating system, and applications.

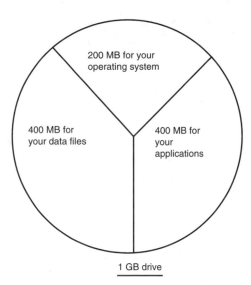

One 400MB partition can be for applications, and the other 400MB partition can be for data. You don't have to separate the application area from the data area, and you don't have to separate the data and application area from the area that contains the operating system (in this case, Windows NT). Some people maintain that doing so makes it easier to recover data

10

after a crash. Other people do it so they can more easily back up the data partition. In fact, Figure 10.3 displays another possible partition scheme. Here, there is a 2GB drive that is divided into two equal parts. The first gigabyte of space is for the operating system and applications, and the second is purely for personal data files. If you have an Iomega Jazz drive, in which each disk holds 1GB of data, you could perform simple backups by periodically dragging the data volume to a Jazz disk. This is not a conventional backup strategy by today's standard, but is becoming more common as removable storage devices fall in price.

Figure 10.3.

A simple partition scheme that divides the drive into two parts: one for data files and the other for the operating system and applications.

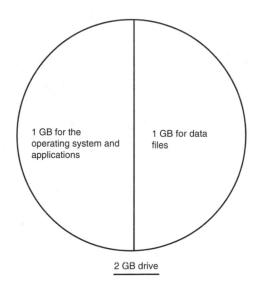

1 GB for the operating system and applications

1 GB for data files

2 GB drive

The more common approach is to install a tape backup system that is programmed to do periodic backups when the computer is not being used. Both methods have their own advantages and disadvantages. The newer Jazz technology is very fast and convenient, making backing up a quick process. Furthermore, the Jazz is inexpensive technology. On the other hand, some tape drives can store more data than can the Jazz drive and are easily configured to do backups unattended.

A volume, on the other hand, can be a single partition, which is typically the case. However, a volume can consist of several partitions. There are a few rules involved with partitioning and volumes that you must think about and use in order to find a configuration that meets your needs.

Primary Reasons for Partitioning

When you are considering hard drive partition strategies, there are a few important items to keep in mind. There are many reasons people have for partitioning their hard drives, but there are two fundamental reasons that attract many computer users:

☐ Installing two or more operating systems that require separate partitions for each (see Figure 10.4). Not all operating systems require their own partition. All of the Microsoft operating systems can be on the same partition, with the exception of Windows NT, if you choose the NTFS file system. In addition, if you are thinking of installing another operating system in the future, it's a good idea to make room now, because the second operating system will probably need a separate partition. And, you cannot create a second partition without deleting the current single partition and then creating two or more partitions. This means wiping the drive clean.

Figure 10.4.

If you want to have two operating systems that use different file formats, you will need to partition your drive.

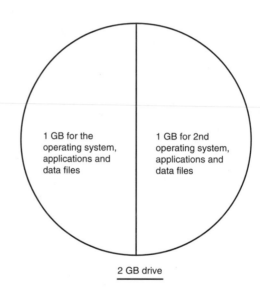

1 GB for the operating system, applications and data files

1 GB for 2nd operating system, applications and data files

2 GB drive

☐ Attempting to reduce the size of the hard drive's clusters. Table 10.1 illustrates that different partition sizes give you different cluster sizes on your hard drive.

In the first case, if you would like to install two operating systems requiring their own partitions, say Linux and NT, you would have to create separate partitions for each because they use different file systems. In a case like this you have no option but to create partitions for both operating systems. IBM's OS/2 is another example of an operating system that has its own file system, HPFS, and therefore requires its own partition. On the other hand, if you plan to have Microsoft Windows NT along with either Windows 95 or Windows 3.*x*, then you do not need separate partitions because they use the same file system (FAT). The only exception here would be if you chose NTFS as the file system for Windows NT, making it incompatible with Windows 95 and Windows 3.*x*.

With regard to the second consideration, partitioning to reduce the cluster size, several points are worth keeping in mind. As mentioned in Hour 9, if you choose the File Allocation Table (FAT) file system, then the smallest unit of storage per file (regardless of size) is one cluster—

10

even if the file does not need an entire cluster. If you choose to format a volume from the command prompt, it is possible to specify the cluster size, but the minimum for different drive sizes is shown in Table 10.1.

Table 10.1. Minimum partition sizes.

Partition	Cluster size
For FAT:	
0 to 32MB	512 bytes
33 to 64MB	1KB
65 to 128MB	2KB
129 to 255MB	4KB
256 to 511MB	8KB
512 to 1023MB	16KB
1024 to 2047MB	32KB
2048 to 4095MB	64KB
For NTFS:	
0 to 512MB	512 bytes
513 to 1024MB	1KB
1025 to 2048MB	2KB
2049 to 4096MB	4KB
4097 to 8192MB	8KB

The maximum drive or partition size for FAT is 4GB. When the drive is larger than 512MB, I recommend either using a different file system or partitioning it to prevent a lot of space from being wasted.

The Disk Administrator

In Hour 9 you looked at the Disk Administrator utility briefly in order to learn how to format a hard drive. The Disk Administrator utility is a fairly comprehensive utility for managing your hard drives. With this utility, you can perform the following functions:

☐ Format and label volumes

☐ Create and delete partitions

☐ Create and extend volume sets (which you learn in "The Disk Administrator's Toolbar" section)

☐ Access the properties sheet for a volume, which presents you with a graphical presentation of the used and free space and enables you to check the disk for errors and set up sharing and set permissions

☐ Set the drive letter that corresponds to each volume

First, look at the options presented in the Disk Administrator window. Look at Figure 10.5, which shows the utility's window. You are given five menu choices: Partition, Tools, View, Options, and Help. You will take a look at the choices listed under these menus in "The Disk Administrator's Toolbar" section.

Figure 10.5.

The Disk Administrator enables you to manage your hard drives. Here is a Volume view of your hard drives.

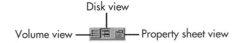

The Disk Administrator's Toolbar

Below the menus, you'll find a toolbar with three icons (see Figure 10.6). Each of the icons gives you a different view of the drive configuration of your computer.

Figure 10.6.

Below the menus of the Disk Administrator is the toolbar, which contains three icons that enable you to select different ways of presenting information about your volumes.

Disk view

Volume view ——— ——— Property sheet view

Volume View

Clicking the first icon in the toolbar gives you the Volume view of your hard drives (refer to Figure 10.5). The Disk Administrator conveniently displays information at the bottom of the screen when a particular volume is selected. Note in Figure 10.5 that the L: drive is selected (you can tell by the fact that the letter L is highlighted). Because it is selected, the information at the bottom of the window tells you that it is partitioned, it is 201MB large,

10

it uses the FAT file system, it is designated as the L: drive, and that its name is New200. If you select another volume, this information will change to reflect the characteristics of the volume.

You can also right-click any of the volumes displayed to get the pop-up menu. This menu lets you format, assign a drive letter, delete, or get the properties sheet of the volume (see Figure 10.7).

Figure 10.7.

The Disk Administrator lets you right-click volumes to bring up the menu seen here.

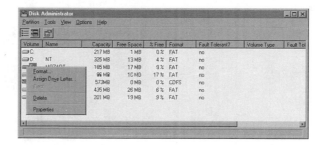

When you are using the Volume view, notice below the toolbar the description bar containing the following descriptors: Volume, Name, Capacity, Free Space, % Free, Format, Fault Tolerant?, Volume Type, Fault Tolerance Overhead, and Status. These descriptors are important because they enable you to view the data in different ways. Notice in Figure 10.8, for example, the Free Space descriptor in the description bar. If you click this descriptor, it will reorganize the volumes so that the volume with the largest amount of free space is listed at the top, followed by the volume with the second largest amount of free space, and so on. If you click on the Free Space descriptor a second time, it will reverse the order of the drives so the drive with the smallest amount of free space is first. Similarly, clicking other descriptors will also reorganize the volumes, depending on the descriptor that you click.

Disk View

The second icon will give you a Disk view of your hard drives (see Figure 10.8). If you click one of the volumes, the bottom of the screen will tell you whether it is a partition, active partition, logical drive, or CD-ROM drive. In Figure 10.8, notice that the L: is highlighted, and the bottom of the window informs you that it is the logical partition. Because Figure 10.8 is black and white, you cannot see this, but the bottom of the window has a color differentiation for volumes that are of different types. You can see two designations: primary partition and logical drive. You can select the color designation for each type of volume. Go to the Options menu and select colors and patterns, and choose a color of your choice along with a pattern.

Figure 10.8.

The Disk view enables you to see the volumes graphically, instead of the text-based table that the Volume view provides.

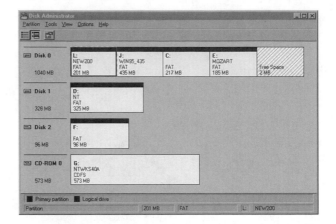

As with the Volume view, here you can also right-click one of the volumes and open the pop-up menu, as shown in Figure 10.9. One new option you will notice is the Mark Active option. This is used to select the primary partition (the C: drive), which has the operating system on it. By making it active, the operating system on the primary partition will be started when your computer is rebooted.

Figure 10.9.

In the Disk view, you can open the pop-up menu, which enables you to perform various functions on the volume.

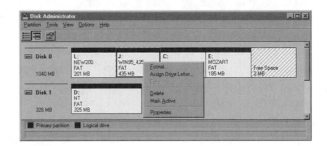

Property Sheet View

The last button in the toolbar enables you to see the property sheet for whichever volume is currently selected (see Figure 10.10). The property sheet for a volume displays some redundant information; for example, you can already see the amount of space on the disk that is used and the amount that is free, as well as the volume label. But here you can change the volume label, set up sharing, and set permissions on the volume.

The Property Sheet view also has a Tools tab. If you select this you will find tools for checking your hard drive for errors, backing up the hard drive to a tape drive, and an unimplemented defragmenting tool (which you can't use because it wasn't available when Microsoft released Windows NT 4 Workstation). The Check Now button will run a utility to check your system files and also check the hard drive for errors. The Back Up Now button will start up a utility that checks for the presence of a tape backup system and lets you back up files to the tape.

Figure 10.10.
The property sheet for a volume gives you additional capabilities.

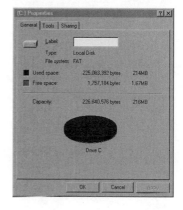

Managing Partitions

The Disk Administrator enables you to format a partition, using either FAT or NTFS, discussed in Hour 9 and Hour 13, "File Systems and Windows NT 4." The Disk Administrator also lets you assign a letter to each volume created. Most of the time, your disk will be partitioned already, and if you want to create additional partitions, either you need specialty software, such as Partition Magic, or you must reformat the drive. (If you reformat the drive, everything on it is lost.) Therefore, knowing how many partitions you need is one of the first things to determine after you receive your computer (or put a new drive into your current computer).

Creating a New Partition

Assuming you already have a primary partition that has Windows NT on it, you can then create additional partitions on the drive. However, this assumes that you did not use all of the space on the drive for your primary partition. If that is the case, then, as mentioned in the "Managing Partitions" section, you need special software to make another partition on it. If there is unformatted space on the drive, then select it by clicking it (it will be labeled "free space," meaning that the space is unformatted). Then follow these steps:

1. Open the Disk Administrator and select the Disk view in the toolbar.
2. Using the mouse, select the free space on the appropriate drive.
3. If you are creating an extended partition, select Create Extended. The Create Extended Partition dialog box appears showing the maximum and minimum size for the partition. Select the appropriate size for the partition.

4. If, on the other hand, you are creating a primary partition and there can be a maximum of only four primary partitions on any single drive, choose Create. You will now see the Create Primary Partition dialog box. It will display the maximum and minimum partition sizes and let you choose the size (in megabytes) for the new partition (see Figure 10.11).

Figure 10.11.

When you use the Disk Administrator to create partitions, you will get this dialog box. By default, it chooses the maximum space available for the new partition.

5. Next, select the size for the partition and then choose OK. You now have created the partition; the final step is to format it, which you learn in the "Formatting Partitions" section.

Creating Logical Drives

It is possible to create a logical drive, in addition to primary and extended partitions, using the Disk Administrator. However, a logical drive (here *logical* is synonymous with *virtual*, because you can't "create" a drive) can be made only from within an extended partition. To create a logical drive, follow these steps:

1. Open the Disk Administrator and, using the mouse, choose the area in the extended partition. This area cannot be formatted yet.

2. Go to the Partition menu and choose Create. You will now be presented with the Create Logical Drive dialog box, which is similar to Figure 10.11.

3. Select the desired size for the logical drive, which must be within the minimum and maximum shown.

4. Choose OK, and you now have a logical drive in the extended partition space, which you can use as you would any other volume.

Saving the Changes: You Must Commit

Now you must commit to the changes that you have made to your disk partition structure before you can format the new volumes you have created. If you decide to skip this step, then your changes are not saved.

10

To commit to the changes, go to the Partition menu of the Disk Administrator and select the second item from the bottom: Commit Changes Now. After selecting this, the changes are written to the Registry.

Formatting Partitions

Now that you have created the types of partitions you need and the correct number of partitions, the final step is to format them so that they can be used. During the process of formatting, you must decide which file system to use (either FAT or NTFS). (If you are uncertain, see Hour 13.)

You will also be presented with the option of labeling the volume. This last step isn't crucial and can be skipped, but it can help you to identify what the volume is used for or what the contents are.

To format your newly created partition, first select the partition by clicking it. This lets the Disk Administrator know that you want to perform an action on this particular partition. Go to the Tools menu and choose Format. This action brings up a dialog box in which you can choose the label for the partition and the file system type (see Figure 10.12). Now follow these steps:

1. After choosing the file system and the label for the volume, click Start, and the formatting process begins. If you select the checkbox Quick Format, the Disk Administrator will not scan the volume for bad sectors. It is a good idea to have the scan performed, because the utility will mark bad sectors so they are not used. This process could save data, because storing data to an area of the drive that contains bad sectors can result in loss of data.

Figure 10.12.

The Disk Administrator Format dialog box enables you to enter a name for the volume and choose a file system type.

2. After choosing Start, a confirmation dialog box appears. If you are certain you want to continue, click OK.

3. When the process is completed, a final dialog box will appear informing you that the format is complete and how much space was formatted.

Deleting a Partition

Disk Administrator lets you delete partitions and logical drives to enable you to create a new partition strategy. If you delete a partition, it will become free space and must be partitioned and reformatted before it can be used.

CAUTION

Do not confuse deleting a partition with the idea of deleting the data on a partition. If you want to delete the data on a partition, simply select all the items on the volume and drag them to the trash. You will now have a blank volume that is ready to hold new data. Contrast this to the process of deleting a partition, described in this section.

To delete a partition or logical drive, follow these steps:

1. Using the Disk Administrator, and select the area that you would like to delete.
2. Go to the Partition menu, and choose Delete. NT will now ask you to confirm your choice. Again, all the information on this volume will be deleted. Choose Yes if you are sure you want to delete the partition or volume.

The area is now turned into free space and can be repartitioned. Follow the partitioning steps presented in this lesson to be able to use this area of your drive.

Creating Volume Sets

You create a volume set by using free space on multiple drives. The advantage of using a volume set is that you may find you have small areas of free space, which might be less useful individually, but if you combine them into a single larger volume they are easier to use. Furthermore, instead of partitioning and formatting them, thereby creating a bunch of smaller volumes, you can create one additional volume by creating a volume set. Follow these steps to do so:

1. Using the Disk Administrator, select multiple areas of free space. To do this, hold down the Ctrl key after you have selected the first free space area.
2. Next, choose the Partition menu, and select Create Volume Set. This brings up a dialog box in which you can select the size of the new volume. Probably you will want to choose the maximum size in order to use all the space in each free area.
3. Choose OK. A new volume is created and assigned the next unused drive letter.

Summary

This hour has shown you how to plan and manage volumes, and you learned different strategies for using the volumes. You also learned how to use the Disk Administrator utility to manage partitions and retrieve data about the volumes. The Disk Administrator is useful during and after the volume creation stage.

Workshop

The Workshop helps you solidify the skills you learned this hour.

Glossary

extended partition An area of your hard drive that is beyond the primary partition. Within this space, you can create additional partitions, called logical drives.

hard drive The physical mechanism that stores your data and applications even when the computer is turned off.

logical drive See *extended partition*.

partition Parts or areas into which a hard drive can be divided.

volume A partition that has been formatted; it is assigned a drive letter at this point.

volume set Unused areas of partitions combined together into a single volume.

Exercises

1. Open the Disk Administrator, examine your hard drive, and note the current partitioning strategy.
2. Can you think of alternative partitioning strategies?
3. Again using the Disk Administrator, use the different toolbar options to look at your volumes in the various ways provided by the utility.

10

Hour 11

Security: Planning a Secure System

by Robert Bogue

You've made it to the 11th hour. In this lesson, you learn what security for Windows NT Workstation is and the things that you need to know about it. Here you will learn the following:

- [ ] How to create, rename, and delete users
- [ ] How to create and delete groups
- [ ] How to establish password policies
- [ ] How to set up auditing

One of the best ways to understand security is to think of it like the locks that you have on your home, your car, and even your desk drawers. Some people never lock anything, they have no concern that anyone will come in and take what they have earned. Other people lock everything: They lock their homes— sometimes with more than one deadbolt—they lock their cars, and they lock their glove compartments.

NT security is a lot like this. All of the locks are there; the question is, which ones do you feel you need to use?

JUST A MINUTE

> If you're using NT Workstation at home on a local network or without any networking and don't share your computer with anyone you don't completely trust, you might want to skip this hour for now and come back to it another time. By default, the Administrator account has full access. You can just use this account to log into NT Workstation and leave all the security concerns behind.

Security for the Home and Business

There are some basic elements to NT's security strategy that you need to know, whether you're trying to set up a small home network with some limitations for children or working in a 1,000-employee company. You must know how to identify users and what security they should have. You also need to understand how NT uses groups to simplify managing users, and security.

Users

The Windows NT security system is based around users and identifying who has authority to what resource. Each user in NT is assigned a user ID and a password, which he or she uses to gain access to the system. The combination of the user ID and password signifies to NT who you claim to be and that you are that person. This kind of security system assumes that only the user knows his or her password.

JUST A MINUTE

> Although it is possible to use a single user ID for more than one user, I don't recommend it because it makes it harder to set up each person with the exact security he or she needs and reduces your ability to audit what has happened on your system.

NT manages users through the User Manager program. This program is located in Start | Programs Folder | Administrative Tools.

When you first open the User Manager it will open with two windows, as shown in Figure 11.1. The window on top is the user window, which will list all the users that NT knows about.

11

Figure 11.1.

User Manager lists all the users and groups defined on the system.

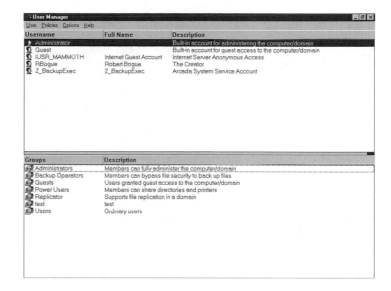

You'll see that NT has created a few users for you. These users should not be deleted (although some of them can be). These users are special for NT and are used as a part of the system's operation. They are explained in Table 11.1.

Table 11.1. Special users and their uses.

Username	Purpose
Administrator	Can do everything in the system. This account is created for you to administer the system.
Guest	Created to allow people who do not have user accounts to access the system. By default, this account is disabled.
IUSR_*	Used by the Peer Web Server and related services to determine what access Internet users should have. You might not have an IUSR_* account. This account appears only if you installed Microsoft Peer Web Server.

Creating a New User

Creating user accounts in NT is very easy. To do so, select User | New User. NT opens the New User dialog box shown in Figure 11.2.

Figure 11.2.

The New User dialog box.

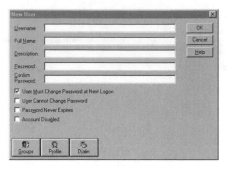

NT just needs a few things to get this user set up. The first is a unique username for the user.

In larger networks, it's very important that all of the users' IDs be generated the same way so that the administrator can easily guess what a username is if he knows the person's name. The username is also important because, generally, a user's home directory and e-mail username are the same as the username. Some examples of naming conventions appear in Table 11.2.

Table 11.2. Naming conventions.

Name	First letter of the first name plus last name	First name plus the first letter of the last name	First three letters of the first name plus first three letters of the last name
Cindy Morrow	cmorrow	cindym	cinmor
Kim Spilker	kspilker	kims	kimspi
Lynette Quinn	lquinn	lynetteq	lynqui
Jane Doe	jdoe	janed	jandoe
John Doe	jdoe1	johnd	johdoe
John Denver	jdenver	johnd1	johden

The first standard (first letter of the first name plus the last name) is the most common in corporate environments because it's normally unique and is easy. In this scheme, you have a problem if two people have the same last name and a first name that starts with the same letter, as in the example of Jane Doe and John Doe in Table 11.2. This is always possible; the key is to minimize it.

The second standard (first name plus the first letter of the last name) is popular in UNIX environments but tends to have more problems of the scheme not generating unique user

11

IDs, because people's first names generally are less unique than their last names. In Table 11.2, the problem shows up with John Doe and John Denver.

I've only seen the final standard (first three letters of the first and last names) used one time, but it does seem to provide more unique IDs than either of the other two methods. It's probably not what you want to do for your naming convention.

Remember that you don't have to use any of these naming standards; you can do anything you want. NT doesn't care.

JUST A MINUTE

> If you're in a highly secure environment, you might not want usernames to be guessed by knowing a person's name. In situations like this, the best thing to do is just assign user IDs at random.

After a username has been selected, NT asks for the full name of the user and a description. Both the full name and the description appear in the User Manager window, as shown in Figure 11.1. Normally, the description is a person's title and department. In a home environment it might be their relationship to you or a nickname.

Next, NT provides a Password and Confirm Password text box. This is the password assigned to a user. As you will learn in Table 11.3, this can be a temporary password that the user uses only to log onto NT one time. The password you enter here does not have to conform to the password rules that you'll learn about in the "Password Security Settings" section except that it must meet the minimum password length requirement.

Next, NT has a series of checkboxes relating to passwords and whether the account is disabled. These options are described in Table 11.3.

Table 11.3. User options.

Option	Description
User Must Change Password at Next Logon	Determines whether the user will be forced to set his or her own password when he or she logs on next. Useful when administrators want to make sure that users set their own unique passwords. When this option is set, the password that is entered in the password and confirm password text boxes is a temporary password.

continues

Table 11.3. continued

Option	Description
User Cannot Change Password	Prevents a user from changing his or her password. Useful when multiple users share the same account and you need to prevent a single user from changing the password.
Password Never Expires	This overrides the Account policy described in the "Password Security Settings" section and enables an account to use the same password indefinitely. Useful for service accounts needed for software that isn't used. If this isn't specified, then some services might mysteriously break when their password expires.
Account Disabled	This turns off the account. The account is still in the system, but when this option is checked, the user will be unable to log in. Useful when you want to delete an account, as explained in the "Deleting a User" section. Also useful for consultants or temporary employees when you want them to have access only occasionally, but don't want to have to re-create the account each time.

NT presents three buttons on the bottom of the new user form, which take you to other forms so that you can fill in additional information. The first of these is the Groups button.

When you press the Groups button, you're presented with a dialog box that lists all of the current groups on the system, as shown in Figure 11.3.

Figure 11.3.

Groups are a quick way to add authority to a user.

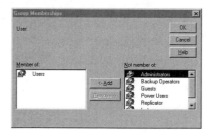

NT enables you to create groups and assign users to those groups. In the "Adding Access" section, you will see that NT enables you to assign permissions to access resources to groups rather than to users. Users inherit the permission to use a resource from the group.

11

Groups are useful when you have a set of resources that should be available to a group of people. For example, the Accounting department might be given access to the accounting records, but other groups are not allowed to see them. If there are 15 people in Accounting and you can't create a group, you must assign 15 people the same set of permissions.

With a group, however, you assign those permissions once to the group and then make the users members of the group. This simplifies administration and makes it much easier to create a new accounting user.

It gets even more complicated when you consider someone who belongs to several groups, such as a shared administrative assistant. With the capability of creating groups, the administrator only needs to add the administrative assistant to the appropriate groups instead of trying to track down all of the security settings that each of these groups may have.

To add the new user to a group, select the group on the right and press the Add button. Repeat this as many times as is necessary. When you're finished, click OK to return to the New User form.

Pressing the Profile button displays the form shown in Figure 11.4. This form enables you to set profiles and home directory settings.

Figure 11.4.

Profiles specify the environment the user will get when he or she logs on.

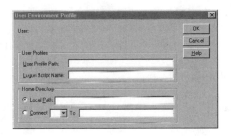

A *profile* is a group of settings that determine what the user's interface looks like and potentially restricts the user's options. Generally, this is left blank for NT Workstation accounts.

The logon script name is the name of a batch file (.BAT or .CMD), which runs every time you log on. This batch file can run any reminder programs, set your time to an atomic clock, or anything else that you want to happen for the user when he or she logs on.

Next, NT enables you to specify a home directory. A home directory is where you are put by default if you open a DOS prompt or try to save a file. This is important because NT enables you to move from one computer to another and keep access to your files no matter what computer you are on. This requires some network setup but is very useful in large computer environments.

If you're on a computer that isn't attached to a network, just select Local Path and fill in a directory where this user will keep his or her files. This directory can be anything but is normally something like C:\USERS\%USERNAME%.

TIME SAVER

> You can use %USERNAME% to fill in the username for the user you are adding. This can be useful when you are adding a bunch of new users or going back and establishing home directories for users you've previously created.

If you are on a network, specify to connect to a drive and the path to connect to. I recommend the H: drive as the drive to connect to; it's easy for users to remember that their home directory is the H: drive. The connect path should be in Universal Naming Convention (UNC) format. This should look something like \\BEAST\USERS\RBOGUE.

When you've entered a logon script and home directory, select OK to return to the New User dialog box.

The third and final button on the New User dialog box is Dialin. Press this button to display the dialog box shown in Figure 11.5. This dialog box enables you to determine whether the user will be able to call into this computer and gain access to its resources over a phone line. In Hour 8, "Remote Access to Your Work and Setting Up Laptops," you saw this dialog box and how to set up the Remote Access Service (RAS) for dial-in access. We'll quickly review this information here.

Figure 11.5.

Setting dial-in access.

To refresh your memory, the Grant dialin permission to user checkbox enables you to say that the user can call in. If this is not checked, the user will not be able to call in remotely regardless of what you set the call back settings, discussed next, to be.

Call Back settings are designed for added security, because someone could call in and steal your information or cause harm from anywhere. Without remote access, all the users to your system must be close at hand—where you can discuss the problem if they do something wrong. With remote access, you might not even know where the user is.

Call Back calls the user back after he or she logs onto the system and is verified as a user.

Setting Call Back to No Call Back means you are saying that you do not need this added security feature or that you can't use it because of your environment.

The Set By Caller option enables the user to be anywhere when he or she calls. This has the advantage of transferring the cost of the phone call to the RAS. It also provides an audit log of where the user was. That way, if a problem arises, you know where the call came from.

The final option, Preset To, requires that the person be at a specific location. This is good for when you want to let users access the system, but you only want them to be able to call in from home. Another option is that you can allow the administrator dial-in access, but only from your house.

JUST A MINUTE

> The one problem with Call Back is that it doesn't normally work if the user is staying in a hotel. Because very few hotels offer automated operators, there's no way to have the RAS dial directly to the user's room.

Click OK on the Dialin Information dialog box, and then again on the New User dialog box to finish setting up the user.

This will take you back to the New User dialog box to add another user. Press Cancel to exit.

Deleting a User

Sometimes it becomes necessary to delete a user: Someone has left your company, or you kicked Uncle Joe out of the family. (Personally, I think that's a bit extreme.)

But before you go in and delete a user, consider that you might just want to turn off his or her access, at least for the short term. If there's a chance that Uncle Joe will get back together with Aunt Molly, you could just disable his account for now.

One of the strong suits of NT is its capability to build an audit trail of what happens on the system. This audit trail can tell you what files someone opened, when he or she logged on, and what permissions he or she used, among other things. One somewhat unfortunate thing about the audit trails is that sometimes they show you the Security Identifier (SID) for the user instead of the username. So you need to know what username corresponds to the SID. If you delete Uncle Joe's record, you won't be able to match his username to the SID and can't positively pinpoint that he wrote the love letter to...well, never mind.

The other reason to leave a user on the system is because he or she might come back. Every user in the system is assigned a unique SID. Therefore, if you delete a user and create another user with the same username, the SIDs will be different, and as a result the user won't be able to get back into the files that he or she once could.

If you decide that you still want to delete a user, here's how you do it:

1. Select the user in the User Manager's user window.
2. Press the Delete key, or select User | Delete.
3. Acknowledge the NT warning message shown in Figure 11.6 and press OK.

Figure 11.6.

NT warns you that you won't be able to re-create this user.

4. Click Yes in the dialog box shown in Figure 11.7 to delete the user.

Figure 11.7.

Your last chance to cancel deleting the user.

Here's how to disable the account instead:

1. Select the user in the User Manager window and press Enter, or double-click the user.
2. Check the Account Disabled checkbox as shown in Figure 11.8.

Figure 11.8.

A disabled account.

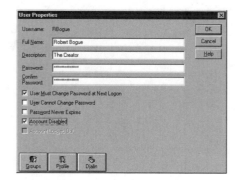

Renaming a User

Every once in a while people change their names, sometimes because they get married or divorced. And most people want their usernames changed when they change their full names so that they match.

Renaming a user in NT is absolutely painless. Renaming a user in application programs can be very painful. In NT, a few simple steps will do it, but sometimes there are dozens of applications that the user uses that also need some changes. Here's how to change the user's name in NT:

1. Select the user from the User Manager window.

2. Select User | Rename.

3. Enter the new username in the dialog box as shown in Figure 11.9.

Figure 11.9.

Rename users; don't delete them and attempt to re-create them.

4. Press OK.

One catch to this is that if you specified that the user has a home directory with his or her username as a part of the directory name, it will still have the old name. To change this, follow these steps:

1. Select the user in User Manager and press Enter, or double-click the user.

2. Press the Profile button.

3. Change the user's home directory to specify the correct username.

4. Press OK to close the Profile dialog box.

5. Press OK to update the user.

6. Open Windows NT Explorer.

7. Select the directory in which the user's directory is located. For example, if the user's home directory is C:\USERS\JSMITH, select the C:\USERS directory.

8. Right-click the user's folder on the right side of the display; for example, the JSMITH directory.

9. Select Rename from the Context menu.

10. Enter the user's new name and press Enter.

Groups

When you looked at setting up a user in the "Setting Up a New User" section, you learned briefly about how groups fit in and how you can use them to simplify administration.

NT comes with five predefined groups for you. It also has one group defined for a system function. Each of these groups represents a specific type of user that Microsoft thinks you might have on the computer. They're explained in Table 11.4.

Table 11.4. Built-in groups.

Group Name	Purpose
Administrators	Enables you to easily create administrative users. Users who are members of this group can do anything.
Backup Operators	This group is designed for special user accounts that are used for performing backups. Workstation users rarely use this group.
Guests	This group is for users without accounts on the NT system and normally should not be used.
Power Users	This group is for those users who know a lot about the system and fix things like printer problems, but don't need to have full access to everything.
Replicator	Used internally by NT to provide replication services between an NT server and an NT workstation. You should never add users to this group.
Users	These are the normal users of the system. They receive more access than a guest would but not normally any additional access.

Creating Groups

As mentioned in the "Creating a New User" section, you can create your own groups to make providing security easier. You can group people by departments at work, adult/child at home, or any way that makes sense to you. Ask yourself the following questions before creating your groups:

☐ How many people will be in the group? If there's only going to be one member of the group, don't bother creating a group; just assign rights to the user. There are some exceptions in which you want to create a group anyway, but consider that sometimes it doesn't make sense to create a group.

☐ Do I need to be more specific? If your Accounting department does payroll internally, you might want to create a separate payroll group from the accounting groups.

☐ Do I need to assign resources to the group? If you have a group for which you don't need to assign resources, you might want to wait until later to set the group up.

When you've decided the groups you need to make, you can create them by following these steps:

11

1. Select the User menu, then the New Local Group option. This will display the New Local Group form as in Figure 11.10. If you select users before selecting New Local Group, the users will be listed in the members of your new group automatically.

Figure 11.10.

The New Local Group dialog box.

2. Enter the name of the group and a description.
3. Click the Add button to show the Add Users and Groups form, as shown in Figure 11.11.

Figure 11.11.

Adding users to the group.

4. Select the user you want to be a member of the group and press Add. Repeat for each user you want to be a member of the group.
5. Press OK to return to the New Local Group dialog box.
6. Press OK to create the group.

Deleting Groups

When you delete a group, you have the same considerations that you have when you delete a user. There is a unique SID assigned to each group. If you delete the group and create another group with the same name, NT doesn't restore the permissions because the SIDs aren't the same.

This isn't as big a deal when you are dealing with groups because audit logging is always done at a user level, not a group level. It's not possible to disable a group, so your only option might be to delete the group. You do this by following these steps:

1. Select the group in User Manager.
2. Press Delete, or select User | Delete.

JUST A MINUTE

You cannot rename groups; as a result, you might need to delete a group and create a new group.

System Policies

NT has a few user security settings that take effect on all users on the system. These settings define, to a large extent, how secure your system will be.

These settings are administered through the Policies menu | Account item. If you select this option, you will see a form like the one in Figure 11.12.

Figure 11.12.

Account Policy determines how secure your system will be.

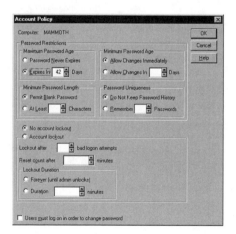

Password Security Settings

The first part of the screen enables you to change settings on how NT deals with passwords. Table 11.5 explains what each of these settings does.

Table 11.5. Password restriction options.

Option	Function
Maximum Password Age	Requires that a user change his or her password after the specified number of days. Normally used to make sure that someone can't continue to use a password he or she found or stole.
Minimum Password Age	Prevents the user from changing his or her password too many times. This is generally used to prevent users from trying to defeat the Password Uniqueness option.
Minimum Password Length	Requires that all passwords be at least a certain length. The longer the password, the harder it is to guess. By requiring a certain length, you prevent users from selecting passwords that are very easy to guess.
Password Uniqueness	This prevents the user from defeating the Password Age by requiring that he or she set a different password than the last one. Some users try to defeat this setting by changing their password several times in a row so that they exceed the number of passwords saved here. Setting a Minimum Password Age prevents this.

Now that you have all the options, how should they be set? That depends on how security conscious you are. My recommendations for a lightly secure environment are to require that passwords expire every 180 days, passwords be six characters in length, passwords be one day old before they can be changed, and 24 passwords be kept.

In a tightly secure environment, you should reduce the number of days before the passwords expire and increase the minimum length requirement.

Account Lockout

We now define how NT responds to invalid login attempts. This determines what NT does to an account if someone tries logging onto it with the wrong password. I strongly encourage you to turn this option on.

One of the easiest ways for a hacker to gain access to a system is to set up a program to try a database of words on every account. This brute-force method generates a lot of invalid logon attempts but might eventually get a correct password. The best way to deal with these brute-force attacks is to lock out the account after a certain number of invalid logon attempts have been made.

When you've selected the Account Lockout radio button, you'll be given the opportunity to set the number of attempts to accept in a period of time before locking the account out, and the length of time to lock the account out for.

My recommendation used to be to set the invalid login attempts to five to ten. This was normally more than enough for a user to realize that he had forgotten his password and to come for help.

Unfortunately, Microsoft made some changes in how it deals with passwords when it released Windows 95. Windows 95 tries a series of passwords that it has before asking the user for a password. The password the user used to log into Windows 95 is tried, as well as a blank password, and any password that might have been in the user's password list. As a result, Windows has tried to log in three to five times before the user knows that something is wrong. If the user doesn't get the password right on the first try he or she ends up locked out.

The solution is to set the count to a much higher number, such as 20 or 25, before an account is locked out. This isn't that much more of a threat really, because a password guessing program will generally need many more attempts (like hundreds or thousands) before it can find a match.

The next questions are how close the attempts must be to be considered multiple logon failures and how long to lock the account for. My recommendation is to set these each to five minutes. That's long enough to discourage a hacker and not too long for the user to wait.

The reason that you want to set this number low instead of setting the lockout to forever is because, if you're like me, as an administrator you don't want to get called unless you have to be. A short lockout time will encourage the user to try again before calling you.

The final checkbox on this form is to require users to log on to change their passwords. Checking this box prevents users from changing their expired passwords themselves. Because I don't normally like to be bothered, I don't check this box; you probably won't want to check it either.

When you have finished setting Account Policies, click OK. Your changes take effect immediately.

Users' Rights

For the most part, you won't have to worry about Users' Rights in NT Workstation. NT assigns these rights to the predefined groups you learned in the "Groups" section.

What you should know is that you can prevent users from logging onto your workstation directly by removing the Everyone, Guests, and Users groups from the Log on Locally Right.

11

NT Server, by default, enables only Administrators and Server Operators to log on. This prevents users from trying to use the server as a workstation.

Auditing

People sometimes associate auditing with the IRS. This gives auditing a bad name, but it doesn't deserve it. Auditing can help you to determine what is happening and when—and more importantly, who's doing it.

Auditing is just keeping track of everything that has happened. If you have a security guard at your work who signs in visitors, you have one form of auditing that is not unlike the auditing NT will perform if you want it to. Another way to think about it is that the traditional security in NT is like the door and lock that you learned about at the beginning of the hour. Auditing is the card-access system that provides access but logs it so that people can be questioned later if there is a problem.

JUST A MINUTE

Just in case you didn't know, every time you use an access card it is logged to a central computer. Whoever administers this at your place of business knows that you come in at 2 a.m. in the morning on Sunday so you can get some peace and quiet.

To turn on auditing, select Policies | Audit. This will display the form shown in Figure 11.13.

Figure 11.13.

Auditing options send their results to the Security Log.

You can choose to audit everything on this list, but that will create a huge log. I'd suggest that you limit what you audit to things that you think are really important.

Normally, I log all failures and successes for Restart, Shutdown, and System, as well as Security Policy Changes.

This yields a security log that is manageable but provides enough information to identify who's doing things that he shouldn't. When you've turned on audit logging you'll be able to see events in the security log. Figure 11.14 shows a few events in my security log.

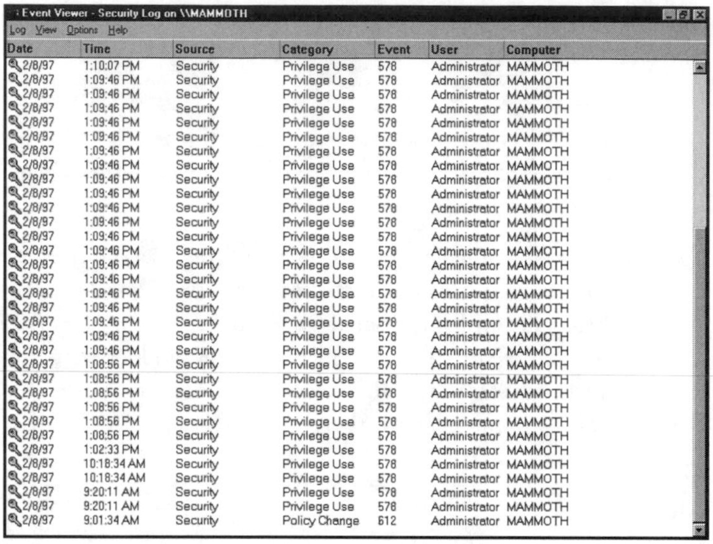

Figure 11.14.

An example of a security log.

File and Folder Permissions

Now that you've set up NT to know who the users are, to what groups they belong, and how to audit their actions, I'll bet that you're anxious to start setting up some permissions so that the users you set up don't do something they're not supposed to.

This is the traditional good news/bad news story. The good news is that this is all possible, and there are now some pretty easy ways to make this happen with the new Explorer interface. The bad news is that you can't take advantage of this if you're using a FAT-formatted partition.

You'll remember from Hour 9, "Working with Hard Disks," that NT supports two different types of hard disk formats. One is the old FAT system that was used in DOS and Windows. This file system does not support security information. The other file system is NTFS (NT File System), and it does support security information, in addition to other benefits. Everything you learned in this section applies to those drives that you've formatted as NTFS; it won't work for FAT formatted drives.

Setting permissions for files is very easy. You can do it through either My Computer or Explorer. The first step is to display the Security tab of the file's properties. This can be done as follows:

1. Select the folder that contains the file or folder you want to change.

2. Right-click the file or folder to display the context menu. If you're in the Explorer, make sure that you right-click the file or folder in the right-hand pane of the window, not in the tree view on the left.

3. Select Properties; the form as shown in Figure 11.15 will appear.

Figure 11.15.

A folder's properties tell you how much space is taken up by the files in it.

4. Select the Security tab (see Figure 11.16).

Figure 11.16.

The Security tab enables you to set permissions, configure auditing, or take ownership.

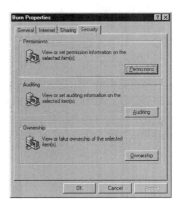

Permissions

If you press the Permissions button on the form shown in Figure 11.16, you'll get a dialog box, shown in Figure 11.17, which shows the current permissions for the file or folder you selected.

Figure 11.17.

All the users with permission to the current file or folder are shown here.

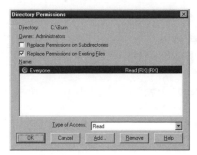

In this case, you can see that Everyone has full control of the C:\Burn folder on my hard drive. This means that everyone can access these files. They can create new files in the directory and delete existing files.

One thing to remember when you are reviewing the type of access that a person has to a file or folder is that access is additive. By this I mean that if you give users read access, and they belong to a group that has been assigned full control access, users will have full access.

The exception to this rule is the No Access type of access. This explicitly removes access from a user or group. None of the other access permissions are checked for the user.

If you drop down the Type of Access list box you'll see a list of possible options, explained in Table 11.6.

Table 11.6. Types of access.

Access	Result
No Access	Prevents access to a file or folder, overrides any other settings.
List	The ability to list subdirectories and files within a directory.
Read	The ability to see directories and see and read files.
Add	The ability to create new files in a directory.
Add & Read	The ability to create new files and read existing files.
Change	Allows everything Add & Read does and enables a file to be changed or deleted.
Full Control	Allows everything Change does plus enables the user to change permissions or take ownership (discussed in the "Ownership" section).
Special Directory Access	Allows you to set specific directory accesses.
Special File Access	Allows you to set specific file accesses.

11

Changing Existing Access

Changing some users', or groups', access to a file or directory is very easy. Follow these steps:

1. Select the user or group for which you want to change access.

2. Select the new type of access from the Type of Access drop-down combo box.

Removing Access

Removing access is just as easy as changing existing access. Follow these steps:

1. Select the user or group that you want to delete.

2. Press the Remove button.

Adding Access

Adding new access is only a little more complicated.

1. Press the Add button. The dialog box shown in Figure 11.18 will appear.

Figure 11.18.

Adding new access for a user or group is easy, too.

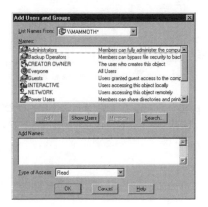

2. Press the Show Users button if you want to add access for a user instead of a group.

3. Select the group or user you want to add access to by double-clicking or clicking once and pressing Add.

4. Repeat step 3 for any other users or groups to which you want to give the same access.

5. Select the type of access to give in the Type of Access drop-down listbox.

6. Press OK to return to the Permissions menu.

Options for Directories

If you're working on a directory, there are two checkboxes displayed that you must consider before pressing OK.

☐ Replace Permissions on Subdirectories: The checkbox Replace Permissions on Subdirectories is a very dangerous option. If done at the root of your system drive, it replaces all the permissions on the drive—including ones that NT set up for its use in the system directories.

This option is convenient if you want to replace the permissions on a set of user directories, but remember that it replaces the permissions; it doesn't add the new users that you've selected, it tries to make an exact match of the permissions you've listed.

☐ Replace Permissions on Existing Files: This box normally should be checked. This takes your current settings and makes all the files in the directory match them.

When you're finished with these two options, or if you're modifying the permissions on a file, press OK to exit the dialog box and return to the file or folder's Security tab.

Auditing

The next item displayed on the Security tab is Auditing. This enables you to control which files and directories are audited. These settings take effect only if you turn on File and Object Auditing in User Manager.

If you press the auditing button, a dialog box as shown in Figure 11.19 appears.

Figure 11.19.

Determine the users to audit on this directory.

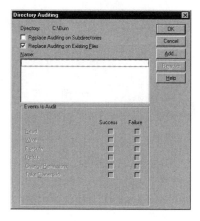

To turn auditing on for this file or directory, you must first add a user or group to audit on.

1. Press the Add button; a dialog box as in Figure 11.20 appears.
2. Press the Show Users button if you want to add auditing only for a user.
3. Select the group or user by either double-clicking or clicking once, and then pressing the Add button.

11

Figure 11.20.

Adding users to audit.

4. Click OK to return to the auditing dialog box.

5. Next, you must select which activities you want to audit. Remember to keep what you audit to a minimum so that your security log does not fill too quickly.

6. Press OK to return to the Security tab of the File or Directory Properties dialog box.

Ownership

The final option on the Security tab is Ownership. Every file is owned by a user. The user that owns a file has complete control over it, no matter what the permissions are set to.

You as an administrator have the take ownership right, which allows you to gain access to a file that you don't have permissions to. When you have done this, you will gain the ability to change the permissions of the file so that you do have access to it.

JUST A MINUTE

NT requires you to take ownership so that the original user can determine whether you've been tampering with his or her files. This is one area in which NT protects the users from the administrator.

To take ownership of a file, follow these steps:

1. Press the Ownership button on the Security tab. A dialog as shown in Figure 11.21 appears.

Figure 11.21.

The Owner dialog shows both the file or folder name and its current owner.

2. Press the Take Ownership button. This displays a warning, as in Figure 11.22.

Figure 11.22.

Should NT go through all the subdirectories under the current directory and change their ownership?

3. Normally you will press Yes so you have access to all the files and subdirectories.

Security for the Business

Up to this point, you've learned things that apply whether you use NT at home or in a business. In this section you're going to take a left turn and learn about only those things that apply to a business user.

The NT Domain

The defining thing that big businesses have that most home users don't is an NT *domain*. This is a special arrangement of NT servers that work as one unit.

A domain uses one security database for multiple computers. The benefit of this is that you don't have to set up every user on every computer. You define the user to the domain, and all of the computers in the domain recognize that user.

In a small network, or one without an NT server, you don't have domains; you have workgroups. In a workgroup, each machine must know all the users who will be accessing it. This represents a lot of administrative overhead if you have to set up each new user on 10 machines.

The key to being a part of a domain is trusting—trusting other domains and, in the case of a workstation, trusting the domain to identify users.

JUST A MINUTE

NT describes the relationship between two domains as a trust. The domain membership of a workstation or server is not considered a trust by NT. However, the member workstation or server does accept the security information provided to it from the domain.

11

Security Concerns for NT in a Domain

When your machine is attached to a domain, it adds new members to your Administrators group and your Users group. These are the Domain Admins and Domain Users global groups from the domain. Figure 11.23 shows the Users group with the domain's (THORPROJ) domain users group.

Figure 11.23.

The domain's domain users group is automatically added to the NT Workstation users group when it is attached to the domain.

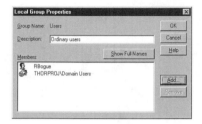

These are global groups, as opposed to the local groups that you set up earlier. These groups are defined automatically when NT Server is installed as a domain server. They are designed to allow the domain administrator to administer all the systems in the domain and for a user in the domain to be able to access resources on all of the systems transparently.

Most of the time, keeping these domain groups in your local administrator and user groups is fine. The domain administrators are trustworthy, and the users are appreciative of the access they will gain to your system (if you share resources). There may be some times, however, when you can't trust users or administrators in your company.

You can break the connection from your computer by removing the domain's groups from your local groups. This will render the users or administrators unable to control or use your computer.

Setting Security or Adding Users to Groups in a Domain Environment

One other thing changes when your computer is a part of a domain. Instead of just seeing users from your machine when you establish security or create groups, you also have the option of selecting users from the domain of which your computer is a part. Figure 11.24 shows an Add Users and Groups dialog box showing the domain's users.

When your computer is part of a domain, it's normal for the users to be set up at the domain instead of locally. Therefore, it's important that you be able to assign access to files and folders on your system to the domain's users.

Figure 11.24.

*Add domain user to a
local group.*

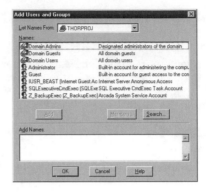

Summary

You've covered a lot of ground in this hour. You've learned how to set up users, groups, and
permissions. You've also learned how to make changes to the system to make it require
passwords and to audit those events that you want to know about.

Workshop

The Workshop helps you solidify the skills you learned this hour.

Glossary

account lockout   A temporary lockout used by NT to prevent brute-force attacks. An
account is locked out for the time period defined in User Manager | Policies | Account.

auditing   The process of logging activities so that actions can be associated with the user
ID that performed them.

ownership   Every file in NT has a specific owner, usually the creator of the file. Ownership
can be taken by those with the Take Ownership user right. Administrators have this right by
default.

security identifier (SID)   The unique ID that NT uses to identify a user or group. Always
unique.

11

Exercises

1. Create a new user.
2. Create a new group and make your user from exercise 1 a member.
3. Create a directory and set the security so that your group from exercise 2 has no access.
4. Log on as your user from exercise 1 and try to access the file from exercise 3. You shouldn't be able to open the directory.

11

PART III

The Evening

Hour

Hour 12

Migration Considerations

by Jeff Perkins

Migrating to NT Workstation is a complicated decision. This hour covers the following migration paths:

- ☐ From DOS/Windows
- ☐ From Windows 95
- ☐ From Windows NT version 3.51
- ☐ From OS/2

Each section covers hardware, software, installation, and operating system considerations. The hardware and software sections show the hardware and software need for a particular migration path. The installation section contains tips and traps that lay in your migration path. Within each migration path, in the section, "Operating System Considerations," you learn all the other considerations you need to successfully complete your migration to NT 4. Each migration path is self contained.

Migrating to Windows NT Workstation: An Overview

The first question you need to ask is, "Why Migrate to NT?" Hours 11, "Security: Planning a Secure System," and 13, "File Systems and Windows NT 4," describe what NT 4 does. It is also important at this point to consider some of the things NT does not do.

Compared with DOS, Windows 3.1, and Windows 95, which count their users in the hundreds of millions, Windows NT Workstation installations number in the hundreds of thousands. This means that there is a smaller pool of users finding errors. This also means there is a smaller number of software developers working on programs specific to Windows NT Workstation.

On the positive side, the number of NT Workstation installations is growing, and NT is one of the primary building blocks of Microsoft's short- and long-term business strategy. The fact that Microsoft has merged its Windows 95 and Windows NT development groups into a single Operating Systems group also promises a high level of support for NT in the short and long terms.

There are also some specific hardware and software incompatibilities to consider (covered in detail during the section on each upgrade path).

JUST A MINUTE

> Each of the migration paths covered in the following sections are self contained. For example, all of the information about migrating from Windows 3.x is in the "Migrating from DOS and Windows 3.x" section. When you have read the section covering your migration challenge, then you can go on to the next hour without missing any additional data.

Migrating from DOS and Windows 3.x

This section covers the hardware, software, installation, and operating system considerations for migrating from DOS and Windows 3.x to Windows NT 4. This is the most common migration path and presents several challenges.

Hardware Considerations

The required hardware configuration for Windows NT Workstation is listed at http://www.microsoft.com/ntworkstation/Datasht.htm. In short, Microsoft says the minimums are as follows:

- ☐ 486/25 MHz (or faster) or Pentium-based system (Intel system)
- ☐ 12MB of random access memory (RAM) (Intel systems); 16MB all others
- ☐ 110MB of available hard-disk space
- ☐ CD-ROM drive or access to a CD-ROM over a computer network
- ☐ VGA or higher-resolution display adapter
- ☐ Microsoft Mouse or compatible pointing device

These minimums will run NT but will not provide acceptable system performance. Experience shows that the following will provide average system performance:

- ☐ At least a Pentium 100 or its non-Intel equivalent
- ☐ 32MB of RAM
- ☐ 2GB of hard-disk space
- ☐ 6X CD-ROM drive or higher
- ☐ SVGA display adapter with hardware graphics accelerator and a 17-inch monitor

When moving from DOS/Windows 3.*x* to Windows NT, you might find your existing hardware base to be inadequate. You will be tempted to upgrade your computers by buying more RAM, faster central processing units (CPUs), and bigger hard drives. This upgrade will look better on paper than replacing your existing PCs, but it is only a short-term fix. New systems will also include new system BIOS chips, improved bus architecture, preinstalled software, and a warranty. (The advantages of the preinstalled software are discussed in the "Software Considerations" section.) The other, hardware-related, features will pay for themselves during setup and maintenance. If, for some reason, you cannot buy new systems, at least consider replacing the motherboards. Replacing the motherboards will give you a state-of-the-art BIOS and bus. A new motherboard will also normally have a built-in, enhanced disk drive controller capable of handling up to four 2GB+ drives or a combination of drives and CD-ROMs.

If you decide you want to dual boot your existing DOS/Windows 3.*x* installation with Windows NT (details of creating a dual boot installation are in Hour 15, "Installation and Setup of NT 4 Workstation"; software considerations that would drive you to a dual boot are in the "Software Considerations" section), then you must decide how to configure your disks. If you have decided to install NT, then you will probably decide to install NTFS (New Technology File System, detailed in Hour 13). Your DOS/Windows 3.*x* installation will not be able to read the disk or disk partitions you format with NTFS. This means you need to place your DOS/Windows 3.*x* files in a separate partition or on a separate disk. You will be able to read this partition or disk from the NT installation (unless they are compressed) but will be unable to use NTFS security, compression, and long filenames on the DOS/Windows 3.*x* partition/disk.

12

Software Considerations

Windows 3.*x* and DOS software are 16 bit. The software industry spent quite a bit of time and money developing thousands of titles for DOS and Windows 3.*x*. But the money and time spent on mainstream software development has now moved on to 32-bit software, supported by operating systems like Windows NT. Fortunately, most of your DOS and Windows software will run under NT. Unfortunately, some of your most vital or interesting software will not.

Any software that tries to access hardware directly will not run under Windows NT. For example, many DOS-based game programs read and write directly to the video board to improve the speed of graphics. Windows NT does not allow this kind of hardware access.

If you have DOS/Windows 3.*x* programs that are mission critical (or just too interesting to lose), you should create a dual boot. (The physical limitations of a dual boot are outlined in the "Hardware Considerations" section.) From the DOS/Windows side, the NT side (assuming you use NTFS) will be invisible. The NT side (assuming your DOS/Windows 3.*x* partition is not compressed) will show your DOS/Windows files but will only be able to execute the ones that do not interface directly with hardware.

Installation

The hardest part of moving from DOS/Windows 3.1 to NT Workstation is the installation. Hour 15 covers installation in detail; this section covers installation as it applies to migrating from DOS/Windows 3.*x* to Windows NT.

Making a Boot Disk

The Windows NT installation process is centered on the CD. One of the smartest things you can do before you start the installation process is to make a boot disk that gives you access to the CD-ROM. This disk should include himem.sys, drivers to the CD-ROM (normally called something like mydrive.sys), mscdex (the Microsoft CD-ROM extensions), an autoexec.bat file, and a config.sys file. Your autoexec.bat should look like the following:

```
mscdex.exe /d:mvcd001 /m:10 /v
```

Your config.sys file should look like the following:

```
DEVICE=HIMEM.SYS
DOS=HIGH
devicehigh=slcd.sys /D:mvcd001 /B:1F88 /M:P /v /c
```

Notice the use of loadhigh and devicehigh to free up as much of the 640KB primary memory as possible. The setup program on the Windows NT CD requires at least 428KB to run.

You can use this disk to initiate an install from the CD-ROM regardless—even if your NT installation will not boot or you can't find the boot disks you created.

Creating the Boot Disks on the Target Machine

When connectivity to the CD is established, change to the appropriate directory for your hardware and type winnt. This will create the three boot disks (detailed in Hour 15) on the target machine and start the setup process.

Creating the Boot Disks on Another Machine

To create the boot disks on another machine, change to the appropriate directory on the CD-ROM for your hardware and type winnt /ox. This will create the disks without running the setup program.

Setup Without Boot Disks

Establish a connection to the CD-ROM and type winnt /b. This will bypass the creation of the boot disks, copy their information to the hard drive, and start the installation process.

Hot-Wiring the Setup Process

You might find that the current setup disk does not include the same mass storage drivers that the last one did. It might be that your device has to be renamed or rewritten, or it might just be an oversight. If this happens to you and you can't get the installation to sense your particular hard drive or CD-ROM, then it might be possible to copy your driver from the old disks to the new one. Examine the txtsetup.sif file from the first installation disk in Listing 12.1.

Listing 12.1. Excerpt from the txtsetup.sif file from the first NT installation disk.

```
atapi.sys    = 1,,,,,,,_3,4,0,0
atdisk.sys   = 1,,,,,,,_3,4,0,0
atkctrs.dll  = 1,,,,,,,2,1
atsvc.exe    = 1,,,,,,,,2,1,0
attrib.exe   = 1,,,,,,,2,1,0
audiocdc.hlp = 1,,,,,,,2,0,0
autochk.exe  = 1,,,,,,,_x,2,0,0
autoconv.exe = 1,,,,,,,,2,1,0
```

To include your file from the old disk, copy the appropriate .sys files to the new disks and make an entry in the new txtsetup.sif file that looks like the entry in the old txtsetup.sif file.

Use this procedure as a last resort. If you have access to the Internet, the correct file could already be on the Windows NT home page.

Common Mass Storage Device Drivers

Most of the current motherboards and CD-ROM installations are covered by the ATAPI driver. This driver covers the standard used for the Extended IDE interface, which drives both CDs and hard drives. If you have an older set of hardware in which the CD-ROM has its own controller and you cannot remember or discover from the outside of the CD-ROM what brand it is (not an uncommon occurrence), then choose the Panasonic driver during the Mass Storage Detection Phase of the installation. If that doesn't work, choose the Sony. If neither choice works, it is probably more cost-effective to buy a newer ATAPI-compatible CD-ROM (discount-priced at about $100) than to try to find a compatible driver.

Operating System Considerations

If you have chosen to migrate your Windows 3.*x* applications to your NT installation, then install Windows NT in the same directory in which your current Windows files reside. This directory is normally named Windows. This doesn't affect your DOS programs.

If you install Windows NT in the same directory as your current Windows 3.*x*, then Windows NT will be able to support many of the features of your current applications (with the constraints you have already seen involving NT and writing directly to the hardware).

The first time you log onto Windows NT after installing it to the same directory as your current installation of Windows 3.*x*, NT will migrate parts of the many *.ini files that are so common in Windows 3.*x* to the Windows NT Registry (see Hour 21, "The Windows NT Registry," for the detailed working of the Registry). When this first login occurs, you will be asked if you want to migrate the *.ini files and the *.grp files (program group files) to the Registry. Windows NT will set up win.ini and system.ini files to facilitate your 16-bit Windows programs. The win.ini file will be similar to Listing 12.2.

Listing 12.2. A Windows NT win.ini file.

```
; for 16-bit app support
[fonts]
[extensions]
[mci extensions]
[files]
```

```
[Mail]
MAPI=1
MAPIX=1
OLEMessaging=1
CMC=1
CMCDLLNAME=mapi.dll
CMCDLLNAME32=MAPI32.DLL
Exchange=C:\Program Files\Windows NT\Windows Messaging\exchng32.exe
MAPIXVER=1.0.0.1
[WinZip]
win32_version=6.1-6.2
Name=Jeff Perkins
SN=12307597
[WINFAX]
ExePath=C:\WINFAX\
Fax Path=C:\WINFAX\DATA\
PhoneBook=Default
Cover Path=C:\WINFAX\COVER\
VERSION=3.0
imodemclass=Class2
imodemdesc=Generic CLASS 2 Send/Receive Fax/modem
imodeminit=AT&F&C1&D2\
Paper Format=Letter (8.5 x 11 inches)
Orientation=Portrait
Resolution=Standard
Registered=Yes
[AnyFax]
OP30=C:\WINFAX\
FileView=C:\WINFAX\ocrlink.dll
Autoloadocr=NEVER
Memsize_200=1000
Memsize_300=1800
Memsize_400=2800
[mciwave.dll]
WaveAudio=4
[Solitaire]
Options=69
Back=11
[IDAPI]
DLLPATH=C:\DELPHI16\IDAPI
CONFIGFILE01=C:\DELPHI16\IDAPI\IDAPI.CFG
[Borland Language Drivers]
LDPath=C:\DELPHI16\IDAPI\LANGDRV
[BWCC]
BitmapLibrary=BWCC.DLL
[Interbase]
RootDirectory=C:\DELPHI16\IBLOCAL
[Paradox Engine]
UserName=PxEngine
NetNamePath=C:\
MaxTables=64
RecBufs=64
MaxLocks=64
MaxFiles=64
SwapSize=64
```

12

continues

Listing 12.2. continued

```
[DDE Servers]
DBD=C:\DELPHI16\DBD\DBD
[DBD]
WORKDIR=C:\DELPHI16\DBD
PRIVDIR=C:\DELPHI16\DBD\DBDPRIV
[Collage Capture]
Save On Exit=1
Prompt On Entry=0
Collage Capture Settings File=C:\COLLWIN\ORIGINAL.SET
[programs]
Winword.exe="C:\Program Files\Microsoft Office\Office\Winword.exe"
[Oracle]
ORA_CONFIG=C:\WINNT\ORACLE.INI
[Btrieve]
Options=/m:40 /p:4096 /f:16 /l:20 /t:btrieve.trn
[MAPI 1.0 Time Zone]
Bias=168
StandardName=Central Standard Time
StandardBias=0
StandardStart=00000A00050002000000000000000000
DaylightName=Central Daylight Time
DaylightBias=ffffffc4
DaylightStart=00000400010002000000000000000000
ActiveTimeBias=168
```

Your system.ini file will look something like Listing 12.3.

Listing 12.3. A Windows NT system.ini file.

```
; for 16-bit app support

[drivers]
wave=mmdrv.dll
timer=timer.drv

[mci]
[386enh]
woafont=dosapp.FON
EGA80WOA.FON=EGA80WOA.FON
EGA40WOA.FON=EGA40WOA.FON
CGA80WOA.FON=CGA80WOA.FON
CGA40WOA.FON=CGA40WOA.FON
device=dva.386
```

Notice in Listing 12.2 the 16-bit Delphi and the Oracle entries. These entries are mirrored in the register. During your first login to Windows NT, entries are made into the system log showing what was moved into the system.ini and win.ini files. These entries can be read using the event viewer. After initial login, system.ini and win.ini are updated each time you log off Windows NT.

12

If you don't specify that the .ini and .grp files be migrated during initial login but want to migrate them later, delete the following two keys from the registry:

```
HKEY_CURRENT_USER\Windows 3.1 Migration Status
HKEY_LOCAL_MACHINE\SOFTWARE\Windows 3.1 Migration Status
```

When you log back on, the system will think it is your first login and ask if you want to migrate the .ini and .grp files.

If you choose not to install Windows NT into the same directory as your Windows 3.x installation, then there will not be an automated relationship between the Windows 3.x .ini files and the Windows NT Registry. Installing Windows 3.x after installing Windows NT will also make the two systems run independently, unaware of each other.

If you do install Windows NT in the same directory as Windows 3.x and then install a program while running Windows 3.x, the new program will not be installed under Windows NT. If you need it to appear in Windows NT, you can delete the two registry keys discussed previously, and NT will incorporate the new program during the next login, or you can reinstall the program while running Windows NT.

Regardless of where Windows NT is installed, changes made to the desktop or to the arrangement of the program groups are not synchronized with the previous version of Windows.

JUST A MINUTE

> Windows NT uses a common directory to store TrueType font and font header files for both 32- and 16-bit applications. This directory is %*SystemRoot*%SYSTEM\FONTS, where *SystemRoot* is usually named winnt or windows. Don't delete the files from this directory.

12

Migrating from Windows 95

This section covers the hardware, software, installation, and operating system considerations for migrating from Windows 95 to Windows NT 4. These two operating systems might look the same, but there are a few things that can jump up and bite you.

Hardware Considerations

The required hardware configuration for Windows NT Workstation is listed at http://www.microsoft.com/ntworkstation/Datasht.htm. In short, Microsoft says the minimums are as follows:

- ☐ 486/25 MHz (or faster) or Pentium-based system (Intel system)
- ☐ 12MB of RAM (Intel systems); 16MB all others
- ☐ 110MB of available hard-disk space
- ☐ CD-ROM drive or access to a CD-ROM over a computer network
- ☐ VGA or higher-resolution display adapter
- ☐ Microsoft Mouse or compatible pointing device

These minimums will run NT but will not provide acceptable system performance. Experience shows that the following will provide average system performance:

- ☐ At least a Pentium 100 or its non-Intel equivalent
- ☐ 32MB of RAM
- ☐ 2GB of hard-disk space
- ☐ 6X CD-ROM drive or higher
- ☐ SVGA display adapter with hardware graphics accelerator and a 17-inch monitor

If you are migrating from a typical Windows 95 setup, you will probably have all of the items recommended here except the memory. Most Windows 95 users find 16MB acceptable. The extra 16MB of RAM will cost you about $100.

If you got your Windows 95 hardware by upgrading an older machine, then you should strongly consider replacing the hardware as you migrate to Windows NT. The increased RAM, faster CPUs, and bigger hard drives you bought to upgrade your systems to Windows 95 are already obsolete. Upgrading again might look better on paper than replacing your existing PCs; but it will be only a short-term fix. New systems will also include new system BIOS chips, improved bus architecture, preinstalled software, and a warranty. You might not need the preinstalled software (because you already upgraded your software to 32-bit versions), but in the long run, replacing instead of upgrading will pay for itself during setup and maintenance. If, for some reason, you cannot buy new systems, at least consider replacing the motherboards. Replacing the motherboards will give you a state-of-the-art BIOS and bus. A new motherboard will also normally have a built-in, enhanced disk drive controller capable of handling up to four 2GB+ drives or a combination of drives and CD-ROMs.

Windows 95 and Windows NT 4 might look similar, but they are completely different underneath. Because of these differences, Microsoft doesn't support a dual boot option for Windows 95 and NT.

Another hardware consideration is what boards installed on your Windows 95 machine will be supported by Windows NT. Windows NT doesn't yet support plug-and-play (Microsoft plans to add plug-and-play to NT in 1997), so that the new 32-bit plug-and-play sound card you paid part of last month's rent for may clobber both your network card and your floppy drive (happened to me) and leave you mute and disconnected. In general, until plug-and-play

12

is supported, you must use cards that have user-configurable IRQ (Interrupt Request), DMA (Direct Memory Access), and address settings with your NT system.

Software Considerations

If you were lucky enough not to sell that 16-bit sound card and have installed it as part of your new NT installation, you might still have problems finding an NT driver that supports all of your card's bells and whistles—or supports your card at all. The problem is, from the software developer's point of view, a company can write a Windows 95 driver, making its hardware accessible to millions of software installations, or it can divert its efforts toward making an NT driver that will make its hardware accessible to hundreds of thousands of software installations. Economics has dictated that the probability of finding off-brand NT drivers is small. Stick to name brands or boards that support name-brand software standards.

Installation

The hardest part of moving from Windows 95 to NT Workstation is the installation. (Hour 15 covers installation in detail.) This section covers installation as it applies to migrating from Windows 95 to Windows NT.

Making a Boot Disk

The Windows NT installation process is centered on the CD. One of the smartest things you can do before you start the installation process is to make a boot disk that gives you access to the CD-ROM. This disk should include himem.sys, drivers to the CD-ROM (normally called something like mydrive.sys), mscdex (the Microsoft CD-ROM extensions), an autoexec.bat file, and a config.sys file. Your autoexec.bat should look like the following:

```
mscdex.exe /d:mvcd001 /m:10 /v
```

Your config.sys file should look like the following:

```
DEVICE=HIMEM.SYS
DOS=HIGH
devicehigh=slcd.sys /D:mvcd001 /B:1F88 /M:P /v /c
```

Notice the use of loadhigh and devicehigh to free up as much of the 640KB primary memory as possible. The setup program on the Windows NT CD requires at least 428KB to run.

Windows 95 and DOS/Windows 3.x are very similar when it comes to boot disks. This disk could be made using either a bootable DOS or a bootable Windows 95 disk. Whichever one you use, make sure the system files come from the same operating system. In a DOS setup, the system files are often in a directory called bin or DOS. In a Windows 95 setup, the system files are located in the windows, windows\system, and windows\command directories.

12

You can use this disk to initiate an install from the CD-ROM regardless—even if your NT installation will not boot or you can't find the boot disks you created.

Creating the Boot Disks on the Target Machine

When connectivity to the CD is established, change to the appropriate directory for your hardware and type `winnt32` if you used Windows 95 to boot your machine or `winnt` if you used DOS. This will create the three boot disks detailed in Hour 15 and start the setup process.

Creating the Boot Disks on Another Machine

To create the boot disks on another machine, change to the appropriate directory on the CD-ROM for your hardware and type `winnt32 /x` for 32-bit platforms like NT or Windows 95, or `winnt` for 16-bit platforms like Windows 3.*x* or DOS. This will create the disks without running the setup program.

Setup Without Boot Disks

Establish a connection to the CD-ROM and type `winnt32 /b` if you booted through Windows 95 or `winnt /b` if you booted through DOS. This will bypass the creation of the boot disks, copy their information to the hard drive, and start the installation process.

Hot-Wiring the Setup Process

You might find that the current setup disk does not include the same mass storage drivers that the last one did. It might be that your device has been renamed or rewritten, or it might just be an oversight. If this happens to you and you can't get the installation to sense your particular hard drive or CD-ROM, then it might be possible to copy your driver from the old disks to the new one. Examine the `txtsetup.sif` file from the first installation disk shown in Listing 12.4.

Listing 12.4. The `txtsetup.sif` file from the first NT installation disk.

```
atapi.sys    = 1,,,,,,,_3,4,0,0
atdisk.sys   = 1,,,,,,,_3,4,0,0
atkctrs.dll  = 1,,,,,,,2,1
atsvc.exe    = 1,,,,,,,2,1,0
attrib.exe   = 1,,,,,,,2,1,0
audiocdc.hlp = 1,,,,,,,2,0,0
autochk.exe  = 1,,,,,,_x,2,0,0
autoconv.exe = 1,,,,,,,2,1,0
```

12

To include your file from the old disk, copy the appropriate .sys files to the new disks and make an entry in the new txtsetup.sif file that looks like the entry in the old txtsetup.sif file.

CAUTION

Use this procedure as a last resort. If you have access to the Internet, the correct file could already be on the Windows NT home page.

Common Mass Storage Device Drivers

Most of the current motherboards and CD-ROM installations will be covered by the ATAPI driver. This driver covers the standard used for the Extended IDE interface, which drives both CDs and hard drives. If you have an older set of hardware in which the CD-ROM has its own controller and you cannot remember or discover from the outside of the CD-ROM what brand it is (not an uncommon occurrence), then choose the Panasonic driver during the Mass Storage Detection Phase of the installation. If that doesn't work, choose the Sony. If neither choice works, it is probably more cost-effective to buy a newer ATAPI-compatible CD-ROM (discount-priced at about $100) than to try to find a compatible driver.

Operating System Considerations

The fact that Windows 95 and Windows NT look alike on the surface hides how different these two systems are underneath. Your migration from Windows 95 to Windows NT will underline these differences.

You have already seen that there is no dual boot option for Windows 95 and Windows NT. This is because of the vastly different ways their registries are structured and their different approaches to supporting hardware.

Because of these differences, your migration to Windows NT must be manual. No programs or register values will be transferred automatically. When you install Windows NT, install it in a different directory; winnt is the default. After the installation, you will need to reinstall all of your other software, and then the old Windows 95 directory will be deleted. Microsoft is working on a more automated migration but has not released a target date for an automated migration.

About the only common feature of Windows 95 and Windows NT, aside from some common interface elements, is that they both support long filenames; you will not lose the descriptive filenames you have given your documents under Windows 95 when you make the transition to Windows NT.

12

The things you will gain by migrating to NT are the following:

☐ Better security. For example, you cannot log onto an NT workstation without an account on the machine. Windows 95 enables anyone to log on.

☐ NT file system (NTFS). Not only does it support long filenames, but it also supports access, logging, and compression features down to the file level. For example, by setting a file's attribute to compressed, you can compress that one file and leave all other files in the directory uncompressed.

☐ Distributed common object model (DCOM) support. Component object model (COM) support is critical to the inter-application communication and manipulation that makes object linking and embedding (OLE) possible. Windows 95 currently supports the COM model on the local machine, and add-on DCOM support for Windows 95 is currently available from the Microsoft Web site. Windows NT supports DCOM. This enables OLE objects to exist on different machines. Windows 97 is scheduled to support DCOM.

☐ Multimedia application programming interfaces (APIs). Windows NT provides a path for multimedia software developers to use to move away from hardware-specific programs. DirectX, which is implemented on both Windows 95 and Windows NT, is the main Multimedia API. Check out the Windows implementation of Doom to see how well this approach works. (Convince your boss you need this on your machine to evaluate trends in hardware-independent computer graphics software!)

☐ Multi-processor support. Windows NT supports more than one processor per motherboard, an advantage if your application lends itself to faster execution through the use of more than one processor.

This is the migration path that requires the most deliberation because of the diverse nature of both operating systems.

Migrating from NT 3.51

This section covers the hardware, software, installation, and operating system considerations for migrating from Windows NT 3.51 to Windows NT 4. The user interfaces of these two operating systems look completely different, but under the hood they are the same system. This makes the migration from NT 3.51 to NT 4 more of a update than a migration.

Hardware Considerations

The required hardware configuration for Windows NT Workstation is listed at http://www.microsoft.com/ntworkstation/Datasht.htm.

In short, Microsoft says the minimums are as follows:

- ☐ 486/25 MHz (or faster) or Pentium-based system (Intel system)
- ☐ 12MB of RAM (Intel systems); 16MB all others
- ☐ 110MB of available hard-disk space
- ☐ CD-ROM drive or access to a CD-ROM over a computer network
- ☐ VGA or higher-resolution display adapter
- ☐ Microsoft Mouse or compatible pointing device

These minimums will run NT but will not provide acceptable system performance. Experience shows that the following will provide average system performance:

- ☐ At least a Pentium 100 or its non-Intel equivalent
- ☐ 32MB of RAM
- ☐ 2GB of hard-disk space
- ☐ 6X CD-ROM drive or higher
- ☐ SVGA display adapter with hardware graphics accelerator and a 17-inch monitor

If you are migrating from a typical Windows NT 3.51 setup, you will probably have all of the recommended items.

If you got your Windows NT 3.51 hardware by upgrading an older machine, then you should strongly consider replacing the hardware as you migrate to Windows NT 4. The increased RAM, faster CPUs, and bigger hard drives you bought to upgrade your systems to Windows 95 are already obsolete. Upgrading again might look better on paper than replacing your existing PCs; but it will be only a short-term fix. New systems will also include new system BIOS chips, improved bus architecture, preinstalled software, and a warranty. You might not need the preinstalled software (because you already upgraded your software to 32-bit versions), but in the long run, replacing instead of upgrading will pay for itself during setup and maintenance. If, for some reason, you cannot buy new systems, at least consider replacing the motherboards. Replacing the motherboards will give you a state-of-the-art BIOS and bus. A new motherboard will also normally have a built-in, enhanced disk drive controller capable of handling up to four 2GB+ drives or a combination of drives and CD-ROMs.

Because this is more of an upgrade than a migration, there is no need for a dual boot. Plus, all your existing cards should move seamlessly from NT 3.51 to NT 4.

Software Considerations

Software will be the least of your worries during the update from NT 3.51 to NT 4. The biggest change is the Windows NT 4 interface; the soul of the operating system has not changed.

12

Installation

This is the simplest of all the installations. This section covers installation as it applies to upgrading from Windows NT 3.51 to Windows NT 4.

Making a Boot Disk

The Windows NT installation process is centered on the CD. Because Windows NT does not make a bootable system disk, there are advantages to creating a boot disk that gives you access to the CD-ROM. This disk will enable you to install from the CD-ROM if the boot-up gets mangled beyond all recognition. This disk should include himem.sys, drivers to the CD-ROM (normally called something like mydrive.sys), mscdex (the Microsoft CD-ROM extensions), an autoexec.bat file, and a config.sys file. Your autoexec.bat should look like the following:

```
mscdex.exe /d:mvcd001 /m:10 /v
```

Your config.sys file should look like the following:

```
DEVICE=HIMEM.SYS
DOS=HIGH
devicehigh=slcd.sys /D:mvcd001 /B:1F88 /M:P /v /c
```

Notice the use of loadhigh and devicehigh to free up as much of the 640KB primary memory as possible. The setup program on the Windows NT CD requires at least 428KB to run.

Windows 95 and DOS/Windows 3.x are very similar when it comes to boot disks. Make this disk using whichever operating system—a bootable DOS or bootable Windows 95 disk—is convenient for you. Whichever one you use, make sure the system files come from the same operating system. In a DOS setup, the system files are often in a directory called bin or DOS. In a Windows 95 setup, the system files are located in the windows, windows\system, and windows\command directories.

Creating the Boot Disks on the Target Machine

When connectivity to the CD is established, change to the appropriate directory for your hardware and type winnt32 if you used Windows 95 to boot your machine or winnt if you used DOS. This will create the three boot disks detailed in Hour 15, "Installation and Setup of NT 4 Workstation," and start the setup process.

Creating the Boot Disks on Another Machine

To create the boot disks on another machine, change to the appropriate directory on the CD-ROM for your hardware and type winnt32 /x for 32-bit platforms like NT or Windows 95, or winnt for 16-bit platforms like Windows 3.x or DOS. This will create the disks without running the setup program.

12

Setup Without Boot Disks

Establish a connection to the CD-ROM and type `winnt32 /b` if you booted with Windows 95, or `winnt /b` if you booted with DOS. This will bypass the creation of the boot disks, copy their information to the hard drive, and start the installation process.

Hot-Wiring the Setup Process

You might find that the current setup disk does not include the same mass storage drivers that the last one did. It might be that your device has be renamed or rewritten, or it may just be an oversight. If this happens to you and you can't get the installation to sense your particular hard drive or CD-ROM, then it might be possible to copy your driver from the old disks to the new one. Examine the `txtsetup.sif` file from the first installation disk shown in Listing 12.5.

Listing 12.5. The `txtsetup.sif` file from the first NT installation disk.

```
atapi.sys    = 1,,,,,,,_3,4,0,0
atdisk.sys   = 1,,,,,,,_3,4,0,0
atkctrs.dll  = 1,,,,,,,2,1
atsvc.exe    = 1,,,,,,,2,1,0
attrib.exe   = 1,,,,,,,2,1,0
audiocdc.hlp = 1,,,,,,,2,0,0
autochk.exe  = 1,,,,,,x,2,0,0
autoconv.exe = 1,,,,,,,2,1,0
```

To include your file from the old disk, copy the appropriate .sys files to the new disks and make an entry in the new `txtsetup.sif` file that looks like the entry in the old `txtsetup.sif` file.

CAUTION

Use this procedure as a last resort. If you have access to the Internet, the correct file could already be on the Windows NT home page.

Common Mass Storage Device Drivers

Most of the current motherboards and CD-ROM installations will be covered by the ATAPI driver. This driver covers the standard used for the Extended IDE interface, which drives both CDs and hard drives. If you have an older set of hardware in which the CD-ROM has its own controller and you cannot remember or discover from the outside of the CD-ROM what brand it is (not an uncommon occurrence), then choose the Panasonic driver during the Mass

Storage Detection Phase of the installation. If that doesn't work, choose the Sony. If neither choice works, it is probably more cost-effective to buy a newer ATAPI-compatible CD-ROM (discount-priced at about $100) than to try to find a compatible driver.

Operating System Considerations

This upgrade will cause all of your register information to be placed in the new Registry. Because the user interface has changed, you will lose some of the values that contained the 3.51 user interface information; but you won't miss them because they don't contribute to the new interface.

Migrating from OS/2

This section covers the hardware, software, installation, and operating system considerations for migrating from OS/2 to Windows NT 4. Given the zealots that populate all aspects of operating system wars, migrating from OS/2 to Windows NT is more of a religious conversion than a software migration. Religious conversions are beyond the scope of this book, so we will deal only with the migration aspects.

Hardware Considerations

The required hardware configuration for Windows NT Workstation is listed at `http://www.microsoft.com/ntworkstation/Datasht.htm`. In short, Microsoft says the minimums are as follows:

- ☐ 486/25 MHz (or faster) or Pentium-based system (Intel system)
- ☐ 12MB of RAM (Intel systems); 16MB all others
- ☐ 110MB of available hard-disk space
- ☐ CD-ROM drive or access to a CD-ROM over a computer network
- ☐ VGA or higher-resolution display adapter
- ☐ Microsoft Mouse or compatible pointing device

These minimums will run NT but will not provide acceptable system performance. Experience shows that the following will provide average system performance:

- ☐ At least a Pentium 100 or its non-Intel equivalent
- ☐ 32MB of RAM
- ☐ 2GB of hard-disk space
- ☐ 6X CD-ROM drive or higher
- ☐ SVGA display adapter with hardware graphics accelerator and a 17-inch monitor

12

If you are migrating from a typical OS/2 setup, you will probably have all the recommended items except the 32MB of memory. Buying additional memory will cost you about $100.

If you got your OS/2 machine by upgrading an older machine, then you should strongly consider replacing the hardware as you migrate to Windows NT 4. The increased RAM, faster CPUs, and bigger hard drives you bought to upgrade your systems to OS/2 are already obsolete. Upgrading again might look better on paper than replacing your existing PCs; but it will be only a short-term fix. New systems will also include new system BIOS chips, improved bus architecture, preinstalled software, and a warranty. You will probably need all the preinstalled software. In the long run, replacing instead of upgrading will pay for itself during setup and maintenance. If, for some reason, you cannot buy new systems, at least consider replacing the motherboards. Replacing the motherboards will give you a state-of-the-art BIOS and bus. A new motherboard will also normally have a built-in, enhanced disk drive controller capable of handling up to four 2GB+ drives or a combination of drives and CD-ROMs.

Because of the file systems involved, HPFS versus NTFS, any dual boot scheme will involve separate partitions or hard drives. Unless you are setting up the machine as a test platform for one or both operating systems, separate storage will not be very cost-effective. You also will have to consider replacing any plug-and-play or OS/2-specific cards.

Software Considerations

The only software you will be able to migrate from your OS/2 setup will be the 16-bit Windows software and a small subset of your OS/2 software (see the "Operating System Considerations" section for details on OS/2 software). There is no automated migration. You will have to go back to the original disks and install the software on your Windows NT machine.

Installation

Your installation will probably consist of backing up your 16-bit Windows software and the few OS/2 programs you can run under Windows NT 4, reformatting your hard drive, and installing Windows NT. This might sound a little severe, but in the long run, it is the least painful way to go. If you have an NT version 3.51 lying around, you might try installing 3.51 (which reads HPFS) and then upgrading to 4, but your OS/2-specific programs still will not work.

Making a Boot Disk

The Windows NT installation process is centered on the CD. Because Windows NT does not make a bootable system disk, there are advantages to creating a boot disk that gives you access to the CD-ROM. This disk will enable you to install from the CD-ROM if the boot-up gets mangled beyond all recognition. This disk should include `himem.sys`, drivers to the CD-ROM (normally called something like `mydrive.sys`), `mscdex` (the Microsoft CD-ROM extensions), an `autoexec.bat` file, and a `config.sys` file. Your `autoexec.bat` should look like the following:

```
mscdex.exe /d:mvcd001 /m:10 /v
```

Your `config.sys` file should look like the following:

```
DEVICE=HIMEM.SYS
DOS=HIGH
devicehigh=slcd.sys /D:mvcd001 /B:1F88 /M:P /v /c
```

Notice the use of `loadhigh` and `devicehigh` to free up as much of the 640KB of primary memory as possible. The setup program on the Windows NT CD requires at least 428KB to run.

You must generate a boot disk from a machine running either Windows 95 or DOS (especially if you reformatted your hard drive). Windows 95 and DOS/Windows 3.x are very similar when it comes to boot disks. Make this disk using whichever operating system—either a bootable DOS or a bootable Windows 95 disk—is convenient for you. Whichever one you use, make sure the system files come from the same operating system. In a DOS setup, the system files are often in a directory called `bin` or `DOS`. In a Windows 95 setup, the system files are located in the `windows`, `windows\system`, and `windows\command` directories.

Creating the Boot Disks on the Target Machine

When connectivity to the CD is established, change to the appropriate directory for your hardware and type `winnt32` if you used Windows 95 to boot your machine or `winnt` if you used DOS. This will create the three boot disks detailed in Hour 15, and start the setup process.

Creating the Boot Disks on Another Machine

To create the boot disks on another machine, change to the appropriate directory on the CD-ROM for your hardware and type `winnt32 /x` for 32-bit platforms like NT or Windows 95 or `winnt` for 16-bit platforms like Windows 3.x or DOS. This will create the disks without running the setup program.

Setup Without Boot Disks

Establish a connection to the CD-ROM and type `winnt32 /b` if you booted with Windows 95, or `winnt /b` if you booted with DOS. This will bypass the creation of the boot disks, copy their information to the hard drive, and start the installation process.

12

Hot-Wiring the Setup Process

You might find that the current setup disk does not include the same mass storage drivers that the last one did. It might be that your device has been renamed or rewritten, or it might just be an oversight. If this happens to you and you can't get the installation to sense your particular hard drive or CD-ROM, then it might be possible to copy your driver from the old disks to the new one. Examine the following `txtsetup.sif` file from the first installation disk, as shown in Listing 12.6.

Listing 12.6. The `txtsetup.sif` file from the first NT installation disk.

```
atapi.sys    = 1,,,,,,,_3,4,0,0
atdisk.sys   = 1,,,,,,,_3,4,0,0
atkctrs.dll  = 1,,,,,,,2,1
atsvc.exe    = 1,,,,,,,2,1,0
attrib.exe   = 1,,,,,,,2,1,0
audiocdc.hlp = 1,,,,,,,2,0,0
autochk.exe  = 1,,,,,,,_x,2,0,0
autoconv.exe = 1,,,,,,,2,1,0
```

To include your file from the old disk, copy the appropriate `.sys` files to the new disks and make an entry in the new `txtsetup.sif` file that looks like the entry in the old `txtsetup.sif` file.

CAUTION

> Use this procedure as a last resort. If you have access to the Internet, the correct file could already be on the Windows NT home page.

12

Common Mass Storage Device Drivers

Most of the current motherboards and CD-ROM installations will be covered by the ATAPI driver. This driver covers the standard used for the Extended IDE interface, which drives both CDs and hard drives. If you have an older set of hardware in which the CD-ROM has its own controller and you cannot remember or discover from the outside of the CD-ROM what brand it is (not an uncommon occurrence), then choose the Panasonic driver during the Mass Storage Detection Phase of the installation. If that doesn't work, choose the Sony. If neither choice works, it is probably more cost-effective to buy a newer ATAPI-compatible CD-ROM (discount-priced at about $100) than to try to find a compatible driver.

Operating System Considerations

There is a set of OS/2 programs that you can run under Windows NT 4:

- ☐ OS/2 1.*x* 16-bit applications on *x*86 computers only
- ☐ Character-based applications

You will not be able to run the following:

- ☐ OS/2 2.*x* applications
- ☐ Presentation Manager (PM) applications (unless you install the Windows NT Add-On Subsystem for Presentation Manager, which can be ordered separately from Microsoft)
- ☐ Advanced video I/O (AVIO) applications (unless you install the Windows NT Add-On Subsystem for Presentation Manager)
- ☐ OS/2 applications on RISC-based computers
- ☐ Applications that directly access hardware memory or I/O ports at Ring 2 or lower

Additional Resources

The following are some additional resources that could help you overcome your migration challenge:

- ☐ `http://www.microsoft.com/NTWksSupport/`: Microsoft's Internet page for NT Workstation
- ☐ `http://www.microsoft.com/NTWksSupport/content/faq/`: Frequently asked questions about NT Workstation
- ☐ `http://www.microsoft.com/windows/common/aa2692.htm`: URL for Comparison of Windows 95 to Windows NT Workstation

Summary

In this hour, you have learned four migration paths to Windows NT 4: from DOS/Windows 3.*x*, Windows 95, Windows NT version 3.51, and OS/2. You should now be aware of the hardware, software, installation, and operating system considerations for each path. This information will help you to plan and implement your migration to Windows NT 4.

12

Workshop

The Workshop helps you solidify the skills you learned this hour.

Glossary

High Performance File System (HPFS)   The native file system for OS/2. Supported on NT versions before NT 4. Not compatible with NT 4.

New Technology File System (NTFS)   The native Windows NT file system that provides security, logging, and compression to NT users.

winnt and winnt32   The Windows NT setup programs.

Exercise

Build a boot-up disk that gives you access to the CD-ROM of your machine. Use either DOS or Windows 95.

12

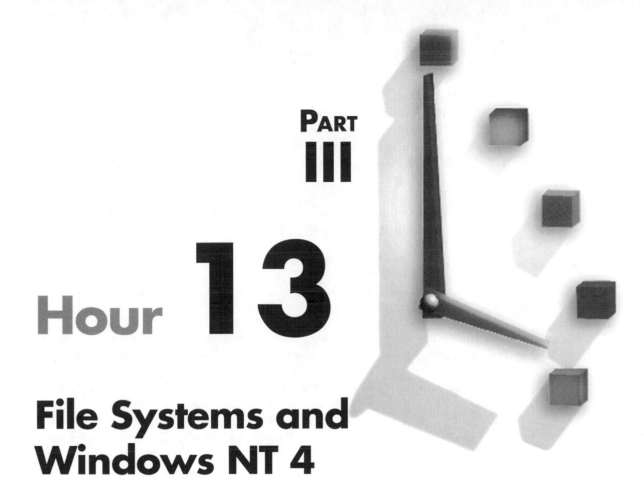

Hour 13

File Systems and Windows NT 4

by Gary Neely

NT has a very compelling strength over other operating systems: It can support more than one type of *file system*. NT implements file systems as modules similar to device drivers used for video cards or sound systems. The module NT will use is determined by your choice of file system when you install NT. Choosing which file system to use is one of the most important choices you must make when you install NT. To be prepared for making the best choice, you must understand what a file system is and what the choices can do for you.

Disks and Volumes

To understand file systems, it is helpful to understand how an operating system like NT or DOS sees a hard disk. Hard disks are split into divisions called *partitions*. There are two kinds of partitions: primary and extended. The primary partition is always the location of files necessary to start the computer and is usually labeled C:. Hard disks typically have one primary and one extended partition. An extended partition can be further divided into multiple units called *logical drives*, each having its own drive letter like D:, E:, and so on. It is possible to have many logical drives on one hard disk.

JUST A MINUTE

Sometimes a hard drive is configured with only one partition (the primary partition) that occupies the entire drive and is labeled C:. This is very common with machines purchased from department stores or electronics superstores. As you will see in the "Disadvantages of FAT" section, this often is not the best solution.

The amount of space to be allocated to each partition or logical drive is determined when partitions and logical drives are created by the owner or system administrator. For example, a 1GB hard disk could be partitioned as a single logical device (the primary partition) and called C:. The same hard disk could also be split into one primary partition of 256MB and one extended partition of 768MB. The extended partition could then be broken down into three logical drives of 256MB each. The hard disk would then have four logical devices: C: (the primary partition), and D:, E:, and F: (the logical drives of the extended partition). Other combinations are possible; see Chapter 9, "Working with Hard Disks," for more information on partitioning strategies.

The primary partition and all logical drives must be individually formatted to accept data. When a partition or logical drive is formatted and ready to be used for file storage, it is called a *volume*.

CAUTION

Experimenting with disk partitions and volume formatting is not a good idea unless you are an experienced user. It is very easy to make a mistake and suddenly and irrevocably lose all information on your hard disk. Be very sure of what you are doing, and as always, back up, back up, back up. For more information on the details of partitioning and formatting, see the related discussions in Hour 9 and Hour 10, "Volumes and the Disk Administrator."

Special Partitions

Two formatted volumes are particularly important to NT: the *system partition* and the *boot partition*. The system partition must contain the files necessary to boot the computer. For NT these include `BOOT.INI`, `NTDETECT.COM`, `NTLDR`, and the NT boot manager. In many cases, this partition will also contain the NT system files. The boot partition will contain the system files required to start NT. The name is a bit of a misnomer until you realize that "boot" in this case refers to starting NT, not the computer. Note that the system and the boot partition might be one and the same, but they don't have to be. The system partition could be C:, and the boot might be on logical drive F:. You will choose where you want your NT system files to go during the NT setup process, and that determines your boot partition. The setup process will automatically set up your system partition.

The concept of the boot partition becomes important should you decide to have NT coexist with other operating systems on the same machine (see Chapter 15, "Installation and Setup of NT 4 Workstation"). If NT will be the only operating system on your machine, then it will likely reside on your system partition, and you can safely ignore the distinction.

File Systems

Now you know about drives and volumes, but what about file systems? A file system is simply a method for organizing information on a partition or logical drive for storage and retrieval. The idea is similar to a library's system of cataloging books or the postal service's method of organizing mail for delivery. When the logical drive or partition is formatted, it is being prepared with a system to accept files in a structured way. All volumes have a file system, including volumes on hard disks, floppies, or CD-ROM. A file system not only enables the operating system to answer the question, "Where the heck did I put that file?" but also determines how that file can be named or what programs or users have access to that file.

In the "Disks and Volumes" section, you learned that each volume is individually formatted with a file system to prepare it for accepting data. If you're quick (or you've seen this stuff before), you might have figured out one of the advantages of splitting your hard disk into multiple logical drives: You can have different file systems on the same hard disk. You learn some of the advantages of this as this lesson progresses.

There are four file systems that involve Windows NT 4:

☐ File Allocation Table (FAT): The simplest and least powerful file system available for use with NT 4. FAT is the native file system for DOS and Windows 3.x. Note that Windows 95 uses an augmented version of FAT known as VFAT.

☐ New Technology File System (NTFS): The native file system for NT designed for large volumes, high reliability, security, and performance. It is the file system of choice for the Server version of Windows NT.

☐ High Performance File System (HPFS): The older cousin of NTFS, native to IBM's OS/2 operating system.

13

☐ CD-ROM File System (CDFS): A file system designed for use with read-only CD-ROM devices.

Only the first two file systems will be important to most readers. CDFS is used only for CD-ROM access; there are no decisions for NT users to make, so you won't learn it here. I'll touch on HPFS but won't spend much time on this topic, because most readers will not be concerned with HPFS.

FAT—The Venerable PC File System

Back in 1976, a young man named Bill Gates designed a file system that enabled a programming language called BASIC to store data on floppy disks. That file system became known as FAT for its characteristic feature: the File Allocation Table. In the early days of FAT, a 360KB floppy disk was considered a lot of storage for a small computer. Even Bill Gates could never have envisioned that FAT would be used for managing information on today's compact and fast multi-gigabyte hard disks; yet it has survived for many years as the native file system for DOS and Windows 3.x.

FAT's file allocation table is stored at the beginning of the volume to keep track of files and directories. The table format is fairly simple: Its entries are simply sequential pointers to where files and directories are stored on the volume. FAT maintains a redundant copy of this table as a hedge against the primary table being corrupted. The table is often updated, so hard drive heads must constantly bounce back and forth from wherever they are to the start of the disk volume. On big volumes, this can greatly increase the time required to read and write files.

Advantages of FAT

Despite FAT's age, there are still good reasons to think about using it even when given the alternative of a modern operating system such as NT 4. Don't be too quick to discount using FAT on NT volumes. Consider its strengths:

☐ Compatibility: NT, DOS, Windows 95, Windows 3.x, and OS/2 can all use FAT volumes. Even if you decide to make NT your only operating system, using FAT gives you the ability to boot DOS from a floppy and access your files. In addition, you can take comfort in the ability to use commonplace DOS utilities to examine and manipulate the volume. If your computer will have other operating systems available and the partition with NT has a lot of space available, you can still use that space for other non-NT applications rather than have it sit wasted.

☐ Simplicity: The FAT system is simple and reliable. It will not consume much of your disk space for its own overhead, and does not require a lot of memory. FAT has more than 20 years of proven reliability behind it.

13

☐ File access on small volumes: Because FAT is fairly simple, it has a low overhead for operations. It is not the optimal file system for large volumes, but for small volumes it actually performs quite well, in many cases better than modern feature-rich file systems.

The main point to remember is the compatibility issue. Keep this strength in mind as you read on.

Disadvantages of FAT

FAT shows its age when contrasted against such feature-rich file systems as NTFS. Here are the disadvantages of FAT that are likely to cause you the most grief:

☐ Limited naming convention: FAT is responsible for the 8+3 character DOS naming convention. Although NT's implementation of FAT is capable of giving files and directories longer names, DOS is still going to see only 8+3 characters. Many people find this convention tiresome. In addition, there is no support for uppercase/lowercase characters or *Unicode*, a 16-bit convention that is useful for supporting non-English language characters.

☐ Poor security: There are no built-in provisions for controlling the access of files on a volume. If you require this kind of protection for certain files or directories, FAT is not the solution. If yours is a multiuser system, be aware that FAT offers zero security.

☐ Inefficient use of large volumes: FAT wasn't designed to manage today's big hard drives, so use of disk space on large volumes can be very wasteful. File access on large volumes with lots of files can be very slow, because FAT uses an unsophisticated procedure to search for files.

Given the increasingly large size of hard drives, the latter weakness of FAT is one of the greatest. This is particularly true of those single-partition hard drives that come from electronic superstores. To see why, you must understand how files are saved on a volume. (Yes, get ready for yet another definition.)

Clusters and File Systems

Most computer users are familiar with that part of a directory listing that gives the size of a file in bytes or kilobytes. That is how much space the file takes up on the drive, right? Not necessarily. In fact, very likely it is not even close. Try this: On a machine on which you have access to DOS, make a little text file and save it to disk. Do a DIR on the directory where you saved the file and record the size of the file and the number of bytes available on the hard disk. Now, delete the little text file. How many more bytes would you expect to have available on the disk? Do a DIR again. Surprise!

You've just discovered the effect of *clusters*. A cluster is the smallest unit of space that can be allocated for file storage. The size of a cluster is measured in bytes and varies with the file system and the size of the volume. Look at Table 13.1 and notice how the size of FAT clusters increases as the volume size gets bigger.

Table 13.1. Cluster size comparisons.

FAT Volume Size (MB)	Cluster Size (Bytes)	NTFS Volume Size (MB)	Cluster Size (Bytes)
0–15	4096	Up to 511	512
16–127	2048	512–1023	1024
128–255	4096	1024–2047	2048
256–511	8192	2048 and up	4096
512–1023	16384		
1024–2047	32768		
2048 and up	65536		

If you look closely at the table, you might notice an odd break in the cluster size sequence of a FAT volume with a size of 0–15MB. This is not an error; on small volumes, FAT uses 12-bit addressing rather than 16-bit, meaning there are fewer possible clusters, so each cluster must be larger.

Every file requires at least one cluster of disk space and very often more than one cluster. If a file doesn't use all of a cluster's disk space, that space is wasted. For example, if you save a little 400-byte text file on a relatively small 240MB FAT volume, that file will occupy 4096 bytes of actual physical disk space. The same file on a 1.2GB drive with a single partition will hog a whopping 32,768 bytes of disk space. Imagine having a bunch of tiny little files such as e-mail messages on such a drive. Disk space begins disappearing quickly.

You have two options for dealing with this situation: Partition a big disk drive into smaller volumes, or use a file system that has more efficient cluster sizes for big volumes. There is nothing wrong with creating smaller volumes, and doing so can help you organize your computer. If you have a big hard disk and would rather deal with a single volume, then using a file system like NTFS makes more sense.

TIME SAVER

Creating FAT volumes that give a cluster size of 4096 bytes is a good compromise for minimizing the number of volumes on your hard disk as well as cluster size. I have several 1GB hard disks that I've split into four

> 255MB partitions. Whatever you decide, don't make volumes that use cluster sizes of 16384 or more. The amount of disk space you will waste is guaranteed to be hideous.

NTFS—Microsoft's New Technology Answer

As Microsoft's Windows 3.x family of operating environments became increasingly popular as business computer solutions, the business community began requesting better support for security and networking. Microsoft was motivated to come up with a file system that offered such features and more.

NTFS was designed to support the large volumes typical of business applications. Whereas FAT is a 16-bit file system, NTFS is a 32-bit file system. This means it can support larger volumes with smaller cluster sizes. Take another look at Table 13.1 and compare NTFS with FAT using the same volume size. FAT can use a volume size of 4GB, which is pretty big—but it does so very inefficiently. NTFS can support a maximum volume size of 16 exabytes, or 2^{32} times the maximum volume size of FAT. (An *exabyte* is 2^{60}, a number that is simply huge.)

The NTFS file system can access files on a big volume much faster than FAT because it uses a more advanced search algorithm on a sorted list of filenames rather than FAT's simple lookup on a list of unsorted filenames. The difference is similar to using a telephone book as it was intended instead of starting with the first name and going through the entire book sequentially until you find the name you wanted.

With NTFS, you can assign security features to files and directories, and you have increased ability to recover from system failures without losing data. NTFS is the way to go for the Server version of Windows NT—any other choice is silly.

Advantages of NTFS

Here is a comprehensive glance at the major benefits of using NTFS with NT 4 Workstation:

- ☐ Efficient support of large volumes: As you learn in the "NTFS—Microsoft's New Technology Answer" section, NTFS manages files on large hard disk partitions very efficiently, resulting in fast file access.

- ☐ Efficient use of disk space: NTFS uses relatively small cluster sizes so less disk space is wasted when storing files.

13

☐ Security: NTFS enables you to set permissions on files and directories and won't let users bypass security features by booting from a floppy or another operating system. In addition, NTFS enables you to maintain a file access log that records who accessed (or tried to access) a file or directory. NTFS boasts of meeting U.S. government C-2 security standards.

☐ Robustness: NTFS makes a record of file transactions to help protect you against the loss of data in the event of a system crash or hardware failure. If a transaction fails before it can be completed, NT will be aware of the problem when the system is restarted and will make the necessary corrections. NTFS also features disk fault tolerance, which protects data against loss of a hard disk on a multidisk system, but this feature is normally available only on the Server version of NT 4.

☐ Automatic compression: NTFS lets you enable automatic compression of a specific file or even a directory of files. (With other file systems, you must run a utility every time you want to compress or decompress a file.)

☐ Advanced filename support: NTFS supports the use of uppercase and lowercase characters, Unicode (a format that allows 16-bit characters and is useful for support of foreign languages), and long filenames of up to 254 characters.

Disadvantages of NTFS

There are some pitfalls to the use of NTFS for your volumes. NTFS consumes about 5MB on any volume on which it is used. Because of all the activities it performs for you, it is not very fast when used with small volumes, particularly those under 512MB. You should also remember that NTFS volumes can't be accessed by other operating systems. The latter is a very important consideration, especially if you plan on using a dual-boot configuration in which several operating systems will share your computer.

HPFS and Windows NT 4

HPFS was originally developed by Microsoft for OS/2 Version 1.2. HPFS is optimized for volumes of moderate size, 256MB–512MB. It features automatic disk caching, and the cluster size is always 512 bytes regardless of volume size. It is a good file system in its own right, and Microsoft developers incorporated many of its features into the more advanced NTFS.

Previous versions of Windows NT came equipped with support for HPFS, but with the release of NT 4, Microsoft developers decided to discontinue this practice. This is a puzzling decision, because it makes it more difficult for OS/2 users to move to NT, and HPFS would otherwise be a good file system choice for NT 4 Workstation users with intermediate-sized volumes. Unfortunately, HPFS is not an option with the stock NT 4 package.

13

JUST A MINUTE

OS/2 and HPFS fans take heart! Although NT 4 doesn't support HPFS out of the box, it is possible to use HPFS with NT 4. The solution involves importing some HPFS files from NT 3.51 and modifying your NT 4 registry. This is beyond the scope of this introductory book, but (shameless plug follows) interested readers are encouraged to look into more detailed NT 4 reference works from Sams such as Windows NT 4 Workstation Unleashed and Peter Norton's Complete Guide to Windows NT 4 Workstation. A step-by-step solution for HPFS support can be found in the October 1996 issue of Windows NT Magazine.

Converting FAT Volumes to NTFS

Microsoft provides a utility program with NT 4 that enables you to convert FAT volumes to NTFS painlessly—in other words, without losing your data. You can do this after you've installed NT. When completed, all your files and directory structures are converted. Backing up your data is not required, but it is always a good idea when you do this type of operation.

JUST A MINUTE

NT won't let you change the file system of a volume containing the Windows NT 4 system files.

The process of converting a FAT volume to NTFS without data loss must be performed from the command prompt:

1. Access the command prompt from the Programs menu of the Start button.
2. At the command prompt, enter the following, where *drive*: indicates the volume you want to convert. You should see something like the example in Figure 13.1.

```
convert   drive:   /fs:ntfs
```

Figure 13.1.

The command prompt with an example of the conversion command.

13

3. Press Return. One of two things will happen: Either the drive will be immediately converted, or you will be informed that the drive is in use and asked if you want to convert the drive the next time the system starts. A drive could be in use for several reasons: an application could have a file open on that drive, or you might have an NT page file on that drive. If you agree, then when the system next starts you'll see a message telling you the volume is being converted.

You can also convert a volume to NTFS using the Disk Administrator | Tools | Format option.

1. Access the Disk Administrator from the Administration Tools submenu of the Start button Programs menu.

2. In the Disk Administrator, select the volume you want to format by clicking the appropriate volume display.

3. Select the Format option under Tools. A dialog box similar to the one shown in Figure 13.2 will appear.

Figure 13.2.

The conversion utility built into the Disk Administrator. This is not the same program as the one run from the command prompt.

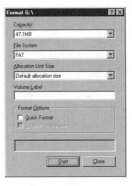

4. Click the File System box and change it to NTFS. You will also see an option for specifying the Allocation Unit Size. This lets you change the default cluster size for NTFS. Although it is interesting that Microsoft enables you to play with this, there is really no point in changing it. The default size is recommended.

5. Click Start. You will get a warning that the volume is about to be reformatted and all data will be lost. At this point you can abort the operation or continue.

CAUTION

The conversion program invoked by the Disk Administrator actually formats the disk to do the conversion, so you will lose all your data on that volume.

13

The Disk Administrator Format utility is an entirely different program than the one used at the command prompt. It is more flexible and powerful, but it does not have the capability to change a FAT volume to NTFS without losing everything on the volume. Use this program with great care. If you are wondering why Microsoft included two programs for very similar tasks, you are not alone.

Additional File System Topics

This section answers some of the more common questions related to file systems and Windows NT.

If I decide to use NTFS for a volume but change my mind after installation, what can I do about it?

Unfortunately, there is no way to painlessly change back to another file system. Your only solution is to back up the files and the applications you want to retain and reformat the volume. There's a good chance that this will involve reinstalling a lot of applications. Remember that when you reformat a volume, you lose all information on the volume.

What about floppies? Do I have to choose FAT or NTFS every time I want to use a new floppy disk?

No. NT uses FAT for floppies. As you've seen, NTFS was designed for large-scale storage devices, whereas FAT was originally designed for floppies. FAT is simpler and more efficient for use with relatively small-capacity media such as floppy disks. In fact, the disk space required for NTFS system overhead would exceed the capacity of a 1.44MB floppy.

I've heard about something called "disk fragmentation." What is this, and is this a problem with NT?

Yes, unfortunately it is a problem. Disk fragmentation is a side effect of writing and deleting files on your disk. When a file is deleted, the space it frees up might be too small for the next file written to the disk, so the operating system keeps looking for a bigger space and can be forced to use many little spaces linked together rather than one large continuous space. As a result, many files are broken down into small chunks scattered over the disk. The heads of the disk drive are forced to bounce all over the place to read a single file (which takes time) rather than smoothly read contiguous information. This can slow the reading of files considerably, sometimes drastically. Most operating systems don't monitor or correct this problem, but there are utility programs available to enable you to periodically reorganize your disk.

13

TIME SAVER

Disk fragmentation is not limited to hard disks. The effect can cause problems on commonly used floppy disks as well. If you have a defragmenting utility that works with FAT, you might consider occasionally using it on your most commonly used floppies.

NTFS is more clever about writing files to disk than FAT. NTFS examines the available disk space to select a reasonably efficient way to store a file, whereas FAT takes available space on a first-come, first-served basis, without looking ahead. As such, disk fragmentation is less of a problem with NTFS than with FAT, but nevertheless it is still a problem.

Now for more bad news. As of this writing, Microsoft (for reasons known only to Microsoft) has not provided a defragmenting utility for NTFS with any NT release. (If you poke around in the Disk Administration section of NT's administration programs, you'll see that Microsoft did provide a place to install a defragmenting utility. You have to wonder what Microsoft developers do when their disks get fragmented.) Fortunately, there are third-party solutions to fill this hole in NTFS disk maintenance. One advantage to using FAT with NT 4 is that you can use the DEFRAG.EXE program provided with DOS to defragment your hard disk. You can't use DEFRAG.EXE on an NTFS partition, because DOS can't read that partition.

How will DOS see a volume formatted with NTFS?

It won't. If you boot DOS on a system with one of its volumes formatted with NTFS, DOS will simply skip over that volume when assigning drive letters. You'll never see it as any of your logical drive options.

Summary

So which file system should you use? No book can make this choice for you, because only you know your requirements and system configuration. As of this writing, no file system does everything, so any choice you make will be a compromise. Table 13.2 summarizes the basics and might help you make your choice.

Table 13.2. When a file system is clearly superior.

Situation	The Best Choice
Need to share the volume with DOS, Windows 3.x, or Windows 95	FAT
Your disk volume is relatively small (less than 512MB, especially those 200MB or less)	FAT

13

Situation	The Best Choice
The volume is large (512MB or more)	NTFS
Need to control access to files or directories	NTFS
Need to share the volume on a network	NTFS
NT is the only operating system you will be using	NTFS
You are using NT Server	NTFS
Your computer has a RISC-type CPU	FAT

JUST A MINUTE

A RISC machine actually needs only a 2MB FAT partition for booting. Other partitions can be formatted using the same criteria as an Intel machine.

Workshop

The Workshop helps you solidify the skills you learned this hour.

Glossary

cluster   The smallest unit of disk space that can be allocated for file storage. Cluster size is dependent on volume size and the file system used. In general, the larger the volume size, the larger the cluster size. Sometimes a cluster is called an "allocation unit."

file system   A method for organizing information on a partition or logical drive for storage and retrieval.

logical drive   A subdivision of an extended partition. Each logical drive is identified by a drive letter.

partition   Structured divisions of a hard drive. There are two types: primary and extended. An extended partition can be further subdivided into logical drives.

volume   A partition or logical drive that has been formatted with a file system and is ready to accept data.

13

Exercises

1. Find a computer using FAT and try the experiment described in the first paragraph of "Clusters and File Systems" earlier in this hour. How much space is your system wasting with your current partition structure?

2. If your system will be using FAT or you intend to have a multiple-operating system configuration, what number of partitions will be the best solution for your hard disk or disks? This is likely to be a compromise that keeps cluster size small while minimizing the number of hard disk partitions.

Hour 14

Pre-Installation Concerns with NT 4 Workstation

by Gary Neely

You might have heard scary things about installing NT. The truth is that Windows NT 4 Workstation is not difficult to install if you approach it systematically and do a little research before you start. NT 4 Workstation is large and has many options, but if you've been through the installation of a big software package such as Microsoft Office, you won't find the installation of NT much more difficult. In fact, you will probably get NT working on your first attempt. You will have a few more decisions to make and might need to learn more about your system, but for most potential NT users this should not be a challenge.

When preparing to install NT, you should do two things if you do nothing else. The first is to make sure you meet the absolute minimum system requirements for installation of NT. Few things are more frustrating than acquiring a wonderful new program only to learn that it requires more RAM than the amount on your system. To help prevent this situation, Microsoft provides the following list of its recommended minimum requirements:

- ☐ Platform: An Intel-type 486 or better processor or a RISC-based processor such as a Digital Alpha-based system, a PowerPC, or a MIPS R4x00. (Note that Windows NT 4 Workstation supports up to two processors.)

- ☐ RAM: NT 4 Workstation on an Intel *x*86 platform requires at least 12MB of RAM. RISC-based machines like the PowerPC, Digital Alpha-based systems, and MIPS R4x00 systems require a minimum of 16MB of RAM.

- ☐ Video display adapter: You will need a VGA or better video display adapter.

- ☐ CD-ROM drive: A CD-ROM is required to install NT unless you are installing NT over a network connection.

- ☐ 3.5-inch high-density disk drive: You will need a 3.5-inch high-density floppy drive. High-density 5.25-inch floppy drives are not supported.

- ☐ Pointing device: A mouse or other pointing device is optional but highly recommended.

- ☐ Free disk space: Intel-type platforms will require a minimum of 117MB of available hard disk space for NT Workstation system files. RISC-based systems will require a minimum of 148MB of free disk space.

- ☐ Network adapter card: If you will be using Windows NT with a network, you will need a network adapter card.

You should be aware that Microsoft's ideas for minimum requirements are not entirely realistic. Yes, you can run NT 4 Workstation on such a system, but using it productively is another matter. As this hour progresses you'll learn these requirements in more detail. By the end of this hour you will be better equipped to make your own judgment.

I stated there were two things you should be absolutely certain to do. The second item is a simple recommendation, but one that is commonly ignored: Take the time to read the setup literature. Read the "Basics and Installation" section of the *Start Here* installation book that came with your copy of NT 4, any release notes that might have been provided, and any READ.MEs or other text files on your distribution disk.

Some people love to tear open a new box of software, throw the literature in a pile in the corner, slam the disk in the drive, type SETUP.EXE, and go to it. (Naturally, this author has *never* done anything like that...) With a system like NT, this is not a good idea. NT's installation requires you to prepare a few things in advance and make some important decisions during the setup process. The rest of this hour will help you to be ready for those decisions and will help make your NT installation painless.

14

TIME SAVER

There is a lot of NT setup information available on the Internet. If you have Internet access, search for any documents relating to NT's installation. You'll find many references, examples of NT configurations, and recommendations by other people who have installed NT.

Hardware Considerations

Before installing NT, you will need to know what hardware NT requires and what hardware it can use. In addition, you'll need to have a reasonable working knowledge of personal computers if for no other reason than to be able to ask the right questions should you get in trouble. A car owner does not need to know how the engine works but does need to know the car has an engine, the engine uses gasoline and needs to be kept cool, for example. The same is true of a personal computer. You don't need to know all the computer-nerd details, but you are installing an operating system, which is a complex piece of software; it helps to know the basics. If you are not interested in this, you might seek out a knowledgeable friend to help you through the setup process.

To prepare your system for NT, you should have all your system documentation handy, including any documentation and files that came with your hardware devices. Setting up an operating system involves every aspect of your computer. Chances are there will be some device in your computer that you will need to know more about before the installation is complete. Many components such as network and sound cards will have settings that you need to be aware of as you install NT. If you gather this information before you start the installation, you will avoid frustrating delays when the installation is under way.

JUST A MINUTE

It might surprise you to learn that the capability of Windows NT to automatically detect and configure hardware is not as good as Windows 95. Windows NT does not yet support the plug-and-play standard, but this is likely to be an option for future versions of NT. (Some readers familiar with the shortcomings of plug-and-play might not be happy to hear that.) Because NT doesn't do as much autodetection and configuration for you, you might have to learn a little more about your hardware and be familiar with things like jumper settings and interrupt requests (IRQs).

14

If your computer is to be part of a computer network, then you should be familiar with your networking requirements. NT will give you the option of installing and configuring network options during the installation process, but you can safely bypass this step and return to it after NT is installed. This would be a good time to have a chat with your network administrator if you've never dealt with this situation before.

JUST A MINUTE

Another difficulty you might face with hardware devices and NT is that Windows NT does not support the use of real-mode and 16-bit device drivers. If you have an old device that you can't afford to replace, try to find a device driver that is compatible with NT. Because of the growing popularity of NT, many hardware vendors are increasingly motivated to provide such drivers.

The Hardware Compatibility List

Microsoft developers spend a great deal of resources testing various hardware devices for compatibility with NT. Because they can't test everything and they don't even bother to test some devices, they maintain a document that describes all the devices that have been certified as compliant with NT. This is called the *Hardware Compatibility List* (HCL). If a device is on the HCL, you can be sure that Microsoft supports it and has a device driver written specifically for Windows NT.

Your Windows NT package should contain a paper copy of the HCL. There is also a copy on the distribution disk in the SUPPORT directory. The latter copy is distributed in Windows NT .HLP format, so you probably won't be able to look at it until after you've installed NT. (That seems to be a slightly strange decision on the part of Microsoft. How does a DOS user look at the HCL before installing NT?) A Windows 95 user should be able to view the file, because Windows 95 and NT share the same help file format. The HCL is frequently updated because Microsoft makes an effort to test new devices as they hit the market.

JUST A MINUTE

The latest and greatest HCL is available at Microsoft's Internet site. You can find it on the Web at http://www.microsoft.com/isapi/hwtest/hsearchn4.idc. A self-extracting version is available on Microsoft's FTP server at ftp://microsoft.com/services/whql/hclnt4.exe.

When buying hardware, first check to see if that device is on the HCL. This will reduce your risk of an evening of frustration spent getting a device to work with NT, because you will be guaranteed to have a device certified to work with NT. However, if a device is not listed on the HCL, it doesn't mean the device won't work with NT—only that there will be no support and possibly no driver for that device. If you are considering a device that is not on the HCL, at least look at the manufacture's literature or Web pages to see if it has released an NT driver for that device. It could be that the device will work with NT but is too recent to have been tested by Microsoft.

14

TIME SAVER

Microsoft provides a free program that can help you determine whether your computer's components are compatible with NT Workstation. It is called "The Microsoft Compatibility Tool Version 1.0 for Windows NT Workstation." According to Microsoft, the program will examine your computer's hardware and give you a report on compatibility with NT Workstation. You might find this tool useful if you have problems installing NT. The program can be downloaded from Microsoft's Web site at `http://www.microsoft.com/windows/common/ntcompto.htm`.

The Hardware Abstraction Layer

One of NT's great strengths is the capability to run on various types of CPUs. Microsoft designed NT to be independent of the system platform. NT 4 is NT 4 on a 486 or a PowerPC. Microsoft accomplished this by isolating the machine-specific parts of NT into modules that can be plugged into the main body of the operating system based on what platform is being used. It is easier to rewrite small parts of the operating system than to have a different operating system for each platform. (And easier on Microsoft's overworked support staff, too!) This isolation of the hardware-specific components is called the *Hardware Abstraction Layer* (HAL).

The HAL is clearly a good thing, but it has a downside. (Are you surprised?) Programs run on NT must go through the HAL interface to access devices like video cards and sound cards rather than talk directly to the device. This is both good and bad. The HAL protects your system against an application doing something dumb with a device. How often have you seen DOS or Windows lock up or crash while running a program? This type of incident is rare when working with NT. (No, really! I'm serious!) Remember that NT is designed primarily for business environments that demand reliability (reliability = money). The disadvantage of the HAL approach is the increased system overhead required for calls to use a device. This can result in the sluggish response of some applications that would otherwise benefit from direct access to hardware. Games are perhaps the most outstanding example of such applications, because they often ride the very cutting edge of the desktop computer's capabilities.

The HAL is a big reason behind Microsoft's NT HCL. Application developers no longer need to include drivers with their programs. The responsibility for *device drivers* (programs that give an operating system the capability to speak the device's language) falls on the shoulders of Microsoft and hardware developers. Microsoft carefully tests these drivers before distributing them with NT or otherwise recommending their use. With NT, you might give up a little of the cutting edge, but you gain robustness and reliability.

14

Hardware Requirements

Earlier I promised to take a closer look at Microsoft's recommended minimum requirements for Windows NT 4 Workstation. Here is a more realistic view of what you need to run NT 4 Workstation.

CPU

Microsoft says you can use any Intel *x*86 or Pentium processor with Windows NT 4. In the real world, don't even try to use NT Workstation with anything less than a 66MHz DX2. You are likely to be very disappointed with the results of a slower processor. I have had NT 4 Workstation running on a 100MHz DX4 with good results, but if you will be running any processor-intensive applications on your computer, then you should consider running NT on a 90MHz Pentium or better.

JUST A MINUTE

> Note that with release 4 of Windows NT, Microsoft discontinued support of the 386 processor. Even if you could run NT 4 on a 386 the performance would be too sluggish to do any real work.

RAM

Microsoft's recommendation of a minimum of 12MB for an Intel-based machine is simply not enough. It is possible to run NT 4 Workstation on 12MB, but I wouldn't be too surprised if your hard disk begins to plead for mercy.

NT 4 is well-designed with a great deal of attention to optimization, but it is still a big system that does a lot behind the scenes. NT uses a special file on your hard disk as a kind of substitute for memory (a really slow kind of substitute): a swap file. (NT refers to this as a *pagefile* or a *paging file*.) This is also known as *virtual memory*. The sum of your real memory and the swap file size gives the total system memory that NT thinks it has. The less real memory on your machine, the more NT relies on the swap file, constantly moving "memory" contents back and forth from real memory to the swap file according to an algorithm that maximizes efficient use of memory. On systems that are light on memory, the hard disk will be working very hard.

For situations in which NT isn't expected to run many applications or services, 16MB of RAM is sufficient, but you should strongly consider moving to at least 24MB. NT gets very comfortable at 32MB, particularly in situations in which you have three or four big applications open at once.

14

TIME SAVER

One way to get by if your system is light on RAM is to minimize use of those "frills" that let you customize your copy of NT. Background wallpaper, shortcut icons, sounds, and fonts all consume precious memory resources, even when they are not currently in use. Consider the following ideas: Don't run unnecessary applications or services, use a small tiled image for wallpaper or none at all, disable sound support, and reduce the number of installed fonts down to those that you actually use.

Hard Disk

NT supports most modern hard disks. Be sure to check the HCL if you are in doubt. If your current hard disk is fairly old, you might consider buying a new one. Modern disks are substantially faster and provide a lot more disk space for the dollar, and disk space can be at a premium with large operating systems like NT.

JUST A MINUTE

Windows NT will not properly detect the majority of old hard disk types such as MFM, RLL, and ESDI. Most such hard disks have small capacities and all are slow by today's standards, so this type of hard disk wouldn't be very useful with NT in any case.

Windows NT has good support for Small Computer System Interface (SCSI) drives. Although SCSI devices are normally found on servers, there is no reason why they can't be used with NT 4 Workstation. Using SCSI hard disks requires a SCSI adapter, which can cost as much as a hard disk but provides an increased level of performance and versatility to your system. Standard SCSI can have up to seven additional devices on the bus, and wide SCSI can have up to 15 additional devices. That is a lot of hard disks, tape drives, or CD-ROMs connected to your system. SCSI is fast, and devices on the SCSI bus can exchange data independently of the system's CPU. For these reasons, SCSI is becoming increasingly common on high-end workstations. Make sure you check Microsoft's HCL for support of both the SCSI hard disk and the SCSI controller card.

Video Adapter and Monitor

Any video adapter/monitor combination that lets you work in 640×480 resolution with 256 colors is fine. If you need a little more workspace for things like graphics or spreadsheet applications, a combination that allows 800×600 resolution or better may be desirable. If you make extensive use of graphics applications or enjoy viewing photographic-quality pictures over the Internet or other sources, you might want to use an adapter capable of displaying

14

64K or even 16.7 million colors. Keep in mind that the higher the resolution and the more colors you display, the more work your system is doing. With a high-resolution display, you might notice a significant performance drop on slower systems.

CD-ROM

NT 4 requires that you have a CD-ROM. Windows NT has excellent support for SCSI CD-ROM devices but somewhat less support for non-SCSI CD-ROMs. Be certain to check the HCL for your CD-ROM. Most common devices are supported. A relatively fast CD-ROM of 4x or greater will help speed the installation of NT, but any speed device will do. Note that if you are installing NT over a network you won't need a CD-ROM.

Pointing Device

You will definitely want a mouse or some other pointing device when you use NT. It is possible to work with NT without a mouse, but it is difficult to imagine why anyone would want to do so voluntarily. Note that NT does not (yet) support three-button mouse configurations such as those provided by Logitech.

3.5-Inch High-Density Floppy Disk Drive

For Intel-based installations you will need a 3.5-inch high-density floppy drive for the three boot disks required for the installation. All NT users will want a 3.5-inch drive for making a recovery disk.

Modem

You will need a modem if you intend to use NT to remotely connect to a network or log in to a remote host. Microsoft is increasingly using the Internet to provide support for its products, so using a modem with NT Workstation to connect to an Internet Service Provider is a very good idea. Most name-brand 28Kbps or faster modems should work fine with NT. NT 4 has very good modem support but you would be wise to check the Hardware Compatibility List to make sure NT will support your modem.

Uninterruptible Power Supply and NT Installation

If your computer is fortunate enough to be connected to an uninterruptible power supply (UPS), you must disconnect the UPS from your computer's serial port. The NT installation program attempts to detect devices connected to the computer's ports but doesn't properly recognize a UPS during the setup procedure. You can safely reconnect the UPS after installation is complete.

14

Testing Your Hardware

NT 4 Workstation is big and complex; a lot can go wrong or be improperly configured with strange results. Sometimes it is difficult to trace a problem because everything is related to everything else. When installing a new operating system this situation is compounded because so many things are being configured within a short period of time. To minimize your potential for misery, do yourself a favor and make certain that all your hardware devices are working correctly before you install NT 4.

You can, of course, skip any kind of hardware testing, particularly if you are familiar with your equipment and your machine isn't performing any mission-critical operations. Testing can be tedious, but when you are installing a new operating system it can be extremely frustrating to recognize and resolve a problem that is in fact caused by a quirky device.

Testing Hardware Under DOS

There are many diagnostics available to test various common hardware components but relatively few designed exclusively to support NT. Because NT uses the HAL to prevent applications from directly manipulating a device, it can be difficult to thoroughly test hardware within NT. One way to get around this problem is to test your hardware under DOS. Simply boot your machine from a floppy disk formatted as a DOS system disk and run the diagnostics that came with the hardware device or whatever other testing program you want to use. Booting the system into a simple, clean DOS configuration gives you a system free of any program that might otherwise interfere with your test. If the device works well under DOS, you can be reasonably certain it will work well under NT (assuming you can get the proper NT driver for the device).

Testing Hard Disks

If you are running NT, there is a good chance you are doing so at least in part because you need a stable, crash-resistant operating system. An operating system is only as good as the devices it depends on. If your hard disk is quirky in any way, then your implementation of NT is likely to be quirky. More than once I've been called in to help someone with a computer exhibiting "weird errors" and ultimately traced the problem to bad regions on their hard disk. Hard disks are easily taken for granted as they quietly whir away in their cabinets, but a lot of your time and effort is sitting in that little box. (Have you performed a backup lately?)

You should periodically and thoroughly test your disks if you are relying on your computer for critical data. Programs like CHKDSK and SCANDISK can find major problems and are worth running, but if your operation is truly critical (particularly if your business is relying on your computer or you are running any kind of file server), then you should consider using a more thorough disk-testing program on your volumes. I use SpinRite from Gibson Research for my testing purposes. In addition to being a good utility, SpinRite's documentation is excellent and will teach you nearly everything there is to know about hard disks.

14

Time is the disadvantage of testing your volumes with a program like SpinRite. A large hard disk can take several days to test (SpinRite is meticulous!). Be prepared to have your system unavailable for a while.

Testing Memory

Like hard disk errors, memory errors can also be responsible for a quirky system. Memory errors can occur from a memory card that is not seated properly in its slot, from memory cards that are not properly matched for speed or simply because a chip is bad. Errors caused by memory problems can be hard to trace, because they often refuse to cooperate by conveniently repeating themselves in the same way or time. The only sure method to be certain your memory is working as well is to run a diagnostic designed to put your memory through a sequence of special tests designed to check for a variety of problems. There are several good memory-testing packages available as shareware or from commercial vendors.

JUST A MINUTE

When you power up your computer, the system might appear to be testing your system's memory. There might even be a message reporting something like "Testing memory, please wait..." The system is not testing your memory, it is taking a roll call of what memory is available. This "test" might find a simple problem like a memory card not being seated properly on the motherboard, but it won't find more subtle ailments.

Hardware Devices and Interrupts

There are 16 interrupt channels (IRQs) that can be used by various devices to flag the attention of the CPU. Most of these IRQs have predefined uses, either by convention or by the standards of CPU and motherboard design. Table 14.1 shows the typical uses of a PC's IRQs. The table shows the priority of each IRQ as seen by the CPU; lower numbers are seen and handled first.

Table 14.1. IRQs and their standard assignments.

Channel	Priority	Standard Assignment
IRQ0	1	System timer.
IRQ1	2	Keyboard.
IRQ2	n/a	Used to add eight additional IRQs to the original eight employed in early PCS. IRQ2 tells the CPU to look for an interrupt in the IRQ8–IRQ15 range.

Channel	Priority	Standard Assignment
IRQ3	11	COM2.
IRQ4	12	COM1.
IRQ5	13	LPT2; most users don't need a second printer, so this IRQ is commonly used for sound card support.
IRQ6	14	Floppy controller.
IRQ7	15	LPT1.
IRQ8	3	Real-time clock.
IRQ9	4	Required for the IRQ2 scheme; cannot be used separately.
IRQ10	5	Not used.
IRQ11	6	Not used.
IRQ12	7	Often used for PS/2 mouse support.
IRQ13	8	Math co-processor support.
IRQ14	9	Hard disk controller.
IRQ15	10	Not used.

Table 14.1 shows that your safest course is to use IRQs 5, 10, 11, and 15 for adding devices to work with NT. Some devices are picky about which IRQ they will want to use. For example, I have an older sound card that absolutely refuses to use anything but IRQ5. Consult the documentation that came with the device for information on how to configure the device and which IRQs the manufacturer recommends.

Disk Space and File System Considerations

Windows NT 4 is much larger than DOS or Windows 3.*x* and will need correspondingly larger amounts of disk space. You will have to make several choices and perhaps a few compromises before you complete your installation of NT.

Disk Space Requirements

Microsoft recommends 117MB (148MB for a RISC-based system) as the minimum available amount of disk space you should have for the volume where you will install NT. The

14

actual amount you will need is highly dependent on your customization choices when you install NT. I have found a very modest NT installation actually requires less than Microsoft's claim (under 100MB in one instance), but this is likely irrelevant if you want to make productive use of NT. Unless you are installing NT just to explore the operating system, you will want much more room in which to install additional utilities, services, applications, and data. You can use other volumes for this purpose, but in general you would be wise to make your NT system volume 256MB or larger.

Choosing File Systems

In Hour 13, "File Systems and Windows NT 4," you learned about NT and the various file systems that are supported. You should have enough information to make your decision regarding what file system you want NT to use. The NT installation procedure will ask what volume you want to use for NT's files and what file system you want to use on that volume. It is not a lot of fun to change a volume's file system after installation of NT, so be certain your choice is best for you.

Disk Compression

Disk compression is a method by which files are automatically compressed into a smaller size as they are written to the hard disk and decompressed when read from the disk. They work by treating a volume as one gigantic compressed file and showing you an index of what is contained in the big file disguised to look like a normal directory structure. Hard disk compression was popular a few years back when applications began to have bloated disk space requirements and big hard disks were still rather pricey. You might be familiar with Stacker, Drivespace, or Doublespace—three of the most popular compression utilities. Although less frequently used now, many systems with smaller disk drives are still configured with a disk compression utility.

NT 4 doesn't support compressed volumes; you will not be able to use a compressed volume to run NT. If you want to use the volume for NT, you must remove the compression system from the volume. Consult the documentation that came with your compression program for details on how to do this.

Because NT can't access volumes using one of these disk compression utilities, you won't be able to use files or programs on those volumes. You can get around this if you are using a multiple-operating system environment by booting an operating system such as DOS that can access the compressed volume and copying the desired information to a noncompressed volume.

14

When NT 4 is installed it does give you plenty of options for file compression if you are using the NTFS file system. You can set NT to automatically compress and decompress a given file or even entire folders.

Backing Up Your System

You've heard it many times before: Back up your system. Well, hear it again: Back up your system. Why? When you install a new operating system, particularly a stand-alone operating system like NT (by which I mean an operating system that doesn't sit on top of another system such as DOS), you are making major changes to your computer. The NT setup program will make many of these changes without consulting your opinion. Disaster probably won't happen to you, but ask yourself this question: What if it did?

If you are installing NT on a fresh system with a hard disk free of any data, then you have nothing to worry about. If you are installing NT on a system that has previously installed operating systems, applications, or data that you definitely want to keep, then you must consider how you would restore everything should something disastrous occur. Not only should you think about your ability to restore your files, but consider the time required to do so, particularly if you are working in a business environment.

Common Local Backup Devices

There are a variety of methods available to perform backups on personal computers. The following are the more common devices and their applications:

Floppy Backups: It is possible that there are only a few files that are critical to your needs. A collection of 3.5-inch high-density floppies might be sufficient to back up items such as your word-processing documents, system configuration files, spreadsheet data, and copies of personal e-mail. Floppy backups have the advantage that nearly every personal computer has a floppy drive—there are no added expenses for additional hardware. For major applications or large quantities of big files such as graphics files, however, floppy disks might not be practical.

TIME SAVER

Judicious use of a good file compression program like PKZIP can make a floppy disk go a long way for backups. Learn to use PKZIP's options for disk-spanning and compression of entire directory structures, and you will find even fairly large applications can be squeezed into only a few disks.

14

Tape Backups: For serious backup requirements, tape drives are a good solution. A single tape is capable of storing several gigabytes of data. Tapes are small and easily stored, but the backup and restoration procedure can be relatively slow because a tape drive is a sequential-access device rather than a random-access device, which means the device might have to read through a lot of data before it finds the specific information you want to retrieve.

Hard Disk Backups: If you have access to a second hard disk with lots of available space, you can directly connect the hard disk to your system as a second drive or use a cable and a program such as LapLink or the DOS application INTERLNK to connect your system to another computer with the second hard disk and start transferring a complete copy of your volumes to the second hard disk. Once again, use of a compression program like PKZIP can really speed this process.

Zip Drive Backups: Devices such as Iomega's Zip drives are increasingly popular. They are much like floppy drives but are usually externally mounted through your computer's parallel port, and their removable disks can store up to 100MB of information and programs. These devices are a very good alternative or companion to tape drives for professional backups.

Backing Up to a Network

If your computer is on a network, then you might have the option of saving your backups on a server or another computer on the network; consult your network administrator to learn if this is an option. If your network is a busy one, your administrator is likely to ask you to perform the backup during off-hours so that you don't overload the network during the critical business hours.

Summary

If you are comfortable with all the topics mentioned in this hour, then you are probably ready to get on with the installation of NT. Before you go on, take a moment and ask yourself the following questions:

- ☐ Have you checked that your hardware meets NT's requirements?
- ☐ Are you prepared with all the details of your computer and peripheral devices?
- ☐ Have you read all the setup documentation that came with NT 4?
- ☐ Have you backed up anything that should be backed up?

If you can answer yes to all of these points, then you are ready to install Windows NT 4 Workstation!

14

Workshop

The Workshop helps you solidify the skills you learned this hour.

Glossary

device driver   A program that gives an operating system the ability to speak the language of a given hardware device. For example, a video driver enables an operating system or application program to manipulate the video card to correctly display information on the screen.

Hardware Abstraction Layer (HAL)   A modular interface built into NT that handles all hardware-specific activities. The HAL enables NT to be largely independent of what hardware is used to run it.

Hardware Compatibility List (HCL)   A list of all devices thoroughly tested by Microsoft and known to be compatible with Windows NT. Devices not on the HCL are not supported by Microsoft.

IRQ (interrupt request)   A prioritized signal from a peripheral device to the CPU informing the CPU that the device requires immediate attention.

plug-and-play   A standard designed by a consortium of hardware and software vendors that enables an operating system to automatically detect and configure devices designed to conform to the standard. Theoretically, this saves the user the hassle of having to learn about the device and configure it so that it both works and doesn't adversely affect other parts of the system.

real mode   This is a Windows 3.0 operating mode that is backward compatible with older Intel processors. Real mode forces programs to operate within conventional memory (the first 640KB of RAM), which is very constrictive to the operating environment. Newer operating systems use protected mode, which allows access to all available memory but surrenders support for older processors.

virtual memory   A special file on a hard disk used to supplement memory when real memory is insufficient. Because virtual memory relies on a mechanical device it is very slow compared to real memory. Also called a swap file or a pagefile.

Exercises

1. Run SCANDISK (or preferably SpinRite) on a floppy disk. This will demonstrate how the program works and what you can expect to learn before you invest the time performing the operation on a hard disk.

14

2. On a computer with Internet access, go to the sites listed in the "The Hardware Compatibility List" section and familiarize yourself with Microsoft's Windows NT HCL.

3. Take a moment and answer how you would respond if you just lost all files on your hard disk. If your answer was something like "scream and holler," then take another moment and make a backup plan for your system before you install Windows NT or make any other major change to your computer.

14

Hour **15**

Installation and Setup of NT 4 Workstation

by Gary Neely

If you've never installed an operating system before, you might be a little intimidated by the process. Fortunately, the installation of NT is largely automated and shouldn't present any difficult choices assuming you've done your homework. This hour briefs you on what to expect, including how to run the installation program, the various stages of the process, the questions you'll need to answer, and how to install NT so it can coexist with an existing operating system. You're going to walk through the complete process so you will encounter no surprises during installation.

Hour 14, "Pre-Installation Concerns with NT 4 Workstation," should have prepared you for the installation process, but there are a few final items to check or have ready before you actually run the installation program:

☐ Time: Make certain you have at least three hours to spend on the installation. More is better.

☐ Disks: You will need four floppy disks. Three will be used to make boot disks necessary for the installation. The fourth will be used to make a recovery disk.

☐ Free disk space: About 90MB of available hard disk space is required.

☐ BIOS settings: In your computer's BIOS configuration routine, disable video, BIOS, and hardware shadowing. These features consume system memory and because NT doesn't use them, you might as well get rid of them. If NT will be your only operating system, then disable plug-and-play support if possible.

Windows NT and Multiple-Boot Systems

Windows NT 4 Workstation can coexist nicely with other operating systems on the same machine. Making use of this feature of NT is an excellent way to learn NT while retaining all the capabilities of your previous operating system. You can experiment with NT and move your applications over at your leisure without worrying about loss of productivity as you learn to use a new operating system.

When NT is installed, you will have the option of upgrading a previous Windows installation or installing NT in another directory or volume. If you choose to have NT coexist with another operating system, NT will employ its *boot loader* to manage a multiple-boot environment. This enables you to select from a menu of operating system choices when you start your computer. The NT installation program will set up the multi-boot loader to make NT the default operating system if you make no selection within a specified number of seconds, but you can change this configuration after the installation process (see the "Troubleshooting the Installation" section).

JUST A MINUTE

If you suspect you might want to uninstall NT at some future time, you are much better off to install NT separately from your previous operating system. If you do this, removing NT is relatively easy. If you install NT over an existing Windows operating system you will have to rely on a complete copy and backup of your original Windows. (See the "Troubleshooting the Installation" section for more on the problem of uninstalling NT.)

If you have many operating systems or simply want better control over the boot process, you might want to use a product like System Commander from V Communications. System Commander enables you to easily integrate Windows NT, DOS, Windows 95, OS/2, Linux, and many other operating systems all on the same computer. If you have security requirements, you can assign passwords to each operating system to control unauthorized entry of

15

operating systems that lack this feature. NT's boot loader is sufficient for most situations, particularly if you have only two or three operating systems on your computer.

Walking Through the Setup Process

You install Windows NT 4 in three stages:

- [ ] The first stage is to run the WINNT program to start the installation process.
- [ ] The second stage reboots the computer with the first of three boot disks and begins a text-based sequence of steps for making fundamental hardware checks and loading the necessary NT files.
- [ ] The third stage begins with a second reboot that brings up a *graphical user interface* (GUI). This final stage guides you through the configuration of NT's many options with an easy-to-use program that enables you to change your mind at any point in the process.

Running WINNT

WINNT is the DOS-based installation program that creates the boot disks necessary for NT installation and begins the installation process. To run WINNT, first make sure your NT distribution CD is in the drive. At a DOS prompt, change to the drive letter of your CD-ROM, and then change to the directory corresponding to your computer platform. For most people, this will be i386 for Intel-based platforms. In that directory, type WINNT followed by any desired command-line *switches*—options that modify the use of the WINNT program. Table 15.1 gives a description of the more useful switches.

Table 15.1. WINNT command-line switches.

/?	Displays a list of available switches.
/O	Runs the WINNT program to create a set of boot disks. Running WINNT with this option does not install NT. Use this option if you want to create additional boot disks.
/OX	Causes the installation program to automatically create boot floppies. Note that unlike /O, this switch will start the installation process.
/X	Begins the installation of NT without creating boot disks. Use this switch if you already have a set of boot disks.
/F	The boot disk creation process is done without file verification. Don't use this switch if you suspect your disks are questionable.

continues

Table 15.1. continued

/C	Omits the free disk space check for the boot disks. Saves time.
/T:*path*	Specifies an alternative destination drive and path for WINNT to use for storage of temporary files necessary for installation. WINNT will default to the current drive. Use this switch if the current drive isn't supported by NT or doesn't have the approximately 100MB of free space necessary for temporary files necessary for the installation process.
/B	This switch enables you to install NT without using boot floppies. Installation will go faster, but you will need much more disk space for the installation. Approximately 200MB is required for temporary installation files.

Here's an example of how to use WINNT with switches:

```
WINNT  /T:f:  /X
```

This runs WINNT with two switches. The first switch tells the installation program to use drive F: for the temporary files. The second instructs the program to skip the creation of boot disks.

Just a Minute

> If you are using a previous version of Windows NT, you must use another version of WINNT called WINNT32. This program is designed for 32-bit operation and uses a graphical interface for the installation process but is otherwise similar to WINNT.

When you run WINNT, the program will first prompt you for the location of the Windows NT 4 source files. For most people, this will be the i386 subdirectory. The program will then begin copying many files from the CD-ROM to a temporary directory on your hard disk. If you should have to abort your installation for some reason, you can see this temporary directory as WIN_NT.~LS on your hard disk. Moving all the necessary files to your hard disk will take some time, so be prepared to wait. The temporary files will be removed after the installation process is complete. When this step is finished, you will be prompted to insert the first of three boot disks into your floppy drive. Be sure to label each disk as you are instructed.

When the boot disk creation process is finished, you will be prompted to restart your computer. This begins the second stage of NT 4 installation.

The First Reboot: The Text Stage

This stage of the setup process will prepare your hardware and install NT 4 from the temporary files on your hard disk. After your computer restarts, the first thing you will see

15

is the following message at the top of your screen as Setup determines what processor and memory is on your system:

```
Setup is inspecting your computer's hardware configuration.
```

The screen will then turn blue, and you will see the "Windows NT Setup" message. A series of messages will begin flashing by at the bottom of your screen informing you that Setup is loading various files. These text messages look a little like error messages but don't worry, nothing is wrong. In a few moments, you will be prompted to insert the second boot disk—more loading of files. Eventually, you will see a message at the top of your screen very similar to the following:

```
Microsoft (R) Windows NT (TM) Version 4.0 (Build 1381).
1 System Processor [16 MB Memory] Multiprocessor Kernel
```

Your hardware might be different, so you might see a slightly different message.

In a few moments, you will be shown the "Welcome to Setup" screen. At this step, you'll be given four choices:

☐ To Learn more about Windows NT Setup before continuing, press F1.

☐ To set up Windows NT now, press ENTER.

☐ To repair a damaged Windows NT version 4.0 installation, press R.

☐ To quit Setup without installing Windows NT, press F3.

Press F1 to spend a few moments reading what Microsoft has to say about the setup procedure. F3 is a good opportunity to bail out if you are uncertain that you want to continue the setup process at this time. If you're ready to go on, press Enter to continue the installation process.

JUST A MINUTE

By the way, make a mental note of the third choice in this list, "To repair a damaged Windows NT version 4.0 installation." You'll see this again and learn how it is useful in Hour 23, "Recovery Tips."

Detection of Mass Storage Devices

Setup will now begin the Mass Storage Device Detection phase, in which it looks for what sort of floppy drives, hard disks, and CD-ROM drives are mounted on your system. You can press Enter to begin the auto-detection process, or you can select S to manually select SCSI adapters, CD-ROM drives, and other disk controllers. It is best to let Setup attempt to detect your hardware; if it doesn't succeed, you will be given another chance to manually select your devices.

After you make your selection, Setup will prompt you for the third boot disk (if you are working with boot floppies). Setup runs through a list of devices it knows how to recognize until it finds those that match your devices. It then displays a list of your devices that it has successfully recognized. At this point, you can select S to manually select other devices, or you can accept Setup's work and press Enter to continue to the next installation step. If you pressed S, you will be shown a list of devices. Highlight the one you want, and press Enter. You can select others or continue with the Setup process.

The Microsoft Licensing Agreement

After loading a series of device driver files, Setup will present you with the Microsoft Licensing Agreement. At the end of the agreement you are asked to press F8 to accept the agreement. Do so—you wouldn't want to stop now, would you?

Hardware Component Verification

Setup's next step presents you with a list of the hardware components that have been detected for your system:

Computer:	Standard PC
Display:	Auto Detect
Keyboard:	XT, AT, or Enhanced Keyboard (83-104 Keys)
Keyboard Layout:	US
Pointing Device:	Logitech Serial Mouse

You can change the configuration of each category by using the arrow keys and pressing Enter to make your selection. Here is a description of the possible choices:

☐ Computer: Most users will have an Intel 486 or Pentium processor, so Standard PC will be the typical choice. If your processor is unusual, you might need to select from one of the other provided options.

☐ Display: The default option "Auto Detect" should be sufficient to detect your display hardware. You might want to select "Standard VGA" (640×480, 16 colors) if you are uncertain that your display will be recognized; a standard VGA video driver is almost certain to work with nearly any video card. You are also given the option to provide a manufacturer's driver for your display card.

☐ Keyboard: You probably won't have to change this default setting unless you are using a very unusual or specialized keyboard.

☐ Keyboard Layout: Choose the layout that best fits your country.

☐ Pointing Device: Setup will detect most common pointing devices. If you do not have a mouse or similar device installed, you will see the message "No Mouse or other Pointing Device."

15

15

When you are finished with this menu, select "The above list matches my computer" and press Enter to move on.

Checking for Existing Windows Version

Setup will now check your hard disk for existing versions of Microsoft Windows. If you do not have an existing version, Setup will continue with the next step; otherwise, you will see the following screen message:

```
Setup has found a previous version of Microsoft Windows on your hard disk
in the directory shown below.
```

If you want to install NT separately from your existing Windows installation, press N and specify the desired volume when prompted. If you do not do this, Setup will install NT over your existing Windows installation. Choose the latter option if you intend to upgrade your previous Windows version.

JUST A MINUTE

If you decide to install NT separately from an existing Windows installation, the NT installation program will construct a dual-boot configuration for your machine. When you start your computer, a menu will be displayed giving you a choice of which operating system you want to boot. After NT is installed, you can further configure this multiple-boot program to default to an operating system of your choice.

Selecting an Installation Volume and File System

If you are not upgrading from a previous Windows version, Setup will give you a list of all the available volumes on your computer. You are given the opportunity to pick the one you want to use for your NT installation. If you've read Hour 13, "File Systems and Windows NT 4," then you are probably prepared with your decision; all you have to do is highlight the volume you want and press Enter.

At this point, you are given the opportunity to select a file system for the volume. Again, you should already be prepared with your choice. If you are not, take a moment and return to Hour 13 to review the material on file systems.

JUST A MINUTE

The safest course of action at this stage is to select FAT. You can easily change a FAT volume to NTFS after NT is installed. Changing NTFS to FAT after installation is a very tedious process, so if you are in doubt, choose FAT.

CAUTION

The Setup program gives you the capability to repartition your hard disk. Be very careful if you decide to use this feature. Changing the partition structure of your hard disk can easily result in loss of all data on the partition. Know what you are doing before you do it.

Selecting a Directory for NT Files

After you have selected a file system for your NT volume, Setup will now prompt you to name the directory where you want NT installed:

```
Setup installs Windows NT files onto your hard disk. Choose the location
where you want these files to be installed:
```

The default location is the WINNT directory on your selected volume. For most people, this recommended default is fine. Press Enter to select it and continue.

Hard Disk Surface Scan

Setup will now give you the option to test your hard disk for problems:

```
Setup will now examine your hard disk(s) for corruption.
```

Press Enter if you want to go ahead with the examination process or Esc if you want to skip it.

If you took the advice from Hour 14 and already performed a thorough examination of your hard disk with a utility such as SpinRite, you can safely skip this test. If not, you might want to let the NT installation process perform this test now. Be aware that this test will take a lot of time.

Installation of NT Files

After the disk examination step is completed or skipped you will see this message:

```
Please wait while Setup copies files to your hard disk.
```

The Setup program is copying NT's installation files from the temporary files to their final destination in the WINNT directory (or whatever alternative directory you chose). This procedure can take a while, so sit back and relax for a few minutes. The Setup program displays a progress bar at the bottom of the screen to keep you aware of its current situation.

When the file transfer process is completed, you should see the following message:

```
This portion of Setup has completed successfully.
```

15

15

At this point, you will be prompted to remove any floppy disk or CD-ROM from the computer and press Enter. Your computer will then restart and boot up into the final graphical user interface (GUI) stage of the installation and configuration process.

The Second Reboot: The GUI Stage

When your computer reboots, it will go through a brief hardware detection process and load necessary drivers. In a few moments, you'll see the Welcome to Windows Setup screen. This screen begins Microsoft's Setup wizard, a program that will guide you through the process of configuring the features of your NT Workstation.

You can't do much in the Welcome screen, so click Next to move on to the first step in the process. The wizard will let you back up by clicking Back at any time, so don't be too concerned about getting ahead of yourself.

Customizing Setup

You're finally getting into the more interesting part of the Workstation setup. Here you can begin customizing your installation of NT to fit your needs and space requirements. Setup gives you four options for whichever type of installation you want:

- ☐ Typical: This is Microsoft's recommended installation. A standard list of features will be installed with very few questions asked during setup. This is the easiest and fastest setup option.

- ☐ Portable: This option is designed specifically for those people who want to install NT on a portable computer. Your NT setup will be optimized for use on a portable PC.

- ☐ Compact: Select this option to install a minimal NT configuration on your computer. Only those files and programs absolutely necessary for NT to run will be installed. If you are tight on disk space, you might consider using this option for your initial installation, and then add NT's other features later as needed. There are no frills with the Compact option. This is not a good choice for those people who are new to NT, because it does not enable you to dive in and play with all of NT's features.

- ☐ Custom: This option enables you to specify exactly what NT components you want to install. This option is similar to many other installation packages, such as Microsoft Office, in which you can pick and choose from a variety of package options. I strongly recommend this option if you are comfortable with exploring these kinds of decisions and have at least an average amount of computer experience. You will benefit from the ability to choose what you want to install rather than what Microsoft believes you will want to install. Custom will also give you a chance to see many of the program packages that are included with your NT disk.

The first three options are largely automated. These are the simplest installation procedures because there are not many decisions required on your part. People not very familiar with Microsoft Windows products might want to go ahead and choose Typical. I suggest those with any familiarity with Windows products choose Custom. There is really nothing challenging about the Custom option, and you might find it interesting.

TIME SAVER

The Compact option has an interesting side benefit for people who have the time and resources to play with NT a little bit. By choosing the Compact installation and then exploring NT's directory and file structure, you can learn quite a lot about what files are essential to NT. This can help when you are troubleshooting problems or making future decisions about installing NT to a small-system environment.

Don't be too concerned about which option you choose at this time because you can easily add or remove components after NT is installed. (Refer to the "Troubleshooting the Installation" section for information on how to do this.) You won't have to go through the installation process again to change your components. When you've made your choice, click Next to continue.

Name and Organization

Setup now wants you to enter your name and organization. Use your mouse or the Tab key to move between the entry fields, or press Alt+M to select the Name field or Alt+O to select the Organization field. Organization is optional, but you must enter a name in order to continue the Setup process. Setup uses this information to create an identification number unique to your NT installation. When you've completed this information, click Next to continue.

Registration

You will now be prompted to enter your ten-digit registration or "CD Key." This key should be prominently displayed on your distribution disk. Enter the key in the space provided and click Next to move on.

CAUTION

Be certain not to lose your registration key. You'll need it any time you must run the installation process. Don't assume you'll do this only once.

15

Computer Name

Setup will now ask you to enter a name for your computer. This name will be used to identify your computer on a network. Your network administrator might want you to enter a specific name according to some scheme used by that network. If you are allowed to choose the name, be sure it is something unique and descriptive. The name can be up to 15 alphanumeric characters long and will automatically be converted to uppercase. When you have entered the computer name, click Next to continue.

Administrator Account

You are now prompted to enter a password for the system's Administrator Account. If your system will be shared with other users, it will be important to control access to various important components of the system. If security is not a factor, you can omit the password, but this is not recommended. Enter the password you have selected in the first field, and then press Tab to move to the second field and re-enter the password for confirmation. Be certain to record your password in a safe place.

TIME SAVER

> If you are using NT Workstation at home and are tired of going through the login sequence every time you use NT, you will be happy to learn there is a method to automate the login by modifying the Registry. Although you do not need to supply a password for the Administrator account, you must supply a password for the automated login to work. If NT doesn't find a password, it will reset the Registry and force you to log on the next time you boot NT.

Click Next to continue to the next step in the Setup process. Note that the Setup wizard will not let you continue until the passwords in both fields match.

Emergency Repair Disk

Setup will now ask you if you wish to create an emergency repair disk. If you like, you can skip this process and use the RDISK utility to make a repair disk at any time after installation of NT. You learn this in greater depth in Hour 23, "Recovery Tips," but it is a good idea to go ahead and tell Setup to make the repair disk.

Click Yes to proceed with the repair disk creation process or No to skip this step. To create the repair disk, you will need a blank, formatted disk. The repair disk isn't actually created at this time, so for the moment, you can continue the Setup process without having a disk available. However, when the Setup wizard is completed, you will be asked to insert the disk, so you might want to go ahead and find an available disk. Make sure to label it.

Select Components

Here is where your selection of the Custom Setup option will make a big difference. This step in the Setup process lets you select which NT components you want to install. If you did not select Custom, NT will still give you a chance to install optional components. If you decide not to install any optional components, skip this step and move immediately to the "Network Setup and Configuration" section.

Setup shows you six component categories from which to select. Use your mouse to put a check in the box next to each category if you want to install components in that category. Click the component category to select it, and then click the checkbox to add or remove that category. Setup gives you a rough approximation of how much disk space is required when you choose to install a component category.

Most categories actually contain multiple subcomponents. If you want to see and select each subcomponent individually, click the Details option. If the Details option is gray, there are no subcomponents to select. Click Details on each category to familiarize yourself with what components you are installing. You will see a brief (all right, *very* brief) description of each subcomponent and a display of the approximate disk space required if you select that component. You can individually add or remove each subcomponent as desired.

Here's a list of the components Microsoft is providing with the current release of NT 4 Workstation:

☐ **Accessibility:** This component includes options to modify the mouse, display, and keyboard for people with physical impairments.

☐ **Accessories:** This category contains many standard packages that you will want to include with your NT installation.

Calculator: The familiar Windows calculator package.

Character Map: A utility that enables you to insert special characters and symbols into your documents.

Clipboard Viewer: The clipboard is the temporary storage space used when you cut something from a document and paste it to another application. This a handy utility that enables you to examine and manipulate the contents of the clipboard.

Clock: This package enables you to display the time and date in either analog or digital format.

Desktop Wallpaper: Various images that you can use as a background for your desktop display. Images used for wallpaper can consume a lot of disk space. One solution is to load these images, pick out the ones you like, and delete the rest.

Document Templates: Standard templates for creating new documents for many common programs.

15

Imaging: A basic image viewer with the capability to scan and annotate images. Note that as of this writing, the Image Viewer does not support the very popular GIF image file format, considerably reducing its value.

Mouse Pointers: Various schemes you can use to change the appearance of the little images associated with your pointing device. For example, you can enlarge the mouse pointer or give it a three-dimensional appearance.

Object Packager: This utility lets you create objects that can be embedded into your documents.

Paint: Microsoft's simple program for working with graphics images.

Quick View: A utility that enables you to open a document for viewing without opening the application that created the document. This feature makes viewing documents much faster.

Screen Savers: Windows NT comes with a nice variety of screen savers, many of which have a lot of customizing options. More fun than many games.

WordPad: More than the old Windows NotePad but less than a full-featured word processor. Think of WordPad as a poor man's Word. Worth loading.

☐ **Communications:** This category includes programs that help you use your modem and computer to talk to other computers. Hyperterminal is probably the most important utility in this group. If your computer does not have a modem, you can skip this category.

Chat: This utility is designed to let you talk with other NT users on a network.

Hyperterminal: If you intend to use a modem to connect your computer to other computers or online services, you should load this easy-to-use package.

Phone Dialer: A phone book on your computer. Use this program to hold your most commonly dialed numbers. At the touch of a key, it will dial your phone for you!

☐ **Games:** Of course, NT Workstation comes with the usual suite of time-killing games. Curiously, Microsoft chose not to distribute Hearts with NT 4.

Freecell: Part Solitaire and part logic puzzle.

Minesweeper: Microsoft's interesting and addictive strategy game. Clear hidden mines from all map squares using clues revealed as you clear each square.

Pinball: A well-done rendition of a pinball game on the computer written for Microsoft by the noted game design and distribution company Maxis. Pinball loses a lot of its appeal without sound, so if your system does not have a sound card, you might want to skip this program, particularly because it is rather large.

Solitaire: The ubiquitous Windows solitaire game.

☐ **Multimedia:** This accessory group includes utilities to add sound and video to your computer. You will need a sound card to benefit from these applications and resources. If you are operating NT Workstation in a business environment, you can safely skip the multimedia group.

CD Player: This utility enables you to play music CDs on your computer's CD-ROM drive.

Jungle Sound Scheme: A theme-oriented collection of sounds that will be associated with various activities of your computer.

Media Player: If you intend to play video or audio clips using Windows NT, you will need this utility package.

Musica Sound Scheme: Another theme-oriented sound collection.

Robotz Sound Scheme: Yet another sound collection.

Sample Sounds: A basic collection of short sounds that can be associated with various system activities.

Sound Recorder: This utility lets you record and save sounds on your computer. Of course, you will need a sound card and some form of input device such as a microphone.

Utopia Sound Scheme: Another sound theme to try.

Volume Control: A utility to adjust the volume on sound cards that support software control of volume. Many older cards do not support this function.

☐ **Windows Messaging:** This category includes Microsoft's electronic mail and messaging applications.

Internet Mail: Microsoft's application for accessing mail from the Internet. Note that this is not the Internet Mail and News application freely available from Microsoft's Web site. It is the Internet Mail service for Windows Messaging, essentially a scaled-down Exchange client.

Microsoft Mail: You will need this service if you will be using Microsoft's Mail Post Office services.

Windows Messaging: This package is the integrated messaging program necessary for using the other message-related applications.

When you have completed your component selections, click Next to continue with Setup.

Network Setup and Configuration

The next step in the Setup process is configuring NT to work with a network. This is a fairly involved process that requires you to have a lot of information and knowledge prepared before you attempt it. The configuration of a network can be done at this time or be delayed to some time after NT is installed.

15

15

If you want to install networking components at this time, select "This computer will participate on a network" and refer to Hour 16, "Networking NT," for this step in the Setup process. If you want to skip the network setup process at this time or your computer won't be involved with a network, select "Do not connect this computer to a network at this time." Click Next to continue.

Setting the Time and Date

After the network setup process is completed (or after the Select Components option if you skipped the network setup), Setup will prompt you to configure the date and time properties for your computer. You probably will not need to change the date and time for your computer, but you will want to select the time zone for your region. Clicking the Time Zone tab will bring up the Time Zone selection screen, as shown in Figure 15.1.

Figure 15.1.

Selecting your time zone using the Date/Time Properties screen.

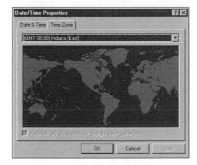

Select the list of time zones and pick the one that matches your region. The map display will then snap to your region. When you are finished configuring the time and date, click the Close button to continue.

Configuring Your Display

Setup will now present you with a Display Properties screen similar to the one shown in Figure 15.2.

This screen shows you the display characteristics selected for your computer, including selections for the number of colors displayed, the display resolution, and the display's refresh rate. You probably will want to change some of these settings. Click the Color Palette setting to display a list of color options supported by the NT driver for your video card. To adjust your screen resolution, place your mouse on the Desktop Area slidebar and hold the button down to move the bar. Change the video refresh rate by selecting the Refresh Frequency box and choosing the highest refresh rate supported by the driver. The refresh rate controls how many times your screen is updated each second; higher rates reduce screen flicker and are easier on the eyes. When you are finished with your selections, click Test to make sure your choices are supported. If everything worked, click OK to finish this step in the Setup process.

Figure 15.2.

The Display Properties screen enables you to choose the settings that best match your needs and video hardware.

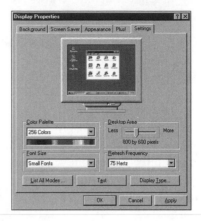

Finishing Setup

If you've managed to get this far, you're almost finished. If you told Setup to make an emergency repair disk, you will be prompted to insert the disk at this time and click OK. Setup will then prepare the disk and copy the necessary files. After this is completed, Setup will begin copying the remaining NT files from the temporary files and then remove the temporary files from your hard disk. You will be prompted to remove all disks from your computer and click Restart to have all your setup changes take effect. Your computer will reboot, and in a few minutes, you will see NT's Welcome screen. Your installation of NT is complete.

Installing Sound Card Drivers

Many NT Workstation owners, particularly those using NT at home, will want to install a sound card or might already have a sound card. You might have noticed NT's Setup program walks you through the important steps to get NT up and running but does not help you install sound cards or printers. Installation of printers is discussed in Hour 7, "Setting Up Printers with NT Workstation." In this section, we'll address the installation of sound cards.

JUST A MINUTE

If you are purchasing a sound card for installation into an NT machine, make certain it is on the Hardware Compatibility List. Some sound cards do not yet have drivers for Windows NT 4.

15

To install a sound card, you will need to have NT installed and running, a source for your sound card drivers (many are included on your Microsoft distribution disk), and a little knowledge of what resources are required and available for the sound card's use.

Before you try to install the sound card, run the Windows NT Diagnostics program. This is a useful utility found by clicking Start | Programs | Administrative Tools. Click the Resources tab of the Diagnostic program. The results will look something like that shown in Figure 15.3.

Figure 15.3.

The Windows NT Diagnostics program showing user-available IRQ usage. In this example, note that nothing is using IRQ 5 so it is available for use.

You can use the Diagnostic program with your sound card documentation to find which system resources are required and available for the sound card. Take a few moments and explore the Diagnostic program. It's an interesting utility.

After checking the necessary requirements, make certain your sound card is properly physically installed. If you have not yet installed your sound card, shut down your machine now and install the card according to the manufacturer's instructions.

When you are confident that the card is properly installed, restart your machine back into Windows NT. Go to the Control Panel, and click the Multimedia icon. In Multimedia, click the Devices tab. Your screen should show something similar to Figure 15.4.

The display will show a list of multimedia-related drivers currently available. Next, click the Add button to open the Add dialog box (see Figure 15.5).

Scroll through the list of available drivers until you find one that matches your card. Select the driver and click OK. You will now be asked where the driver software can be found. For drivers supplied with NT 4, this is likely to be the \i386 directory of your CD-ROM distribution disk. If you have another driver you want to use, such as one provided with your sound card (assuming it is certified to work with NT), you can provide the drive letter and location of that file. NT also will look for previous drivers installed on your system; if it finds one, it will ask you if you want to use that existing driver instead of one on a source disk.

Figure 15.4.

Multimedia properties—
Adding multimedia
devices.

Figure 15.5.

Adding an audio
device driver.

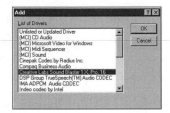

When you have selected your sound card driver, NT will ask you for information necessary to configure the card, such as the port address and IRQ setting. When you have completed this information, you will be asked if you want to restart Windows NT in order to have your driver changes take effect. You can do so now or later, but your sound card will not work until you do this.

When you restart NT, you can verify that your sound card's driver is installed by returning to the Multimedia Properties screen and checking the Devices tab. You should see an appropriate sound driver under the Audio Devices category similar to that shown in Figure 15.6.

Troubleshooting the Installation

Not every installation is going to be this smooth. This section answers some of the more frequently asked questions and needs that new NT users have.

My system locks up when I begin to install NT. What can I do?

Your system is probably hanging during the hardware detection process. Try removing any nonessential hardware device and run the installation program again. After NT is installed, you can try to reinstall your miscellaneous hardware devices.

15

Figure 15.6.

*Multimedia properties—
Verifying that the driver
was properly added.*

My choices during installation led to a dual-boot configuration. The startup choice defaults to NT, but I want it to default to DOS. How can I change the boot program?

There are two ways to do this. You can edit the BOOT.INI file in your root directory, or you can use the System Properties screen to change your boot configuration. Editing boot files is beyond the scope of this book, so I'll concentrate on the much safer method provided within NT.

In the Control Panel, select System Properties, and then click the Startup/Shutdown tab. You'll see a screen like the one shown in Figure 15.7.

Figure 15.7.

*Select the Startup/
Shutdown tab to change
the startup properties of
a multiple-boot install-
ation.*

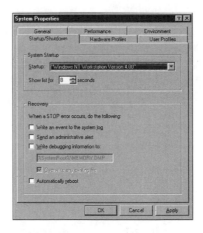

The Startup option enables you to choose which operating system will be the first on the startup menu and thus the default option. Click this box and choose from the list of possibilities. The Show list for: option enables you to change the amount of time that can elapse before the default operating system option is automatically booted. You have the indicated number of seconds to make your own selection from the list. Use the arrows to adjust the number of seconds desired. Click OK and the changes will take effect the next time you restart your system.

How do I add components after I've installed NT?

In the Control Panel, select Add/Remove Programs. Click the Windows NT Setup tab. You'll see a dialog box like the one in Figure 15.8.

Figure 15.8.

Using the Add/Remove Programs utility is similar to using the Custom installation procedure.

You can use this dialog box in the same manner described in the installation process. When you are finished, click OK to have your changes take effect.

My video card supports more colors, resolutions, and refresh rates than NT let me select during installation. What is the problem?

Remember that NT's hardware support is intentionally conservative to promote a stable, crash-resistant system. Microsoft's drivers for hardware reflect this. You should make a habit of checking Microsoft's Web site for improved hardware support. Another good idea is to check the manufacturer of your card to see if it has released a new driver specifically written for NT. Many manufacturers keep a list of downloadable drivers on their Web site. Because NT's popularity is growing quickly, you are likely to see much better hardware manufacturer support of NT in the near future.

How do I uninstall NT?

Oops. Unfortunately, Microsoft did not provide an easy way to do this. Imagine the folks at Microsoft scratching their heads and looking at each other in puzzlement: *Uninstall* NT? Why would anyone want to do *that*?

15

15

If you installed NT over a previous version of Windows without making a full backup of your original system, you are out of luck. You will have no choice but to rebuild your system from scratch. You'll have to boot DOS from a floppy disk so you can repartition or reformat your hard disk and then copy the system files back to your hard disk. Next, you will have to go back to your original DOS, Windows, and application installation disks and set up everything all over again. Even hardened computer veterans groan when confronted by this sort of thing.

If you installed NT to its own directory, leaving all your original files intact, you are in good shape if you are careful. Follow these steps:

1. Boot your system from a floppy disk formatted as a DOS system disk.

2. If you were using a dual-boot configuration, enter the following command at the DOS prompt: FDISK /MBR. This will restore the Master Boot Record of a system that was using a dual-boot configuration. (In case you noticed, the /MBR switch isn't a documented feature of FDISK. Microsoft probably didn't want Jack or Jill User fooling with the Master Boot Record of a hard disk.)

3. Enter the following command at the DOS prompt: SYS C:. This will restore the usual DOS system files IO.SYS, MSDOS.SYS, and COMMAND.COM to your hard disk.

4. Remove the DOS floppy from your computer and reboot. You should get the familiar DOS prompt. You can now access your system and wipe out any files related to NT. In addition to the files installed in the NT directory, you will find some or all of the following files in the root directory: BOOT.INI, NTDETECT.COM, NTLDR, and BOOTSECT.DOS. You may have to use the /AH switch with the DIR command to see some of these files because Microsoft likes to hide them. You can safely delete these files. You may also find a gigantic file called PAGEFILE.SYS, which is the NT swap file. You can delete it, too.

If you used NTFS on a separate NT volume, you will be forced to use a utility such as FDISK to reformat that volume to FAT to regain use of that volume for non-NT operating systems. Do not reformat all of your volumes or you will lose your original operating system, too!

Summary

If you made sure your hardware supports NT 4 and you were prepared for each step before you encountered it, installation of NT Workstation should proceed smoothly. (I believe this qualifies as "famous last words.")

When you have NT up and running, you'll want to customize your desktop and install your favorite software. While you're at it, take the time to explore NT's many features. NT 4 Workstation is a big system that gives you many features and flexibility. Indulge yourself, and learn what it can do for you.

Workshop

The Workshop helps you solidify the skills you learned this hour.

Glossary

boot loader   A program that controls the loading of an operating system or systems when your computer is started, or *booted*.

graphical user interface (GUI)   This term is applied to a program that enables a user to interact with the computer using images and a pointing device rather than typing commands on a text-only screen.

multiple-boot   Also known as multi-boot or dual-boot. This refers to a configuration that allows a choice of operating environments when you start your machine. Multiple-boot configurations give the owner the flexibility of using one computer platform to use several different operating systems.

switch   An option tacked onto the end of a command that modifies or controls how the command is performed.

wizard   A Microsoft word for a GUI program that guides you through a process, letting you go back or advance through the process until you are ready to accept your choices.

Exercises

1. After installation is complete, click every icon on the Desktop and every menu selection in the Start button. Observe what program appears. If you are not familiar with this program, take a moment and read the available Help or otherwise find out what it does. You might be surprised how many useful utilities NT provides for you.

2. Use the Windows NT Diagnostics program to observe the difference in IRQ usage with a sound card driver installed and with no sound card driver installed. You can use the Control Panel Multimedia function to easily add or delete the sound card driver.

3. Use the Display function of the Control Panel to change your display configuration after installation. Experiment with the Desktop Area and color options to find the settings that make you the most comfortable. Experiment with NT's many graphical options for controlling your desktop appearance. Try using Paint to make your own image for your desktop background.

15

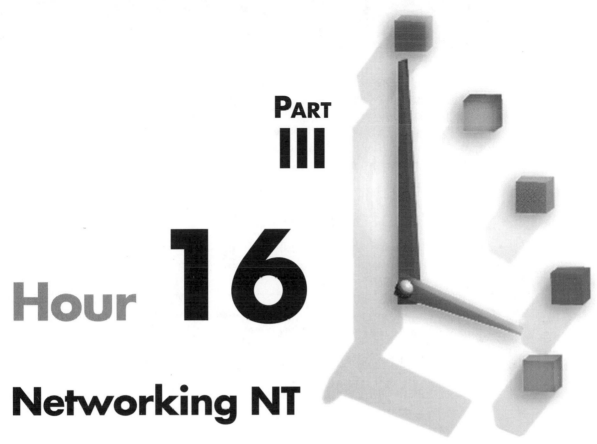

Hour **16**

Networking NT

by Martin Kenley

This hour, Hour 17, "Configuring Network Components," and Hour 18, "Peer-to-Peer Networking," involve networking. This lesson gives an overview of networking concepts and describes Microsoft's networking strategy as employed in Windows NT. Hour 17 walks through setting up the networking components, which you can install either during the installation process or later.

Introduction to Networking

To better understand the networking components of Windows NT, look at how a local area network functions. A network is simply several computers connected together by cable. Sometimes, there are additional devices connected to the network, such a printer, that all the computers can share.

For a simple network like this to work, you need several items. First, you need cable that will connect each of the computers. Two general types of cabling are common today: coaxial cable and twisted pair. "Coax" cable is made with a solid copper core surrounded by insulating material, a metal shield, and an outer coat of plastic. Common types of coax are 10Base2 and 10Base5. Every form of cable has specifications that determine how long any segment of cable can be until the signal that runs over it is so weak (or attenuated) that the next computer can't interpret it. With 10Base5, the maximum distance is 500 meters; with 10Base2, it is 185 meters.

Twisted pair cable is more common, and it is likely your office is wired with some of it. The most common type is unshielded twisted pair (UTP). 10BaseT is a common form of UTP. The maximum distance of any segment is 100 meters.

Both coaxial and twisted pair are capable of running Ethernet over them. Ethernet is a protocol developed for carrying data over cables between computers.

TIME SAVER

Look at the back of your computer and determine what type of cabling your office uses. If you see a metal "T" connector that connects to the cable, you are using coaxial cable.

If the connector looks similar to a telephone jack, you are using twisted pair cabling.

Network Cards

In addition to the cable connecting the machines, you will need an Ethernet card for each computer you want connected to the network. The network interface card (NIC), also known as a network adapter card, translates the data you are sending over the network into a format that enables the cable to handle it.

There are many manufacturers selling NICs; I recommend getting a name-brand card to save you the time of trying to configure the card. Cheap cards often come with software drivers that are less than reliable.

You can determine what type of Ethernet card your computer uses. To do this, you must find out what software driver it is using, which corresponds to the type of card it is. Then follow these steps:

1. Go to the Start menu | Settings | Control Panel.
2. Now open up the Network control panel (see Figure 16.1).
3. You will notice some tabs at the top of the Network control panel window. Select Adapters, and you should see what type of card you have in your computer, assuming that it has been correctly identified (see Figure 16.2).

Figure 16.1.

The Network control panel lets you configure various network settings.

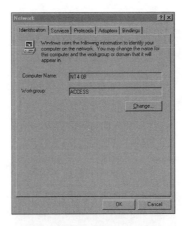

Figure 16.2.

The different tabs in the Network control panel provide information on your adapter and network settings.

Networking Models: Peer-to-Peer and Client/Server

So far, you have seen that you need network cable, network interface cards, and a software driver that works with the network cards. The next element in understanding networks is the software that makes it all happen. Look at an example of several computers that are linked together and share a printer (see Figure 16.3). In this example, the various computers are sharing their resources (such as files on their hard drives, space on their hard drives, CD-ROM drive, and the printer connected to Hannah's computer) by peer-to-peer networking. To do peer-to-peer networking, each computer must be running software that enables it to handle requests from other computers that want to use its resources. In Figure 16.3, the printer is connected to Hannah's computer, but the networking software enables her to share it with the other computers in the office. In this structure, no single computer controls the requests made by the computers; therefore, there is no central management.

Figure 16.3.

A basic local area network setup.

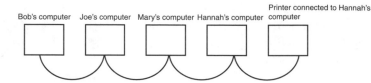

Peer-to-peer networking is less expensive because you do not need to purchase a server. However, the performance of your network will suffer because you do not have a dedicated file and print server. Moreover, a peer-to-peer network does not have the same security that a client/server structure provides. (You look more at peer-to-peer networks in Hour 18.

In a client/server model, the server, or rather the software running on it, controls the network. The two primary pieces of software are the network operating system (server software) on the server, and the networking software (client software) on the workstations. Both of these together compose the network operating system, which is responsible for providing connections to all the computers and other devices (for example, printers).

The network operating system also is responsible for coordinating the requests of the different computers. For example, in Figure 16.4, what if Bob's computer wanted to send a job to the printer at the same time that Mary's computer wanted to access a file on the server? The network operating system would coordinate this activity.

Figure 16.4.

A model of a client/server network structure.

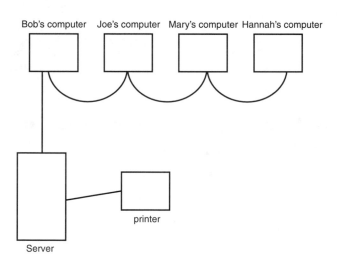

The server can perform a variety of functions. The most basic type of server is a print server, which functions only to take print jobs from workstations and process them by passing them to a printer connected to it. A more complex type of server is a file and print server. In this case, the server is capable of storing files for individual workstations and enabling them to access these files on request. This type of server has security built into it so that the system administrator can determine who can access what files and what types of privileges they have when accessing different files (for example, if they can change or delete a document or just read it).

Networking Software

Here is where things begin to get more complicated. In the example in Figure 16.4, there are several computers, a server, and a printer networked together. When one of the workstations makes a request, it must be passed to the appropriate location for the request to be carried out. Look at the previous example: Bob wants to send to the printer a memo he just typed. In his word processor, he tells it to print. This request is intercepted inside his computer by the redirector, which then must determine whether this request can be handled locally or if it must be routed to the network.

The OSI Seven-Layer Model

The OSI seven-layer model is the most important concept in networking. All networking software must adhere, however loosely, to this model. The International Standards Organization (ISO) is responsible for developing standards for networking data. The seven-layer model it developed describes what happens when one computer exchanges data with another (see Figure 16.5). The model was developed so that different types of software and hardware could communicate with one another. As long as each computer (along with its networking software) followed a set of standards, there would be no obstacles for communication.

Each layer uses *protocols* to communicate with the layer either directly above it or below it. A protocol is a set of standards that describes how the layer will interact with the layers above and below it. If these other layers understand the protocol, the layer will be able to understand the data passed to it, and so on down the seven layers. Let's take a quick look at the seven-layer model.

Layer 7: The Application Layer

The top layer of the model, the application layer, is the layer with which you interact directly. The application can be a word processor; although not usually thought of as a network application, if you attempt to save a text file to a file server, then it must interact with the network. More commonly, the applications that use network functions include your electronic mail package and file transfer applications. In reality, sometimes the application layer will handle lower-layer functions as well.

Figure 16.5.

The OSI seven-layer model.

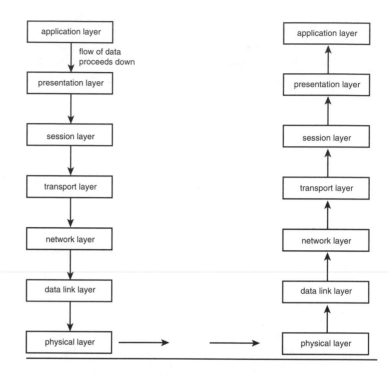

Layer 6: The Presentation Layer

As mentioned in the previous section, the user will not interact with any of the lower layers, with the exception of the network and transport layers, where some configuration might be necessary. The presentation layer receives data from the application layer and formats the data.

Layer 5: The Session Layer

The session layer's job is to manage a connection with the remote host. This layer is, in practice, tied very closely to layer 4 because the two work hand-in-hand. An example of a layer 5 protocol is NetBIOS.

Layer 4: The Transport Layer

The transport layer manages the packets of information to ensure that the contents of each packet arrived error free. The transport layer builds an error-checking device into the packets; although lower levels also have error checking, this is the last place errors can be checked and remedied. This layer also breaks the data or file given to it from the upper layer into small packets; the transport layer on the receiving computer reassembles the packets.

16

Layer 3: The Network Layer

The network layer builds on the connection provided by layer 2. Often, the network layer will not occur inside your computer, but rather out in the network in switches (computers that route data on the Internet). Therefore, the network layer determines the physical path that the packets will take. An example of a layer 3 protocol is Internet Protocol (IP).

Layer 2: The Data Link Layer

The data link layer is in charge of managing the data stream between the source (your computer) and the destination. This layer may use several protocols to achieve its goals. It builds on the transmission capability of layer 1 by grouping the data together into frames, which are put into an "envelope" that is marked with header information for error checking, address information (sender's and receiver's addresses), and a control field (which marks different types of data link frames). The two most common protocols associated with this level are Ethernet and Token Ring.

Layer 1: The Physical Link Layer

The physical link layer is responsible for actually transmitting data over the cable. The data at this stage is in the form of bits (0s and 1s). This layer handles mechanical and electrical exchanges as the data travels to its destination.

Summary of the OSI Model

Figure 16.5 shows how information moves down the layer, across the wire, back up the layers, and to the application on the receiving computer. Each layer adds some formatting, and often a header, and encapsulates its packet in an envelope, which is passed to the next layer. Each layer can only communicate with the layer above and below it and is unaware of the other layers.

Let's pick an example of how data moves: Here are the steps involved in transferring a file from your computer to a remote computer:

1. Begin by launching the application that will assist in performing the transfer, such as WinFTP. Connect to the computer to which you will upload the file by using your FTP application. When this occurs, a lot has happened already, but we're interested in just a small part of the picture. The top layer, the application, passes the file down to the next layer.

2. The presentation layer is skipped because most FTP applications handle this function by themselves. Therefore, the session layer receives the file, which is broken up into smaller chunks; error correction and other header information is added. This packet or envelope is passed down to the next layer.

3. This continues until the packet arrives at the data link layer, where it is put inside an even larger envelope, an Ethernet frame. It is then passed over the wire to the receiving computer.

4. The receiving computer opens the Ethernet frame envelope, discards the header information, checks for accuracy and other measures, and passes it up to the next layer.

5. The next layer opens the packet, checks the information for accuracy, discards its header information, and passes it up until it reaches transmission control protocol (TCP).

6. TCP combines the packets back into a file and passes it up to the application. Obviously, most of this is transparent to users, whose only interaction is with the FTP application.

Activity

Now take a look at the protocols installed on your computer. You should have at least a passing familiarity with the protocols used in your office or work environment.

1. Go to the Network control panel, and open it.

2. Click the Protocols tab, and write down all the protocols that your computer is using (if you are reading this to configure your networking, skip to Hour 17, which discusses configuring your NT Workstation).

3. How many of the protocols can you currently define from the lesson so far?

4. Use the Properties button to get information on the different protocols and see how much information makes sense.

Networking NT Style

Now look at some particulars now that you have a general framework for understanding networking. With Windows NT Workstation, the capability both to operate as a client and to handle peer-to-peer requests is built into the operating system itself. In the past, computer users had to install separate software on top of their operating system to acquire networking capabilities.

16

Another unique feature of NT networking is the fact that it is able to function well in a multi-network environment, where there are Macintosh computers, UNIX, NetWare 3.*x* and 4.*x*, Remote Access Services, as well as Windows NT 3.*x* and Windows for Workgroups. NT networking is constructed in such a way that a component can be replaced by a newer version without affecting other network components. NT is fully capable of running multiple protocols simultaneously.

The capability to run multiple protocols simultaneously provides a great amount of flexibility. Because you have several protocols bound to each other, it is possible, for example, to attach to a Novell server and open a file at the same time that you can use TCP/IP and run a Web browser. NT networking is also flexible because it can work with different file systems.

16

Network Topologies

There are two common network topologies used today in local area networks (LANs): the bus topology and the star topology (see Figures 16.6 and 16.7). A bus topology consists of each computer being connected to the computer next to it, with the cable forming a line from one computer to the next. (For example, Ethernet uses a bus topology.) The disadvantage of this network topology is that if one segment of the cable is broken, the entire network goes down.

Figure 16.6.

A typical bus topology.

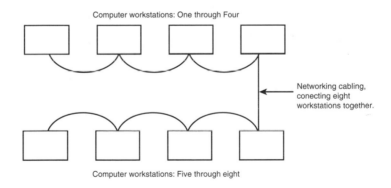

A star topology has a central unit sometimes called a *central wiring hub*, to which all the computers are connected. The advantage of this type of network is that if one part of the network goes down—for example, because of a break in a cable segment—the rest of the network will not be affected.

Figure 16.7.

A second example of a bus topology. Although this may look like a star network, it is not a true star because the hubs simply pass the signal along in a broadcast fashion to all the computers connected to the hub.

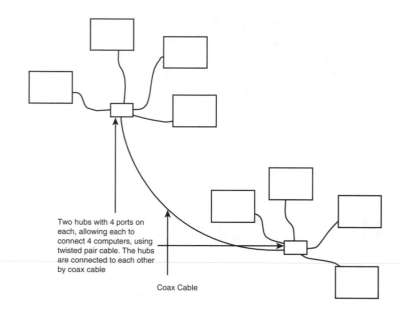

Two hubs with 4 ports on each, allowing each to connect 4 computers, using twisted pair cable. The hubs are connected to each other by coax cable

Coax Cable

Summary

In this hour, you learned the basic elements of a local area network: the cabling, network cards, protocols, and the OSI model. It is important that you understand these concepts before you read the other lessons on networking.

Workshop

The Workshop helps you solidify the skills you learned this hour.

Glossary

10Base-2   A network coax cable known as thin Ethernet. It uses RG-58 media and supports distances up to 185 meters. The 10 in the name refers to its transmission rates of 10 megabits per second (Mbps). The Base refers to it being a baseband media as opposed to broadband.

10Base-5   A network coaxial cable known as thick Ethernet, it supports distances of up to 500 meters.

10Base-T   A network cable known as twisted pair or UTP (unshielded twisted pair).

100Base-T   A network cable known as twisted pair capable of transmission rates of up to 100 Mbps. Also called fast Ethernet.

16

100Base-FX   A network cable very similar to 100Base-T, except it uses fiber-optic.

attenuation   The process of an electronic signal weakening as it travels down the cable.

client   In a network, a client computer makes a request to another computer, which acts as a server.

coaxial cable   A network cable consisting of a copper core surrounded by a protective coating.

Ethernet   An implementation of a media access method; it is at level 2 of the OSI model to transmit bits to the cable.

fiber-optic   A network cable that uses glass as a transmission medium and is used for high-speed transmission.

file server   A computer that is dedicated to providing and storing files for the workstations on a local area network.

header   Information added to a packet by one of the seven layers of the OSI network model.

International Standards Organization (ISO)   The organization responsible for developing the OSI model of networking.

Internet address   Often referred to as an IP number, it is the unique identification number that each computer or device on Internet Protocol networks must have.

Internet Protocol (IP)   A protocol used on the Internet to help route packets from one computer to another.

local area network (LAN)   A small network of computers.

network driver interface specification (NDIS)   A protocol interface used by NT to provide a standard method for LAN driver and protocol development; it also enables various NICs and protocols to function together.

network interface card (NIC)   Also called network adapter, it is used by PCs to transfer material from the PC to the network cable and operate at the physical level of the OSI model.

OSI seven-layer model   A seven-layer networking model describing standards for each of the layers involved in networking.

peer-to-peer network   A network setup where there is no server; each computer can request resources from the other computers. When one computer makes a request, it is behaving as a client, and the destination computer behaves similar to a server while it fulfills the request.

protocol   Sets of standards or rules that dictate how something functions. Because TCP is a protocol and the other layers that interact with it understand the set of rules governing how TCP operates, the layers above it and below it understand how to interact with it.

server   A computer on a network that functions to provide services to other computers on the same network. The types of services are varied, such as providing access to applications, files, or a printer.

transmission control protocol (TCP)   The protocol responsible for taking information from higher-level protocols and breaking it up into datagrams; on the destination computer, TCP reassembles the datagrams. TCP is also responsible for packet delivery, error checking, and flow control.

Workshop

1. Learn more about your network. To what type of server is your computer attached? What type of protocols are necessary to send and receive data to your server?

2. Is your computer doing any peer-to-peer networking?

3. What are the advantages and disadvantages of peer-to-peer networking compared with using an NT server?

4. With regard to the OSI seven-layer model, can layer 7 communicate directly with layer 3?

5. Again, thinking about the OSI model, which layer is responsible for routing your data on the network?

6. Why are protocols so important with regard to networking?

Hour 17

Configuring Network Components

by Martin Kenley

If you have installed Windows NT on a workstation that is not connected to a network by network cable, then you can skip this hour. If you plan to connect to a network by a modem, then you will want to read Hour 8, "Remote Access to Your Work and Setting Up Laptops."

At this point, you should have a plan for the type of network environment you want to create, whether it be a mixed client/server and peer-to-peer environment, or perhaps a straight client/server environment using Internet protocols (TCP/IP).

When you install Windows NT, you can configure your network components then, or wait until after you have finished the installation. This lesson guides you through the process; although I assume you are doing it after the installation, the instructions in this lesson are suitable for configuring your network settings either during the installation or later.

Installing Network Components on Multiple Computers Unattended

If you are going to set up numerous workstations and you want to install the networking during the installation of Windows NT without having to answer all the questions that accompany the install process, you can create an *answer file*. This type of file is simply a text file that provides automated answers for the install Setup wizard during installation. It is an excellent way for a computer specialist to save time, but you only benefit if you have numerous computers to set up.

Using an answer file will enable you to install device drivers and a network interface card and even join a domain if any exist on your network. To create an answer file, follow these instructions:

1. Use any text editor and save the result as a text file.
2. Use the information in the section "Answer Files," which divides the answer file into parts.
3. Below each section you must enter keys, or lines of code that tell the Setup program to enter the values you specify.

A uniqueness database file (UDF) works along with an answer file, having a similar structure, and is used to handle unique characteristics of a particular computer. Elements or values therein will override those in the answer file. Thus, the UDF enables you to customize the automatic, unattended install process that the answer file provides you with, customizing it for the particular needs of each computer. For example, it would be possible to specify a username and computer name in a UDF. Take a look at the section "Answer Files."

Preconfiguration Checklist

Before you begin, there are several pieces of information you will need to make the network installation go smoothly (the following information assumes you are using TCP/IP and Ethernet):

- ☐ Internet protocol (IP) number: A unique identification number assigned to every computer on the Internet or an IP-based network
- ☐ DNS and WINS address numbers: Servers that assist you in Internet activity
- ☐ The type of networking: peer-to-peer or client/server
- ☐ The type of servers you will need to connect to
- ☐ Which protocols your system administrator prefers you to use
- ☐ The type of network interface card that is installed in your computer

17

☐ What resources your Ethernet card uses

☐ What resources your computer has free

If you are not certain what resources are and which ones your computer has open or free, you might want to read this lesson first before you begin the installation. When you understand more about resources, you might be able to check your current operating system, if you already have one installed on your computer, to determine what is being used. If you don't have an operating system on your computer, you will want to read this lesson first, install NT, and follow these instructions as you configure your networking components.

If you are doing the network setup during the installation process, NT's Setup wizard will prompt you for certain information; the windows you get are identical to those you would get if you chose to do the setup later.

Answer Files

As mentioned in the "Installing Network Components on Multiple Computers Unattended" section, answer files enable you to perform unattended installations of NT and are relevant here because you might want to have information about the network setup and other appropriate information typed up so you can do the install unattended. I have presented enough information to get you going. For additional information, consult the *Microsoft Windows NT Workstation Resource Kit* (Microsoft, 1996).

The sections of an answer file, shown in brackets, are shown in the following code. Below each section is a key or line of code that tells the Setup program what to do. You can remark out lines using a semicolon. UDFs use the same sections and keys as answer files, with the exception of the unattended OEMBootFiles, MassStorageDrivers, KeyboardDrivers, PointingDeviceDrivers, and DetectedMassStorage, which are used only in answer files.

```
[unattended]
OemPreinstall = no
ConfirmHardware = no
NtUpgrade = no
Win31Upgrade = no
TargetPath = WINNT
OverwriteOemFilesOnUpgrade = no
[OEMBootFiles]
; for x86 computers; if this section is included, $OEM$\OEMFILES\TXTSETUP.OEM
➥and all the files therein must be included in this section.
[MassStorageDrivers]
;here you can indicate which SCSI drivers are used.
[KeyboardDrivers]
;if you need to indicate a special keyboard driver, do it here.
[PointingDeviceDrivers]
;if you need to indicate a special pointing device driver, do it here.
[DisplayDrivers]
;if you need to indicate a specific display driver, do it here.
```

```
[Display]
;here you can indicate settings for your video.
ConfigureAtLogon = 1
;since it is set to 1, no video settings occur until the installation is
➥done and it is booted for 1st time.
;if you wanted to set up video, you could use the following syntax:
BitsPerPel = 16
XResolution = 800
YResolution = 600
VRefresh = 70
AutoConfirm = 1
;the last line instructs the installer to save the settings automatically.
;A zero value prompts the user before continuing.
[DetectedMassStorage]
;indicate here which mass storage device is to be recognized.
[GuiUnattended]
;indicate any keys to use during the GUI portion of the Setup.
TimeZone = "(GMT-07:00) Arizona"
[UserData]
FullName = "BJones"
OrgName = "ABC Company"
ComputerName = Bob's Computer
ProductID = "19955999569884383"
[network]
;here is where you can indicate network configuration settings.
Attend = yes
;the above line specifies that you would like this section to be interactive;
;otherwise leave this key out.
DetectAdapters = DetectParams
;InstallAdapters = AdaptersList
InstallProtocols = ProtocolsSection
;InstallServices = ServiceList
JoinDomain = Accounting
CreateComputerAccount = BobJ, GreenEggs
[DetectParams]
DetectCount = 1
LimitTo = ELNKIII
[AdaptersList]
ELNKIII = 3comParams
[ProtocolsSection]
TC = TCPIPParameters
[TCPIPParameters]
DHCP = NO
IPAddress = 129.79.110.23
Subnet = 255.0.0.0.
Gateway = 129.79.110.254
DNSServer = 198.56.43.1
WINSPrimary = 179.43.2.34
WINSSecondary = 179.43.2.35
[3ComParams]
interrupt = 5
IoChannelReady = 4
IoAddress = 500
[Modem]
;indicate whether or not you want Setup to intall a modem.
```

17

Network Adapter Cards: Part I

One of the first items you'll encounter during your network configuration is your network card (see Figure 17.1). Network interface cards (NICs) plug into an expansion slot on your computer's bus. Network cards are sold by many vendors, and most come with their own special software driver, which interacts with the operating system; in fact, they help the operating system "talk" to the network card. The network adapter translates or converts PC bus signals into a format that the network cable can understand, and the adapter on the receiving computer converts the data back into its original format. Just a few of the large number of manufacturers include Western Digital, 3Com, Intel, SMC, Gateway Communications, Eagle/Novell, D-Link, and National Semiconductor.

Figure 17.1.

An Ethernet card, which can be seated into an expansion slot inside your PC.

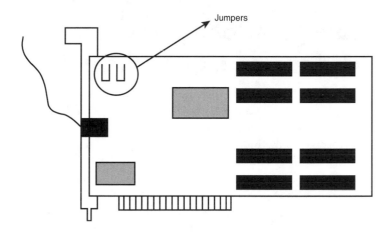

Jumpers

17

If it is a good card, you should be able to configure the settings through its software, rather than having to actually set the jumpers (see Figure 17.2). What settings are we talking about? Every network interface card will need an interrupt request (IRQ) line, a direct memory access (DMA) channel assignment, and an I/O range (that is, an input/output memory address range). You will learn how to resolve such conflicts, which work for all devices in your computer, and then you'll return to setting up the network card.

Figure 17.2.

Jumpers such as these are common on many devices inside your PC.

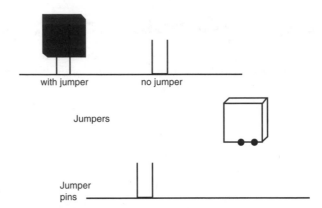

with jumper   no jumper

Jumpers

Jumper
pins

Troubleshooting Resource Conflicts: IRQs, DMAs, and I/O Address Ranges

The skills needed to find resource conflicts have not gone away with the so-called plug-and-play, whereby you purchase, for example, a sound card, bring it home, plug it into your computer's expansion slot, and away you go: You are now ready to "play." In fact, many people in the industry refer to it as "plug-and-pray." For this technology to work, your operating system must be plug-and-play, the motherboard must be plug-and-play capable, your BIOS must support plug-and-play, and the device you are installing must support it as well. Windows NT 4 Workstation does not support plug-and-play. If one of these factors is lacking, beware: It is often easier to disable plug-and-play and install it the old-fashioned way. The old way involves determining which resources the device needs: one, maybe two DMA channels; an IRQ; or one or more I/O memory address ranges. Then you have to know which of these resources are free so you can assign them to your new device.

JUST A MINUTE

While you learn to troubleshoot your hardware, prepare yourself for the inevitable resolving of resource conflicts for your computer:

1. Make a list of all the devices inside your computer. Such devices can include sound cards, modems, video cards, network adapter cards, SCSI cards, and so on.

2. Look for any documentation on these devices to help determine the resources they use.

3. If the devices came with any utilities, run them to see if they will show what system resources they are using. If now is not a good time to run these diagnostics, at least have them close by so you can do so when you have time.

17

IRQ: Interrupt Request Line

The IRQ, or interrupt request line, is a method hardware devices have for getting the attention of the central processing unit (CPU). Special chips handle the IRQs and pass them to the processor in a way that keeps data flowing the best way possible.

The important point is that your PC has 16 IRQ lines. Of these 16 lines, you are only allowed to use those that are free. Look at Table 17.1, which shows how most computers use IRQs.

Table 17.1. How most computers use IRQs.

IRQ #	Component that uses the IRQ
0	Is for the system
1	Is for the keyboard
2	Connects to IRQ 9
3	Is dedicated to COM ports 2 and 4
4	Is dedicated to COM ports 1 and 3
5	Often used by a sound card
6	Is for the floppy disk controller
7	Is for LPT1
8	Is for the real-time clock
9	Is connected to IRQ 2
10	Is for general use
11	Is for general use (may be the default for SCSI adapter)
12	Is for general use (unless you are using a PS/2 mouse port)
13	Is for the math coprocessor
14	Is for the hard drive controller
15	Is for general use (but may be used by a SCSI adapter)

Network interface cards are generally happy with IRQ 5 or 10, as long as no other device is trying to use them.

Although these IRQ line designations are true for most computers, you can confirm that it also holds true for your PC. You must become familiar with the tricks of troubleshooting device-driver conflicts. First, take a quick look at DMAs and I/O address ranges, and then you'll see how to find out what is happening with the resources in your computer. Be aware that some Adaptec SCSI controller cards use IRQ11 as a default.

TIME SAVER

Create a table that will enable you to determine what devices are using which system resources. One side of the table should list the device names: sound card, network card, modem, and so on. At the top of the table, list your system resources: IRQ, DMA, I/O, and COM port.

Fill in as much of the table as is currently possible. You will be able to fill in more after you read the next section.

DMA: Direct Memory Access

On the motherboard (the main circuit board) inside your PC is special hardware that gives some devices the capability to transfer data from them directly to the computer's memory, bypassing the CPU. This is an advantage because the CPU can continue chugging along completing its tasks without being interrupted. PCs have eight DMA channels and a channel can be assigned to only one device, or—lo and behold—you have a device conflict. Note Table 17.2. It shows the eight DMA channels inside the PC and which resource commonly uses each line.

Table 17.2. How most computers use DMA channels.

DMA Line	Resource that likely uses that line
0	Used for memory refresh
1	Used for 8-bit transfer (often used for sound cards)
2	Used for the floppy disk controller
3	Used for 8-bit transfer
4	Used by the system
5	Used for 16-bit transfer
6	Used for 16-bit transfer
7	Used for 16-bit transfer

From this, you can see that those used for transfers are free. If you have a sound card, it is likely that it is using DMA channel 1. So for your NIC, you can try channels 3, 5, 6, and 7. However, your card might come with diagnostic software that you can run to tell you what resources it is set to use. Another caveat: DMA channel 5 is the default for some Adaptec SCSI adapter cards.

17

I/O Addresses

An I/O address is a three-digit hexadecimal (using the base-16 numbering system) number that indicates the address at which a device is signaled. Each device needs its own unique address. You are definitely seeing a pattern here: The best way to set up your PC is to assign unique resources (as far as possible) to each device.

Most network adapter cards will use one of the following memory addresses: 280h, 300h, 320h, 340h, and 360h. It is not uncommon for SCSI devices to use 300h, 320h, 330h, or 340h, so if possible, avoid these addresses.

Checking for Free Resources

Armed with this knowledge of what IRQs, DMAs, and I/O addresses are, you are now ready to determine how your system resources are being used. If you have already installed NT 4, you are in luck, because it comes with a fairly reliable, built-in program for checking resource use: Win NT Diagnostics (see Figure 17.3). However, it is rare but possible that a driver for a specific device might not accurately report what resources it uses and it will therefore cause NT Diagnostics to incorrectly report what resources are being used for that device. Therefore, install only one device at a time and make sure it is working properly before you install another component. To launch the Win NT Diagnostic, follow these steps:

1. Go to Start | Programs | Administrative Tools | Win NT Diagnostics.

Figure 17.3.

The Win NT Diagnostics utility shows IRQ usage.

2. Select the Resources tab at the top of the screen.
3. Select the IRQ button at the bottom of the screen. You can now see how all 16 of your IRQs are being used and which are still free to use.

4. Now fill in the portion of your table that you began earlier. When you have filled in the IRQ portion, continue to step 5.

5. Now, select the DMA button at the bottom of the screen, and note how your eight DMA channels are being used. The screen you see should look similar to that displayed in Figure 17.4. Again, fill in the corresponding part of your table.

Figure 17.4.

The Diagnostics utility also shows DMA usage, as well as I/O address usage.

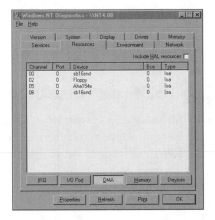

6. Now, click the Devices button on the bottom-right side of the screen. The Device Manager will give you a comprehensive listing of resources used by each device in your PC. The screen you see should look similar to that displayed in Figure 17.5. This is a great way to quickly find out a lot of information on a single device. You can see what resources my sound card is using.

Figure 17.5.

The resources each device uses are summarized in the device's property sheet. Shown here are the resources I use for my SoundBlaster card.

7. Finish filling out your table, which should look like Figure 17.6.

17

RESOURCES

DEVICES	IRQs	DMAs	I/O
Sound Card			
Network Adapter Card			
Modem			
Video Card			

Figure 17.6.
To organize the resources your devices use, construct a table like this one.

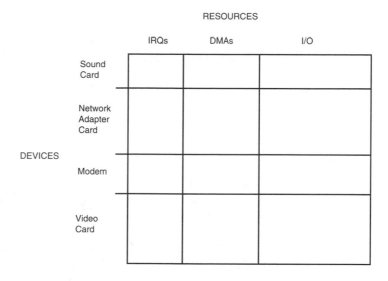

Network Adapter Cards: Part II

Installing network adapter cards is not difficult, and if you have taken the time to consider your purchase and have selected a card that has good driver support, you should not experience any problems. The following list will help you during the installation:

1. To install a network adapter card, you can let the NT installer attempt to automatically detect the card during the install process or, if NT is already installed, go to the Control Panel folder and double-click the network icon. You will now see something similar to Figure 17.7.

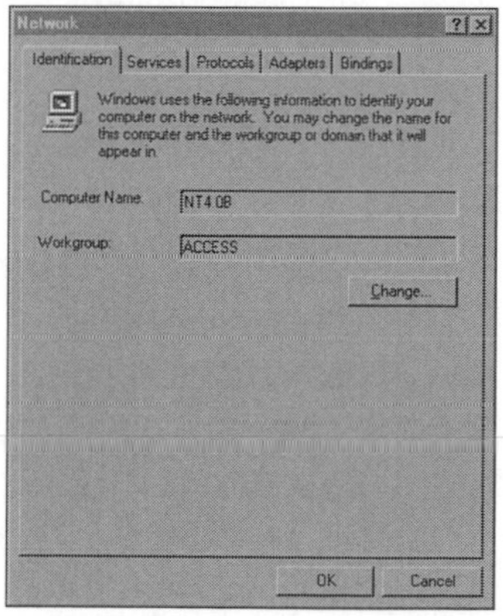

Figure 17.7.
The Network control panel enables you to configure your network settings.

2. Select the Adapters tab at the top of the window.

3. Now you must add an adapter unless it was automatically recognized (see Figure 17.8). Click Add if it was not detected.

Figure 17.8.

The Network control panel makes it easy to install the driver for your network adapter card.

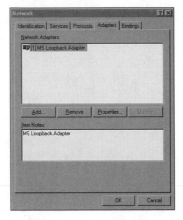

4. NT will now build a list of NICs. Scroll through the list, which is in alphabetical order, and click your NIC. If you don't see it and you have an NT 4–compatible (this is very, very important) driver for it on a disk, insert the disk and click Have Disk.

5. If you are using NT native drivers (those that come with NT), the Setup Wizard will ask you where the drivers are. Point it to the i386 file, which is normally on the CD-ROM drive. Thus, the path would be D:\i386.

6. Click the card; then click Properties to see what resources the card is using. If the card comes with a diagnostic utility, run it now to verify which resources the card is using (be aware that most of these utilities will not work with NT, but card manufacturers are developing new utilities). If these resources are free, you are in business and can continue.

7. Select the Protocols tab at the top of the window. At this point, you might need some assistance from your system administrator. If you are connected to the Internet, you will definitely need to add some protocols.

8. Click Add and select TCP/IP. You will now need that IP address that was mentioned in the "Preconfiguration Checklist" section. In addition, you will need to know the numbers of your DNS server and WINS servers if you have any.

9. Now, if you will be connecting to any Novell NetWare servers, you will want to add IPX/SPX.

10. If you plan to do any peer-to-peer file sharing, you might want to click the Services tab and add Server and Workstation.

17

Workshop

The Workshop helps you solidify the skills you learned this hour.

Glossary

answer file   Enables you to do an unattended install of NT by providing NT with the answers to the install process.

direct memory access (DMA)   Enables a component to send and receive data directly to the RAM without interrupting the CPU (central processing unit). PCs have a total of eight DMA channels.

I/O addresses   Many peripheral devices will require their own unique I/O addresses, a hexadecimal number pointing to an area in the computer's memory used by the device.

interrupt request line (IRQ)   Also called hardware interrupt, it is used internally by a computer to get the attention of the process. Every PC has 16, numbered from 0 to 15.

plug-and-play   A new standard for hardware that enables the hardware to use special technology to configure its resource settings without the assistance of a user. At this point, there are still problems with the technology.

uniqueness database file (UDF)   This type of file works in conjunction with an answer file and enables you to customize the install of NT on multiple machines, specifying unique elements on a particular machine.

Exercises

1. Complete the table that shows which resources all of your devices use. You should now be able to fill in the data for the network adapter card.

2. Get your hands on the NT Workstation Resource Kit, published by Microsoft, and learn more about protocols. This book is available at most bookstores. The important ones you'll commonly hear of are TCP/IP, IPX/SPX, NetBIOS, and NetBEUI.

3. Again, using the Resource Kit, learn more about services you can install in the Network control panel.

17

PART IV

The Midnight Session

Hour

Hour 18

Peer-to-Peer Networking

by Martin Kenley

This lesson looks at peer-to-peer networking, considerations in using this type of network plan, and setting up a peer-to-peer network. It also reviews the advantages and disadvantages of peer-to-peer networks in contrast to client/server networks. Finally, this lesson explains sharing directories so other users can access them.

Peer-to-Peer Network Basics

Peer-to-peer networks do not solve the needs of larger organizations due to the inherent limitations of this networking paradigm. However, many small offices with modest networking needs and minimal security needs will find peer-to-peer networking sufficient and inexpensive. You still need network adapter cards and cabling, but no server is necessary. Peer-to-peer networks work by having a peer-to-peer capable operating system, such as Windows 95 or Windows NT, on all the computers. Both of these operating systems have the capability to enable every computer on the peer-to-peer network to share files, printers, and other resources.

Background

Peer-to-peer networks have been around for a while. A slow start was made, in fact, with early versions of DOS, which permitted you to lock files. Microsoft saw the need for something more powerful and released MS-NET in 1984, a product that faded quickly and was replaced with Microsoft's LAN Manager, a more substantial product.

At the same time, Apple introduced AppleTalk. Not only was it a fairly complete peer-to-peer network operating system, but it was built right into the Macintosh operating system. In its implementation, no additional hardware other than cables was required because AppleTalk could use the built-in printer port for cabling Macs and printers together.

However, client/server networking dominated the network model. Even as new peer-to-peer products entered the market, Novell's NetWare, based on the client/server model, was the market leader.

A company by the name of Artisoft released a product by the name of LANtastic, which was one of the alternatives to Novell in the limited and small network market. LANtastic is a DOS-based peer-to-peer network operating system. Novell even created its own version of peer-to-peer networking when it released NetWare Lite in the early 1990s. Shortly thereafter, Microsoft released Windows for Workgroups, which implemented peer-to-peer technology. Both the Microsoft and Novell products helped to legitimize this networking strategy.

The Microsoft product had the advantage over other peer-to-peer products in that it was designed for Windows, and as such gave users a GUI that was not available in other packages. In fact, Windows for Workgroups was simply an enhanced version of Microsoft Windows that incorporated some networking functions. The File Manager was given additional capabilities that assisted in managing remote drives. The Print Manager also received a facelift so it could now handle network printers.

TIME SAVER

If you are considering setting up some type of network in your organization, the starting point is determining what your needs are: sharing files, sharing a printer or two, sharing a CD-ROM device, running applications off a central computer, electronic mail, and so on.

Draw up a specific list of short-term, immediate needs as well as long-term, future needs.

Hold a meeting with your company's computer specialist or a reliable consulting firm on what hardware and software it would take to meet your current needs.

Draw up a list of expenses.

Make sure to budget for computer support personnel if needed. Many organizations spend large sums of money on technology and have it go to waste because no one in the organization can use it effectively or even maintain it. New systems need maintenance, and you usually have to train others to maximize your benefits.

An Overview of Peer-to-Peer Networks

If you are part of a small organization and are currently not networked, and you are not sure what type of network you need, there are some basic considerations listed in this section that will help you decide. Perhaps you are part of a large organization, but your department is not networked and there is very little money in the budget for equipment. In such a situation, you might want to consider a peer-to-peer network initially and later, if your needs grow, move to a more comprehensive network solution.

In a peer-to-peer network, each workstation has the capability to behave like either a server or a client. Take a look at an example. In Figure 18.1, there are 10 workstations and a printer. If workstation 2 requests a file from workstation 9, a redirector takes the request from workstation number 2, which is acting as a client, and passes it on the network. Workstation number 9, acting as a server (because it will serve the file to the requesting computer), receives the request, and a virtual server driver (SVR.SYS) will grant access to the local resources.

Figure 18.1.

A peer-to-peer network; each workstation is running NT 4 Workstation.

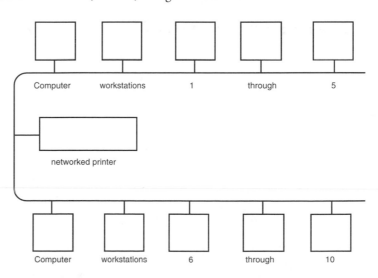

The virtual server is the first and most important element in NT Workstation's set of server functions.

Keep in mind that a few computers might have special functions and still play the role of a peer-to-peer workstation. As you can see from Figure 18.2, a workstation can act as a mail server; a Remote Access Server (which would enable people to dial in from home and connect to the network, or the Internet if your network is connected to the Internet); or even a Web server. Given these examples, you can see that the flexibility of peer-to-peer networking has increased dramatically with the release of NT 4.

Figure 18.2.

NT Workstation allows significant enhancements to what peer-to-peer networks have previously been capable of.

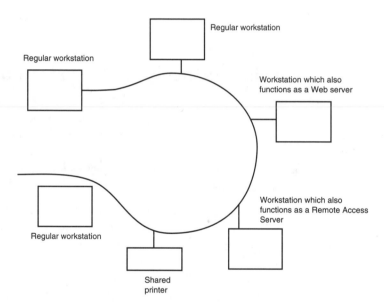

Peer-to-Peer Versus Client/Server Networks

When you are planning a network for your office or department, you will want to consider several elements. The model you choose will have long-term consequences on the capabilities and functionality of your local area network, so plan carefully.

1. Size of the organization: If the number of workstations is limited and you don't foresee the need for adding more than a few workstations in the near future, then a peer-to-peer network might be feasible, depending on other factors.

2. Needs of the organization: If the organization needs to share a database that several users need to access, or you plan to share applications from a central computer, you should consider a client/server arrangement. If the needs are more modest, a peer-to-peer network might work.

3. Security considerations: If you will be sharing sensitive data of a confidential nature, a client/server network may better meet your goals. Thus, if you are sharing data with other departments in your organization, then almost certainly you are looking at setting up a true server to perform these functions.

4. Type of business: If your organization has special needs, perhaps a sales force that must be able to remotely connect and retrieve updated information, again a server might be in order if the sales force is large. You don't want to overburden a peer-to-peer network, and unfortunately, growing organizations can do this without too much effort.

5. Network usage patterns: Here again, this refers to the volume of traffic on the network. A peer-to-peer network in which workstations send electronic mail, do some file sharing and printer sharing is reasonable for modern computers, but when you begin to add additional duties to the network, additional computers, or increase the current network work load, productivity might slip because you can saturate the network with too much traffic.

6. Network budget: A big concern for all organizations is the amount of money they can commit to their computer system. The good news is that powerful equipment is dropping substantially in price due in large part to the decrease in price of components such as RAM, hard drives, CPUs, and motherboards. Don't hesitate to at least price out what you think you need. You might be surprised at what you can buy with a modest expenditure.

7. Level of computer support: If your organization does not have a person whose sole function is to maintain your computer system, and you want to avoid the need to hire such a person, then you don't want to have a server with critical data on it in your office. The reason is simple. Without an "expert" to maintain it, back it up, troubleshoot it, and so on, you are asking for one giant headache. When the server encounters some problem, as all equipment is bound to do, and you don't have someone who is familiar with it inside and out (not someone who knows only enough to be dangerous), you will wish you had hired a "computer person." Servers are complicated beasts; it's as simple as that.

Peer-to-peer networks, on the other hand, have the decided advantage of being much more simple to maintain. When the computer users become familiar with sharing directories, and granting persons or groups permissions to their resources, you are most of the way there. The topic of sharing resources is covered in the section, "Sharing Resources."

It is worth mentioning, however, that with the ease of use, relatively speaking, that comes with peer-to-peer networks, you sacrifice the centralized control that a server provides.

18

Here's a summary of the benefits of this networking typology:

- ☐ It's easier to administer.
- ☐ No server is required.
- ☐ Users are given more control over resources.
- ☐ Peer-to-peer networks are less expensive.
- ☐ Peer-to-peer networks can handle more functions than in the past.

However, peer-to-peer networking has some disadvantages, too:

- ☐ It provides no centralized control over security.
- ☐ Security measures are less comprehensive.
- ☐ The size of the network must be limited.
- ☐ It lacks the flexibility a server provides.
- ☐ You cannot install applications remotely.
- ☐ Backing up data is more problematic.

Setting Up a Peer-to-Peer Network

In order for a peer-to-peer network to function, you still need network adapter cards, cabling, and protocols (protocols were described in Hour 17, "Configuring Network Components"). Protocols still function in a similar fashion: preparing the data, addressing it, and passing it down the network layers until it reaches the wire.

When setting up a peer-to-peer network with Windows NT, there are six primary steps to follow before you begin to share resources.

1. First, make sure NT has detected your network adapter card correctly. To do so, go to the Control Panel folder and open the network configuration window by double-clicking the network icon. This brings up a window (see Hour 17 on the details of installing an NIC).

2. Connect cables to each PC's network adapter card. In general, the type of cable you need to use is determined by the type of adapter on the NIC. Be careful to plan ahead so that the network cards and cabling match. If this seems a bit confusing, you can buy network starter kits that include cabling and cards that match and are usually capable of networking two to four computers.

3. Next, again go to the Network control panel and click the Services tab at the top of the configuration window. Make sure you see both the Server and Workstation service here (as shown in Figure 18.3).

18

Figure 18.3.

The Network control panel provides you with all the necessary items for installing a peer-to-peer network.

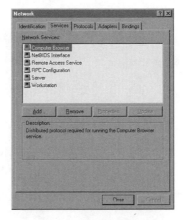

4. If you don't see the Workstation and Server, click the Add button, which opens a window similar to that shown in Figure 18.4. Scroll down until you see Server. Click it and click OK. Repeat again in order to add Workstation.

Figure 18.4.

Adding additional services to NT 4 is easy.

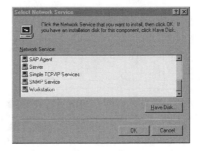

5. You can now establish a workgroup by going to the Network control panel and selecting the Identification tab at the top of the window. This brings up the Network dialog box shown in Figure 18.5. Type in the name for your workgroup, and make sure every other computer that is part of the workgroup has the exact same name typed in this location.

6. If your workgroup is connected to the Internet, you will want to add TCP/IP protocol.

Figure 18.5.

*Establishing a workgroup
with NT 4 is simple.*

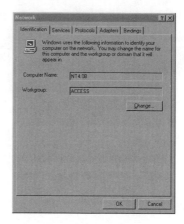

Sharing Resources

Sharing in a peer-to-peer environment is very similar to sharing in a client/server environment.

1. To share an item such as a subdirectory, right-click it. This action brings up the pop-up menu. Move your cursor so that you have selected Sharing, and then click the mouse button. You now see the Sharing dialog box as shown in Figure 18.6.

Figure 18.6.

The Sharing dialog box.

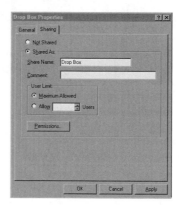

2. Select the Shared As button by using either your mouse or the Tab key.
3. Type in a name for the share, or accept the default name.
4. Choose either to limit the number of users who can use the share simultaneously, or accept the default maximum allowed. The important point here is that if many users are attaching at the same time, their performance will diminish, as will the performance of your computer.

18

5. Click the Permissions button. You now see the dialog box shown in Figure 18.7.

Figure 18.7.

Setting the permissions on a share involves using the Permissions dialog box.

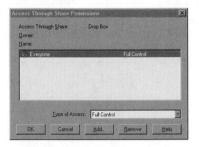

6. Notice that the default is to give everyone full control. You may want to change this depending on the share you are setting up. If you need to add a group or individual, click Add. (More information is provided on setting up sharing in the next lesson.) If you need to, and it does not present a security problem, you can share an entire hard drive by following these steps.

Now you are ready to connect to shared items.

1. You can connect to a shared resource by browsing the Network Neighborhood or by using the UNC (Universal Naming Convention) that gives the complete name of the resource. A UNC looks like the following:

   `\\servername\sharename`

   or

   `\\servername\sharename\directory\filename`

   The *servername* is what you expect: the name of the server (in the context of peer-to-peer networking, it would be the name of the workstation). The *sharename* can be the name of the hard drive or shared directory.

   Of course, for you to be able to attach or map any shared resource, the share must be set up so that you have permission to use it.

2. If you don't see an item to which you want to attach, make sure the computer that owns the share is turned on and logged into Windows NT. If it is, the sharing might have been turned off.

JUST A MINUTE

Keep in mind that if you are sharing folders with DOS or Windows for Workgroups users, you have to be cautious about the file and directory names you choose. Although Windows NT and 95 operating systems can handle long filenames (and spaces in the names), Windows 3.11 and DOS cannot. In fact, the maximum filename in NT is 155 characters including periods. With NTFS file systems, you can have filenames up to 255 characters long.

Windows for Workgroups and DOS systems are limited by the 8.3 convention: eight letters or numbers, with no spaces, followed by a period and three more characters. For example, a document named Marketing report quarter 1 97 would be a valid name under NT, it would have to be changed to something like Mrkt1_97.xls under DOS or Windows for Workgroups.

CAUTION

> The default NT sets for shared folders is to give everyone full control. This default often gives more users more control than you intend.

Controlling the Ability to Share Resources

As an administrator, you can control what is shared.

1. Log into the computer that needs a share set up. Make sure you log in as an administrator.

2. Set up sharing for any directories as needed.

3. Log off. Even after you log off, the items will be shared as long as the computer is running. However, no one else can modify the shares or add new shares unless you give them the permission to do so. (See the next lesson for information on how to do this.)

Monitoring Your Peer-to-Peer Network Performance

As mentioned earlier in this lesson, when your peer-to-peer network grows much beyond 15 or more users and the network traffic increases substantially, you might find that your resources are being pushed to their limits. It is possible to monitor the traffic and predict when the network is being pushed to its upper limits.

1. Open the Performance Monitor by going into the Administrative Tools group, and clicking Performance Monitor. You will see a window similar to that shown in Figure 18.8.

2. Go to the Edit menu and select Add to Chart. You should now see something similar to Figure 18.9.

3. Pull down the Object window by clicking in it with the mouse. You want to select Server.

4. In the Counter window, you want to select Bytes Total/Sec. This will measure the amount (in bytes) of data that the server sends to and receives from the network. Knowing how busy the server is on the computers that do the most networking gives you a good indication of resource use.

18

Figure 18.8.

Performance Monitor even lets you check network traffic.

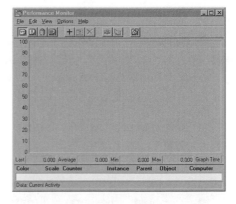

Figure 18.9.

The Add to Chart dialog box.

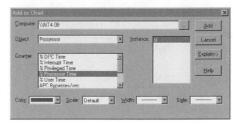

5. Click Add.

6. Now, add the Bytes Transmitted/Sec., which is another counter. This measures the amount of data the server has sent to the network.

7. You can measure other objects as well: Server Session and Redirector. Server Session can show the number of active sessions, while the Redirector Object can measure its activity. If you recall, the redirector is responsible for watching your computer's bus and taking data that is bound for a remote computer, or printer, and redirecting it to the network.

Summary

In this hour you learned about the elements you need to consider when you are planning a network and trying to determine a strategy for your office network. It is important to consider both your short- and long-term needs when planning. The choices you make will have long-term consequences.

Workshop

The Workshop helps you solidify the skills you learned this hour.

Glossary

client/server network   In a client/server network, you have a computer acting as a dedicated server, which "serves" the workstations on the network. The server provides security so only those authorized can log onto the network.

GUI   A graphical user interface.

NIC   A network interface card (NIC) is an electronic expansion card that you put inside your computer. It provides a port on the back of the computer to which you attach a network cable.

peer-to-peer network   In this network structure, there is no server: All the computers are equals and are capable of behaving as a client (when requesting a service) or a server (when another computer requests a service from it).

redirector   The redirector is responsible for taking network requests from your computer's bus and redirecting them onto the network.

remote access server   A service under Windows NT that enables your NT Workstation to behave as a server, using its modem so remote computers can dial in and access files and other resources.

shares   Under Windows NT, when a resource is shared, it is known as a share.

Exercises

1. If you are on a local area network and have the system administrator's permission to experiment with some peer-to-peer networking concepts, share a folder on your hard drive to all the members of your workgroup or domain (whichever your administrator has set up for you and your colleagues). Create a folder and name it Drop Box. This will be a folder in which colleagues can pick up and drop off documents for you. Set the privileges so everyone has full control. This assumes that no one will be dropping in confidential or sensitive material, because anyone who is a member of domain or workgroup will have access to it.

2. Create another folder on your hard drive and label it Docs: READ ONLY. Give your colleagues the permission to read items stored here. This will be a location in which you can put documents that others might need to read, but won't need to change.

3. Create a folder on your hard drive and set it up to be shared. What are the default settings NT provides for shares?

18

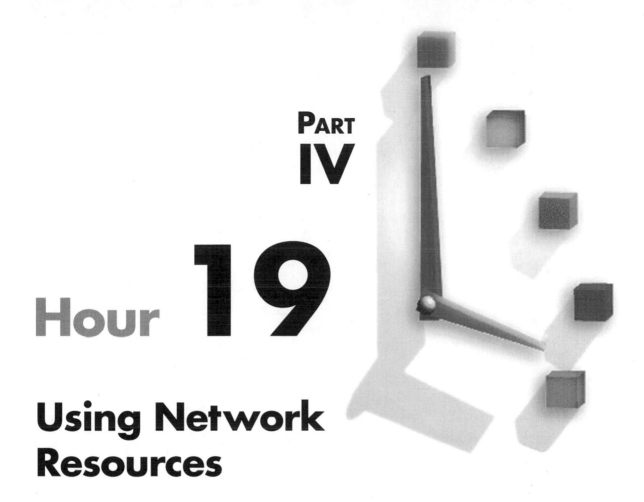

PART
IV

Hour 19

Using Network Resources

by Martin Kenley

You have already seen the flexibility of Microsoft networking as implemented in Windows NT 4 Workstation. It can run several protocols simultaneously and successfully route the information through them. In today's networks, the most common protocols you are likely to see include TCP/IP and IPX/SPX.

This lesson is intended for people who are integrating NT 4 Workstation into a Novell NetWare environment. You will be glad to learn that the process of integrating NT machines is fairly easy. In fact, if you upgraded from a previous version of NT or Windows 3.*x*, NT will detect the network configuration and install the Client Service for NetWare. If you have installed NT Workstation fresh and no network protocols are set up, you can set them up easily.

Novell networks are more numerous than any other network operating system. The core of the NetWare environment, in terms of the transport protocols, has been IPX/SPX. This lesson examines some of the features of NetWare.

The Layers of NetWare

In Hour 17, "Configuring Network Components," you looked at the OSI seven-layer model of networking. Beginning at the bottom of the OSI model, the seven layers are the physical, data link, network, transport, session, presentation, and application layer. Now, compare it to the way it is actually implemented by Novell. In Figure 19.1, you can see that NetWare follows the OSI model loosely, which is not unusual. Take a look at the more important layers.

Figure 19.1.

Note how the seven-layer OSI model compares to Novell's implementation of networking layers.

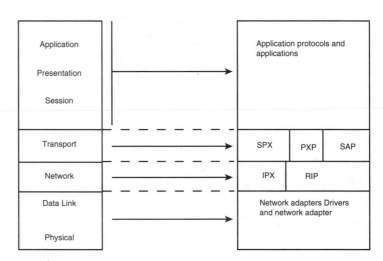

The Application Layer

The application layer under NetWare incorporates the top three layers of the OSI model: the session layer, the presentation layer, and the application layer. Examples of NetWare application services include file and application sharing, printer sharing, and network management.

The Transport Layer

The transport layer of the NetWare stack approximates the transport layer of the OSI model. It supports a connection-oriented link between the two computers. Additional protocols that work at this layer include the following:

☐ SPX, or Sequenced Packet Exchange protocol, establishes a connection before packets are sent and assists in error checking. This protocol also numbers the packets and adds additional "header" information that enables the packets to be put back together by the destination computer.

19

☐ SAP, or Service Advertising Protocol, utilizes a broadcast scheme to tell the client workstations that the server is there and has X, Y, and Z services. Broadcasts are made periodically to routers and workstations.

☐ Echo and Error Protocol assists in routing packets to the destination and reports errors when encountered.

The Network Layer

In the NetWare world, the network layer functions are handled by two protocols: IPX and RIP. IPX, or Internet Packet Exchange protocol, assists in transmitting the data and routing the data. RIP, or Routing Information Protocol, is used to communicate with routers, which are computers on the Internet that make decisions on how to route or ship packets—they decide which paths are best.

Connecting to a NetWare Server

Let's move away from the world of theory and down to how you would actually connect to a NetWare server with Windows NT 4 Workstation.

1. Go to the Network control panel. Note the tabs at the top of the window.

2. Click the Services tab.

3. Now select Client Service for NetWare. The window you get should look like the one shown in Figure 19.2. Click OK.

Figure 19.2.
*NT builds a list of
services from which
to choose.*

4. NT now needs to know where the install files are located. For most people, that will be on the CD-ROM, so you would enter a path similar to the following:

D:\I386

If your install files are on your hard drive, point it to the location on the hard drive.

5. If you have other protocols or services installed, you might get a message similar to the one in Figure 19.3. The correct answer lies in how your office network is set up.

Figure 19.3.

Installing protocols when other services are loaded might invoke questions such as this.

You have now successfully loaded the Client Service for NetWare. When you go through the steps just outlined, several other items are installed at the same time in order for the client to work properly: NWLink IPX/SPX Compatible Transport protocol along with NWLink NetBIOS. You need to make sure that they were installed, however. Go to the Network control panel and click Protocols. If you see both of them, then everything is OK. If not, follow these instructions:

1. Open the Network control panel.
2. Click the Protocols tab at the top of the window.
3. Click the Add button. You should see a window that looks similar to the one shown in Figure 19.4.

Figure 19.4.

Adding protocols is easy with Windows NT.

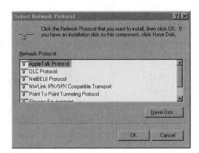

4. Locate the NWLink IPX/SPX Compatible Transport, click it, and click Add.
5. You will then need to point the installer to the location of the install files (i386).
6. Click Continue.

Network Bindings

Now that you have installed the service and protocols, take a look at how to set up bindings. When you establish bindings, you are essentially telling NT which protocols and services should be tied or linked to what other protocols and services. Follow these four steps to set the bindings for NetWare:

19

1. Go to the Network control panel.
2. Select the Bindings tab at the top of the window (see Figure 19.5).

Figure 19.5.

*When setting bindings,
you have to use this
configuration box.*

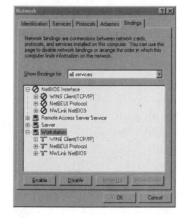

3. Make sure that the Show Bindings for: list is displaying "all services."
4. Look at Client Service for NetWare and make sure there is not a circle with a line drawn through it next to it. This would indicate that the service was disabled. If it is disabled, click Enable at the bottom of the window.

NT now has both your protocols and your bindings correctly set, and you can identify your computer. Follow these steps:

1. Open the Network control panel.
2. Select the Identification tab at the top of the window. You should see a window similar to the one shown in Figure 19.6.

Figure 19.6.

*Identifying your com-
puter is very easy.*

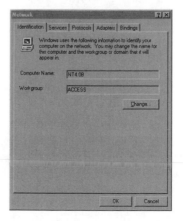

3. Select the Change button and you will see something that looks like Figure 19.7.

Figure 19.7.

At the same time that you assign a name to your computer, you can join a workgroup or domain.

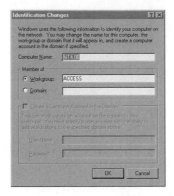

4. Type a name for your computer. If you are also planning on doing peer-to-peer sharing with Windows 3.*x*, Windows 95, or NT computers, then you'll need to join either a workgroup or domain.

5. Choose OK. You are now finished with the major part of configuring your network settings.

6. Restart your computer.

Choosing a Preferred Server

Now when you log on to NT, it will ask you to set a preferred server. Your choices are to select a preferred server (a NetWare server that will authenticate your user name and password), or you can choose a Default Tree and Context.

The preferred server will enable you to authenticate with a NetWare 3.*x* server using bindery emulation (the bindery is a file used by 3.*x* and 2.*x* NetWare servers and is used to authenticate users). If you choose None in the preferred server area, NT will go ahead and use the nearest NetWare server to authenticate you.

On a NetWare server that is running 4.*x* and has been configured to run NDS (a kind of parallel to the bindery), you'll want to select the second option: Default Tree and Context. You might need to talk to your system administrator about this part of the setup. The first part here, the tree, will locate the server in your organization's hierarchy, and the context will determine the manner in which you interact with the server.

Using the Microsoft Client to Connect to Resources

Fortunately, connecting to NetWare file and printer servers is not much different than connecting to other servers. This section discusses mapping drives and other ways of connecting.

1. Launch the Network Neighborhood by double-clicking the Network Neighborhood icon.

2. You will see two sets of icons: one for Microsoft networks, and another for NetWare networks.

3. By double-clicking the Microsoft Windows Network icon, you can see all the servers and workstations under that category. The Microsoft Windows Network includes Windows for Workgroups, Windows 95, and Windows NT computers.

If you want to see what is available on a particular Microsoft server, double-click it, and you will see what volumes and printers it is sharing. Of course, you will need permissions to see what is available.

After you double-click the server icon, you will also see that the title bar to the new window informs you what server you are looking at. This is very useful because it is easy to have your screen so cluttered with windows that it is difficult to tell where you are.

In order to copy files to your local machine from a remote computer, follow these steps:

1. By double-clicking the NetWare or Compatible Network icon, you can see all the servers and workstations under that category. To find out what is available on any item, double-click it.

2. To copy a file to your local machine, arrange the windows so you can see the file you want to copy, and you can see the destination on your computer's hard drive. Then, simply drag the file to its destination.

3. Another method of copying files is to position the mouse pointer on top of the file, and then click the *right* mouse button, not the left, and select the Send To option. In fact, you can use this same method to copy any file, whether it is local or remote.

To add additional locations to the Send To folder, follow these steps:

1. Find the Send To folder by going to the Start menu, to Find, and then to Files or Folders. When the dialog box comes up, type Sent To. Click Find Now.

2. Make a shortcut to any common places you send files to. For example, a temp folder on your C: drive would be one possibility.

3. Drag these shortcuts to the Send To folder.

4. Make sure the new items appear by right-clicking an object, and then going to the Send To option to see if they are there.

When you connect to a NetWare volume, your user name and password must be authenticated by the server that "serves" that volume.

1. To map a drive, open the Network Neighborhood and locate the directory you want to map.

2. Go to the File menu and select Map Network Drive.

3. A dialog box appears, and if you click the Drive box, you can select a drive letter. Make sure you choose a letter that is not currently in use (which means you cannot choose A:, C:, or D: if you have a second drive or CD-ROM drive).

4. Type in your username in the Connect As box. You need to type a name here only if you want to connect as a different user than the one you're logged in to the server as; otherwise, you can leave this field blank.

5. If you would like to be automatically reconnected the next time you log on to this workstation, make sure Reconnect at Logon is checked. Otherwise, click it to take the check mark off.

6. Finally, choose OK, and the drive is now mapped to the drive letter you assigned to it.

Workshop

The Workshop helps you solidify the skills you learned this hour.

Glossary

application layer   In reference to the OSI seven-layer model, the application layer is the top layer, layer seven. This is the layer that you interact with directly. It might be WordPerfect (saving a file to a remote server), or it might be FTP, Telnet, a Web browser, and so forth.

IPX   IPX is a protocol used in the seven-layer model. It stands for Internet Packet Exchange and operates at the network layer, which is layer three. It is responsible for transmitting and routing data.

NDS   NetWare Directory Service, or NDS, is a naming service used by NetWare 4 and higher servers. It is based on X.500, enabling it to be compatible with other directories. This database contains information about users, groups, servers, printers, and so on. As opposed to the bindery, used by earlier NetWare systems, NDS enables you to log on to a network rather than a certain server.

19

NetWare   NetWare is the name Novell gave to its family of network operating systems.

network layer   The third layer in the OSI seven-layer model. Examples of layer three protocols include Internet Protocol, IP, and Internet Packet Exchange, IPX.

OSI model   A model developed by the ISO group to develop standards that protocols should adhere to at each of the different network layers.

protocols   At each layer of the OSI model, protocols handle different functions. Standards have been set for how each of the layers is to function in order to enable them to be compatible with other protocols.

SPX   SPX, or Sequenced Packet Exchange, is a protocol used on NetWare networks. It operates at the fourth layer, the transport layer.

transport layer   The transport layer of the OSI model is layer four and is responsible for breaking up the data (or reassembling it on the receiving end), error checking, and handling certain aspects of the connection between the two computers.

Exercises

1. If you are on a network that contains both Microsoft machines and NetWare machines, click the Network Neighborhood. Can you tell by looking at the icons which computers are running Microsoft software and which are running Novell software?

2. Practice sharing a directory on your computer using the information in this lesson and in Hour 11, "Security: Planning a Secure System." What important issues should you keep in mind when sharing a resource?

3. If there are any Novell servers that you use on a regular basis, map a drive to them. Do you know how to make the connection permanent?

19

Hour 20

Browser Services

by Darren Schubert

When some of the resources (file directories and printers) are shared for use by the other users on your network, how can you be sure that those network users who need to use your resources will know that the resources exist or know how to make a connection to them? How, in fact, are you to know what other computers and resources exist on the network and are accessible to your Windows NT Workstation computer?

Assume for a moment that your network is composed of hundreds of computers. If you had a list of all of these computers, including their shared resources and descriptions, to look through (or *browse*), then you could see what was available and decide what you wanted to use. However, if each of these computers attempted to create its own list, there would be a great deal of inefficiency because each computer would have to perform the same work that every other computer had already performed. Fortunately, Windows NT Workstation (and even the general Microsoft Windows Network architecture) provides a method of collecting and distributing a centralized list of computers and shared resources known as a *browse list*. In other words, only one or a few computers on a network are assigned the tasks of collecting and distributing the browse list. Computers that perform these collection and distribution tasks are known as *browser servers*. Computers that do not collect or distribute the browse list are simply *browser clients*. When a browser client needs that list, it just sends a request to those computers that are maintaining the browse list.

A reality about computers and networks is that computers can be turned off, resource shares can be changed or unshared, and many unexpected things can happen to routers, bridges, and hubs—all of which could make some shared resources on a network unavailable to those who might want to use them. Therefore, you would want any changes to be reflected in that browse list, and done so in a timely manner.

Another reality involves how computers are deployed and grouped throughout an organization. Some computers are members of an NT domain, whereas others are part of a workgroup. To you, the user, it should not matter whether an organization is centralized into one domain or decentralized into multiple workgroups and domains; if you need to use a resource of a computer on another workgroup, then you will need to see that computer in the browse list.

Computer users must place high demands on this browse list so that the preceding realities do not hinder their work. These are very stringent demands, and they are not always met, but the browse list should conform to the following requirements:

- ☐ Accuracy and timeliness. The browse list must include only those computers and shared resources that exist and are currently available for use.

- ☐ Completeness. The browse list must include other domains and workgroups (in fact, all domains and workgroups of which the network is aware).

- ☐ Redundancy. The storage and replication of the browse list must be such that you can see an accurate listing even if some computers are shut down or if a network hardware device fails.

- ☐ Low Overhead. The collection, maintenance, and distribution of the browse list should not adversely affect the performance of the user's computer or the network.

- ☐ Scalability and adaptability. Browser services must function regardless of the complexity of the network or the network protocols in use by the network.

With this browse list, you can view all the resources that are available on your network. Instead of displaying the shared resources in one flat list, each individual resource (whether it be a printer, directory, and so on) is logically grouped under the computer from which it is shared. Also, each computer is grouped under the domain or workgroup to which it belongs.

TIME SAVER

If you want a shared resource to be omitted from the browse list, append the $ character to the share name when you first create it. When any resource ends in $, it is a hidden share. You can still connect to it and use it, but you must know the resource's computer and share name.

The browse list is used when you are performing an action in which you want to use a shared network resource but you do not know how to refer to it, such as the functions in the following list. In other words, you don't know the name of the share name or which computer is sharing the resource.

☐ Network Neighborhood. If you double-click this icon, a window such as in Figure 20.1 appears in which you can see the other computers in your workgroup or domain.

Figure 20.1.

The local browse list in the Network Neighborhood window.

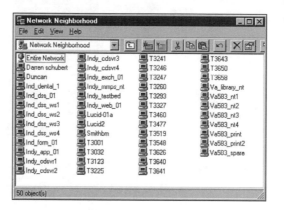

By double-clicking the Entire Network icon, you'll see all of the domains and workgroups (as in Figure 20.2). If you click the icon of a different domain or workgroup, you can view its computers and resources. This example assumes that you have no other network client installed. If you've also installed the Client Service for NetWare network service, the window will contain two listings or icons: Microsoft Windows Network and NetWare or Compatible Network. Domains and workgroups—and their members—are found within the Microsoft Windows Network while NetWare servers are found within the NetWare or Compatible Network.

20

Figure 20.2.

The list of all domains and workgroups in the Microsoft Windows Network window.

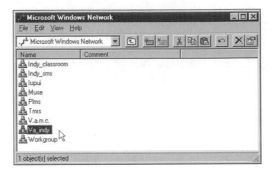

If you click a computer's icon, a window such as Figure 20.3 appears from which you are able to see what resources it is sharing.

Figure 20.3.

A computer's list of shared resources window.

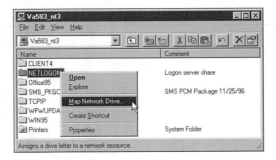

☐ Windows NT Explorer. The browse list is used when you attempt to map a network drive using NT Explorer. First, NT Explorer can be launched by clicking Start | Programs | Windows NT Explorer. There are two methods to map a network drive using NT Explorer. In the first method (shown in Figure 20.4), you click Tools in the menu bar, and then select Map Network Drive. In the second method, you right-click the My Computer icon, and then select Map Network Drive. With either method, you can view the shared directories of each computer in the browse list (as in Figure 20.5).

JUST A MINUTE

Hidden shares (sometimes known as administrative shares) will not be visible in the browse list—even to users with Domain Administrator privileges. If you want a resource to show up in the browse list, do not make it a hidden share.

20

Figure 20.4.

Mapping a network drive from the NT Explorer window.

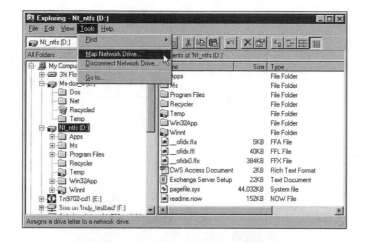

Figure 20.5.

The Map Network Drive window.

☐ Add Printer wizard. The easiest way to add a printer is by using this wizard. To set up a printer, select Start | Settings | Printers | Add Printer. At this point, you have two options: My Computer or Network Print Server. Select the My Computer option only if you have a printer attached directly to your computer. If you select the Network Print Server option, you will see the browse list of the entire network, modified so that you see all the shared printers first (as in Figure 20.6) followed by the computers in the browse list.

☐ Command prompt. If you must be old-fashioned, you can exit to a DOS command prompt and issue a net view command, which will result in the display of the computers in the browse list. In order to view the available shares, you must then issue another command, net view \\computer_name.

Figure 20.6.
The Connect to Printer window showing all shared printers.

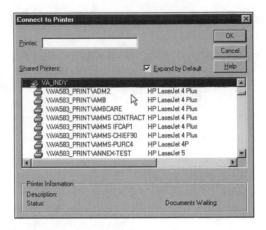

Both Windows NT Workstation and Server are capable of maintaining this browse list (of all available domains, workgroups, and computers) by running the NT service known simply as the *Computer Browser service*.

Installing the Computer Browser Service

By default, Windows NT 4 Workstation installs the Computer Browser service at the Network Services Setup during the Windows NT Workstation installation. To verify that the service is installed (or to install, deinstall, or reinstall it), you can go to the Services tab of the Network setup dialog box, which you can open from the control panel. From here, you may add or remove the service. You may not, in any way, configure the Computer Browser service from this location. The only method of doing so is by modifying the NT Registry (see "Configuring the Computer Browser Service," later in this hour).

JUST A MINUTE

In order to install a service (such as Computer Browser), you must be logged on to your NT Workstation computer with an account that has administrative privileges (is a member of the Administrators local group).

JUST A MINUTE

Under Windows NT Server, you can configure the Computer Browser service from the Network Service setup windows by double-clicking the service. The only added functionality from this location is the ability to add other specific domains (and workgroups) for the Browser service to track.

20

Browser Roles and Functions

Ever hear the saying "Nothing's easy?" Well, true to form, understanding the concepts and names relating to browsing is no exception. As discussed earlier, there are some computers that must create the browse list and send it to others when requested. The best way to understand what is occurring is to know what your computer is capable of versus what your computer is assigned to do right now. For example, your Windows NT Workstation computer is capable of doing it all: it can be the primary caretaker of the browse list, it can play a secondary role in just distributing the list, and it can do as little as request the browse list from others. In order to meet the requirements of adaptability and redundancy, computers are assigned roles and responsibilities based on the outcomes of *Browser Elections* (see "Browser Elections," later in this lesson). The following is a list of the classifications into which computers can be divided based upon their roles and actions:

- Non-Browsers
- Potential Browsers
- Backup Browsers
- Master Browser
- Preferred Master Browser
- Domain Master Browser

The following sections explain the responsibilities held by each of these types of computers and the actions they perform.

Non-Browsers

Non-Browsers are computers that do not maintain, or store, the browse list. They are also known as *browser clients* because they issue requests to other computers that then serve the browse list to them. When the browser client receives that browse list, the client is able to see the available network resources. All computers running Windows (Windows for Workgroups, Windows 95, Windows NT Workstation or Server) are capable of being browser clients. A computer is considered to be a non-browser when it is specifically configured to not play the role of a *browser server*. (See "Configuring the Computer Browser Service," later in this lesson.) The functions of Non-Browsers include the following:

- Announcements: At regular intervals, every computer will announce itself to the Master Browser so that it can be included in the browse list. The message to the Master Browser includes the computer's name and its shared resources. Every computer, no matter what its role, will make these announcements to the Master Browser.

20

☐ Browse requests: When a computer's user performs an action that is dependent on the contents of the browse list, then the computer sends out a message requesting it.

TIME SAVER

If you do not have a small network, you should make sure that your slowest machines are specifically configured to be Non-Browsers. If an underpowered machine were ever to be elected a Master Browser, the entire network's browsing performance could seriously suffer, if not become unavailable altogether.

Potential Browsers

Potential Browsers are computers that are capable of maintaining and distributing the browse list, but only as needed. If there are no "better" computers that are configured to be Backup Browsers, a computer that is configured to be a Potential Browser may be promoted by the Master Browser computer to be a Backup Browser. Following the same logic, if there is no "better" computer to be the Master Browser, then the Potential Browser computer will assume that responsibility. For example, if your Windows NT Workstation computer is part of a small workgroup consisting of Windows for Workgroups 3.11 (WFW) and Windows 95 computers, it is most likely that your computer will become the Master Browser.

JUST A MINUTE

If a Potential Browser is not assigned to be a Backup Browser or Master Browser, then it does not maintain its own browse list. Instead, it functions as a browser client.

JUST A MINUTE

By default, a Windows NT Workstation computer is configured to be a Potential Master Browser.

Backup Browsers

Although their name might imply a secondary role, Backup Browsers play an active part in distributing the browse list to browser clients that issue requests. Backup Browsers receive and store the browse list after they request it from the Master Browser. In other words, they do not play an active role in collecting information from every computer. Periodically, an updated browse list is sent to the Backup Browsers by the Master Browser. This updated list is *maintained*, or stored, until the next list arrives. When the Backup Browser receives a request from a browser client, it sends the browse list, or serves it, to the browser client.

Master Browser

The Master Browser is the computer that collects and maintains the centralized browse list and distributes it to the Backup Browsers. This computer is responsible for collecting information from all the computers in its domain or workgroup, as well as collecting a list from all of the other domains and workgroups that might exist on the network. With this information, it forms the browse list that contains the available resources. Depending on the characteristics of the network (see the section "Number of Browsers in a Domain or Workgroup"), the Master Browser computer can serve the browse list directly to browser clients or indirectly through backup browsers. Simplified, the functions of a Master Browser include

- ☐ Receiving announcements.
- ☐ Building the browse list using the information received in the announcements.
- ☐ Distributing the browse list to its Backup Browsers, if any exist.
- ☐ Responding to clients that request the browse list or the list of Backup Browsers.
- ☐ Promoting Potential Browsers to Backup Browsers, when needed.
- ☐ If the Master Browser is also the Domain Master Browser, it will announce itself to Master Browsers of other domains and workgroups.
- ☐ If the Master Browser is also the Domain Master Browser, it will receive announcements (and browse lists) from other domains and workgroups and incorporate those remote browse lists into its own.

Preferred Master Browser

The Preferred Master Browser is a computer that is configured so that it has preferential treatment when the Master Browser is being elected (see "Browser Elections," later in this lesson). Making a computer a Preferred Master Browser does not mean that it will necessarily become the Master Browser. By default, when an NT Server is configured to be the Primary Domain Controller of an NT domain, it is also configured to be the Preferred Master Browser. The default for all other computers, including Windows NT Workstation, is that they are not the Preferred Master Browser.

20

Domain Master Browser

In a Windows NT domain, there is always one computer, the Primary Domain Controller, that will be responsible for the centralized browse list of all computers in that domain, especially for use when computers in its domain are on different TCP/IP subnetworks (see "WAN Browsing and Network Protocol Considerations," later in this lesson). For NT domains that are on "simple" networks, the Domain Master Browser and the Master Browser will be one and the same: the Primary Domain Controller.

JUST A MINUTE

> There should never be a case in which the Primary Domain Controller is not the Domain Master Browser. If the Primary Domain Controller were to be shut down or otherwise network-disabled, problems would occur (see "Browser Service Failures," later in this lesson).

TIME SAVER

> If your domain's Primary Domain Controller fails (or will otherwise be unavailable for an appreciable amount of time), a Backup Domain Controller (BDC) should be promoted by an administrator to be the Primary Domain Controller. Not only will domain administration continue, but the new PDC will also become the new Domain Master Browser, and the domain's browsing functions will not be affected.

Browser Operations

The Browser Service functions through elections, announcements, requests, distribution, and shutdowns. Failures also occur. Following are detailed explanations of each occurrence.

Announcements

In order for a Master Browser to create a list of computers, it must be aware of what computers exist on the network. Awareness occurs when a computer (network-enabled) sends a message to the Master Browser known as an *announcement*. Windows NT Server, Windows NT Workstation, Windows 95, Windows for Workgroups, or LAN Manager computers are all capable of sending these announcements. When the Master Browser receives the announcement, which contains the computer's name and shared resource information, it adds that computer to the browse list.

Non-Browsers, Potential Browsers, and Backup Browsers all announce themselves in the same manner. A computer will announce itself to the Master Browser initially every minute for the first five minutes, but it then extends that interval to once every two minutes, then to four, then to eight, and then finally to once every 12 minutes. If the Master Browser does not hear from the computer for three consecutive announcement periods, the Master Browser will remove the computer from the list.

Browser Requests

At some point in your use of a computer, you will probably perform some action that requires your computer to view the browse list. The first time that this occurs, your computer is unaware of who it should turn to. It does know enough to send a very general request to the Master Browser, but not for the browse list. Instead, the request (called a *GetBackupList* request) is for a list of computers to which to send a browse request. This is where it gets tricky. If there aren't any Backup Browsers for the workgroup or domain, the Master Browser will respond with only the name of itself. Your computer will store the name of, and make all browse requests to, the Master Browser.

If there are one or more Backup Browsers in a workgroup or domain, the Master Browser will respond to the request with the list of all existing Backup Browsers. The requesting browser client will choose up to three of these computers to store in its memory. It will then issue a request to one of the three Backup Browsers for the browse list. Thereafter, any time that the client needs an updated browse list, it won't even bother to ask the Master Browser. It will simply send its request to one of the Backup Browsers, which it chooses at random. By delegating some responsibility (that of sending the browse list to clients) to the Backup Browsers, the Master Browser computer ensures that it is not overloaded in trying to service all of the browser clients. If your NT Workstation computer's current role is as a browser client and it does not receive a reply to its browse request, it will log a Warning Event in your computer's event logs. The following is an Event Detail of type Warning from the author's NT 4 Workstation's System Event log: "The browser was unable to retrieve a list of servers from the browser master \\INDY_TESTBED on the network \Device\NetBT. The data is the error code."

JUST A MINUTE

NetBT = NetBIOS over TCP/IP. This refers to the network protocol of that particular browse list. See "WAN Browsing and Network Protocol Considerations," later in this lesson.

20

Distribution of the Browse List

In order to provide the redundancy, accuracy, and completeness that are required from the Computer Browser service, Master Browsers must periodically be reminded to send an updated browse list to their Backup Browsers. Every 15 minutes (but not all at the same time), a Backup Browser will send a request to the Master Browser stating that it wants the Master Browser's current browse list, whose contents will include not only its own domain or workgroup but also those computers and resources of other domains and workgroups on the network.

Browser Service Shutdowns

When a Backup Browser computer is shut down gracefully, it should send an announcement to the Master Browser stating that the computer will no longer be available. When a Master Browser computer is shut down gracefully, it should broadcast an election datagram message so that a new Master Browser will be elected. It will also log a System Event in your event logs. For example, on the author domain's PDC (the Domain Master Browser), a Shutdown and Restart command will result in two System Event log entries of type Information: one during the shutdown and one during the restart. The first will be "The browser has forced an election on network \Device\NetBT because a Master Browser was stopped." In fact, the PDC was that Master Browser. The second log entry will be "The browser has forced an election on network \Device\NetBT because a Windows NT Server (or domain master) was started." Again, the PDC is referring to itself.

Under all but the worst circumstances, a Windows NT Server or Workstation computer will shut down gracefully and successfully remove itself from the browse list. Windows 95 is "rumored" to do this as well, but don't hold your breath. The Windows for Workgroups and Windows 95 "operating systems" are not Windows NT. Enough said.

Browser Service Failures

A failure occurs when a computer on the network fails to perform an action on which other computers are depending. When a client requests a list of Backup Browsers from a Master Browser, it expects a reply. If it does not receive a reply to its request, then the Master Browser has "failed" and the client will force the election of a new Master Browser. When a non-Master Browser computer (including browser clients, Potential Browsers, and Backup Browsers) fails, it no longer sends announcements to the Master Browser. When the Master Browser does not receive an announcement from a computer for three consecutive announcement periods, the Master Browser will remove the computer from the browse list.

If a Backup Browser fails and its name has been given to any clients, any subsequent attempts made by a client to contact this Backup Browser will fail when the client does not receive a

20

reply. The client will then randomly choose one of the other Backup Browsers in its list and re-attempt the request. If all of the Backup Browsers in a client's list have failed, then the client will reissue another GetBackupList request to the Master Browser in order to get a current list of Backup Browsers.

Because Backup Browsers request the browse list every 15 minutes from the Master Browser, they will notice a Master Browser failure within 15 minutes of its occurrence. When a Backup Browser does not receive the browse list after making a request for it, the Backup Browser will issue an election datagram to force an election.

JUST A MINUTE

For testing purposes, I disabled the network functionality of my Master Browser, an NT 4 Server named INDY_TESTBED. Upon inspection of the event logs of my NT 4 Workstation computer (which had been functioning as a Backup Browser), I found that my computer had actually issued a total of ten requests (two requests every two minutes over a period of eight minutes—yes, that is ten requests) and logged ten System Event Warnings: "The browser was unable to retrieve a list of servers from the browser master \\INDY_TESTBED on the network \Device\NetBT. The data is the error code." Only after the last pair of failed requests (a full eight minutes after the first failed request) did my NT Workstation log the System Event of type Error: "The browser service has failed to retrieve the backup list too many times on transport \Device\NetBT. The backup browser is stopping."

CAUTION

If a Master Browser were to fail on a network with no Backup Browser (and no Potential Browsers), then browsing services in the domain or workgroup would be unavailable. If browsing is the least bit important, you should make sure that your network has a Backup Browser or a few Potential Browsers.

CAUTION

In a multisubnet TCP/IP network, the failure of a Domain Master Browser would effectively cut off intersubnet browsing because each subnet's Master Browsers would not be able to see any other subnet's Master Browser and could not distribute the browse list. The Master Browser of each subnet would only be capable of seeing computers on its own "local" subnetwork. Although it would take up to 15 minutes, all computers on "remote" subnetworks would eventually be removed from the browse list. (See "WAN Browsing and Network Protocol Considerations," later in this lesson, for a detailed explanation.)

20

Browser Elections

Proper and efficient browsing assumes that every computer on the network knows its place and behaves properly. With hundreds of machines on a complicated network, there has to be a simple and effective method to assign every computer a role. Otherwise, there would be chaos. The method used by the Computer Browser service is called an *election*. Elections will occur under the following circumstances:

- ☐ The Computer Browser service starts on a computer configured as a Preferred Master Browser.
- ☐ The Computer Browser service starts on a Windows NT domain controller.
- ☐ The Computer Browser service stops on a Master Browser (such as when the computer itself is shut down gracefully).
- ☐ A computer cannot locate a Master Browser.

The Election Process

An election begins when a computer broadcasts an *election datagram*. An election datagram is a message that has a computer's name and *election criteria*. Because all browser servers can receive these election datagrams, each one will examine the issuing computer's election criteria. If a computer determines that its own election criteria is not greater than that of the datagram that it received, it will essentially "give up" and wait until the election is over before it attempts to determine which computer is the new Master Browser. All the browser servers whose election criteria is greater than (or better than) the computer that issued the first election datagram will send out their own election datagram. This is referred to as an *election-in-progress* state.

Eventually, there will be one computer that sends out an election datagram to which no other computer will be able to respond, as no other computer has higher election criteria. The remaining computer then enters the *running election* state in which it sends out up to four more election datagrams, just to be sure that it is the true winner. If no other computer responds with an election datagram, then it wins the election and becomes the Master Browser.

The following tables show the computers in order (from highest to lowest) of their election criteria.

Hierarchy of primary election criteria

Primary Domain Controller (Windows NT Server)
Windows NT 4 Server
Windows NT 3.51 Server

20

Hierarchy of primary election criteria

Windows NT 4 Workstation
Windows NT 3.51 Workstation
Windows 95
Windows for Workgroups

Hierarchy of secondary election criteria

Preferred Master Browser
Currently a Master Browser
MaintainServerList=Yes
Currently a Backup Browser
Length of time the Browser has been running
Lower alpha-numerical name

As you can see, a Primary Domain Controller has the highest election criteria and will always win an election. After that, the next highest criteria is the type and version of operating system that a computer is running. The only purpose for the secondary election criteria are for instances in which two or more computers' primary election criteria are in a tie (such as two Windows 95 computers).

JUST A MINUTE

The Network Operating System version does not matter for a PDC. A Windows NT 3.1 Server that is a PDC will win an election over a Windows NT 4 Server.

TIME SAVER

If you believe that browsing services are unreasonably slow, use the NT Event Viewer to look at your Windows NT Workstation's System Event logs to see if there is Browser contention. The logs may show that other computers, usually those pesky WFW computers, are issuing election datagrams when they shouldn't. (See "WFW Computers Acting as Browser Servers," later in this lesson).

20

Browser Election Scenarios

Now that you understand the theory of browser elections, take a look at how an election might actually play out in some assumed computer environments.

Scenario 1

Your coworker has a Windows NT 4 Workstation that is functioning as the Master Browser of a workgroup whose other computers consist of mere Windows for Workgroup machines. After you've read this book completely, you install Windows NT 4 Workstation on your computer as well, and you configure it to be a Preferred Master Browser by setting IsDomainMaster = Yes (see "Configuring the Computer Browser Service," later in this lesson). When your computer starts the Computer Browser service, an election will be held. Both of your computers will tie in regards to the Network Operating System and Version, but your computer will barely win the election because a Preferred Master Browser has priority over a running Master Browser.

Scenario 2

Take Scenario 2 a bit further by assuming that your Windows NT 4 Workstation computer, now the current Master Browser, has a MaintainServerList = Auto. Your coworker is jealous and decides to modify his Registry so that his computer is also a Preferred Master Browser (IsDomainMaster = Yes) and its MaintainServerList = Yes. His computer will force an election, but your computer will still come out on top and win the election as the Master Browser. Why? The NOS and version are the same, the Preferred Master Browser settings are the same, and even though the MaintainServerList settings are in your coworker's favor, your computer is currently the Master Browser and so it has higher election criteria.

Scenario 3

Finally, assume that your two NT 4 Workstation computers have all of the same criteria (except for their names). One is named Alpha while the other is named Bravo; Alpha will win the election because A is lower in value than B.

Timing Issues

The Computer Browser service is not perfect by any means, and the requirements mentioned earlier are not always met. For example, there could be instances in which a browser client will attempt to connect to a shared resource from the browse list only to find that it is unavailable or does not exist. Because changes are not instantaneously transferred to the browse list and distribution occurs periodically, it can take up to almost an hour (actually about 51 minutes) before a specific change is reflected in what a browser client sees. You may read on if you want to understand how this could happen; otherwise, just take my word for it.

A Master Browser will not remove a computer from its own browse list until that computer has not announced itself for three consecutive announcement periods. For example, if your NT Workstation computer announces itself at 1:00 p.m. and at 1:12 p.m., the Master

20

Browser would be expecting additional once-every-twelve-minute announcements at 1:24 p.m., 1:36 p.m., and 1:48 p.m. If the Master Browser does not receive at least one announcement by 1:48 p.m., it will remove your NT Workstation computer from its browse list. Now assume that a Backup Browser has just received the Master Browser's list at 1:47 p.m. A client who requests the browse list from that Backup Browser (at any time before the Backup Browser receives the new list at 1:47 p.m. + 15 minutes = 2:02 p.m.) would still see your NT Workstation in the browse list.

To sum that all up: A change might not be correctly seen in the browse list for (3 announcement periods × announcement interval of 12 minutes) + 15 minutes = 51 minutes.

Configuring the Computer Browser Service

Now that you know how to install the service and the details of how browsing operates, you can learn how to modify your NT Workstation to meet the network's needs. Again, the only way to configure the service is through the NT Registry. You can modify the Registry by typing REGEDT32.EXE from the Start | Run menu.

The two Registry entries that are perhaps the most useful (and safest) to modify for browsing purposes are MaintainServerList and IsDomainMaster. Both entries are located (as seen in Figure 20.7) in the following subkey:

HKEY_LOCAL_Machine\System\CurrentControlSet\Services\Browser\Parameters

There are three possible values of type REG_SZ for the MaintainServerList parameter. There are two possible values of type REG_SZ for the IsDomainMaster parameter. Table 20.1 shows the default values for these parameters.

Figure 20.7.

Browser parameters data in the NT Registry window.

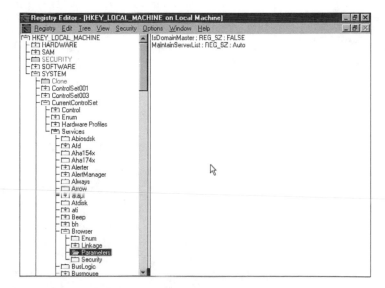

20

The possible values for the MaintainServerList browser parameter are

- ☐ FALSE (or NO). This computer will never function as a browser server, only as a browser client (non-browser).
- ☐ TRUE (or YES). This computer will be a browser server, either as a Master Browser or Backup Browser. It will maintain a browse list and send it to requesting browser clients.
- ☐ AUTO. This computer will be a Potential Browser and may or may not become a browser server, depending on the number of computers and current browser servers. The Master Browser will notify this computer that it should be a Backup Browser, if the Master Browser deems it necessary.

The possible values for the IsDomainMaster browser parameter are

- ☐ TRUE (or YES). This computer is a Preferred Master Browser so that it will receive preferential status over other computers during Master Browser elections.
- ☐ FALSE (or NO). This computer is not a Preferred Master Browser.

Table 20.1. NT Registry default settings for browser parameters.

Parameter	Windows NT Workstation	Windows NT Server
MaintainServerList	Auto	True/Yes
IsDomainMaster	False/No	False (True if PDC)

CAUTION

Be very careful when you modify the NT Registry. One mistake (such as accidentally deleting a key) could result in serious, adverse repercussions on a Windows NT Workstation computer or the entire network. Know what you are trying to accomplish before you run REGEDT32. When you are finished, close the Registry—never leave it open; otherwise, you are just asking for trouble.

Number of Browsers in a Domain or Workgroup

As always, networks can be simple or complex. In this case, there is some added complexity when the number of computers increases in a workgroup or domain. If you have just a few computers, then you can easily get by with one computer (the Master Browser) serving the browse list to those who request it. However, as computers are added to a workgroup or domain, you can expect the number of browse requests to go up as well, causing additional work to be performed by your Master Browser. It is for this reason that a Master Browser needs Backup Browsers. Together, they are able to balance the overhead (CPU utilization) that is needed to build and maintain the list.

The number of Backup Browsers that a Master Browser needs is determined by the total number of computers in the workgroup or domain and can be simplified as shown in Table 20.2.

Table 20.2. Number of browser servers on a domain or workgroup.

Number of Computers	Master Browsers	Backup Browsers
1	1	0
2 to 31	1	1
32 to 63	1	2
64 to 95	1	3

For each additional 32 computers added to the workgroup or domain, the Master Browser will attempt to promote another Potential Browser to the role of Backup Browser.

JUST A MINUTE

The preceding is a guide to the number of Backup Browsers that a Master Browser will attempt to create, not the number to which it will be limited. If there are 10 Windows NT Workstations whose MaintainServerList Registry settings were all set to True, then there would be one Master Browser and nine Backup Browsers even if those 10 computers were the only computers in the workgroup.

JUST A MINUTE

The number of Backup Browsers depends on the existence of computers whose Computer Browser service is configured to enable the computer to become a browser server. For example, if a workgroup consisted of two NT Workstation computers, the only way there could be a Master Browser and a Backup Browser is if both computers' MaintainServerList Registry settings were set to Yes/True or Auto.

20

Technical Issues

If, up to this point, you simply wanted to learn the concepts and general operations of network browsing, then the rest of this hour might be more technical than you need for now. On the other hand, if you're hungry for even more knowledge, read on.

WFW Computers Acting as Browser Servers

If you have machines that are running NT Server, NT Workstation, or even Windows 95, then you most likely do not need any of your Windows for Workgroups (WFW) computers to be configured as browser servers. Think you don't have any WFW browser servers? Don't be so sure. Unless a WFW computer is specifically set to be a Non-Browser, the default seems to be that it is a Potential Browser. I have personally seen instances in which there were "election broadcast storms" on networks (mine, unfortunately) with a large number of WFW computers. These "election broadcast storms" were a result of the contention of multiple WFW computers as they attempted to win the election of the Master Browser. The only way to be sure that this situation is avoided is to add the line `MaintainServerList=No` under the `[Network]` heading in the WFW computer's `SYSTEM.INI` file.

WAN Browsing and Network Protocol Considerations

If this lesson's concepts were not yet complicated enough, understand that there is a completely separate and distinct browse list for *each* protocol in use on the network. Each protocol has its own set of Master and Backup Browsers. For workgroups on simple networks, NetBEUI (NBF) and IPX/SPX might work fine. For larger workgroups and domains on complex, routed networks, TCP/IP is really the best choice.

If your domain uses TCP/IP and consists of multiple IP subnets, each subnet will have its own set of Master and Backup Browsers. Therefore, the "Subnet Master Browser" will maintain the browse list of all computers on its local subnetwork. Inter-subnetwork browsing is functional due to the Domain Master Browser (provided that `WINS` or `LMHOSTS` files are properly set up), which collects or distributes all the lists from or to each Subnet Master Browser. The Domain Master Browser compiles all the lists from each subnetwork to create the browse list of all the computers in the domain. It is also the Domain Master Browser that communicates and exchanges browse lists with other Domain Master Browsers and Master Browsers of other workgroups.

JUST A MINUTE

If your Domain Master Browser were to fail, the browse list would become localized because each Subnet Master Browser would only be able to provide a browse list containing the computers in the local network segment. All computers on remote IP subnetworks will eventually disappear from the browse list.

TIME SAVER

Implement WINS (Windows Internet Naming System) for the most complete, reliable browsing services for your domain.

TIME SAVER

To ensure proper browsing functionality when using RAS, make sure that your remote NT Workstation has the same workgroup name as the workgroup or domain into which you are dialing.

Because the Domain Master Browser is the communications hub for the multiple TCP/IP subnetworks, if your computer is a member of a workgroup spanning subnetworks, you will actually have two distinct, separately functioning workgroups that just happen to have the same name. Workgroups have no Domain Master Browser.

TIME SAVER

In a workgroup setting, it would be wise to configure a powerful computer to have the Preferred Master Browser status because there would be no PDC. This would give you more control over the outcome of browser elections. In a domain setting, it would be wise to "spread out" the placement of your NT Servers and NT Workstations so at least one, if not three, NT computer was running on each TCP/IP subnetwork.

20

IPX/SPX and NBF (NetBEUI Frame) don't have a Domain Master Browser because they need only one Master Browser for the entire network. IPX/SPX does not need it because it is not limited by physical segmentation. In an IPX/SPX domain or workgroup, there will be only one Master Browser, even if it spans multiple physical segments, because its name queries (broadcast messages) can be sent through a router from one physical segment to another. NetBEUI does not get to have a Domain Master Browser because of the protocol's limitation. NetBEUI (NBF) cannot send broadcast messages across routers and therefore requires a separate Master Browser per physical router segment. NetBEUI should not be used in a large, multiple segment, NT domain environment.

Summary

In almost all network environments, the proper configuration of browsing services can be the difference between a network that easily shares resources and one that does not share them at all. The user friendliness of the browse list is its most important attribute, because its technical design and low-level functions should be invisible to most users. Users merely want to see the computers that exist on the network and the resources that those computers are sharing, period.

Workshop

The Workshop helps you solidify the skills you learned this hour.

Glossary

announcement   A network communication packet sent by all computers to notify the Master Browser of the computer's existence and its shared resources.

Backup Browser   A computer that receives and stores the browse list, and then sends it to browser clients that send browse requests.

browse list   The centralized list of all computers and shared resources available on the network.

browse request   A network communication packet sent by a browser client, requesting the browse list.

browser server   Any computer whose role is to "serve" the browse list to other computers (for example, Backup Browsers, Master Browsers, and Domain Master Browsers).

browsing   The act of searching through the browse list to see what shared resources are available to be used.

Computer Browser service   Also known as the NT Browser service, it is an NT service that performs the behind-the-scenes operations so that the browse list is available to all computers on the network.

Domain Master Browser   Collects, maintains, and distributes the centralized browse list for an NT domain that spans multiple TCP/IP subnets.

election   The process of determining which computer on the network is best suited (or specifically configured) to be the Master Browser.

failure   The unintentional stoppage or disruption of the Computer Browser service.

20

hidden share   A shared resource that, by design, does not appear in the browse list. The share name of a hidden share ends in $.

IsDomainMaster   An NT Registry key that is used to denote preferential treatment when browser elections occur.

MaintainServerList   An NT Registry key that is used to configure the browsing role of a computer.

Master Browser   Collects and maintains the centralized browse list and distributes it to the Backup Browsers.

Non-Browser   Also known as a browser client, it is a computer that receives the browse list from a browser server (for example, a Backup Browser).

Potential Browser   A computer that is configured to be a Backup Browser (if a Master Browser says so) or a Master Browser (if there is no better computer).

Preferred Master Browser   A computer that is configured so that it has preferential treatment in browser elections when the Master Browser is being elected.

shared resource   A directory or printer that a computer is "serving" to other users on the network. For example, computer users can print to a printer that is attached to your Windows NT Workstation if you have "shared" it with them.

shutdown   The deliberate and orderly stoppage of the Computer Browser service.

Exercises

1. If you have them available, check to see how the Browser Service is configured on each of the following types of machines: Windows NT Server, Windows NT Workstation, Windows 95, and Windows for Workgroups. Remember, the configuration of a WFW computer isn't always obvious.

2. Create a few shared directories and one hidden directory on your computer. Go to another machine and see what shared resources display under your computer in the browse list.

3. View your NT Workstation's System Event Registry log. Check to see whether there are any warnings or errors in the browser service. Review the hour to see when and why these occur.

20

PART

IV

Hour **21**

The Windows NT Registry

by Martin Kenley

The Registry is a central database in which NT stores configuration settings having to do with both hardware and software. Without a good Registry in working order, NT cannot boot. In the past, with Windows 3.0 and 3.1, the ini files were critical because system settings were stored in them. Clearly, however, this method had inherent limitations. ini files often became saturated with entries from applications long since removed from your computer. There was no easy way to make these files reflect the current state of your system.

Thus, the Registry was born. It took over the job of not only all the ini files but also the config.sys and the autoexec.bat files. At times, NT is lenient enough to permit the existence of ini files, but usually when an older 16-bit application creates them. You'll most likely see a System.ini file and a Win.ini file on your NT system; NT copies the contents of all the ini files to the Registry whenever possible.

With NT 4, you have a new Registry Editor, RegEdit. It presents the information in a more logical way and enables you to hide the keys you don't need (keys are defined in the first section of this lesson). Unfortunately, the Registry is still a very complicated structure.

Keep in mind, however, that the standard mode for making changes to your configuration is through a regular utility, often a control panel utility. Going in and making changes directly to the Registry is not a recommended practice. It's dangerous, and you can do severe damage—severe enough that your system might not even boot.

CAUTION

> If you do need to get into the Registry due to an emergency, make sure you have a backup handy that you can use to restore the current version, if there are problems. Making a backup copy is explained later in the section "Importing and Exporting Registry Files." More important, know what you are doing before making changes. Fortunately, the Registry is guarded against unauthorized access. Users cannot even use the Registry editors without proper authorization. By default, only administrators can use them.
>
> Moreover, the files are stored in an encrypted format so that they cannot be read by any editors except those designed explicitly for this purpose. A word processor would not know how to deal with the encrypted data. As a further safeguard, the files are marked as read-only, hidden-system files.

The Structure of the Registry

At this point, it might be useful to look at the structure of the Registry to see how it is organized. The organizational strategy used by the developers at Microsoft was to divide the Registry into two main bodies:

- USER.DAT: In this part of the Registry, you will find information about the settings that apply to each user's account.
- SYSTEM.DAT: In this part, NT keeps general hardware and software settings. This section is rather large and cumbersome to navigate.

When you open the Registry with RegEdit, you will be presented with a window that looks like the one shown in Figure 21.1. Look at each key shown in Figure 21.1 to see what it contains. To open RegEdit, go to Start | Run, and type regedit.

Figure 21.1.

When you open RegEdit, you will see the keys shown here.

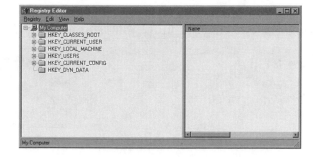

HKEY_CLASSES_ROOT

The HKEY_CLASSES_ROOT key contains information on file associations, extensions, and OLE (Object Linking and Embedding). The following sections cover extensions and object descriptions.

File Extensions

Click the + next to this key to open it up. The first long list of keys presented are the file extension keys. If you've installed many applications, you should see a long, comprehensive listing. This part of the database, for example, maps the three-letter .DOC extension to Microsoft Word files. You'll notice that each key name begins with a period.

You can use the Registry to modify file associations. Normally, you would use the Explorer to change a file association, but because you are going to add an extension type to an application, and the Explorer does not enable you to do this, you will use the Registry.

1. Open the RegEdit application by going to Start | Run, and typing regedit.

2. Open the HKEY_CLASSES_ROOT key by clicking the + next to its folder. In this example, you are going to add .TXT extensions to WordPerfect. Scroll down the list of extensions until you see .wpd. You should see a window similar to that in Figure 21.2.

Figure 21.2.

A typical extension key (this is the key for WordPerfect 6.1).

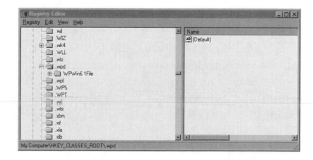

21

3. Click .wpd. If you want to see the value for this extension, click the Default value shown on the right, and you'll see something like what's shown in Figure 21.3.

Figure 21.3.

The Default value for the WordPerfect extension key.

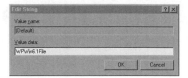

4. Scroll back up to the top so you can see HKEY_CLASSES_ROOT and click it.

5. Go to the Edit menu, choose New | Key, which will add a new key. Name it .TXT. Open the Default value by double-clicking it and type WPWin6.1File. If you forget, look at what the Default type was for the .wpd key.

6. Close the RegEdit utility. Open the Explorer and check to see if it worked. Go to View | Options. This brings up the dialog box shown in Figure 21.4. Click the File Types tab at the top of the window, and scroll down the list until you see the WordPerfect application. Click it, and it will show which file extension types it is capable of opening.

Figure 21.4.

The Explorer is capable of letting you change file associations, but not adding new extension types to an application.

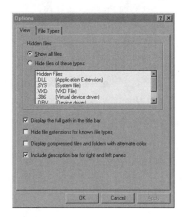

Object Descriptions

Before finishing the section on HKEY_CLASSES_ROOT, you need to look at object descriptions, which are another important part of this section of the Registry. The descriptions are related to the extensions in that the descriptions are additional keys that provide NT with information beyond simply which application is associated with the extension. This information can indicate what the icon type is, for example.

21

HKEY_LOCAL_MACHINE

As the name implies, the HKEY_LOCAL_MACHINE section contains keys that inform NT about the hardware, software configurations, and security.

Hardware

This key of the Registry is compiled each time your computer is booted. See Figure 21.5 for an example of the Hardware Registry key.

Figure 21.5.

The Hardware Registry contains comprehensive information about the hardware in your computer.

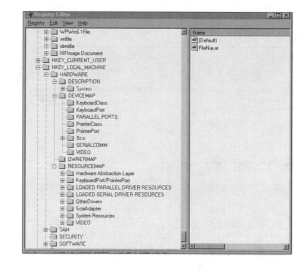

NT stores not only information about hardware installed, but also the resources that the pieces of hardware might be using (see Figure 21.6). You will find three major subheadings under HARDWARE: DESCRIPTION, DEVICEMAP, and RESOURCEMAP. The first item, DESCRIPTION, will be of limited value because most of the entries here are not configurable. This key provides information on peripherals and device settings (in binary). The second item, DEVICEMAP, contains an entry for each system-wide peripheral, such as a SCSI controller. Finally, the RESOURCEMAP stores data on the physical resources used by the hardware.

Figure 21.6.

The HARDWARE key provides information such as that shown here on a SCSI adapter card.

21

Security

This very important key contains information on security. For example, user-privileges information is stored here; so are passwords. If you open this key, nothing appears because this information cannot be edited.

Software

The software key contains information on software installed on the computer. Again, there is not much here that can be configured.

System

Information in this key is critical during the boot phase. Because the data here is of special importance, NT makes multiple copies. You can find them listed as the `ControlSet001` key, `ControlSet002`, and so on. If you ever have to choose the "Last Known Good Configuration" during boot-up, NT will use one of the copies of the hardware configuration found in this key. This is an important area, and improper editing can severely cripple NT.

HKEY_CURRENT_USER

The `HKEY_CURRENT_USER` key stores settings for the user currently logged into NT. It has information on that user's profile, preferences, and network settings. It is used by NT to set up the computer for that user.

You'll probably see that several of these subkeys are also listed in `HKEY_LOCAL_MACHINE`. In the case of duplicates, NT will use the subkey in the `HKEY_CURRENT_USER`. Seven default keys listed in the `HKEY_CURRENT_USER` are

- ☐ `Console`: These configuration settings manage the command line.
- ☐ `Control Panel`: The settings here store all the custom settings done through the control panel. Desktop configuration is one example.
- ☐ `Environment`: These settings are here for compatibility with older applications that have environment settings. Previously, this information was stored in the `autoexec.bat` file.
- ☐ `Keyboard Layout`: Stored here are settings that indicate which language keyboard the user has chosen.
- ☐ `Printers`: Information on each installed printer is kept here. The information is in binary format.
- ☐ `Software`: Here you will find settings for the various applications installed. Previously, this information had been stored in the `Win.ini` file or an application-specific initialization file.

☐ Windows 3.1 Migration Status: You will find this subkey only if you have up-graded from Windows 3.1. This can be a useful subkey because it will show you if .grp and .ini files were successfully migrated.

HKEY_USERS

The Registry stores user profiles in HKEY_USERS. When a user logs in, the Registry moves the profile to HKEY_CURRENT_USER. NT will always have at least two subkeys here: a .DEFAULT as well as a profile for the administrator. The .DEFAULT lists contain the general settings that a new user gets.

HKEY_CURRENT_CONFIG

The HKEY_CURRENT_CONFIG key contains information used by NT that enables it to decide which hardware configuration to use upon startup. It appears that this key points to the HKEY_LOCAL_MACHINE\SYSTEM\CURRENTCONTROLSET\HARDWARE PROFILES\CURRENT.

Editing the Registry

Microsoft does not recommend editing the Registry, but it can be necessary on occasion; you saw one reason already under the section "HKEY_CLASSES_ROOT." Warnings about editing the Registry have been issued elsewhere in this lesson, so be sure you know what you are doing when you attempt to edit the Registry. Make a backup of it before editing parts of it. You can back up the Registry using the information found in the section "Importing and Exporting Registry Files." Furthermore, ask yourself why you are making the changes here rather than to the application or Control Panel applet.

Although the Windows 95 RegEdit utility enables you to edit the Registry from DOS, for security reasons, NT's RegEdit does not. You must run NT in order to be able to edit the Registry.

JUST A MINUTE

Each user has his or her own copy of the Registry, which is found in the user's profile folder. This is good news because it means that if a user screws up his or her copy of the Registry, you can recover by rebooting and logging in as someone else. To recover that user's account, log in as an administrator and copy another Registry file into that user's profile folder.

21

You saw earlier in the "HKEY_CLASSES_ROOT" section how to use the Registry editor, RegEdit.exe. Take a look at how to do more with it.

1. Go to the Start menu and choose Run.

2. Enter the word RegEdit and click OK.

How would you find a key? To do a search, follow these steps:

1. Open the Registry editor.

2. Open the key in which you would like to search: HKEY_CLASSES_ROOT, HKEY_LOCAL_MACHINE, HKEY_CURRENT_USER, HKEY_USERS, or HKEY_CURRENT_CONFIG. Keep in mind that a search will only look inside the open key. For example, if you have the HKEY_CURRENT_CONFIG key open and perform a search, it will look at only the keys inside it.

3. Go to the Edit menu, to Find.

4. Now type in your search entry.

Adding a Key

You can add new keys that contain additional data. For example, if you have a device driver that does have an install program, you could add a key to CurrentControlSet\Services that would load the driver for you automatically.

1. Select the location in which you would like the entry to be added by clicking the appropriate key or subkey.

2. Go to the Edit menu and choose New | Key.

3. When the key appears, type a name for the new key.

4. Add a value by selecting the subkey.

5. Go to the Edit menu, to New, and choose either String Value, Binary Value, or DWORD Value according to the value you want to add.

6. It will now appear in the right side of the window. You can change the name assigned to it simply by typing the new name.

Removing a Key

If you ever need to remove a key, be very careful to open it (by clicking on the + next to it) and look inside it. Make sure it does not contain any more information than you want to delete.

1. Open the Registry editor.

2. Navigate your way to the subkey you want to delete.

3. Right-click the subkey. A pop-up menu appears; choose Delete.

4. A dialog box appears asking if you are sure you want to delete this key. *Be sure you know what you are doing. Deleting a key NT needs could make your system unusable.* Choose the appropriate answer.

Importing and Exporting Registry Files

This section first looks at importing Registry files and then exporting them. NT provides users with several methods of importing files into the Registry. The easiest is to use the Windows NT Explorer.

1. Open the Explorer.

2. Find the Registry file you want to import.

3. Double-click the file; RegEdit will automatically import the file.

Another way to import files into the Registry is to use the RegEdit application.

1. Open RegEdit by going to the Start menu, and choose Run. Type `RegEdit` in the dialog box. Click OK.

2. From the menus at the top, choose Registry | Import Registry File.

3. In the dialog box that comes up, type the filename. Click Open (see Figure 21.7).

Figure 21.7.

When importing a file into the Registry with RegEdit, you must select the appropriate file.

If there are older Registry files with the same keys, the older entries will be overwritten.

Exporting Registry Data

NT gives you the option of exporting a limited portion of the Registry, such as an individual key, or the entire Registry.

21

To export an individual key, follow these instructions:

1. Open RegEdit.
2. Select a Registry key to export.
3. Go to Registry | Export. You will see a window similar to the one shown in Figure 21.8.

Figure 21.8.

The Export Registry File dialog box.

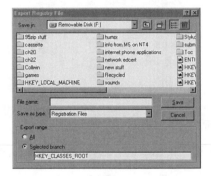

4. Make sure that you choose the Selected branch radio button at the bottom of the screen.
5. Type a name for the file.

To export the entire Registry, follow the same steps just outlined. When you get to step 4, choose All rather than Selected branch.

The entire Registry will take up approximately 2 to 4MB, so it will not be possible to store it on a floppy disk. Even if you save the individual keys, HKEY_LOCAL_MACHINE will probably be too large for a disk (see Figure 21.9).

Figure 21.9.

An example of all the keys saved to a Zip disk.

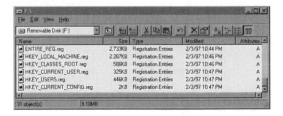

Notice that in the example here, all the keys would fit on a floppy disk with the exception of HKEY_LOCAL_MACHINE. Your only option, if you are determined to use floppies, is to save the subkeys of the HKEY_LOCAL_MACHINE. On my personal computer, all of the subkeys within HKEY_LOCAL_MACHINE are small enough to fit on floppies. The two largest subkeys are the Software and System subkeys, both of which are just over 1MB on my computer.

21

You can also back up your Registry by making an updated copy of your emergency repair disk.

1. Go to the Start menu and choose Run.
2. Type RDISK.
3. Put in either a blank disk (all the data will be erased when NT reformats the disk; you cannot stop it from doing this) or your old ERD.
4. When the copy is finished, label and date the disk.
5. Repeat these steps after changes are made to your system or new hardware is installed.

Summary

The Registry is a complex part of NT, and the developers of NT have designed it so that you should rarely, if ever, need to go into it and edit it. However, if you should have to do so, follow the precautions in this lesson. Be sure you have backed it up, so that if something should go wrong, you can restore the backup copy.

Workshop

The Workshop helps you solidify the skills you learned this hour.

Glossary

Autoexec.bat   The autoexec.bat file is used with Windows 3.x machines, and to a lesser extent with Windows 95 machines, to load DOS commands that are executed every time you boot your computer. It enables the user to add lines to it in order to customize his setup.

Config.sys   This file is also used with Windows 3.x, and to a lesser extent, Windows 95 machines, to load DOS commands every time the computer boots up. The computer operator can edit the file in order to customize how the PC operates. DOS commands in this file often load device drivers.

ini files   Files used by Windows 3.1 and Windows 95 computers. They store hardware and software settings, which are now stored in the Registry in Windows NT.

RegEdit.exe   RegEdit is a utility used to edit the Registry.

Registry   The Registry is a comprehensive database of all your system, hardware, and application settings. For example, when you change your desktop pattern, the change is reflected in a file in the Registry.

21

Exercises

1. Update your emergency repair disk by following the instructions at the end of this lesson.

2. Open the RegEdit utility, and navigate around the HKEY keys. Become familiar with the HKEY_LOCAL_MACHINE, especially the HARDWARE subkey of this section.

3. Export an entire copy of the Registry to either a remote (network) drive, a Zip disk, if you have a Zip drive, or tape backup.

4. Export individual HKEYS to floppy disks. Label the floppy disks.

Hour 22

Troubleshooting Windows NT

by Jeff Perkins

Very few things in life are more frustrating than software that doesn't work. Most of us have spent many hours trying to figure out why our new board doesn't work or our new program doesn't run. The advent of Windows NT does not signal an end to the problems you will have to troubleshoot, but it does offer some good tools for finding out what is wrong. This hour covers the following:

- ☐ Boot errors
- ☐ WinMSD
- ☐ Diagnostic utilities
- ☐ The Event Viewer
- ☐ Network troubleshooting

Rather than being a tour through the world of bytes and registers, this lesson focuses on the most efficient and cost-effective NT troubleshooting techniques for the most common problems.

Troubleshooting Philosophy

Before studying specific problems and their solutions, you need to consider your general troubleshooting philosophy. Many engineers and casual users spend days trying to troubleshoot problems that could have been solved by reformatting, reinstalling, or calling technical support.

The first two options, reformatting and reinstalling, are often avoided because the victim has not made backups. The following is the first rule of troubleshooting:

> Rule #1. Make backups before something bad happens. There are several types of backup schemes. How often you back up should be determined by what data you can afford to lose, afford being measured in money or frustration. I recommend a minimum of once a month. Make payday your backup day. When was the last time you forgot payday (as opposed to the last anniversary or birthday you forgot)?

Yes, a tape drive or another hard drive costs several hundred dollars, but compare that to how much your time is worth. Don't put yourself in the position of looking through the back pages of a computer magazine trying to find a telephone number for a data recovery service (you would normally use the Internet, but your computer is down).

The last option, calling tech support, is often avoided because of cost. But again, consider the cost of your time against the cost of technical support. Also, most software includes one or more free support calls, normally to solve setup problems. Microsoft has a well-trained and well-mannered technical support staff that normally goes to extraordinary lengths to help you solve problems. They also have free online services and for-free subscription services that include hundreds of pages of information on Windows NT troubleshooting. The place to start looking for this information is www.microsoft.com or, if your computer is broken, 1-800-344-2121 (staffed during normal business hours).

Now, learn what the most common problems are and how to deal with them in the most timely and cost-effective way.

Boot Errors

Perhaps the most annoying and time-consuming problems with any operating system are boot problems. Boot problems are especially time-consuming in Windows NT because of the nature of the operating system. For example, suppose you have a problem that occurs during the boot process that prevents you from getting logged into Windows NT. In Windows 3.1 or Windows 95, you could just pop in a boot disk and root around on the disk until you find the problem. If you are using the FAT file system in Windows NT, you can still do boot-up with a DOS or Windows 95 floppy disk and replace any important damaged files (remember rule number one—back things up). But chances are that you are not running the FAT file

22

system. It's far more likely that you will be using the NTFS file system. If you boot up with a Windows 3.1 or 95 floppy, you will not be able to see anything on the hard drive. This brings you to Troubleshooting Rule Number Two:

Rule #2: When in doubt, reinstall.

If you have taken the advice given to you in Hour 12, "Migration Considerations," you will have created a boot disk that has enough on it to create a link to the CD-ROM. The wonderful thing about a CD-ROM is that it can be read from almost any operating system. If you didn't read or heed Hour 12, you might want to reconsider and build this boot disk. If you can get to the winnt.exe or winnt32.exe file on the installation disk, you can start the installation process.

If you find yourself using the boot disk built in Hour 12, you should go through the complete installation process. This process is generally nondestructive to your existing data and programs and will refresh all of the system DLL files, detect hardware, and rebuild the Registry. (Later in this section, you'll learn about some files you might want to have backed up and some numbers you will want to write down and save inside your computer case.)

During the setup process, you are offered an option to either install or use your emergency recovery disk. This emergency recovery disk was created during the installation process, if you asked for its creation, or it can be built using the Rdisk program.

To create a recovery disk, go to the Start menu, choose Run, and type Rdisk. You will get a screen that looks like Figure 22.1.

Figure 22.1.

The Rdisk program.

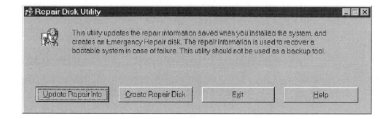

If you have installed new software or hardware and you want to update your existing disk (if you chose to make one), then click the Update Repair Info button. A dialog box will appear, as shown in Figure 22.2, reminding you that all the previous information will be lost.

Figure 22.2.

Saving the data to the repair directory

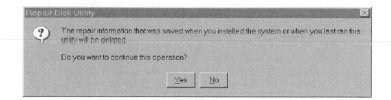

Choose OK. A progress bar will indicate that your configuration information is being saved, and you will be returned to the main screen. This can take a few minutes. This information is written to your hard disk into files located in the repair directory, a subdirectory of the winnt directory. Then you are prompted to create an emergency repair disk, as shown in Figure 22.3.

Figure 22.3.

Preparing to create an emergency repair disk.

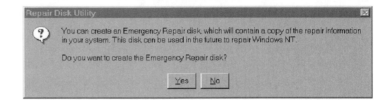

Answering Yes brings you to the warning issued in the next dialog box, shown in Figure 22.4. This dialog box warns you that the disk will be completely reformatted. Don't use your disk that is full of backup files!

Figure 22.4.

The last chance to save your old data.

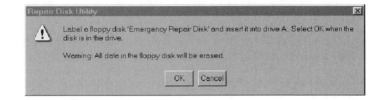

Clicking the Create Repair Disk button doesn't cause new data to be written to the repair directory; it performs the actions associated with Figures 22.3 and 22.4, creating a repair disk.

The files in the repair subdirectory and on the repair disk are identical. Listing 22.1 shows these files.

Listing 22.1. Repair files.

```
Directory of C:\WINNT\repair

02/08/97   11:23p        <DIR>          .
02/08/97   11:23p        <DIR>          ..
05/05/96   09:14p                  438  autoexec.nt
06/29/96   06:35p                2,510  config.nt
01/05/97   01:49a               22,916  default._
02/08/97   11:23p               22,920  ntuser.da_
01/05/97   01:49a                4,610  sam._
01/05/97   01:49a                6,743  security._
02/08/97   11:23p              954,106  software._
02/08/97   11:20p              205,358  system._
```

22

The two files with the .nt postfix are copies of autoexec.nt and config.nt that are used when a command-line session is created. The rest of the files in Listing 22.1 are compressed versions of various Registry and security files. There is one hidden file on both the disk and the directory, setup.log. A portion of that file is shown in Listing 22.2.

Listing 22.2. A portion of the setup.log file.

```
[Paths]
TargetDirectory = "\WINNT"
TargetDevice = "\Device\Harddisk0\partition1"
SystemPartitionDirectory = "\"
SystemPartition = "\Device\Harddisk0\partition1"
[Signature]
Version = "WinNt4.0"
[Files.SystemPartition]
ntldr = "ntldr","2a36b"
NTDETECT.COM = "NTDETECT.COM","b69e"
[Files.WinNt]
\WINNT\System32\drivers\TYNBMNT4.SYS =
➥"tynbmnt4.sys","13eb6","\tyan","Tyan High Performance 32Bit Bus Master
➥Driver","disk1.nt"
\WINNT\system32\drivers\atapi.sys = "atapi.sys","1589b"
\WINNT\Help\31users.hlp = "31users.hlp","12bfc"
\WINNT\Fonts\8514fix.fon = "8514fix.fon","7d29"
\WINNT\Fonts\8514oem.fon = "8514oem.fon","8545"
\WINNT\Fonts\8514sys.fon = "8514sys.fon","c3c2"
...
```

The file goes on to describe all the files critical to the system setup. You really do not want to change this file because of the checksums at the end of each line, but this is a file to add to your list of important files to archive.

So far, the explanation has covered the general situation of something bad happening during boot-up. Take a look at a more specific situation. Suppose that you just changed a video card, or changed monitors. You boot up the system, but where it said Welcome to NT before, there are now rows of Welcome to NT rolling across your screen. To correct this kind of problem, reboot your machine and at the initial NT prompt (where NT asks whether you want to log into NT 4, NT 4 [VGA], or some other operating system), choose to log into the VGA version of Windows NT. This is like the Safe Mode in Windows 95. Like Safe Mode, this brings up Windows NT with a minimum of drivers. Using this option causes the system to boot with a minimum number of drivers and should, if you have changed an item of hardware, enable you to install a new video driver or change hardware settings.

This initial menu is controlled by the Boot.ini file that exists in your root directory. A typical Boot.ini file looks like Listing 22.3.

Listing 22.3. Contents of `boot.ini`.

```
[boot loader]
timeout=30
default=multi(0)disk(0)rdisk(0)partition(1)\WINNT
[operating systems]
multi(0)disk(0)rdisk(0)partition(1)\WINNT="Windows NT Workstation Version 4.00"
multi(0)disk(0)rdisk(0)partition(1)\WINNT=
➥"Windows NT Workstation Version 4.00 [VGA mode]" /basevideo /sos
C:\="MS-DOS"
```

The switches available for use in `Boot.ini` are in Table 22.1.

Table 22.1. `Boot.ini` switches.

Switch	Description
/BASEVIDEO	This boots the computer using the base VGA driver.
/BAUDRATE=nnnn	For Remote Debugging, sets the baud rate to be used for Remote Debugging.
/CRASHDEBUG	Starts the debugger when you start Windows NT but it only becomes active if there is a kernel error.
/DEBUG	Starts the debugger when you start Windows NT and becomes active immediately.
/DEBUGPORT= comx	For Remote Debugging, sets the COM port to use.
/MAXMEM:n	Specifies the maximum amount of RAM that Windows NT can use.
/NODEBUG	No debugging information is being used.
/NOSERIALMICE=[COMx ¦ COMx,y,z...]	For Remote Debugging, prevents the system from trying to detect a serial mouse.
/SOS	Shows the device driver names when they are loaded.

If you look at the `Boot.ini` in Listing 22.3, you will see that the option labeled "Windows NT Workstation Version 4.00 [VGA mode]" will boot up in the Basic Video Mode and display all the device driver names that are loaded during the boot-up sequence.

22

JUST A MINUTE

Notice that there are many options associated with Remote Debugging, which is the option of last resort. The typical user is better off reformatting or reinstalling the system. If you have serious data recovery problems, contact Microsoft tech support. For enough money, they will walk you through it. If you are ever forced to use Remote Debugging, there are several files located under the Support Directory that you will need to use.

A final note before leaving the Boot problems section. You might want to add post office files to your list of files to back up. It's really annoying to lose all the e-mail addresses you have collected over the years. You need to keep a copy of your *.pab file, which is your Personal Address Book. It contains all the addresses and personal information used by the Inbox. If you have space, you might want to back up your .pst files, which are post office files that contain all the correspondence you have not permanently deleted. These files can get quite large, for example, over 50MB.

WinMSD

When you get your system booted up, your next headache is getting all the components on your machine to play with each other. DOS and Windows 3.*x* and 95 use a utility called Microsoft Diagnostics (MSD) to help users find and resolve the resource conflicts that invariably occur. This program has been redesigned for Windows NT. To run WinMSD, click the Start button, select Run, type WinMSD, and press Enter. Its opening screen looks like Figure 22.5.

Figure 22.5.

The WinMSD opening screen.

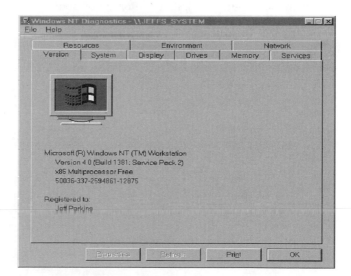

You see nine tabs: Version, System, Display, Drives, Memory, Services, Resources, Environment, and Network. The Version tab is open when you start the program. Here you can check to see what version of the software you are running and what service packs you have loaded.

The System tab shows information about your processors, BIOS, and Hardware Abstraction Layer. This tab is shown in Figure 22.6.

Figure 22.6.

The System tab in WinMSD.

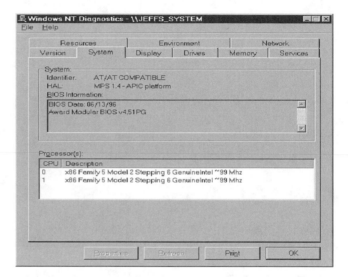

This example shows a dual-processor system with an award BIOS. You would use this information when describing your machine and problems to tech support. The next tab, Display (see Figure 22.7), shows information about your video system.

Figure 22.7.

The Display tab.

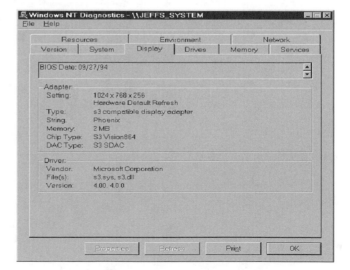

22

The Drives tab shows drive information. Drive information can be shown by type, as depicted in Figure 22.8, or by drive letter.

Figure 22.8.

The Drives tab.

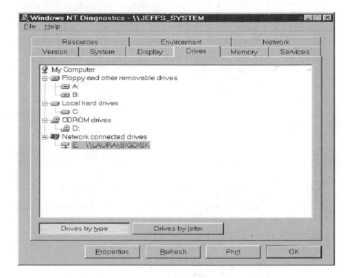

Double-clicking on a drive brings up specific drive information as shown in Figure 22.9. This particular drive is installed on the NT machine. You can see that it is an NTFS drive.

Figure 22.9.

Specific drive information.

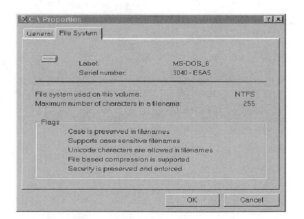

In the Flags section of Figure 22.9, you can see the features supported by the drive (long filenames, compression, security, and so on). Choosing another drive produces a similar screen, Figure 22.10.

Figure 22.10.

Network drive informa-tion.

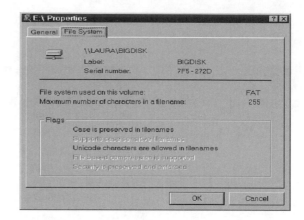

This particular drive lives on a Windows 95 machine and is attached as a network drive to this machine. Notice that the file system is FAT, and it supports 255-character filenames and Unicode characters. However, the drive doesn't support the other NTFS features, which are grayed out in the Flags section.

The Memory tab, shown in Figure 22.11, displays various information about memory. A more usable memory display program is Task Manager, which is discussed in the next section. The next tab, Services (see Figure 22.12), is much more useful for troubleshooting.

Figure 22.11.

Memory information.

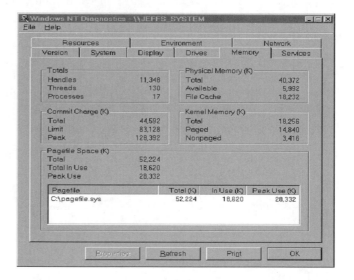

22

Figure 22.12.

The Services tab.

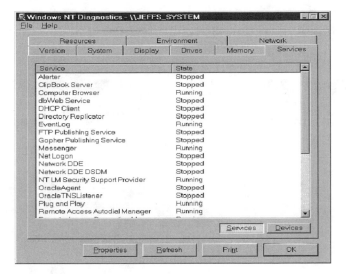

As you know from other parts of this book, NT runs several services that do things such as talk to the disk drive or CD-ROM. These services are provided by devices. The Services tab shows all the services and devices currently on your machine along with their status. From a troubleshooting standpoint, this can be valuable information. Suppose you have a device, such as a scanner, that is not working. Before you explore other solutions, you might want to go to this tab and see if the device is loaded and if the service is running. Double-clicking on a device or service produces the dialog box shown in Figure 22.13.

Figure 22.13.

The General tab for a specific device.

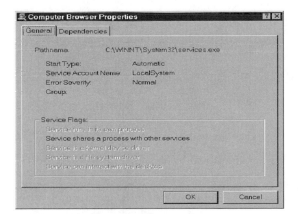

The General tab on this dialog box shows information about the selected service or device, including when the device is activated (boot up, manual, and so on) and how the device plays with the rest of the operating system. Click the Dependencies tab, shown in Figure 22.14.

Figure 22.14.

The Dependencies tab for a specific service.

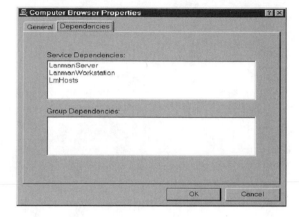

The Dependencies tab shows the other devices and services on which this service is dependent. If this service is not running, check to see whether it has dependencies and if they are running.

The Network tab in WinMSD shows general information, as shown in Figure 22.15, as well as Transports, Settings, and Statistics. Of special interest to the troubleshooter is the Statistics section shown in Figure 22.16.

Figure 22.15.

The Network tab.

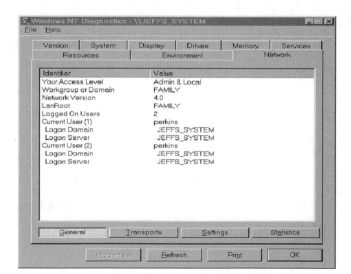

22

Figure 22.16.

Network statistics data.

On the Network tab you can see facts about network problems like network errors, failed operations, and hung sessions. If you are having a problem with a program not finding its resources, then you need to check out the Environment tab, shown in Figure 22.17.

Figure 22.17.

The Environment tab.

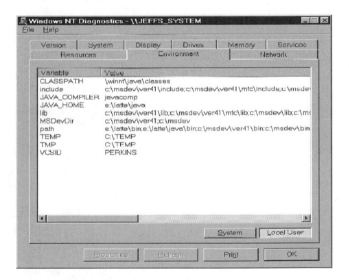

For example, If your Java compiler complains about not finding files, check to see whether you have a CLASSPATH variable and that this variable is set to the correct directory. This tab shows environmental variables for both the system and the current user.

All of the tabs you have looked at so far are valuable in gathering information to use in solving problems on your computer. They will help you solve about 10 percent of the problems you encounter. For the other 90 percent, use the Resources tab, shown in Figure 22.18.

Figure 22.18.

The Resources data.

This is the screen that will help you find and resolve resource conflicts among IRQs, I/O ports, DMA channels, memory, and devices. You will probably use the first three in most of your board-level conflict resolution situations. Double-clicking an entry or clicking the Properties button will bring up specifics, as shown in Figure 22.19.

Figure 22.19.

Resource properties.

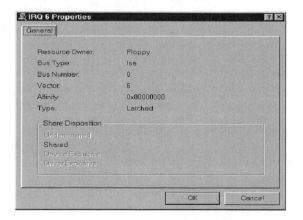

This particular property sheet shows the properties of IRQ 6, which, on the machine illustrated, is assigned to the floppy drive.

You can get a copy of the big picture by clicking the Print button on the bottom of the WinMSD screen. You will get a printout like the one shown in Listing 22.4.

Listing 22.4. The big picture.

```
Microsoft Diagnostics Report For \\JEFFS_SYSTEM
-----------------------------------

OS Version Report
-----------------------------------
Microsoft (R) Windows NT (TM) Workstation
Version 4.0 (Build 1381: Service Pack 2) x86 Multiprocessor Free
Registered Owner: Jeff Perkins
Product Number: 50036 337 2594861-12875
-----------------------------------

System Report
-----------------------------------
System: AT/AT COMPATIBLE
Hardware Abstraction Layer: MPS 1.4 - APIC platform
BIOS Date: 06/13/96
BIOS Version: Award Modular BIOS v4.51PG


Processor list:
    0:  x86 Family 5 Model 2 Stepping 6 GenuineIntel ~99 Mhz
    1:  x86 Family 5 Model 2 Stepping 6 GenuineIntel ~99 Mhz
-----------------------------------

Video Display Report
-----------------------------------
BIOS Date: 09/27/94
BIOS Version: Phoenix S3 Vision864 (16Bit DAC)
➥Enhanced VGA BIOS. Version 1.03-08

Adapter:
    Setting: 1024 x 768 x 256
             Hardware Default Refresh
    Type: s3 compatible display adapter
    String: Phoenix
    Memory: 2 MB
    Chip Type: S3 Vision864
    DAC Type: S3 SDAC
Driver:
    Vendor: Microsoft Corporation
    File(s): s3.sys, s3.dll
    Version: 4.00, 4.0.0


Drives Report
-----------------------------------
C:\  (Local - NTFS) MS-DOS_6 Total: 0KB, Free: 0KB
D:\  (CDROM - CDFS) NTWKS40A Total: 591,322KB, Free: 0KB
E: (Remote - FAT) \\LAURA\BIGDISK BIGDISK Total: 2,096,320KB, Free: 1,472,192KB
```

continues

Listing 22.4. continued

```
Memory Report
-----------------------------------
Handles: 11,349
Threads: 133
Processes: 17

Physical Memory (K)
   Total: 40,372
   Available: 3,808
   File Cache: 16,092



Services Report
-----------------------------------
Computer Browser                                 Running    (Automatic)
EventLog (Event log)                             Running    (Automatic)
Server                                           Running    (Automatic)
Workstation (NetworkProvider)                    Running    (Automatic)
TCP/IP NetBIOS Helper                            Running    (Automatic)
Messenger                                        Running    (Automatic)
NT LM Security Support Provider                  Running    (Manual)
Plug and Play (PlugPlay)                         Running    (Automatic)
Remote Access Autodial Manager                   Running    (Automatic)
Remote Access Connection Manager (Network)       Running    (Manual)
Remote Procedure Call (RPC) Service              Running    (Automatic)
Spooler (SpoolerGroup)                           Running    (Automatic)
Telephony Service                                Running    (Manual)



Drivers Report
-----------------------------------
AFD Networking Support Environment (TDI)         Running    (Automatic)
Remote Access Mac (NDIS)                          Running    (Automatic)
atapi (SCSI miniport)                            Running    (Boot)
Beep (Base)                                      Running    (System)
Cdfs (File system)                               Running    (System)
Cdrom (SCSI CDROM Class)                         Running    (System)
Disk (SCSI Class)                                Running    (Boot)
Fastfat (Boot file system)                       Running    (Disabled)
Floppy (Primary disk)                            Running    (System)
i8042 Keyboard and PS/2 Mouse Port Driver (Keyboard Port) Running    (System)
Keyboard Class Driver (Keyboard Class)           Running    (System)
KSecDD (Base)                                    Running    (System)
Modem (Extended base)                            Running    (Manual)
Mouse Class Driver (Pointer Class)               Running    (System)
Msfs (File system)                               Running    (System)
Mup (Network)                                    Running    (Manual)
```

```
NetBEUI Protocol (PNP_TDI)                              Running   (Automatic)
Microsoft NDIS System Driver (NDIS)                     Running   (System)
Microsoft NDIS TAPI driver (NDIS)                       Running   (System)
Remote Access WAN Wrapper (NDISWAN)                     Running   (Automatic)
Novell NE2000 Adapter Driver (NDIS)                     Running   (Automatic)
NetBIOS Interface (NetBIOSGroup)                        Running   (Manual)
WINS Client(TCP/IP) (PNP_TDI)                           Running   (Automatic)
Npfs (File system)                                      Running   (System)
Ntfs (File system)                                      Running   (Disabled)
Null (Base)                                             Running   (System)
Parallel (Extended base)                                Running   (Automatic)
Parport (Parallel arbitrator)                           Running   (Automatic)
ParVdm (Extended base)                                  Running   (Automatic)
Remote Access Auto Connection Driver (Streams Drivers) Running   (Automatic)
Remote Access ARP Service (PNP_TDI)                     Running   (Automatic)
Rdr (Network)                                           Running   (Manual)
s3 (Video)                                              Running   (System)
Serial (Extended base)                                  Running   (Automatic)
Serial Mouse Driver (Pointer Port)                      Running   (System)
Srv (Network)                                           Running   (Manual)
TCP/IP Service (PNP_TDI)                                Running   (Automatic)
VgaSave (Video Save)                                    Running   (System)



IRQ and Port Report
------------------------------------
Devices                     Vector Level  Affinity
------------------------------------
MPS 1.4 - APIC platform       255   255  0x00000003
i8042prt                        1     1  0xffffffff
Serial                          3     3  0x00000000
Floppy                          6     6  0x00000000
NE2000                         10    10  0x46740843
Sermouse                        4     4  0xffffffff
atapi                           0    14  0x00000000
------------------------------------
Devices                     Physical Address  Length
------------------------------------
MPS 1.4 - APIC platform       0x000000f0   0x0000000010
i8042prt                      0x00000060   0x0000000001
i8042prt                      0x00000064   0x0000000001
Parport                       0x00000378   0x0000000003
Serial                        0x000002f8   0x0000000007
Floppy                        0x000003f0   0x0000000006
Floppy                        0x000003f7   0x0000000001
NE2000                        0x00000320   0x0000000020
Sermouse                      0x000003f8   0x0000000007
atapi                         0x000001f0   0x0000000008
atapi                         0x000003f6   0x0000000001
s3                            0x000003c0   0x0000000010
VgaSave                       0x000003b0   0x000000000c
```

continues

Listing 22.4. continued

```
DMA and Memory Report
-----------------------------------
Devices                    Channel    Port
-----------------------------------
Floppy                        2        0
-----------------------------------
Devices                    Physical Address  Length
-----------------------------------
MPS 1.4 - APIC platform    0xfec00000    0x00000400
MPS 1.4 - APIC platform    0xfee00000    0x00000400
s3                         0x000a0000    0x00010000
s3                         0xe0000000    0x00800000
s3                         0x000c0000    0x00008000
VgaSave                    0x000a0000    0x00020000


Environment Report
-----------------------------------


System Environment Variables
    ComSpec=C:\WINNT\system32\cmd.exe
    Cpu=i386
    Include=C:\INetSDK\Include
    INetSDK=C:\INetSDK
    Lib=C:\INetSDK\Lib
    NUMBER_OF_PROCESSORS=2
    OS=Windows_NT
    Os2LibPath=C:\WINNT\system32\os2\dll;
    Path=C:\WINNT\SYSTEM32;C:\WINNT;C:\EBONY\BIN;E:\ORANT\BIN;
    PROCESSOR_ARCHITECTURE=x86
    PROCESSOR_IDENTIFIER=x86 Family 5 Model 2 Stepping 6, GenuineIntel
    PROCESSOR_LEVEL=5
    PROCESSOR_REVISION=0206
    windir=C:\WINNT


Environment Variables for Current User
    CLASSPATH=\winnt\java\classes
    include=c:\msdev\ver41\include;c:\msdev\ver41\mfc\include
    ➥;c:\msdev\include;c:\msdev\mfc\include;c:\msdev\ver41\include
    ➥;c:\msdev\ver41\mfc\include;c:\msdev\include;c:\msdev\mfc\include
    ➥;C:\INetSDK\Include
    JAVA_COMPILER=javacomp
    JAVA_HOME=e:\latte\java
    lib=c:\msdev\ver41\lib;c:\msdev\ver41\mfc\lib
    ➥;c:\msdev\lib;c:\msdev\mfc\lib;c:\msdev\ver41\lib;c:\msdev\ver41\mfc\lib
    ➥;c:\msdev\lib;c:\msdev\mfc\lib;C:\INetSDK\Lib
    MSDevDir=c:\msdev\ver41;c:\msdev
```

22

```
path=e:\latte\bin;e:\latte\java\bin;c:\msdev\ver41\bin;c:\msdev\bin
TEMP=C:\TEMP
TMP=C:\TEMP
VCSID=PERKINS


Network Report
-----------------------------------
Your Access Level: Admin & Local
Workgroup or Domain: FAMILY
Network Version: 4.0
LanRoot: FAMILY
Logged On Users: 2
Current User (1): perkins
  Logon Domain: JEFFS_SYSTEM
  Logon Server: JEFFS_SYSTEM
Current User (2): perkins
  Logon Domain: JEFFS_SYSTEM
  Logon Server: JEFFS_SYSTEM

Transport: NetBT_NdisWan4, 00-00-00-00-00-00, VC's: 0, Wan: Wan
Transport: NetBT_NE20001, 00-00-B4-72-DC-F7, VC's: 1, Wan: Wan
Transport: Nbf_NE20001, 00-00-B4-72-DC-F7, VC's: 0, Wan: Wan

Character Wait: 3,600
Collection Time: 250
Maximum Collection Count: 16
Keep Connection: 600
Maximum Commands: 5
Session Time Out: 45
Character Buffer Size: 512
Maximum Threads: 17
Lock Quota: 6,144
Lock Increment: 10
Maximum Locks: 500
Pipe Increment: 10
Maximum Pipes: 500
Cache Time Out: 40
Dormant File Limit: 45
Read Ahead Throughput: 4,294,967,295
Mailslot Buffers: 3
Server Announce Buffers: 20
Illegal Datagrams: 5
Datagram Reset Frequency: 60
Bytes Received: 15,584,571
SMB's Received: 11,888
Paged Read Bytes Requested: 15,384,576
Non Paged Read Bytes Requested: 3,075
Server File Opens: 121
```

Save a hard copy of this. The best place to store this hard copy is taped inside the computer case. However, don't put it there yet. There are a few things you might want to write on it that are covered in the "Network Troubleshooting" section.

Other Diagnostic Utilities Included with NT 4

Look at the Tools tab on the Properties page of any of your disk drives to find out what tools are available for your disk and when you last used them. The page will look like Figure 22.20.

Figure 22.20.

Drive tools.

You have already learned about the importance in any troubleshooting situation of backing up data, and the last choice, Defragmentation, shows that there is no disk defragmenter loaded. This is because NT, unlike previous versions of Windows, doesn't come with a disk defragmenter. This doesn't mean that your disks won't become fragmented—they will. When they do, you have two choices. One way is to move your files from one drive to another and then back to their original drive. This will have the effect of defragmenting your files but requires an extra disk with lots of space. The second option is to buy a third-party defragmenter. A trial edition of one third-party defragmenter, Diskeeper, is available on the Web at http://www.execsoft.com.

The remaining entry shown on Figure 22.20 promises to check the drive for errors. Click this button, and you will get a screen that looks like Figure 22.21.

This figure shows the minimalist front end to the Windows NT descendant of ScanDisk. Click the top box, Automatically fix filesystem errors, to have the program do just that. Click the second box, Scan for and attempt recovery of bad sectors, if you want to program it to take a look at the physical part of your hard drive. Seven times out of ten, clicking the Start button will produce the dialog box shown in Figure 22.22.

22

Figure 22.21.

The ScanDisk dialog box.

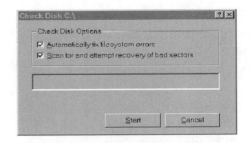

Figure 22.22.

Postponing ScanDisk until the next boot-up.

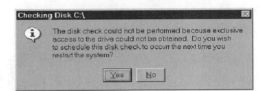

This happens because there is little you can do on your computer that doesn't involve some kind of access to the hard drive. If you are using MS Word, for example, it is normally backing up your document every couple of minutes and has at least one temporary file open all the time. NT wants exclusive access to the disk when it performs this function. Clicking Yes will cause this check to be accomplished during your next boot-up.

The Performance Monitor can also be used in troubleshooting. It is found in the Start menu under Administrative Tools and looks like Figure 22.23.

Figure 22.23.

Performance Monitor.

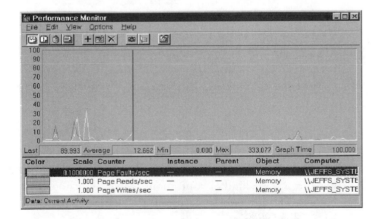

You can set up this tool to monitor almost any activity on your machine. The display shown in Figure 22.23 was created by clicking the plus button on the toolbar, selecting the Memory object, and then selecting the read, write, and error attributes of the Memory object. You could use this setting to check your RAM for excessive errors. You should spend some time playing with this tool to familiarize yourself with what it does. It might save you money in the long run because Performance Monitor can be made to do many things that you might think you need third-party software to accomplish.

A less complicated view of your system and its potential problems is available from the Task Manager. Pressing Ctrl+Alt+Del or right-clicking the Start bar will enable you to choose the Task Manager, shown in Figure 22.24.

Figure 22.24.

The Task Manager.

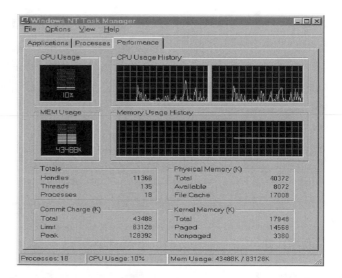

This figure shows the Performance tab of the Task Manager. It produces less detail on memory and CPU usage than the other tools covered so far, but it presents the information it has in an easy-to-absorb graphical format. For example, it would be easy on this screen to see that the installed RAM was too small for the current load.

The next tab, Processes, shows the running processes; these include background operations required by applications. This tab is depicted in Figure 22.25.

If you have an application that seems to have run away and hidden, come to this page and see if it has used any CPU time. If it is using CPU time, either it is still processing or it has gone into some kind of continuous loop. If it is not using CPU time, then it is probably broken. The next tab, Applications (see Figure 22.26), will let you unload an application that has stopped running.

22

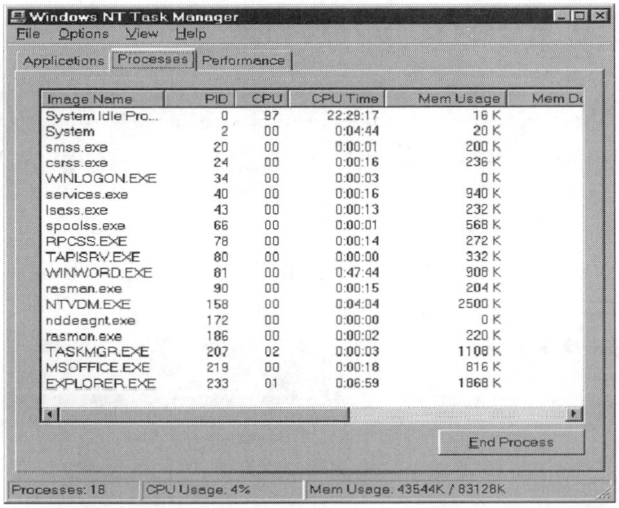

Figure 22.25.

Task Manager processes.

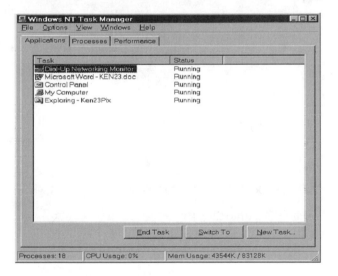

Figure 22.26.

Task Manager applications.

This tab shows the current applications and their status. Normally, if an application has stopped running, it will show a "not responding" status. You can close any application by highlighting it and choosing End Task. If the task refuses to stop on its own, then you will get a dialog that allows you to either give the application 20 more seconds to close or close it immediately. Closing an application this way can result in a loss of data, but if the application has stopped, it is a good way to close it down.

The Event Viewer

Most of the things that happen to your Windows NT computer are recorded in a log. NT lets you look at these events with a tool called Event Viewer, available through the Administrative Tools folder. Event Viewer can be especially helpful in troubleshooting nonfatal boot-up problems. Fatal boot-up problems don't let you into NT far enough to invoke the Event Viewer.

Figure 22.27 shows what the Event Viewer looks like.

Figure 22.27.

The Event Viewer.

Date	Time	Source	Category	Event	User	Computer
2/9/97	9:52:11 AM	Disk	None	7	N/A	JEFFS_SYSTEM
2/9/97	9:52:11 AM	atapi	None	26	N/A	JEFFS_SYSTEM
2/9/97	9:52:11 AM	Disk	None	7	N/A	JEFFS_SYSTEM
2/9/97	9:52:11 AM	atapi	None	26	N/A	JEFFS_SYSTEM
2/9/97	9:52:11 AM	Disk	None	7	N/A	JEFFS_SYSTEM
2/9/97	9:52:11 AM	atapi	None	26	N/A	JEFFS_SYSTEM
2/9/97	9:52:11 AM	Disk	None	7	N/A	JEFFS_SYSTEM
2/9/97	9:52:11 AM	atapi	None	26	N/A	JEFFS_SYSTEM
2/9/97	9:52:11 AM	Disk	None	7	N/A	JEFFS_SYSTEM
2/9/97	9:52:11 AM	atapi	None	26	N/A	JEFFS_SYSTEM
2/9/97	2:21:38 AM	Disk	None	7	N/A	JEFFS_SYSTEM
2/9/97	2:21:38 AM	atapi	None	26	N/A	JEFFS_SYSTEM
2/9/97	2:21:37 AM	Disk	None	7	N/A	JEFFS_SYSTEM
2/9/97	2:21:37 AM	atapi	None	26	N/A	JEFFS_SYSTEM
2/9/97	2:21:36 AM	Disk	None	7	N/A	JEFFS_SYSTEM
2/9/97	2:21:36 AM	atapi	None	26	N/A	JEFFS_SYSTEM
2/9/97	2:21:35 AM	Disk	None	7	N/A	JEFFS_SYSTEM
2/9/97	2:21:35 AM	atapi	None	26	N/A	JEFFS_SYSTEM
2/9/97	2:21:34 AM	Disk	None	7	N/A	JEFFS_SYSTEM
2/9/97	2:21:34 AM	atapi	None	26	N/A	JEFFS_SYSTEM
2/9/97	2:21:18 AM	Disk	None	7	N/A	JEFFS_SYSTEM
2/9/97	2:21:18 AM	atapi	None	26	N/A	JEFFS_SYSTEM
2/9/97	2:21:18 AM	Disk	None	7	N/A	JEFFS_SYSTEM
2/9/97	2:21:18 AM	atapi	None	26	N/A	JEFFS_SYSTEM
2/9/97	2:21:18 AM	Disk	None	7	N/A	JEFFS_SYSTEM
2/9/97	2:21:18 AM	atapi	None	26	N/A	JEFFS_SYSTEM
2/9/97	2:21:18 AM	Disk	None	7	N/A	JEFFS_SYSTEM
2/9/97	2:21:18 AM	atapi	None	26	N/A	JEFFS_SYSTEM

Double-clicking an event, like one of the many Disk events shown on the log, will bring up details about that particular event, as shown in Figure 22.28.

This shows that the system is detecting a bad sector on one of my disks. From this description, you can choose one of the other tools available to fix the problem. This brings up the third rule of troubleshooting:

Rule #3: Read the event log often.

Not every "bad" event that Event Viewer shows is reported to you, the user. For example, the bad sector error was not reported any other way. If you don't regularly read the event log, you might not be able to prevent some problems before you have to resort to troubleshooting.

Figure 22.28.

*Viewing an event in the
Event Viewer.*

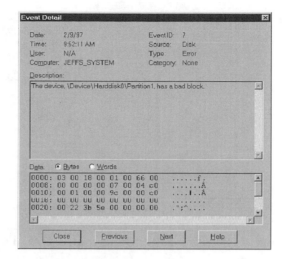

22

Network Troubleshooting

There are generally two areas involved in troubleshooting network problems: hardware and
software settings.

If you suspect a hardware problem, like not being able to talk to your new network interface
card, check the Event Viewer for any events that indicate problems with your card. Also, use
WinMSD to check out possible conflicts. Usually, your problem will involve an IRQ, port,
or memory setting. Most network boards come with diagnostic software that also detects and
displays the IRQ, port, and memory settings for your card. Unfortunately, NT will not
enable you to run these programs because they access hardware directly. You will need to
reboot your system with DOS or Windows 95 and run your board's diagnostic program.

When you get your board de conflicted, write down the settings (a good place is the
WinMSD report described earlier). If you are still having problems, Windows NT has an
extensive built-in network troubleshooting system. You can start this troubleshooter through
the NT Help file. Choose Help from the Start menu and choose the topic, Network
Troubleshooter. You will get a screen that looks like Figure 22.29.

This will lead you, question by question, through common network problems.

Rule #4: Write down your important settings, especially your network settings.

Figure 22.29.

Network Troubleshooter.

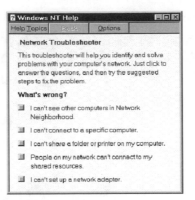

Writing down your network settings sounds like common sense, but I would hate to pay for all the time lost each day rerunning software to find the settings for a network card. And I will bet your systems administrator would like all the time back that was spent telling users for the third or fourth time their IP address and Domain Name Server. Given the Network Troubleshooter to solve the majority of your common networking problems, the next best thing you can do is write down and store your network settings.

Summary

This lesson covered the troubleshooting tools and techniques available to you through a stock Windows NT setup. You learned boot problems, WinMSD, and network problems along with assorted other tools you will find in your NT setup. You also learned four troubleshooting rules:

1. Make backups before something bad happens.
2. When in doubt, reinstall.
3. Read the event log often.
4. Write down your important settings, especially your network settings.

These tools and rules will get you through the majority of the problems you will encounter in Windows NT.

Workshop

The Workshop helps you solidify the skills you learned this hour.

Glossary

disk defragmenter   A program that reorganizes each file on your disk into one contiguous block. Without a defragmenter your hard drive will eventually lose track of the locations of all the pieces of a file.

Performance Monitor   A role of your own performance monitor that enables the user to monitor most of the important aspects of the system. The user must define which details Performance Monitor will display. Good for an in-depth view of system performance.

Task Manager   An NT program that provides both a graphical and textual look at system performance. Offers a few preset views of system performance as opposed to the Performance Monitor's many user-defined views. Good way to get a quick overview of system performance.

WinMSD   An NT utility that will give the user a snapshot of system resource allocation. Especially good for finding resource conflicts.

Exercises

1. Back up all essential information on your machine. Make hard copies of your system settings.
2. Create boot-up disks as described in Hour 13, "File Systems and Windows NT 4," and update or create your emergency repair disk.

Hour 23

Recovery Tips

by Gary R. Neely

Even the best operating system designers in the world can't guarantee that your system won't get corrupted or otherwise messed up. You can make a big mistake in system configuration, delete the wrong file, inadvertently mess up the Registry, or make a bad change to your drive configurations. A poorly installed application can cause problems for your system. You might encounter a computer virus (very possible if you download many executable files from the Internet or other sources). There are many possibilities.

NT is a remarkably stable operating system. You can't expect *never* to have a serious problem, but you can be confident that serious problems are rare with NT. When you do experience the effects of Murphy's Law, you will need to know what you can do about it. That's what this lesson is about.

An Ounce of Prevention

Some readers will be using NT at home for non-critical operations. Others will be planning to use NT for critical business functions. In either case, assume disaster strikes—can you afford to have your system down for long? Run through that scenario a few times and consider how you would survive it. Your best defense is to plan for catastrophe and take steps to avoid problem situations before they occur. This section covers what steps you can take to help prevent a disaster and what you can do to minimize the effects of a system failure.

Limiting Computer Access

Because many problems occur as a result of mistakes on the part of an operator, you should consider limiting access to your workstation to those people who both need to use the system and are competent in its use. You can limit the physical access to the machine, or you can limit system access by creating individual user accounts and employing NT's many security features to place restrictions on what a user can do and access. Learn about the capabilities of the administrator account, and keep these capabilities out of reach of those who don't need them.

Backups: The Best Insurance

Nothing protects you better than a regular backup of your system and critical data. If your workstation is performing business-critical operations, invest in some form of backup device like a tape drive or other removable media device. For critical business applications, backups to a second hard disk are not recommended unless the hard disk is on another machine and preferably at a different physical site. A system administrator should think not just in terms of a system failure, but should consider the possibility of fire or other situations that could destroy the entire site. Keep copies of your important resources in different locations!

Failure Event Recording

Windows NT gives you some capability to record critical system failures, which can help you reconstruct what happened, but you must enable these features in advance of an incident. You can instruct NT to take certain actions in the event of fatal system errors by configuring the Recovery options. To get to this feature, open the control panel and click the System icon. Select the Startup/Shutdown tab. You'll see a dialog box like the one shown in Figure 23.1.

23

Figure 23.1.

*Setting NT's Recovery
options.*

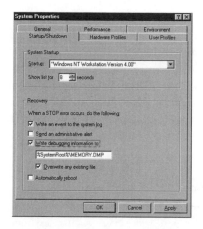

You can make a record of a system failure by having NT write a history of such events to the
system log. The debugging information option probably won't be useful to you, but could
be very useful if you need to call in an NT troubleshooter. I recommend against setting NT
to automatically reboot after an error for two reasons: the error screen can contain
information you might want to record, and you might be booting back into an unstable
system. The administrator alert is useful when the machine is on a network; it will report to
the system administrator that a problem has occurred on that workstation.

JUST A MINUTE

> Changing the Recovery settings might result in the necessity of changing
> your pagefile settings. This is particularly true if you check the Write
> debugging information to: box because this option essentially makes a
> copy of your pagefile as it appeared when the system problem occurred.

If your system has been stable for some time and you are not planning to make any major
system configuration changes, you can turn off the Recovery options and save some system
resources.

The "Blue Screen of Death"

The *Blue Screen of Death* is a system message with a blue background that is displayed when
an NT system experiences the equivalent of a heart attack. You may never see this, but you
should be aware of what it is and what you can learn from it.

If you opted to automatically reboot after a system failure (see the preceding section), then you might not see the death screen. Again, checking this option is not a good idea because you could miss important diagnostic information presented with the death screen. If you get a Blue Screen of Death, carefully record any diagnostic information presented. This can help you discover the source of the problem. Typically, death screens are the result of hardware problems such as flawed devices, improperly seated or bad memory cards, driver resource conflicts, bugs in the operating system, or even a computer virus.

Record Your Experience

Keep your own records of what happened. You might need to describe the situation to someone else. Reporting "Well, it just *crashed*, you know?" isn't going to help a troubleshooter help you. If the event occurred when someone else was using the machine, interview them about the event. Avoid accusations or other negative behavior—most people will try to minimize their involvement at the time when you most need their help.

Even if you solve the problem yourself handily, keeping records can help you in the future if the same problem comes up again. You might discover the solution to some problem, pat yourself on the back for being a genius, and move on, not bothering to write down a short description of the incident (geniuses don't need to write things down, do they?). Months later the problem comes up again, but Mr. Genius can't remember what he did to fix it, so valuable time is wasted re-discovering the solution. Moral: If it's worth fooling with, it's worth recording. A box of 3×5 cards is very useful for this sort of thing.

Diagnosing Disaster

When a problem occurs and you are certain it is system-related, begin collecting all information available to you. Read the system event logs, notes made from a death screen, and details noted by whoever experienced the crash. By that time, it might be clear what happened. If not, determine what recent changes were made to the system.

☐ Is the problem related to software? You can get good clues by recalling what operations immediately preceded the problem. Using beta versions of applications can often cause problems. Running executable files downloaded from the Internet or other sources is a good entry point for a computer virus. Many freely distributed utility or game programs are poorly written or unstable; these can cause problems (NT will intercept many of these problems). Removing the troublesome software might get rid of the problem.

☐ Is the problem related to hardware? A new hardware component or driver is a good clue. Have you recently installed a new memory card? Check that your computer is being properly cooled—this is a common source of strange problems. Has a new peripheral system been added? Is your power system stable? Be certain you have no resource conflicts with your device drivers.

It might help to describe what happened to a friend who might think of something you missed. A clear and logical review of events is very likely to suggest a course for recovery of your system.

The Last Known Good Configuration

In the event that your system does crash, NT provides you with several relatively easy solutions that can help you get things running again. The *Last Known Good* configuration is the first of these solutions.

By now, you have seen the following message when you boot NT 4:

```
Press spacebar NOW to invoke Hardware Profile/Last Known Good menu.
```

You might have wondered what that was all about or even tried it. This is NT's first line of defense against disaster.

Consider this: Suppose you accidentally set up a bad hardware configuration. You already know that NT is picky about hardware installation—a device conflict could cause NT to fail to boot, possibly resulting in the Blue Screen of Death. NT tries hard to save you from this sort of problem. Every time NT is booted and you successfully log in to the system, NT makes a copy of the current (successful) configuration and calls it the Last Known Good configuration. If your hardware changes, you can have several different configurations saved. You have a chance to return to a previous configuration that might not include the troublesome driver. (If only Windows 3.*x* had this feature!)

By pressing the spacebar when you see this message, you are accessing the Last Known Good menu, which will give you the opportunity to pick from a list of historical configurations. You'll see the following message appear:

```
This menu allows you to select a hardware profile
to be read when Windows NT is started.
```

Below this message, you'll be presented with a list of configurations. You can use the arrow keys to select one from this list and press Enter to invoke your choice. You can also press L to go straight to the Last Known Good configuration or press F3 to abort the process and restart your computer. If your hardware and device drivers have remained in their original configuration, you may see only one option.

The Last Known Good solution won't always work. It is largely based on hardware changes, so it might not resolve situations that are not the result of problems like device conflicts. You should also note that it works only if you have not successfully logged into the system since the problem developed.

The Emergency Repair Disk

An *emergency repair disk* is NT's next line of defense, but it relies on you at least in part to take advantage of it. An emergency repair disk is a record of NT's critical system configuration files (including portions of the Registry) saved to a floppy. This record is effectively a "snapshot" of important system files at the time the repair disk was made. For this disk to be really useful, you should make a habit of updating it every time you make a significant change to your system or according to some schedule like a weekly backup cycle. You should consider updating your emergency repair disk any time you add a piece of hardware, change your disk configuration, or add a new user.

JUST A MINUTE

> The emergency repair disk does not make a complete copy of the Registry. The Registry can be larger than the capacity of a floppy, so NT copies only the information necessary to boot the system. You should consider other options to save your Registry information such as the REGBACK and REGREST programs in Microsoft's NT Resource Kit.

Creating the Emergency Repair Disk

There are two ways to create an emergency repair disk. You've already seen one of them back in Hour 15, "Installation and Setup of NT 4 Workstation." The NT installation routine asks you if you want to create an emergency repair disk. If you're lucky, you did so when you first installed NT. The second method is to run an NT utility program called RDISK. This program is found in the SYSTEM32 directory of your NT system directory (normally WINNT).

You can run RDISK from the command prompt by changing to the WINNT\SYSTEM32 directory and entering RDISK.EXE. You'll see a dialog box like the one shown in Figure 23.2.

Figure 23.2.

The main dialog box of the RDISK Repair Disk Utility.

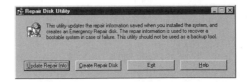

23

The utility's first option, Update Repair Info, scans your system's configuration, updates the backup files necessary for a system repair, and (optionally) makes an emergency repair disk from this information. Click the Update button to update your system's repair files. You will see the warning shown in Figure 23.3.

Figure 23.3.

RDISK warns you that you are about to erase your old system repair information.

Click Yes to continue. The update will require a minute or two to complete. When the update is finished, you will be shown another dialog box, as shown in Figure 23.4.

Figure 23.4.

RDISK asks if you want to make an emergency repair disk from your updated system files.

Click Yes if you want RDISK to create the emergency repair disk. RDISK will then place a copy of the system repair files on your floppy, which will become the emergency repair disk. RDISK will reformat the floppy, and then copy the configuration files. (There seems to be no way to skip the reformatting of the disk.) When this is completed, you are finished making an emergency repair disk. Be sure to label the disk before you store it.

TIME SAVER

It is a very good idea to update your repair disk after installing a Service Pack. If you don't, you'll get a slew of messages about mismatched files during a repair.

You can also use RDISK's other main dialog box option, Create Repair Disk, to format a floppy and copy existing repair files to the disk. Use this button if you want to make an emergency repair disk but don't need to update your system files.

JUST A MINUTE

The emergency repair disk is not a bootable disk, nor is it a substitute for a full system backup. It simply saves those system configuration files necessary to get NT up and running.

Restoring from the Emergency Repair Disk

All right, you've made an emergency repair disk. You feel really comforted now that you have it. But wait... how do you use it? NT's documentation doesn't discuss it. So where do you use the emergency repair disk?

The answer is found back in Hour 15 early in the installation routine. Remember the "Welcome to Setup" screen with the following options?

- ☐ To learn more about Windows NT Setup before continuing, press F1.
- ☐ To set up Windows NT now, press Enter.
- ☐ To repair a damaged Windows NT version 4.0 installation, press R.
- ☐ To quit Setup without installing Windows NT, press F3.

The third option, "To repair a damaged Windows NT...," is the solution—not exactly obvious to casual users.

To restore a messed-up NT system, insert the first of your boot disks and restart your computer. Various files will be loaded from the disk, and then you will be asked to insert disk 2 and more files will be loaded. In a few moments, you'll be shown the "Welcome to Setup" screen with the four options shown. This time, instead of pressing Enter to install NT, press R to begin the system recovery. In a moment, you'll be shown a new screen with the following options:

```
[X] Inspect registry files
[X] Inspect startup environment
[X] Verify Windows NT system files
[X] Inspect boot sector
Continue (perform selected tasks)
```

An X in a box indicates that the recovery procedure will perform that task. Use the arrow keys and Enter to unmark a box or mark it. You can also press F1 to see the help screens for this menu, which is a good idea. F3 will abort the setup procedure and Esc will return you to the Welcome to Setup menu.

The following is a brief description of what each category can do for you:

- ☐ Inspect registry files. This option will check your Registry for corrupted or missing information. You will be given some control over what information is restored.
- ☐ Inspect startup environment. This option will restore corrupted NT system boot files. If your boot files are missing or corrupted, they will be replaced by good versions from your distribution disk.

23

□ Verify Windows NT system files. This option will determine if all necessary system files are present and match the original files. Missing or altered files can be replaced using those on your distribution disk.

□ Inspect boot sector. The option will restore the boot loader files.

When you are comfortable with your selected options, select "Continue (perform selected tasks)" and press Enter. Your experience with the rest of the recovery procedure might not match what is written in the rest of this section if you have not selected all of the four categories, but it will be fairly clear which procedures were omitted.

The recovery procedure begins by detecting your mass storage devices using the same routine described in Hour 15. When this is completed, you will be asked to insert the third boot disk. After some files are loaded, the recovery program will ask you to either insert your emergency repair disk or let the program attempt to find this information on your hard disk. (See the section "The REPAIR Directory," later in this lesson.) If you have an emergency repair disk, insert it in the drive and press Enter. The program continues by briefly examining your hard disk. If you opted to inspect your Registry, it will then ask you if you want to repair your Registry file, showing the following options:

```
[  ] SYSTEM (System Configuration)
[  ] SOFTWARE (Software Information)
[  ] DEFAULT (Default User Profile)
[  ] NTUSER (New User Profiles)
[  ] SECURITY (Security Policy) and
SAM (User Accounts Database)
Continue (perform selected tasks)
```

As in the previous menu, you can use the arrow keys and Enter to mark the components of the Registry you want to repair. Note that the boxes are initially presented unmarked.

CAUTION

Fooling with the Registry is not recommended unless you absolutely know what you are doing. You can easily change or delete critical settings and make your situation worse (or much worse) than it might already be.

You can press F1 to read the help on this menu, and doing so is a very good idea. You'll see Microsoft's warning about messing with the Registry and learn more about the Registry components. F3 enables you to abort the recovery procedure. If you don't have to recover the Registry, simply leave the boxes unmarked, select "Continue (perform selected tasks)," and press Enter to continue.

23

The recovery process continues by examining your system files for possible corruption. A status bar will show you the progress of this examination. When this process is completed, you will be asked to restart your computer.

JUST A MINUTE

When the recovery process examines your system files, it will look for any required file that is not present or does not match the original system files. Some of your applications or support utilities might have modified or upgraded these files. The examination will flag these files and give you the opportunity to restore the original or skip over the file. If you choose to restore to an original, one or more of your applications might have to be reinstalled.

With a little luck, the recovery process will have reconstructed your system and you can successfully boot NT. When you reboot, you might see some strange new messages as NT is loading. The system is simply familiarizing itself with its new configuration; the messages probably won't repeat the next time you boot NT. When NT is up, you might also notice some things have been reset, such as your video mode and (with a multiple-boot system) the configuration of your boot loader. You'll have to go into Control Panel and make the necessary changes to get things back to normal.

TIME SAVER

Did you forget your latest Administrator password? You can use the emergency repair disk to access your system by restoring the User Accounts Database, and with it, your original password.

The REPAIR Directory

As further insurance against disaster, NT saves a copy of the repair disk information in a subdirectory of WINNT called REPAIR. This is the same information that is on the emergency repair disk and is updated when you choose Update using the RDISK program. If you did not bother to make an emergency repair disk, you can direct the recovery program to try to use the information in this directory to restore the system.

Disk Configuration

Windows NT enables you to save information about your disk partitions in case you make a mistake and need to restore your previous configuration.

23

Saving Your Disk Configuration

Saving the disk configuration is a function of the Disk Administrator. You can get to the Disk Administrator by clicking the Programs menu of the Start button, then Administration Tools. In the Disk Administrator, click the Partition menu, select Configuration, and then select Save, as shown in Figure 23.5.

Figure 23.5.

Using the Disk Administrator to make a backup of disk partitioning information.

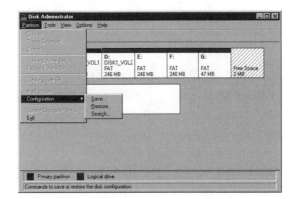

The Disk Administrator will prompt you to insert a floppy disk, as shown in Figure 23.6. The disk must be formatted; the program will not do it for you.

Figure 23.6.

Saving disk configuration to a formatted floppy.

TIME SAVER

You can save your disk configuration information to the emergency repair disk in addition to the disk's normal repair data. Note that if you update your emergency repair disk, you will have to again save your disk configuration because the update process reformats the disk.

Restoring a Disk Configuration

Restoring your disk configuration is very easy. In the Disk Administrator, select Partition | Configuration | Restore. You will be prompted to insert the disk with your restoration information. The Disk Administrator will warn you about overwriting your current configuration, as illustrated by Figure 23.7. Be sure this is what you want to do.

Figure 23.7.
Restoring a configura-
tion will overwrite
your existing disk
configuration.

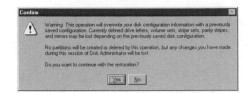

If you want to restore your configuration to the version on the floppy, simply click Yes. The restoration program will do the rest.

Creating Boot Disks

To use your emergency repair disk, you must be able to access the installation Welcome to Setup screen. This is normally accomplished by booting from the three boot disks. If you lose or don't have access to your boot disks, you can create new ones by running the WINNT installation program found on your distribution disk under the directory associated with your platform, probably \i386. If you are doing this under Windows NT, run the WINNT32 program, which is a 32-bit version of WINNT with a graphical interface.

Run the WINNT program using the following format:

```
WINNT  /O
```

The /O switch tells the WINNT program to make boot disks and then quit without installing NT. You should be prepared with three reliable 3.5-inch floppy disks and insert them as prompted. For more information about WINNT and boot disks, see Hour 15.

Summary

By now, you should have some clear ideas on how to prepare for and recover from difficulties with your system. Take a moment to review the options available to you:

- ☐ Limit access, particularly access to Administrator capabilities
- ☐ Back up all critical files
- ☐ Learn to recognize and understand potential problems
- ☐ Keep good records
- ☐ Understand and be able to use the Last Known Good configuration
- ☐ Make an emergency repair disk and keep it up-to-date
- ☐ Back up your disk configuration
- ☐ Keep boot disks handy

23

If you've taken advantage of NT's recovery tools and have protected yourself by the appropriate backup and security precautions, you should not have to face the dreaded Final Option: installing NT and all your applications *again*.

Workshop

The Workshop helps you solidify the skills you learned this hour.

Glossary

Blue Screen of Death   Accepted slang term for the error report generated when NT experiences a critical system failure and cannot continue. The report is presented on a blue background.

emergency repair disk   A floppy disk containing a copy of critical system files that can be used to rebuild an NT system that has suffered damage to the Registry or essential system files.

Last Known Good   A copy of NT's system configuration files made at the time of a successful administrator login. You can use this historical configuration to boot NT if a more recent configuration resulted in problems.

Exercises

1. Consider where you store your backups. Is the location safe? Is it secure from theft? Is the location separate from your computer?

2. The next time you boot NT, press the spacebar to invoke the Last Known Good menu. Take the time to become familiar with this part of NT before you need it.

3. Use the procedures outlined in this hour and actually make an emergency repair disk. After you have the repair disk, try the procedures for using it. An emergency situation can be a lot less scary if you are already familiar with the recovery solutions.

Hour **24**

Using the Internet to Maintain Your System

by Gary Neely

Many resources are available to teach you more about using Windows NT. You're reading one of them right now. Other resources range from Microsoft's support lines to local NT user groups. But one of the best sources is as close as your computer's modem: the Internet. A few hours spent learning one or two common Internet tools will open a vast wealth of information and programs available for no more effort than it takes to find and download them.

In this hour, you'll learn a little bit about the Internet and how it works, and then you'll be introduced to the more common Windows NT programs used to get information from the Internet. After reading this lesson, you should have a good idea of where to turn when you need more information about NT 4 Workstation.

Fundamentals of the Internet

Many computer users are familiar with the idea of a network: a group of computers wired together so they can share information and resources. Despite all the hype and publicity, the Internet is nothing more than a collection of such networks ranging from little ones like those used to manage small businesses to very large networks that span states or even countries, such as those used by Ford, MCI, and the United States government. These networks have two things in common: they all speak the same electronic language called a protocol, and they are all connected to each other in some way. There are no colossal controlling computers and no central authorities other than a modest agency that manages the Internet equivalent to a phone book.

To most people, the Internet appears to be an invention of the 1990s, but it has actually been around in some form since the mid-'70s or so. Back in the late '60s, the U.S. Defense Department initiated a project intended to link military and research sites. The idea was to create a reliable (that is, nuke-proof) means to improve communications and the transfer of data. This network was known as ARPAnet after ARPA, the Advanced Research Projects Agency, which provided much of the funding.

Over time, more facilities were added until most institutions even remotely connected with defense projects or research were on this great network, which became known as the "Internet." The recent explosive growth of the Internet can perhaps be attributed to three things: the increasingly common and powerful personal computer, the movement of the Internet's backbone networks away from government to commercial providers, and the World Wide Web. The Internet has been growing exponentially for several years, and the growth rate shows no sign of diminishing. No one can foretell where it will go, but this medium is here to stay.

The Internet has some really inspiring qualities. Many organizations voluntarily donate expensive resources to help maintain and promote the Internet. (You'll be introduced to some of those resources later in this hour.) There is no central authority, nor is there any way to facilitate the creation of such an authority. It is not a computer fad but a new medium that differs radically from any other medium. It is not run by big broadcasting bosses or controlled by powerful publishing families. No computer on the Internet has precedence over another; a lowly 486SX-based PC has the same rights as a hideously expensive government supercomputer. In many respects, the Internet is representative of the ideals of the country in which it originated.

How the Internet Works (The Nutshell Version)

All computers on a network must speak the same language. There are many such network languages. The language of the Internet is called *Transmission Control Protocol/Internet Protocol*

24

(TCP/IP). TCP/IP was developed specifically for the ARPAnet project. Given its Defense Department requirements, it had to be robust, reliable, easy to maintain, and not be reliant upon a particular contractor. The fact that the explosive growth of the Internet has pushed TCP/IP well beyond its design goals attests to its strengths. TCP/IP is used by every program that relies on the Internet for any purpose. For your computer to use the Internet, it has to be able to speak this same language.

For transmission of its TCP/IP messages, the Internet does not use conventional telephone lines, but relies instead on high-speed dedicated fiber-optic telecommunication lines. Conventional telephone lines are not suited for transferring large amounts of digital information. When you make a telephone call, the line between caller and receiver is dedicated to that call (known as "line-switching"). This is very wasteful because the line mostly sits and twiddles its electrons while the caller talks or types (relatively) slowly. This is one of the reasons why long-distance calls are so expensive. Telephone lines are also rather noisy. An occasional pop or hiss might not affect your voice conversation, but it would be lethal to high-speed transmission of electronic data.

To get around these problems, error-correction protocols and "packet-switching" are used for most data transmission within the Internet. Error-correction protocols make certain that what is received is what was sent. Packet-switching breaks a call down into small pieces, which are reassembled as they accumulate at their destination. With packet-switching, a line can handle many callers; when one caller is not talking or sending data, the line can be busy handling other callers. A packet is a lot like a letter; it is an independent unit with a destination address and a bundle of data. High-speed dedicated computers known as "routers" distributed throughout the Internet act as postal workers for these letters, looking at each packet and checking its address. If the address is not for a computer on the local network, the router hands the packet off to a router on a network closer to its destination. This process is repeated until the packet gets to its destination.

IPs, Domains, and Other Strange Critters

Every computer on the Internet is assigned a number that uniquely identifies it to all other computers. This number is called an *IP address* after the TCP/IP specification. An IP address is a 32-bit number usually expressed as four numbers ranging from 0 to 255 and separated by periods. For example, a computer might have an IP address of 206.31.72.1. When a computer is permanently connected to a TCP/IP network, it is assigned one of these numbers by the local administrator, but in many cases a computer is given a temporary address from a pool of available numbers. This is what happens when you use your modem to connect to an ISP's network for PPP access.

Using 32-bit numbers can be fine for computers, but imagine how annoying the system would be if you had to remember those numbers every time you used the Internet. The TCP/IP specification gives us poor humans a method to assign more meaningful names to computers on the Internet. This is the *domain name* system. A domain is like a neighborhood where each house is a computer. For example, Microsoft's domain is microsoft.com and www.microsoft.com is a specific computer in that domain, one called www that handles Microsoft's World Wide Web traffic. Domain names are categorized by primary usage:

- [ ] com refers to commercial users
- [ ] net refers to networks such as ISPs
- [ ] gov is used for government agencies
- [ ] org is used for organizations (typically non-profit)
- [ ] mil refers to military users
- [ ] edu is used for educational institutions

All domain names are registered with the Internet's one and only central agency, InterNIC. The people at InterNIC keep records of all domain names, making sure all names comply with the TCP/IP standards and no two names are the same. When an organization registers a domain, it has the right to name all the computers that are part of that domain.

JUST A MINUTE

> The Internet use of the word "domain" has nothing to do with the Windows NT Server use of the word, which groups computers on a network for administrative and security purposes.

So how does the Internet use a domain name to find a computer identified by a number? Suppose that you wanted to use the Netscape Navigator Web browser to get a Web page from the author's Web server at www.scigate.net. A browser doesn't care where the server is physically located, but it does care about the server's location on the network. Navigator has no idea where scigate.net is on the Internet, but the InterNIC knows because that information is part of the domain name registration process. (Note that InterNIC does not know where www.scigate.net is.) The Navigator program sends a message to one of InterNIC's Primary Domain Name Servers, computers with well-known addresses that contain directory information for all registered domain names. The message says, in effect, where is this scigate.net place? The reply is the address of scigate.net's own little name server. Armed with that information, Navigator sends out a new message, this time contacting a name server computer on the SCIgate network and asking: where is your "www" computer? SCIgate's name server replies with the exact address of the Web server computer. Finally, Navigator has enough information to contact www.scigate.net and get the Web page you wanted.

This process is called *name resolution* and happens all over the Internet every time someone requests a Web page, sends an e-mail, or contacts an FTP server. It's amazing that everything not only works, but works so fast!

How You Can Get on the Internet

Many people get access to the Internet through university accounts or their office network. Others buy access through commercial enterprises known as *Internet Service Providers* (ISPs). These companies maintain a network that exists only to give their customers' computers a home on the Internet. They have a lot of modems so you can dial in to their network, which in turn is connected to a larger network, like a bigger ISP or a communications company like MCI. This is not the same as a Bulletin Board System (BBS), which typically supports only local file and message exchanges (although many BBSs now offer Internet access or have become full-service ISPs). Companies such as America Online and CompuServe are really gigantic BBSs; most now have full Internet services, but access can be slow due to the large number of users supported.

Internet access has four primary forms: simple dial-up, PPP (or the older SLIP), dedicated PPP, and dedicated line. These forms vary substantially in capability and price.

- [ ] Simple dial-up access enables you to call your provider and use a few services that run on the provider's computers, but you're not actually a part of the provider's network. This service is most commonly used for simple e-mail accounts.

- [ ] A *Point-to-Point Protocol* (PPP) account lets you use your serial port and modem to place you on the provider's network. You are given a temporary IP address from a pool of addresses every time you connect to your provider. This lets you run Internet applications on your computer rather than relying on whatever applications are on the provider's computers.

- [ ] A dedicated PPP account has the same benefits as a PPP account except that your provider gives you a permanent address and generally dedicates a modem for your exclusive use. This has two benefits: You never have to wait to connect to your ISP and (more importantly) you have a permanent piece of Internet real estate. With your permanent address, you can now set up your computer to host your own Internet services. This form of access tends to be rather pricey but is still within the means of many individual users.

- [ ] You can build your own network and connect it directly to an "upstream" ISP using a dedicated high-speed network line. This is the same thing an ISP does, but the scale of the operation varies widely. This form of Internet connection is very expensive and well beyond the knowledge and means of most Internet users, but it is an option, and many ISPs are willing to sell this service.

JUST A MINUTE

A PPP account is necessary if you want to use Internet services such as the World Wide Web and FTP on your workstation. Your ISP may require you to use SLIP, which is an older and simpler protocol than PPP.

When you are looking for an ISP, you should shop around just as you would for any service. Typical prices are $5–$10 per month for an e-mail account, and around $20 per month for a PPP account. Some services base their charges on the time you spend online, whereas others provide unlimited usage. Some ISPs enable you to set up a small World Wide Web home page as part of their package; others require an additional charge. Look for an ISP that does not hide its fees and has a pleasant, courteous staff. As with other services, you get what you pay for. Cheap ISPs often have insufficient modems to handle their customer volume, resulting in busy signals when you try to dial up the ISP's access number. Don't expect a lot of features or help from cheap ISPs.

TIME SAVER

Before you choose an ISP, consider where you will need Internet access. If you are largely a home user, shopping for a reliable local service makes sense. However, if you travel often and need Internet access wherever you may be, you should find an ISP that provides access options in many locations.

Internet Services

Now that you have some idea what the Internet is and how it works, what can you do with it? How can it add to your ability to work with Windows NT?

There are many *client* applications that are used over the Internet. Mail is perhaps the most well-known of these applications. A client program sends and receives information from another program called a *server* that maintains and distributes the information. You run a client application on your computer and use it to request information from another computer running a server. The following client programs and services are likely to prove the most useful for finding more information about NT 4:

☐ World Wide Web browser. A program used to request and read information on the World Wide Web. Typically this is information from Web servers, but most browsers can be used to find and view documents from other servers such as FTP and Gopher.

☐ File Transfer Protocol (FTP). This Internet service is used to move files between computers.

☐ Telnet. This service enables you to log on to a distant computer and use its resources just as if you were a local operator.

☐ Usenet newsgroups. Usenet is a distributed system of discussion groups covering almost any topic imaginable, including Windows NT.

The rest of this lesson is devoted to explaining the use of the Web browser, FTP, and Telnet applications provided with Windows NT 4 Workstation. These programs are well suited to assist you in learning more about NT and the various applications and resources available to you throughout the world. The Usenet and the newsgroups most important for NT support are also mentioned.

The World Wide Web and Microsoft's Internet Explorer

The *World Wide Web* is one of the chief reasons for the Internet's explosion in users over the past several years. The Web can be thought of as the total of all resources that can be accessed on the Internet. These resources are often linked together by means of *HTML* documents containing a link to other (not necessarily HTML) documents. This doesn't sound like a big deal, but the ramifications are tremendous.

HTML is an acronym for HyperText Markup Language, a document-formatting standard designed to let documents be seen in the same way regardless of the reader's computer or operating system. Hypertext enables another file to be associated with information contained within a document. To understand the power of this concept, imagine that you are reading a book with a list of references to other books. To read a referenced book, you must physically go and find the book. With hypertext, you simply click on the reference and suddenly you have the referenced material before you. And the referenced book might have references, which would themselves contain references, and so on until at some point you might encounter an article that refers to the original book! That is the nature of the World Wide Web, except the Web isn't restricted to printed text. Its references can be pictures, sounds, video clips and more—information that can come from computers all over the world.

Before the advent of HTML and the Web, information was viewed as a set of archives; files stored on various computers and accessed by looking at a list of unexciting and often uninformative filenames and then using FTP to download the file you want. Indexing methods such as Gopher were developed to catalog all these resources, and although very useful, they provided about the same degree of excitement as a library card catalog. With HTML and the Web, the same information can be accessed in a more visual and natural way. It is easier to express ideas and make associations that might never have otherwise occurred. Suddenly, it's possible to put things online that were never considered before.

24

If you've had enough of reading about the Web and want to experience it for yourself, why don't you boot up NT and get started using its built-in Web browser: Microsoft's Internet Explorer?

Starting Internet Explorer

Starting Internet Explorer is easy. Just select the Internet Explorer icon from your desktop or choose it from the Programs menu under the Start button. If you are not already connected to a network or your ISP, NT will prompt you to make a connection shortly after starting the Internet Explorer program.

TIME SAVER

> A Web browser such as Internet Explorer can be run without a network connection. This lets you read documents in HTML format or view images locally on your computer. Help and informational literature are increasingly being provided in HTML format because HTML is easy to format and lends itself well to the structured nature of guide documents.

When you start the Internet Explorer program, it will attempt to load an informative page from Microsoft's Web site. You can either wait for the page to download or click the Stop button to halt the process.

Pointing the Browser to a Web Site

Microsoft's slogan asks: "Where Do You Want To Go Today?" You'll have to answer that question, but here's how you can get there. You will find a box labeled Address: in the upper section of the Internet Explorer screen. That box is where you enter an address known as a *Uniform Resource Locator* (URL). A URL is a standard method for identifying many different kinds of information on the World Wide Web. A URL describes the protocol to be used, the computer where the information can be found, the directory path to the desired file, and the name of the file. Web documents use the HyperText Transport Protocol, and so their URLs begin with http:.

In the following example, www.yahoo.com has been entered into the address box. This is the Web address for Yahoo!, a commonly used Internet directory site. After you enter the URL into the address box and press Enter, the browser will request the default or "home" page of Yahoo!. If you did this yourself, you should see something like Figure 24.1.

Figure 24.1.
Using Internet Explorer to view Yahoo!'s resources.

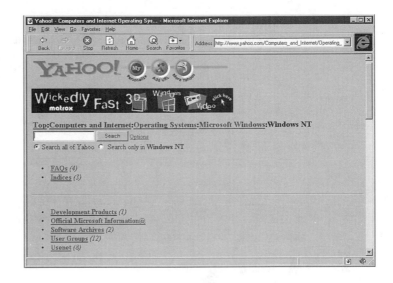

What you see may be different because many Web sites such as Yahoo! often change the content of their pages. In this example, only the computer and domain name of the Yahoo! page was entered; no filename, directory path, or protocol was specified. Because these things were omitted, the browser assumed the default case: The protocol is http and the file is a default file called INDEX.HTML in Yahoo!'s computer's root directory. This is a common case when you want to find the home page for a business, but for many Web pages you will have to be more specific.

Mastering Internet Explorer

Entering URLs is almost all there is to using a Web browser, but there are a few features that will make your use of the program a little more pleasant. Most of these features are common in some form to all the popular browsers, so when you learn one, you will be comfortable with them all.

The Internet Explorer Toolbar

In a row near the top of Internet Explorer's screen, you will have noticed a series of buttons. These buttons are conveniences that help you navigate the Web:

☐ Back. This button takes you back to the previously viewed document. By pressing this button repeatedly, you can continue stepping back through your trail of viewed documents or Web sites. The button will be gray and inoperable if the current document is the first one viewed in that session.

☐ Forward. This button functions like the Back button, but moves you forward through documents you have viewed. It will be gray and inoperable if you haven't yet viewed a page or you are at the end of your list of viewed pages.

☐ Stop. Use this button to stop a page while it is loading. This is useful if you request the wrong page or a page is larger than you expected and you don't want to wait for it to download.

☐ Refresh. This button reloads the page. Use this button if you stopped the original downloading process or want to view an updated version of a page that changes frequently.

☐ Home. The browser's options allow you to specify the default "home" site that is downloaded when you start up the browser. With Internet Explorer, this is initially set to a Microsoft page, but you can change this to any URL you want. Many users change this to their home page or a favorite Web search engine.

☐ Search. You can configure this button to automatically send you to your favorite Web search engine.

☐ Favorites. This button enables you to select from a list of your favorite Web sites, saving you the burden of entering the URL. Use the Add option to add the URL currently displayed in the Address box to your list of favorite sites.

☐ Print. This button is used to make a printed copy of the page you are currently viewing.

Internet Explorer Options

Internet Explorer gives you some capability to customize its features to suit your needs. To get to the Options dialog box, click View | Options. Figure 24.2 shows the Options dialog box.

Figure 24.2.

Using the Options dialog box to customize Internet Explorer.

24

The features under the General tab let you make changes in the general appearance and function of the browser. From here, you can configure the appearance and features of the toolbar and turn off the browser's capability to display images.

TIME SAVER

Turning off the automatic display of graphic images can greatly speed the downloading of Web pages. You won't see all the pretty graphics, but those same pretty graphics account for the majority of time spent waiting for a page to load.

Click the Navigation tab to change the settings for the Home and Search toolbar buttons. Using this screen, you can change Microsoft's default Web pages for these buttons to any Web page you want. The Search button does not necessarily have to point to a search engine but can point to any Web page.

The other tabs show options for more advanced configuration of Internet Explorer. You won't need to mess with most of these, but you might want to take a few minutes to look at what is available.

Viewing the HTML Source of a Document

When a Web page is displayed on your browser, you are not seeing the actual document as loaded from a Web site; you are seeing the browser's interpretation of the document. Internet Explorer gives you the ability to look at the source document of a Web page, showing all the HTML formatting commands. This is a great way to learn HTML by observing how other people crafted their Web pages.

To view the source HTML document, click View | Source. Internet Explorer will use the NotePad to show you the source HTML for the current Web page. You can edit and save the source just as you would any other document. Note that this modifies only your local copy of the Web page; you cannot change the original document unless you have access to that document's server.

JUST A MINUTE

If you've never seen an HTML document before, don't be surprised the first time you see one. Many Web pages give the appearance of some kind of bizarre mating between a text file and a programming language, and in fact that is pretty close to what is happening with elaborate Web pages. Don't let this discourage you from learning HTML. It's quite easy to learn enough basic HTML tags to let you make your own Web page.

Saving Documents

If you find a Web page that you want to save locally to your computer, click File | Save As File. You will be prompted for the location in which you want to save the file. When the file is completely saved, you have a copy of the HTML document on your hard disk. (Note that this will not save any images associated with the document, only the source HTML of the document.)

TIME SAVER

> If a Web page does not offer a convenient way to download an image, you can still obtain it if you're willing to learn a little HTML. View the source of the Web page displaying the image and poke around until you find some text that appears near the image on the page. Near that, you'll find something that looks like `<img src="path/imagename.gif">`. The IMG tag is what pulls in an image to an HTML document. By replacing the filename portion of your currently displayed URL with the path and image filename revealed in the source HTML, you can get your browser to display only the desired image, which you can then save. If your browser can display it, you can save it.

Web Search Engines

You may find yourself staring at the Address box on your browser and have no idea what to type in there. There's so much out there to see, but how do you find it all? Where do you look?

Fortunately, there are many solutions to this problem. There are services on the Web that provide programs called "search engines," which constantly catalog the various Web sites on the Internet. People volunteer the names and URLs of their sites to these services, and the services themselves have automated programs that look for new sites.

The following are a few of the more popular search engines:

```
www.infoseek.com
www.altavista.digital.com
www.lycos.com
www.webcrawler.com
www.excite.com
```

To use any of these Web services, simply enter one of these URLs into the Address box of your browser and wait for the response. You can then use the features of the search engine just as you would look for materials at a library. Most have good online help if you get stuck or confused.

24

In addition to search engines, there are Internet directories that give a menu-like approach to finding information on the Web. The most popular of these is Yahoo!, found at www.yahoo.com. Yahoo! is easy to use and can let you wade into thousands of Web sites quickly without being swamped by too much information.

Many large corporations and universities maintain their own directories of online information. For NT users, the most important of these is the Microsoft Knowledge Base found at www.microsoft.com/kb. This site has large quantities of support material to answer questions and provide new insights into the use of NT. It is definitely worth investigating.

FTP

File Transfer Protocol (FTP) is a standard TCP/IP procedure for moving files between computers. The name "FTP" can refer to the protocol itself or a client program that uses the protocol to perform file transfers. For many people, it has become a common verb: "I'll FTP that file to you before I go home for the evening...." FTP is one of the oldest and most useful Internet tools. Chances are good that you will use it a lot.

In this section, you'll learn to use the FTP program provided with NT to upload and download files from other computers on the Internet. You'll also learn how to use Anonymous FTP to access public FTP servers. At the end of this section, you'll find a list of a few commonly used FTP servers that have valuable NT resources.

Using NT's FTP Program

Microsoft provides a basic FTP program with NT 4. It is simply called FTP.EXE and is found in the WINNT/WINNT32 directory. You can run the program from the Run option under the Start button or from the command prompt by changing to the WINNT32 directory and entering FTP at the prompt. You'll see a basic screen like the one shown in Figure 24.3.

Figure 24.3.
The FTP program's command prompt.

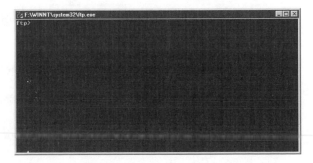

Starting an FTP Session

When the FTP program is up and running, you'll want to tell it what FTP site you want to access. You do this with the OPEN *hostname* command. Simply enter the command OPEN followed by the name of the desired FTP site:

OPEN ftp.microsoft.com

In this example, ftp.microsoft.com is the site name of Microsoft's FTP server. The program will attempt to contact the FTP site. The site will respond with a request for your user ID and then a password. Occasionally, you might be told that the connection is refused. Typically, this is because the site is swamped with too many users trying to access the site. Wait a few minutes and try again.

JUST A MINUTE

> You will often want to use Anonymous FTP to gain access to public FTP sites. Anonymous FTP doesn't sound very exciting but is in fact one of the most wonderful features of the Internet. Through Anonymous FTP, many companies and universities share their resources with the world. In return, they ask for nothing but a little courtesy on behalf of public users, such as avoiding use of the site during business hours and keeping the session as short as possible.
>
> To use Anonymous FTP, simply enter the word anonymous when asked to enter a user name, and then enter your e-mail address or the word guest when prompted for a password. Most FTP servers tend to ask for an e-mail address.

To demonstrate the use of FTP, you'll learn how to log in to Microsoft's FTP site, obviously a very useful place to go if you are seeking NT resources and help. Figure 24.4 shows a typical anonymous access to the Microsoft site.

Figure 24.4.

Logging in to the Microsoft FTP server using Anonymous FTP.

```
F:\WINNT\system32\ftp.exe
ftp> open ftp.microsoft.com
Connected to ftp.microsoft.com.
220 ftp Microsoft FTP Service (Version 3.0).
User (ftp.microsoft.com:(none)): anonymous
331 Anonymous access allowed, send identity (e-mail name) as password.
Password:
230-This is FTP.MICROSOFT.COM.  Please see the
dirmap.txt file for more information.
230 Anonymous user logged in.
ftp>
```

24

TIME SAVER

As an alternative to starting the FTP program and then entering the OPEN *hostname* command, you can provide a site address when you start the FTP program by entering FTP *hostname* at the command prompt. For example, FTP ftp.microsoft.com.

Microsoft's site is almost certain to be powered by NT, but most FTP sites are operated on a UNIX-based system. Figure 24.5 illustrates the difference in views. Even though the NT and UNIX directory schemes appear a bit differently, for purposes of FTP they are functionally the same.

Figure 24.5.

A session with Oakland University's repository, a site based on UNIX.

Navigating an FTP Site

When you have established a connection with the remote FTP host, you will need to know how to get around on its site. FTP provides a standard form of navigation for all FTP hosts. The following commands are used:

cd *directory name*	Changes to the specified directory name on the remote FTP host computer.
lcd *local directory name*	Changes to the specified directory name on your computer.
cd ..	Moves back to the parent directory on the remote computer. Note that unlike DOS, FTP requires a space between CD and the two periods when using the CD .. command.
ls or dir	Lists the contents of the current directory of the remote computer on your screen.

Make sure you enter these commands using lowercase.

Many FTP commands are very similar to their UNIX or DOS equivalents. If you are familiar with either of these command systems, you should have no difficulty with FTP commands. Don't expect the commands to behave *exactly* like their UNIX or DOS cousins.

When you log in to an FTP host, you will be placed in the root directory of the FTP server. Figure 24.6 shows the results of a DIR command on the Microsoft FTP site.

Figure 24.6.

Listing the root directory of the Microsoft FTP site.

A d prefix to an entry distinguishes directories from files. When you can see the directory structure, you can use the CD command to navigate to the directory that interests you.

Transferring Files

When you find a file you want to download, you need to know a few commands to let you set the file type for the download and tell FTP what to do:

ASCII	Sets the file type to ASCII for transferring text files.
BINARY	Sets the file type to Binary for transferring data files.
GET *remote filename*	Downloads a file from a remote computer to your local computer.
PUT *local filename*	Uploads a file to a remote computer from your local computer.

Suppose you want to download the file DIRMAP.TXT, which contains a description of the directory structure of Microsoft's FTP site. FTP distinguishes between standard ASCII files and data files that are not limited to the ASCII character set. ASCII is the default file type mode set by FTP, but if you were previously using the BINARY mode, you could change back by simply entering ASCII at the FTP prompt. FTP will respond with the following:

```
Type set to A
```

Next, to download the DIRMAP.TXT file, you would enter GET DIRMAP.TXT at the prompt. Figure 24.7 shows the procedure for downloading a file.

24

Figure 24.7.

Setting the file type and getting a file from an FTP server.

Getting a file can take some time depending upon the size of the file and how busy the FTP site is at the time of the transfer.

You might be wondering, "Okay, but where did it put the file?" FTP defaults to the directory in which you ran the FTP program, in this case, the WINNT32 directory. This is not a good place to start dumping files. Use the LCD command to change your local directory to some location more appropriate for file downloads.

JUST A MINUTE

> Most FTP systems are UNIX-based and are therefore case-sensitive. It isn't always obvious what operating system the host is using, so take the safe route and always type a command or filename using the exact characters as they appear on the listing.

Use of the PUT command is similar to GET. You must use LCD to change to the directory containing the file you want to upload, and then enter PUT followed by the name of the file you want to upload. Be sure to change to the appropriate file type with the BINARY or ASCII command before you initiate the transfer.

Other FTP Commands

The commands you've just seen will get you started using FTP. Here are a few others that you might need or find useful:

OPEN *hostname*	Opens a new connection to an FTP site.
CLOSE or DISCONNECT	Quits the FTP session with the current FTP host. This command does not quit the FTP program. Use this command if you want to change FTP sites.
BYE or QUIT	Terminates the current FTP session and quits the FTP program.

HELP *command name* or ? *command name*	Prints a brief help message about the command you specified. If you omit the command name, Help provides a listing of FTP commands. Don't expect very verbose help from most command-line FTP programs.
HASH	Prints hash or pound sign (#) for every 2KB block that is transferred during uploads and downloads. This is useful for monitoring the progress of file transfers.

There are additional FTP commands as well. You might want to find a manual on FTP and learn the various capabilities, particularly if you do any system administration.

GUI-Based FTP Programs

Did you find the FTP program shown earlier to be rather crude for today's world of GUI-based point-and-click programs? If so, you're not alone. The standard FTP program is very useful but the command-line interface just isn't very friendly. A little poking around on the Internet will reveal many GUI-based FTP client programs that simplify the FTP process. I highly recommend the shareware program WS_FTP from Ipswitch. Look at Figure 24.8 and compare it with the previous figures.

Figure 24.8.

Using a GUI-based FTP program—a vast improvement over FTP's crude command-line interface.

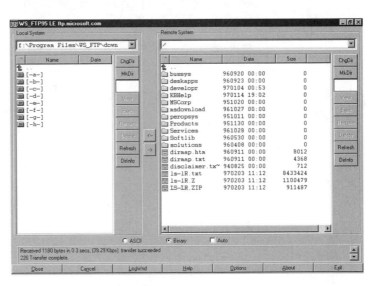

On the left, you see a listing of your current local directory and on the right, you can see a listing of the remote directory. Changing directories is just a matter of clicking the appropriate button. You upload and download files by highlighting the desired files with the mouse and clicking the appropriate movement arrows in the center of the screen. WS_FTP

24

can even be set to autodetect what file type is required. In addition to these features, this program enables you to keep a record of FTP sites including the username and password; you just click CONNECT, select the site you want from the list, and off you go! The program costs very little and is worth every penny if you do much remote Web site administration.

TIME SAVER

Why learn the command-line FTP program when GUI programs are out there? GUI-based FTP programs lay a graphical interface over the same commands used by the basic command-line FTP program—you don't need to learn any FTP commands. But there is the downside: *you don't learn any FTP commands.* The big advantage to the standard FTP program like the one provided with NT 4 Workstation is that it is common to nearly every machine with serious Internet access. FTP is virtually the same whether you are using NT 4 or UNIX. GUI-based programs are wonderful tools for productivity, but they are a crutch. I've known network specialists who could use a GUI-based FTP program but didn't know how to anonymously log in to an FTP site!

Using a Web Browser as an FTP Client

You can use a Web browser such as Microsoft's Internet Explorer or Netscape's Navigator as a poor man's FTP program. Many Web pages have links to FTP sites, so browsers need this functionality. Simply enter the site address in the URL box replacing the usual `http://` protocol prefix with an `ftp://` protocol prefix. Figure 24.9 shows Internet Explorer accessing the Windows NT resource directory of Walnut Creek's public `ftp.cdrom.com` site.

Figure 24.9.

Using Internet Explorer to access an FTP site.

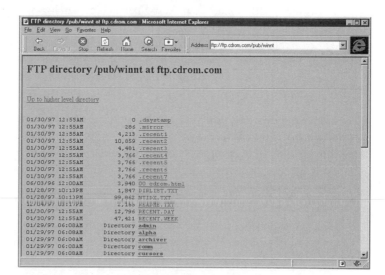

Browsers treat FTP files and directories like Web links. Clicking on the desired file or directory will either begin loading the file or show you the new directory listing. It is very easy to use a browser to visually navigate an FTP site, but you don't have the power and flexibility of a dedicated FTP client.

FTP Sites and Windows NT

Now that you know how to use FTP, scores of sites with countless NT resources are now open to you. The amount of information available can be rather overwhelming at first, but the effort will pay off.

The following is a brief list of some of the FTP sites with significant resources for supporting Windows NT. The list is by no means exhaustive, and you will doubtless find your own favorite sites, but here are some places to start:

ftp.cdrom.com	Walnut Creek CD-ROM Publishing
oak.oakland.edu	Oakland University
ftp.microsoft.com	Microsoft's home FTP site
ftp.cc.utexas.edu	University of Texas
emwac.ed.ac.uk	European Microsoft Windows NT Academic Center

Telnet

Many people who have used a computer have had to "log in" to one at some time. In the old days, if you wanted to use a shared system, you would enter your user name and password on a terminal wired directly to the local computer. But what if the computer you wanted to access was in a different town? With Telnet, you can log in to any computer in the world as long as you have access to a computer on the Internet and the computer you want to talk to is also on the Internet (and you have the required user name and password for that computer). If you've ever used an online service by dialing up with your modem, chances are you've already used Telnet—many of these services have you dial in to a "terminal server" and from there you are connected to your destination host computer via Telnet.

Telnet might seem a little like FTP, but it is quite different. Telnet enables you to control a computer just as if you were sitting in front of that computer as a local operator. You can move files around, change system settings, and run programs all on the host computer. Telnet does not let you transfer information between your local computer and the host you have accessed with Telnet. That's a job for FTP.

24

Using NT's Telnet Program

NT's Telnet program is run very similar to the FTP program, but Telnet has a graphical interface. The program is TELNET.EXE and is found in the WINNT/WINNT32 directory. You can run the program from the Run option under the Start button or from the command prompt by changing to the WINNT32 directory and entering TELNET at the prompt. You'll see a plain screen like the one shown in Figure 24.10.

Figure 24.10.

The Telnet program's work space.

To initiate a Telnet session with a remote host, select Connect | Remote System. The Telnet program will then give you a dialog box like the one shown in Figure 24.11.

Figure 24.11.

The Telnet program's remote system dialog box.

Typically, the only thing you have to do is enter the host name and click Connect. The Telnet program will remember past host names you have used. You can click the down arrow to select from a list of past host names. When you've clicked Connect, Telnet will contact the host and then prompt you for a user name and password. The remainder of your session will take place just as if you were locally typing on the remote host. To end your Telnet session, click Disconnect.

Usenet Newsgroups

Usenet is a compilation of groups each dedicated to the discussion of a topic. There are literally thousands of these discussion groups, called *newsgroups*, and each group can itself be subdivided into more specific topics. Each group consists of sequential e-mail postings by the various readers. Someone will post a comment on a topic and someone else will post a follow-up and then someone will reply to that posting, and so forth. A series of postings related to the same original letter is called a "thread." Because Usenet is an open forum, you can read as much or as little of these postings as you like.

Newsgroups vary tremendously in content and quality of postings. Some newsgroups are moderated, which means they are managed by someone who volunteers their time to do so. Many are not moderated and any kind of postings can be found there. Newsgroups can be an excellent source of information and a great place to post your own questions (and solutions), but expect a fair amount of trash posts and immature behavior because there is no accountability for postings on the Usenet.

Postings to Usenet are distributed to Usenet servers on various computers all over the world. There is no central Usenet authority; the messages circulate until they are timed out based on the capacities of the individual servers and the local administrator's needs.

Messages can last for weeks or only a few days depending on your local server.

How to Access Newsgroups

You may or may not have access to Usenet, and even if your ISP does have a Usenet server, it might not carry all newsgroups. The number of newsgroups is large and the daily volume of newsgroup traffic is vast. Many smaller ISPs do not have the resources to carry such a service. If you are connected to a university or a moderate-to-large ISP, you should be able to access the Usenet and most newsgroups.

To view Usenet newsgroups, you will need a newsreader and the name of your local Usenet server. There are many newsreader programs available, and most major Web browsers can be adapted to read newsgroups. Microsoft's Internet Explorer comes with a newsreader that is more than adequate for the task. Whatever program you use to view the newsgroups will need to know the name of the Usenet server. Your ISP will be able to provide you with this information.

Newsgroups Dedicated to NT Support

You'll find many newsgroups related to discussions of operating systems and Microsoft Windows systems in particular, but the following are the primary newsgroups dedicated to Windows NT:

comp.os.ms-windows.nt.admin.misc	Non-networking administration issues
comp.os.ms-windows.nt.admin.networking	Networking administration issues
comp.os.ms-windows.nt.admin.security	Security issues
comp.os.ms-windows.nt.advocacy	Comparisons of NT and other operating systems
comp.os.ms-windows.nt.announce	News about new NT applications, events and drivers (moderated)

24

`comp.os.ms-windows.nt.misc`	Miscellaneous NT issues not covered elsewhere
`comp.os.ms-windows.nt.pre-release`	Discussions of future NT versions
`comp.os.ms-windows.nt.setup.hardware`	Setup issues related to hardware
`comp.os.ms-windows.nt.setup.misc`	Non-hardware setup issues
`comp.os.ms-windows.nt.software.backoffice`	Discussion of NT and Microsoft's BackOffice suite of products
`comp.os.ms-windows.nt.software.compatibility`	Issues of NT compatibility with Win 95, Win 3.*x*, and DOS
`comp.os.ms-windows.nt.software.services`	Discussions of system service software for NT

24

You might also want to explore Microsoft's news server at `msnews.microsoft.com`. There are many discussion groups dedicated to support and user feedback on Microsoft products including Windows NT 4 Workstation.

Summary

This lesson gave you an overview of the Internet and how it works. There is a lot more to learn than can be included with this book, and the best way to learn is to get on the Internet and explore it yourself. The best material about the Internet can be found on the Internet.

You also learned how to use the most common Internet programs for getting more information about Windows NT. You learned to use a Web browser to download Web pages and other documents from the World Wide Web, and you learned how to use FTP for efficient and fast file transfers. It is very likely that you will use these two programs a lot in the future as you discover just how much material the Internet has to offer on Windows NT.

Workshop

The Workshop helps you solidify the skills you learned this hour.

Glossary

client A program that sends and receives information from a server. Clients are often specific to a kind of server. An FTP client is used only in conjunction with an FTP server. Web clients (also called browsers) are typically used to contact Web servers, but can also be used to contact others such as Gopher or FTP servers.

domain name   A unique name that identifies a group of computers on the Internet. The domain name system gives a structured way to name and group computers that avoids use of unwieldy IP numbers. Note that given a computer name like `www.microsoft.com`, only the `microsoft.com` portion is the domain name.

FTP   A standard protocol or method for transferring files on a TCP/IP network. FTP can also refer to the program that accomplishes this task.

Gopher   An Internet client used for browsing a menu-based directory of Internet resources. Gopher was very popular but is now being replaced by Web-based directory services. Gopher servers are still common and can be accessed using Web browsers. The name is derived from the school mascot of the University of Minnesota, where it was developed.

HTML   Short for HyperText Markup Language. An evolving method of formatting information so that it can be distributed over the Web and read independent of the kind of computer platform used. HTML coding is similar in many ways to old typesetting—a section of text is bracketed by a set of matching HTML "tags," which determine how the text appears on a Web browser. In addition to its use in Web pages, HTML is becoming a standard for creating and formatting help documents.

InterNIC   The agency responsible for registering Internet domain names.

IP address   A unique number assigned to every computer using TCP/IP. Because IP numbers are hard to remember, most computers are assigned names that are mapped to the IP number. For a computer to be on the Internet, it must have an IP number but need not have a name.

newsgroup   An individual discussion group on Usenet. There are many of these groups, often subdivided into more specific topics. Content ranges from interesting and useful postings to nonsense and poorly conceived commercial postings.

Point-to-Point Protocol (PPP)   A method in which a modem and a serial port can be used in place of a true network connection. Typically used to let home users temporarily connect a computer to the Internet.

search engine   A Web-based program that maintains a catalog of Web sites and enables users to search that catalog for documents matching the search criteria.

server   A program that provides a specific service or information to client programs. Note that "server" often refers to a dedicated computer that performs this function.

TCP/IP   An electronic "language" used by all computers on the Internet for communication. A computer on the Internet must be able to use TCP/IP, but because TCP/IP is used for other purposes, a computer using TCP/IP is not necessarily on the Internet.

Telnet   A TCP/IP service that enables you to remotely access a computer.

24

URL   A Uniform Resource Locator is a standard method for identifying many different kinds of information on the World Wide Web. A URL describes the protocol to be used, the computer where the information can be found, the directory path to the desired file, and the name of the file.

Usenet   A decentralized system of discussion groups spread over many computers on the Internet. Usenet is divided into a number of newsgroups that cover various topics. Usenet newsgroups are similar to a collection of e-mail postings oriented (however loosely) around a given topic. A reader can follow the "thread" of a topic as readers reply to each other over time.

World Wide Web   The total of all resources that can be accessed using Web browsers. These resources are often linked together by means of one HTML document containing a URL to another (not necessarily HTML) document. Often abbreviated as the Web.

24

Exercises

1. Use Internet Explorer or another browser to access Microsoft's Web site at `www.microsoft.com`. Explore Microsoft's many online NT resources such as the Microsoft Knowledge Base.

2. Use a Web browser to access a search engine like AltaVista at `www.altavista.digital.com`. Perform a search for NT 4 Workstation resources. You're likely to be buried with results, so learn how to fine-tune your searches.

3. Try using your browser to connect to a news server. Your ISP may or may not have access to Internet newsgroups, but you can always access Microsoft's news server at `msnews.microsoft.com`.

4. Use your Web browser, NT's command-line FTP client, and (if available) a third-party GUI-based FTP client to access an FTP server such as `ftp.microsoft.com`. Which do you find easier to use?

5. If you have a dial-up account with an ISP, set up a PPP network connection with your ISP, and then use NT's Telnet program to log in to your personal account on the ISP.

Appendix A

Control Panel Reference

by Thomas Lee

Introduction to the Control Panel

To many people, the Control Panel is just one of those things you need, but only rarely. When I started writing this appendix, I agreed with this view. As I looked more closely, I saw that the Control Panel is, in many ways, a key component of Windows NT Workstation. To get the best out of Windows NT Workstation, you really do need to know how the Control Panel works. For the power user, some neat features are hidden away in the depths of the Control Panel, which is why this appendix is provided for you: as a single visual reference to the heart of NT Workstation.

Think of the Control Panel as a nice front end for setting the most important system and user preferences. Most users will use some of the options, whereas the true power user will want to come to grips with its full potential.

So What Is the Control Panel?

The Control Panel is a collection object—a collection of a number of smaller applications, or applets, each of which configures some part of your Windows NT Workstation environment. To configure a part of the system, you first invoke Control Panel and then invoke the applet.

Accessing the Control Panel

The two main ways of accessing the Control Panel are from My Computer and from the Start button (click Start, select Settings, and then select Control Panel) as shown in Figure A.1.

Figure A.1.

Two ways to invoke the Control Panel.

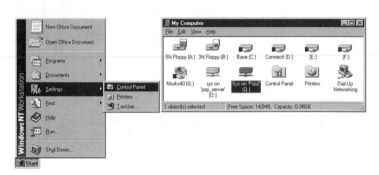

When you invoke the Control Panel, Windows NT displays a folder containing several icons, each one representing a Control Panel applet. As with all folders in Windows NT, you have the option of Large Icons, Small Icons, or Details view. My Control Panel, with Large Icons selected, is shown in Figure A.2. Your Control Panel might look different, depending on what software you have loaded.

What Are Control Panel Applets?

A Control Panel applet is a Windows NT Dynamic Link Library (DLL) stored with the extension .CPL. Each applet is designed to configure one part of your Windows NT System, such as the mouse, the network, or the UPS.

Control Panel applets are found in the %SYSTEMROOT%\System32 directory. If you remove one or more of the applet files from the System32 directory, you will not see the applet's icon in the Control Panel the next time you invoke it. Likewise, you can add Control Panel applets simply by placing their files into the System32 directory.

Figure A.2.

The Control Panel.

A number of Control Panel applets are initially loaded with Windows NT. Adding extra features, such as Dial-Up Networking, or other applications, such as Microsoft Office, results in additional Control Panel applets being installed. Installing Office 95, for example, will install the Find Fast applet, which automatically indexes Office documents.

If you don't see all the Control Panel applets shown in Figure A.2, it might be because you haven't loaded all the related components of Windows NT Workstation.

System Settings Versus User Settings

In using the Control Panel, some settings, such as network configuration, are set up for the system as a whole, regardless of which user is logged in. Other settings are user specific, and you can set them differently for each user with an account on the system.

All the settings controlled by Windows NT's Control Panel are stored in the Registry.

Individual per-user settings are stored below the HKEY_CURRENT_USER\Control Panel key. The subkeys for the user settings match the names of the applets in most cases. The system settings are stored under the HKEY_LOCAL_MACHINE key and are not as easy to find.

Security

Most of the Control Panel applets enable any user to invoke the applet and modify the related settings. Other applets, such as the Date/Time, are considered more secure and cannot be changed by normal users. In general, users cannot modify (change, add, or delete) any device drivers or system services. In order to use these applets, you must be a member of the Administrators local group on your workstation. This is all part of NT's normal security model.

The Control Panel applets that are not available to all users are Date/Time, Devices, Keyboard, Modems, Multimedia, Network, Ports, Printers, SCSI Adapters, Server, Services, System, Tape Devices, and UPS. The specific security restrictions for these applets are noted in the descriptions that follow.

Accessibility Options

Microsoft is committed to making computers easier for everyone to use, including users with physical handicaps and disabilities. Windows NT 4 has a set of features known as the Accessibility Options that let a disabled user use Windows NT more effectively. Although these functions were designed primarily for the disabled, they can be very helpful to the able-bodied, and I regularly utilize a number of them!

When you install Windows NT Workstation, you also have the option to install the accessibility options. If they were not installed when NT was first installed, they can be installed later using the Add/Remove Programs applet, which is described later in this appendix.

Accessibility settings are per-user settings stored in the Registry under the key HKEY_CURRENT_USER\Accessibility. Although most users will never need, or want, to use all these features, the Accessibility applet has a total of 10 separate and interrelated dialogs.

Selecting the Accessibility applet brings up the dialog box shown in Figure A.3. This dialog box contains four separate tabbed dialogs, which control different aspects of the accessibility settings.

Figure A.3.

Accessibility Properties.

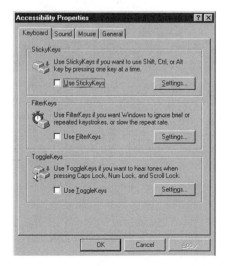

A

The keyboard functions, shown in Figure A.3, allow you to modify the behavior of the keyboard, offering StickyKeys, FilterKeys, and ToggleKeys.

StickyKeys

Many Windows applications utilize one of the modifier keys (Shift, Alt, or Ctrl), pressed in conjunction with some other key. For example, you can press both the Alt and the F keys simultaneously to open the File menu in most Windows applications.

The StickyKeys function enables you to enter these modified keys by first pressing the modifier and then the key to be modified—that is, Alt followed by F. The StickyKey options are set in the dialog box shown in Figure A.4.

Figure A.4.

Settings for StickyKeys.

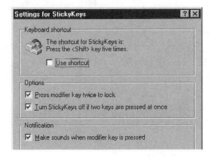

You can turn on the StickyKeys function either by selecting the StickyKeys function in the Keyboard dialog or (optionally) via the keyboard shortcut, pressing either the right or left shift key five times. After StickyKeys is on, you can turn it off by pressing any modifier key and another key simultaneously (for example, Alt and F). This can be useful when you want to use the StickyKeys function only for a short time.

You also can lock the modifier by pressing it twice, which is very convenient for one-hand typing.

The Notification option specifies whether Windows NT should play a sound when the control keys governed by StickyKeys are pressed. The sound is a high-pitched beep when the option is turned on and a low-pitched beep when the option is turned off.

FilterKeys

The FilterKeys function directs NT to filter out keys typed too quickly. The FilterKeys functions are invoked by the dialog shown in Figure A.5.

Figure A.5.

Settings for FilterKeys.

The Filter options directs NT to either ignore repeated keys or to ignore keys typed too quickly by slowing down the keyboard. Like the other accessibility options, FilterKeys can be invoked by a keyboard shortcut, holding down the right shift key for eight seconds.

Both Filter options have Settings buttons that allow the user to control how quickly or slowly the keyboard responds. Selecting the Settings button for the Ignore Repeated Keystrokes feature invokes the dialog box shown in Figure A.6. This dialog enables the user to determine whether keystrokes typed within the range of a half a second to two seconds are ignored.

Figure A.6.

Advanced FilterKeys settings—ignoring repeated keystrokes.

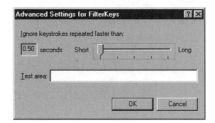

Selecting the Settings button for the Ignore Quick Keystrokes and Slow Down the Repeat Rate option invokes the dialog box shown in Figure A.7. This enables the user to override the keyboard rate specified in the Keyboard Control Panel applet.

The user can direct NT to perform no keyboard repeats (that is, each key must be pressed and then released before the next keystroke is accepted) or to slow down the keyboard repeat rates. You set both the Repeat Delay and Repeat Rate using the slider bars in Figure A.7 within the range 0.3 to 2 seconds.

Figure A.7.

*Advanced FilterKeys
settings—slowing down
the keyboard repeat rate.*

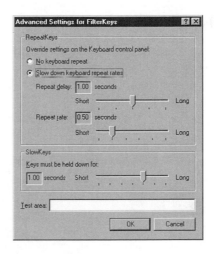

Both of the advanced settings dialogs and the main FilterKeys dialog offer a test area within the dialog box so that you can test the specific filter settings. You should probably test any changes to the settings before applying them.

ToggleKeys

The ToggleKeys function, shown in Figure A.8, instructs your system to make a sound via the system speaker when the Caps Lock, Scroll Lock, or Num Lock keys are toggled. When you turn on ToggleKeys, the system makes a high-pitched sound whenever one of the modifier keys is turned on and a low sound when it is toggled off. The keyboard shortcut is enabled by checking the option as shown in Figure A.8.

Figure A.8.

Settings for ToggleKeys.

The ToggleKeys function is useful for those of us who touch-type but not accurately. It gets so annoying hearing these sounds that after a while, your fingers stop hitting the keys by accident.

Sounds

The Sound functions, shown in Figure A.9, allow you to control how Windows NT informs the user of common error events that are usually signaled by a sound (the beep). The two sound options are SoundSentry and ShowSounds.

Figure A.9.

Accessibility sounds.

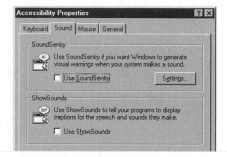

When Windows NT Workstation or a running application detects a user error, it usually indicates the error with a single beep of the system's speaker.

To assist users with impaired hearing, the SoundSentry function instructs Windows NT to flash part of the screen as an alternative to sounding the system speaker. With the Sounds applet, described in the section "Sounds" later in this appendix, you can make WAV files serve as these sounds.

You can choose to make no visual notification (the default), flash the active caption bar, flash the active window, or flash the entire desktop, as shown in Figure A.10.

Figure A.10.

Settings for SoundSentry.

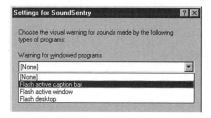

ShowSounds instructs programs that usually convey information only by sound to also provide all information visually, such as by displaying text captions or informative icons. Applications must be specifically written to utilize ShowSounds.

MouseKeys

Selecting the Mouse tab from the main Accessibility dialog invokes the MouseKeys functions, shown in Figure A.11, which enable you to use the numeric keypad as an alternative to a mouse.

Figure A.11.

MouseKeys settings.

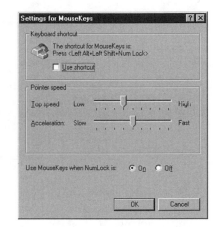

Like the other accessibility functions, the MouseKeys option has a keyboard shortcut, which is Left Alt+Left Shift+Num Lock. Selecting the function either by using the checkbox or the keyboard shortcut enables you to use the numeric keyboard on full-size keyboards as an alternative to using the mouse. This can be very handy for precision work where the mouse might be too crude or in situations where you have no mouse. The Pointer Speed slider bars inform Windows NT how fast to accelerate and move the mouse when you select the numeric keyboard keys.

General Accessibility Features

The remaining accessibility functions are invoked from the General tab, as shown in Figure A.12.

The Automatic Reset function causes NT to reset all accessibility options if they are not used within a certain time period, which can range from 5 to 30 minutes.

The Notification option shown in Figure A.12 directs Windows NT to play a confirmation sound every time you use any shortcut key to turn an accessibility feature on or off. This is very useful as a way of alerting users who might turn on a feature accidentally.

Figure A.12.

*General accessibility
properties.*

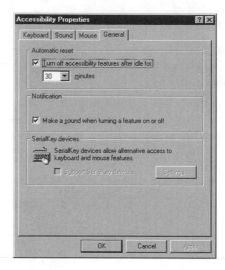

The SerialKeys feature allows you to attach an alternate input device (also called an
augmentative communication device) to your computer's serial port. This feature is designed
for people who are unable to use the computer's standard keyboard and mouse and have
suitable hardware.

Add/Remove Programs

The Add/Remove Programs applet, shown in Figure A.13, provides a simple way to add or
remove Windows applications as well as add or remove Windows NT options.

Figure A.13.

*Properties for Add/
Remove Programs.*

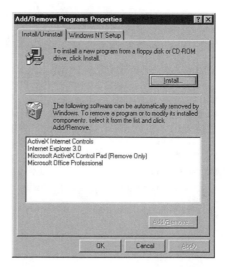

A

The Add/Remove dialog allows you to either install a new application or remove a previously installed application.

Installing or Removing Applications

You usually install most applications by running a vendor-supplied program, and because most application vendors utilize Microsoft's generic setup engine, the installation program is usually SETUP.EXE.

Although most users install applications by running the appropriate install program from the vendor-supplied CD-ROM or disk set, the Add/Remove Programs applet provides an alternative method. Selecting the Install button starts the Install Wizard, which first scans the floppy drive and CD-ROM. If the wizard is unable to find the setup program, another dialog enables the user to browse for the installation program.

The Add/Remove function also provides a consistent way to remove an application or run the setup to add new application components. This option is available only if the application's installation program is based on Microsoft's Install Shield functions. Because not all applications are installed this way, not every application can utilize the Uninstall feature of this dialog. If your application is not visible in the list and you need to update or remove it, consult the vendor's documentation to determine how best to do this.

Installing or Removing Windows NT Core Components

The Windows NT Setup dialog allows you to add or remove various components of Windows NT, as shown in Figure A.14. When Windows NT was initially installed, some or all of the installable options were selected. The dialog box shown in Figure A.14, which is similar to the one displayed by the Windows NT Install process, allows you to add or remove core Windows NT components.

The components that you can install or remove by using this dialog are Accessibility Options, Accessories, Communications, Games, Microsoft Exchange, and Multimedia. With the exception of the Accessibility Options, all the components have subcomponents that you can select individually for installation or removal.

All the components, with the exception of the Accessories, has one or more associated Control Panel applets. If you don't see the related applet within Control Panel, the appropriate component probably was not installed. You should check the Windows NT Installation to ensure that the component was installed.

Figure A.14.

Add/Remove Windows NT components.

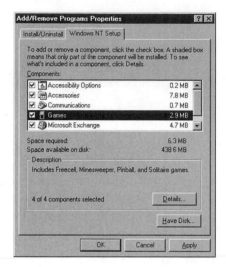

Console

Although most applications run from Windows NT are Windows applications, NT also provides good support for older DOS-based applications. Windows NT comes with a command interpreter, CMD.EXE, which looks and feels like DOS. The code for the command interpreter is based on DOS 5; as a result, CMD.EXE should be familiar to anyone who knows DOS. Command-line dinosaurs like me can even use EDLIN.COM to edit text files if they want!

Windows NT, like Windows 3.*x*, can display applications running under CMD.EXE either full screen or in a window, often referred to as a console window. A console window is a normal window that contains only the console prompt.

The Console Windows Properties applet, shown in Figure A.15, enables you to configure the look and feel of the console windows.

Console Options

The Options dialog, shown in Figure A.15, enables you to specify the following:

☐ Cursor Size allows you to resize the cursor to be Small (the traditional underline cursor), Medium (a solid rectangle at half height), or Large (a solid, full-height rectangle).

☐ Display Options allows you to indicate whether to display the command prompt in a window or full screen, by default.

A

☐ With Command History, you can specify how large a command history buffer to keep, how many of the buffers to keep, and whether duplicate commands should be discarded from the buffer.

☐ QuickEdit Mode enables you to use a mouse to perform cut-and-paste operations without using the command window's Edit menu. If this option is selected, however, you cannot use the mouse to drive any DOS applications, such as EDIT.COM, started in the command prompt window.

☐ Insert Mode gives you the option to start the command prompt with insert enabled; as a result, the text you type is inserted at the cursor. If this is not checked, text typed at the cursor replaces any existing text. After the command prompt is started, you can easily toggle the insert mode off and on by pressing the Ins key.

The command interpreter CMD.EXE maintains a history of the commands entered and allows you to recall them in essentially the same way as the DOSKEY program that came with DOS 5. CMD.EXE automatically sets up this buffer based on the Command History settings noted previously. This is a very useful feature if you use the command prompt often.

Figure A.15.

Console windows properties.

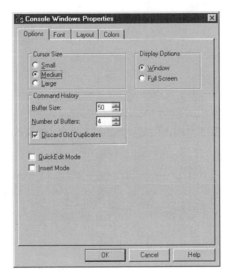

Command Prompt Fonts

The Font dialog, shown in Figure A.16, enables you to specify the font type and size to be used when a command prompt is displayed within a window.

The Font box lists all the fonts on your system that Windows NT uses within a windowed command prompt. The size of TrueType fonts is measured using normal point size; for raster fonts, the measurement in screen pixels indicates how wide and high the character should be generated.

The Window Preview window shows you how much of your physical screen will be taken up by the console window, and the Selected Font box at the bottom of the dialog shows what the selected font will look like when displayed in the window.

Figure A.16.

Console windows fonts.

Command Prompt Layout

The Layout dialog, shown in Figure A.17, allows you to configure how many rows and columns the command prompt screen buffer should contain, how many rows and columns to display, and where to place the window on the screen.

In the Layout dialog, the Screen Buffer Size represents the number of rows and columns Windows NT Workstation reserves for your console session, and the Window Size is how large the console window should be when it is first displayed. If the screen buffer size is greater than the initial display you configure, the window appears with the appropriate scroll bars. This dialog does not let you configure a window size smaller than the buffer. Also, if you increase the window size, Windows NT automatically reduces the size of the window font.

The Window Position option lets you specify where the upper-left corner of the console window should be. You can either specify the exact position by providing the offset relative to the upper-left hand corner of the screen, or let the system position it for you by checking the Let system position window checkbox.

Like the Font dialog, the Layout dialog has a Window Preview to let you see approximately how much of the physical screen will be taken up by the command prompt window.

Figure A.17.

Console windows layout.

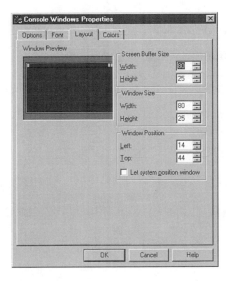

Console Windows Colors

The Colors dialog, shown in Figure A.18, allows you to set and review the foreground and background colors of text displayed at the command prompt.

Figure A.18.

Console windows colors.

This dialog allows you to specify separately the colors used for the normal screen and any pop-up screens. For users with high-resolution video adapters, you can even mix the specific colors by indicating the precise mix of red, green, and blue. You can see any color selections made in this screen in the Layout and Font dialogs described earlier.

Client Service for NetWare (CSNW)

Windows NT Workstation provides full client support for Novell NetWare 2.*x*, 3.*x*, and 4.*x* as a standard part of Windows NT Workstation. This client support is provided by loading the Client Service for NetWare in the Networks applet.

The CSNW dialog, shown in Figure A.19, allows you to specify your default NDS tree and context (for 4.*x* servers using NDS) or your preferred server (non-NDS), as well as control key printing features.

Figure A.19.

Client Service for NetWare configuration.

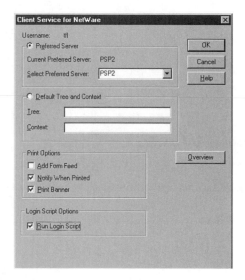

These settings are user specific but are stored in the Registry in HKEY_LOCAL_MACHINE\ SYSTEM\CurrentControlSet\Services\NWCWorkstation\Parameters\Options. If you look at this key, you see a subkey per user (identified by the Windows NT SID), below which you see the CSNW options. This does mean that these parameters are not transportable via roving profiles.

Configuring Client Services for NetWare

If you are using NetWare 3.*x* or 2.*x* (or 4.*x* with Bindery Emulation), you specify an initial server to log into as part of the NT login process. This server, the Preferred Server, is selected from the combo box, which initially contains all bindery-based NetWare servers that were discovered on the network. You also have the option of <None>, in which case no login is attempted until you try to access a NetWare server.

A

If you are using Novell NetWare 4.*x* and NDS, you can alternatively specify the NDS tree and context. As with the Preferred Server, when the Default tree and context are specified, Windows NT Workstation logs you into this context as part of the login process.

Under Print Options, you can configure the following:

☐ Add Form Feed causes the NetWare printer to add a form feed to the end of each document sent for printing.

☐ Notify When Printed provides notification messages when your documents have been printed.

☐ Print Banner generates a printer banner page for each document sent for printing.

Date/Time

NT uses the time and date held in your system's clock for a variety of purposes, such as time stamping files, checking for the latest version of files, and so on. It is important, therefore, that your system clock is set to the correct date and time. One way to do this is using the Date and Time Control Panel applet, shown in Figure A.20.

Figure A.20.

Date/Time Properties dialog.

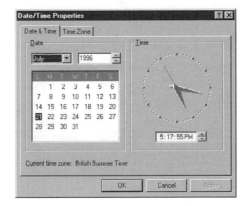

You must be a member of either the Power Users or Administrator's group to change Date/Time settings.

Setting Date and Time

The Date/Time Properties dialog allows you to specify the current day, month, and year, and time of day. This is done using a combination of a pull-down list, several spinner boxes, and a calendar.

Selecting Time Zones

In order to coordinate time around the world, which is vital in large global networks, Windows NT also needs to know your time zone, whether your time zone has a local summer time, and if so, the summer-time starting and ending dates. Time zones are selected using the dialog box shown in Figure A.21.

Figure A.21.

Selecting time zones.

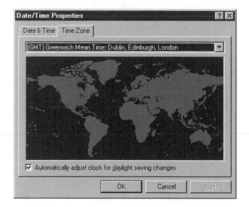

The names and details of all time zones are held in the Registry under the \HKEY_LOCAL_MACHINE\Software\Microsoft\Windows NT\Current Version\Time Zones key.

If the selected time zone information includes details of when local summer time starts and ends, Windows NT automatically adjusts your clock the first time you reboot after summer time starts or finishes. However, the definition of summer time start and finish has changed in some countries recently. NT's understanding of these dates currently appears to be correct, but you might need to edit your time zone information if these dates change.

Devices

Windows NT supports a large number of hardware devices such as network cards, SCSI device drivers, and so on. In order for any device to be useable, it must have a device driver installed and running.

The Devices dialog, shown in Figure A.22, allows you to manage the device drivers on your system if you are a member of the Administrator's local group. With this dialog, you can start and stop individual device drivers, change the startup type for the devices, and include or exclude them from a hardware profile.

A

Figure A.22.

The Devices dialog box.

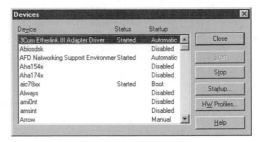

Windows NT automatically starts devices at different times during the loading of the system, depending on the device. The startup types include the following:

☐ Boot: The device drivers for boot types are loaded by the initial loader and initialized as part of the initialization of the NT Kernel. This class includes a SCSI disk controller.

☐ System: These devices, which are essential to the system's operation, start every time the system starts but after the boot devices. Such devices include the floppy disk, the system speaker, the CD-ROM, the disk unidriver, the keyboard, and the mouse.

☐ Automatic: These devices start each time the system does and start after the boot and system devices. Generally, these devices are not critical to basic system operation and include devices such as the parallel port and network drivers.

☐ Manual: These devices are started either by the user or by a dependent device.

☐ Disabled: These devices cannot be started by the user (that is, using the Start button) as they usually relate to devices which you do not have on your system.

Selecting a device and clicking Startup in the Devices dialog invokes the Device dialog shown in Figure A.23, which allows you to select the startup type.

Another important thing to remember is that to change a device driver's startup class or to start and stop a driver, you must be a member of the Administrator's group.

Hardware Profiles and Device Drivers

Using the System applet, you can create hardware profiles. These profiles allow you to specify different hardware configurations that you can choose when Windows NT starts up. Hardware profiles are very useful, for example, for a laptop user who might have a docking station; the user can choose one profile when the laptop is docked and the other when the system is not docked.

Figure A.23.

Configuring a device's startup type.

After the profile is created, you can decide which devices you want to enable or disable for a given profile. You simply select the device and then click the HW Profiles button to invoke the dialog box shown in Figure A.24. From this dialog box, you can enable or disable the device.

Figure A.24.

Including devices in a hardware profile.

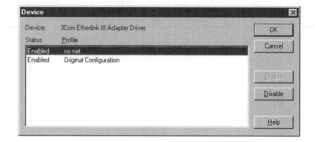

Dial-Up Monitor

Windows NT Workstation includes a powerful set of dial-up networking (DUN) facilities. Using DUN, you can connect to your corporate network or to the Internet via an Internet service provider. These connections are made using a modem, which you set up using the Modem Control Panel applet.

After you have a connection to a remote system, you can use the Dial-Up Monitor to monitor that connection. You also use the Dial-Up Monitor applet to set certain monitoring preferences, such as making a sound when a connection is made or dropped.

Dial-Up Networking Status

The Dial-Up Networking Monitor is shown in Figure A.25. With this dialog, you see details about the active connection. The counters on this dialog are updated in real time as the data is transferred.

A

Figure A.25.

*Dial-Up Networking
Monitor.*

At the top of the dialog, you can select the connection to monitor and see a summary of that connection's current status, which shows the connection speed and how long the connection has been active.

In the lower portion of this dialog, you can see the current statistics for incoming and outgoing communications along with a summary of errors. For both incoming and outgoing data, the Dial-Up Networking Monitor displays the number of characters sent and received and how many network frames the data took, as well as the level of data compression achieved.

Depending on what data is transferred and what modem is used for the connection, the level of compression varies, possibly significantly. Downloading a binary file from a remote file server will probably not result in much, if any, data compression. Downloading a text file, particularly if you're using the right modem, is likely to result in much higher compression.

The Status dialog also displays a set of error counts. In general, any errors seen here are bad news, mainly because they degrade performance. This dialog box shows six types of errors: CRC, Timeout, Alignment, Framing, Hardware Overrun, and Buffer Overrun. These errors are caused by a number of factors, including noisy phone lines, poor modem connections, and badly behaved modems.

Windows NT always attempts to retransmit any data that was lost or transmitted in error. Although a few errors in a long connection are possibly acceptable, each error reduces your throughput. If you get more frequent errors, you should identify the cause and, if at all possible, eliminate it.

Connection Summary

The dialog box shown in Figure A.26 displays a summary of any active connection, showing how long the connection has been active. With Windows NT Server, you can combine multiple physical connections for higher overall throughput. This facility, which you would monitor using this dialog box, is not available in Windows NT Workstation.

Figure A.26.

Dial-Up Networking Monitor summary.

Monitoring Preferences

The Monitoring Preferences dialog, shown in Figure A.27, provides you with a way of setting some monitoring features related to dial-up networking.

Figure A.27.

Dial-up networking preferences.

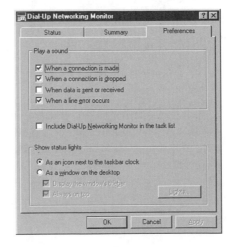

The Play a Sound group enables you to configure a sound to be played whenever a connection is made or dropped, whenever data is sent or received, or whenever a line error is detected. If you are experiencing connection errors, this might assist you in detecting and resolving these errors.

If you select the Include Dial-Up Networking Monitor in the Task List option, when you connect to your remote server, Windows NT starts up the Dial-Up Networking Monitor and includes it on the taskbar. After this is displayed in the taskbar, you can right-click the taskbar to perform certain administrative functions, such as disconnecting the connection.

Dial-up networking also can give you a visual representation of data that is sent or received via the modem. The Show Status Lights section at the bottom of the dialog box enables you to choose whether the set of status lights is a separate icon on the desktop or a small icon on the taskbar next to the clock. Both representations provide a good method of determining how much data is sent and received.

Display

To many people, the display is the computer, and it is vital to the proper operation of their systems. The Display applet configures the properties for the Windows NT desktop, including the background, the screen saver, and so on.

You can select the Display Properties dialog, shown in Figure A.28, either from the Control Panel or more directly by right-clicking anywhere on the desktop and selecting Properties from the shortcut menu.

Figure A.28.

Display properties.

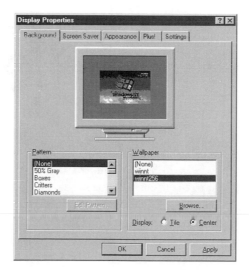

Altering the Desktop Background

The Background dialog allows you to set a background pattern or wallpaper on the desktop. The top of the dialog box displays a thumbnail view of the currently chosen background.

Wallpaper is a bitmap, stored in a BMP file, that you can display on the desktop. My workstation has a wonderful picture of a tropical island—just right for those cold, rainy, winter days here in England! You can use one of the BMPs that come with Windows NT Workstation, download images from the Internet or use a graphics package to create your own. You can opt to show the bitmap at normal size or stretch it to fill the screen.

A desktop pattern is an eight-by-eight pixel pattern made up of either the desktop color, set in the Appearance tab, or black. Each pixel can be either of these two colors. The eight-by-eight pattern is then tiled on the desktop.

You can choose to have either a pattern, the wallpaper, or both displayed on your desktop. If you choose to have both, the wallpaper appears on top of the pattern. If the wallpaper is stretched to fit the desktop (using the Plus! dialog shown in Figure A.33) or the wallpaper is tiled to cover the entire screen, the pattern will not be visible.

You can add new patterns by first choosing an existing pattern and clicking the Edit Pattern button. This action invokes the Pattern Editor, shown in Figure A.29, which you use to edit the pattern.

Figure A.29.

Desktop Pattern Editor.

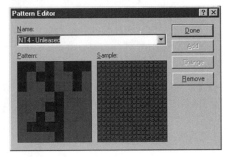

By left-clicking each pixel, you can toggle individual pixels, changing them to black or the desktop color. While you are editing the pattern, Windows NT shows what the pattern looks like at full size in the Sample window. If you type a new name in the Name text box, you can then add it to the list of patterns shown in Figure A.28.

Screen Saver

A screen saver is a program that is set to run whenever the system is idle. Screen savers were traditionally used to avoid phosphor burn-in, caused when a single image is displayed for long periods of time. They also reduce the risk of someone viewing sensitive material when the screen is left unattended. Other screen savers are just plain fun!

The Screen Saver dialog, shown in Figure A.30, allows you to designate and configure a screen saver. Windows NT Workstation comes with five 3D and six 2D screen savers. The 3D screen savers are programmed using the OpenGL graphics library and are quite dramatic.

Figure A.30.

Specifying a display screen saver.

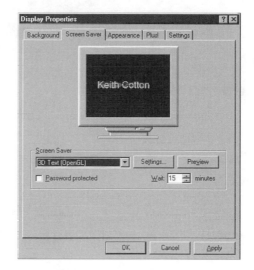

Each screen saver is stored in a file with an SCR extension. The screen savers are located in the %SYSTEMROOT%\System32 directory.

Although they are stored with the SCR extension, screen savers are executable programs. If you execute the file by running it from the command prompt, you see the configuration dialog. However, running the screen saver from the Start/Run dialog runs the screen saver itself. Who needs consistency when you have cool screen savers?

Most screen savers have configuration options you can set by selecting the Settings box. If the screen saver can be configured, a dialog box appears (if not, you get an error message box). The configuration dialog for the 3D Text screen saver is shown in Figure A.31.

Figure A.31.

Configuring a screen saver.

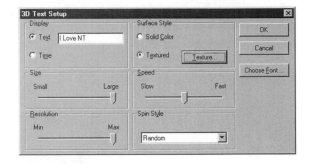

Appearance

The Appearance dialog, shown in Figure A.32, allows you to configure the visual components of the Windows NT environment, such as the desktop color, menu font, icon spacing, and so on.

Figure A.32.

Display appearance.

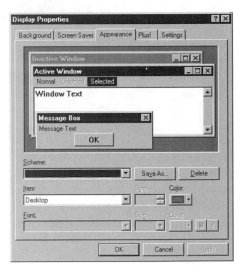

To configure an item, you first select it either by clicking the preview window or by selecting it from the Item pull-down list.

Windows NT comes with a set of predefined display schemes that you can select by using the Scheme pull-down list. If you change the setting on any element, you can then save the new scheme to a scheme name of your choice.

The display schemes are stored in the Registry under HKEY_CURRENT_USER\Control
Panel\Appearance\Schemes. The individual schemes are stored as long binary values and are
probably best edited using the Display dialog.

Plus! Features

The Plus! pack is a set of add-on features for Windows 95, some of which are included as an
integral part of Windows NT version 4. The Plus! dialog, shown in Figure A.33, allows you
to configure some elements of the display.

Figure A.33.

Display Plus! features.

The Desktop Icons enable you to change the default icons for My Computer, the Network
Neighborhood, and the full and empty recycle bin. By selecting one of the four icons in the
preview windows and then clicking the Change Icon button, you can select an alternative
icon to use. By selecting the icon and clicking the Default button, you can restore the default
icons.

The Visual Settings allow you to affect the following aspects of the display:

- [ ] Use Large Icons directs Windows NT Workstation to display larger icons in all
  displays involving icons (for example, the desktop, icon folder views, and so on),
  which can be a help to those with visual impairments or used for demonstration
  purposes.

- [ ] Show Windows Contents While Dragging, known as Full Windows Drag in
  Windows NT Version 3.51, redraws any window that is dragged or resized as it
  moves, rather than just move or resize the window's outline and redraw when the
  window is finally dropped. This makes it easy to see how the window is affected by

the drag. Because this function is very graphics intensive, you should probably use it only on more powerful systems.

☐ Smooth Edges of Screen Fonts improves the appearance of screen fonts by smoothing the jagged edges, particularly with large fonts. To use this option, your video card and display monitor must support 256 colors, although support for high color (16-bit color) is recommended.

☐ Show Icons Using All Possible Colors ensures that icons are displayed using the full color palette available, rather than a 16-color palette. Arguably, icons look better using the full palette, but this requires a graphics card and monitor capable of at least 256 colors. Changing this option requires a reboot before it takes effect.

☐ Stretch Desktop Wallpaper to Fit Screen stretches the selected wallpaper so that it covers your entire screen. You must turn on the Center option in the Background dialog, noted previously, to use this option.

Display Settings

The Display Settings option enables you to specify the color palette depth, the desktop area, font size, and monitor refresh rate. The Settings dialog box is shown in Figure A.34.

Figure A.34.

Display settings.

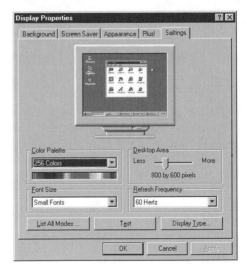

The specific settings available vary according to the video card and monitor in use. On my laptop, for example, I'm only able to get a maximum of 64KB colors, a 640×480 pixel desktop area, and a refresh rate capable of only 60Hz—but my desktop system is capable of 16 million colors, 800×600 pixels, and a 72Hz refresh rate.

After you have selected settings, it is sensible to test them to ensure they work! Clicking on Test displays a simple test pattern using your new settings. After displaying the test pattern for five seconds, Windows NT reverts to the old settings and displays a dialog box asking whether you saw the pattern properly. If you saw the test pattern fully, the new settings are safe, and you can select them. If you didn't see the pattern, select No when prompted (which is the default) and you can try different combinations.

Fonts

The term *font* refers to the way in which characters are formed on an output device. Any given font has a number of specific features, including weight (how thick the font is), slant (whether it's an italic font or not), and so on.

With a large number of fonts available, you can literally find thousands. Microsoft Office loads a number of extra fonts, for example. CorelDRAW! includes nearly 100 fonts (although I've yet to meet anyone who's found a use for more than a handful of these).

Fonts are important because they can reinforce the written message. A flowery, cursive font is probably better for writing poetry or thank-you letters than for a warning sign. Likewise, a bold sans serif font is more useful in a book for topic and chapter headings than for body text.

Windows NT supports a number of different types of fonts:

☐ Printer fonts are built into the printer and vary by printer. Virtually all PostScript printers support a basic set of 35 printer fonts, whereas other non-PostScript printers vary widely in what is supported.

☐ Screen fonts govern how letters appear on the screen and generally come in predefined sizes that cannot be scaled.

☐ TrueType fonts are fully scaleable fonts that can be used both as screen and printer fonts, thus enabling WYSIWYG (what you see is what you get). This is important if you want to proof something onscreen and know it will look like that on the printed page, something that is not always possible with screen and printer fonts.

☐ Bitmap fonts consist of bitmaps for a particular size and weight and do not scale. Often referred to as soft fonts, these can be downloaded to the printer.

☐ Vector fonts hold instructions about how they should be drawn, so they are scaleable. In general, they do not look as nice when scaled as TrueType fonts do.

With Windows NT Workstation, any fonts you install automatically become available from any Windows application, including Windows NT itself. DOS applications, however, are not able to take advantage of these fonts, and their fonts are loaded on a per-application basis.

After a font is loaded, you can use it in any Windows application that supports that font. You can also use it as an element of your desktop by using the Display applet's Appearance function.

Font Folder

The Fonts folder, found in `%SYSTEMROOT%\Fonts`, holds all the fonts that applications running on Windows NT Workstation use. The Fonts option in the Control Panel is really just a shortcut to the Fonts folder. The Fonts folder on my system is shown in Figure A.35.

Figure A.35.

Font folder.

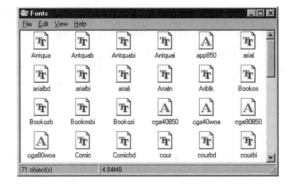

Font Sample Sheet

Selecting one of the fonts shown in Figure A.35 and opening it brings up a Font sample sheet, as shown in Figure A.36. This font sheet displays the font, any copyright information, and a sample of the font. At the bottom of the sample sheet, a sample sentence is displayed using the chosen font, repeated in different font sizes. This sample shows you what the font looks like in larger sizes, and you can print it to view the likely output.

Figure A.36.

Font sample.

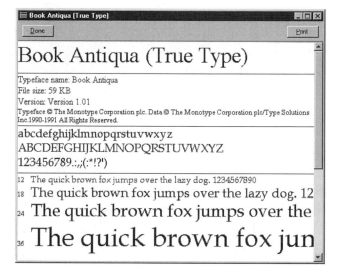

Internet

Windows NT Workstation comes to you Internet-ready, which means that it has the essential components necessary for Internet connectivity. Of course, you need to install a modem, install and configure a dial-up networking connection, get an account with an Internet service provider (ISP), and wrestle through its login procedure. The basic software you need comes fully bundled with NT, and a seasoned hand can connect it all in a matter of five or ten minutes. Getting mail and news is only a little more tricky.

One nice feature of NT Workstation is the WWW browser that is built in. When Windows NT Workstation is shipped (and this sentence was written just minutes after I heard that NT 4 went gold), it will be shipped with Internet Explorer version 2. This is a good, stable build, but the browser market is advancing at an awesome rate. By the time you read this book, Internet Explorer version 3 will have been superseded by version 4!

The Internet Control Panel applet, shown in Figure A.37, configures the Internet Explorer, also know as IE. In the shipping version of NT Workstation, the Internet applet can only configure proxy servers for use with IE, as shown in the figure. Later versions of IE will make greater use of this applet.

Figure A.37.

*Configuring Internet
Explorer.*

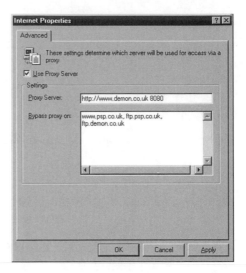

Proxy Servers

A proxy server can provide two general functions. First, it can provide a firewall, enabling you to see outside your local area network without external users being able to see in. Although you tell IE to contact a remote server, say www.microsoft.com, IE sends your request to a proxy server that makes the request on your behalf. In such cases, the actual request appears, at least to the remote server, to come from the proxy server and not your system, thus providing an element of additional security.

The second function some proxy servers can provide is caching. If multiple users all try to get to http://www.microsoft.com/nt, the first person requesting that page causes the proxy to retrieve it, whereas subsequent calls to that page are satisfied from the proxy server's cache. This can significantly improve access time for commonly accessed Web pages or FTP files.

Configuring a Proxy Server

Using the Internet Control Panel applet, you can configure your proxy server. In the example shown in Figure A.37, the proxy for my system is www.demon.co.uk, port 8080. The specific server and port number differs from company to company and from ISP to ISP, so be sure to ask your administrator or ISP for more complete details about proxy server names and port numbers to use. The example shown here is for Demon Internet Systems Limited, an ISP in the United Kingdom.

The Bypass proxy on option allows you to bypass the proxy server whenever you are attempting to access certain servers. In the dialog box shown in Figure A.37, accesses to

A

ftp.psp.co.uk, www.psp.co.uk, and ftp.demon.co.uk all go directly to those servers. The first two are private servers not available on the Internet, and the second is my local provider's FTP server.

Keyboard

Like the display settings mentioned earlier, keyboard settings are a matter of personal taste. Some users might find some settings easier or more difficult to use. The Keyboard Control Panel applet, shown in Figure A.38, allows you to configure your keyboard.

Figure A.38.

Keyboard properties.

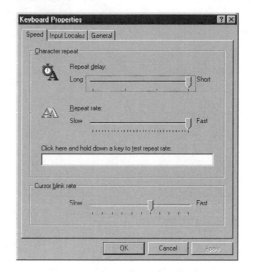

The Speed dialog, shown in Figure A.38, allows the following three adjustments:

☐ Repeat Rate adjusts the wait before a character begins repeating when you hold down any key.

☐ Repeat Delay adjusts how fast a character repeats when you hold down a key.

☐ Cursor Blink Rate allows you to change the speed at which the cursor blinks.

You also can use the test box to check whether the repeat rate and delay settings you've just set are what you want. To the left of the slider in the Cursor Blink Rate setting is a blinking insert cursor that shows the currently selected blink setting. As with all settings, you should test the keyboard settings before accepting them.

If you are using the Accessibility options, the repeat rate set in the Keyboard Properties dialog can be overridden by the FilterKeys functions.

Input Locales

A locale effectively defines your keyboard language—that is, the language and keyboard layout on PCs generally used in your geographic area. Most PC users only ever set up one locale, such as English (U.S.) or English (United Kingdom). Only a member of the Administrator's local group can add or delete input locales.

By selecting the Input Locales tab, you can set up different keyboard configurations, as shown in Figure A.39. This dialog is also a part of the Regional Settings applet.

Figure A.39.

Input locales.

The Input Locale dialog allows you to add or delete locales and configure which keyboard layout to use. The example shown in Figure A.39 shows four locales that have been added, each with a different keyboard.

Keyboard Type

The General tab in the Keyboard applet allows you to define the type of keyboard you are using. This is distinct from the keyboard layout defined using locales, as described previously.

The Keyboard dialog allows you to select a list of keyboards, as shown in Figure A.40. Most users probably use either the PC/AT Enhanced Keyboard (101/102 key) or the Standard 101/102 key or Microsoft Natural Keyboard.

Figure A.40.

Keyboard types.

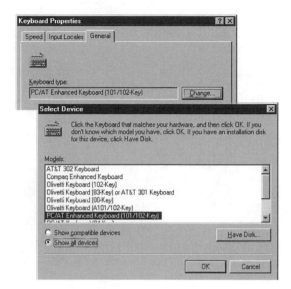

Mail

To many users, e-mail is something they simply cannot live without. A key application for most Internet users is their e-mail, although opinions on what constitutes a good e-mail client are highly charged, to say the least.

Microsoft Exchange is a powerful messaging system and has two main components. The Exchange server runs on Windows NT Server and holds and distributes the individual messages, e-mail items, to Exchange clients. Exchange clients are used to read and create messages sent to Exchange server. You can use Exchange in virtually any size organization, from a small firm to a large multi-national company.

Windows NT 4 has a basic Exchange client, a slimmed-down version of the full Exchange client that is part of the full Exchange product. The Exchange client is a basic mail reader and works in conjunction with Microsoft Mail.

More interestingly for many NT Workstation users, the Exchange client also works and interoperates with the Internet. Out of the box, it communicates with any POP3 Internet mail server, which makes it a good option for home users. If your Internet provider only uses SMTP, you have a variety of SMTP-to-POP3 gateways readily available.

The Mail Applet is used to configure the Microsoft Exchange client shipped with Windows NT 4 Workstation. Selecting the Mail icon displays the dialog shown in Figure A.41.

Figure A.41.

Configuring Exchange e-mail.

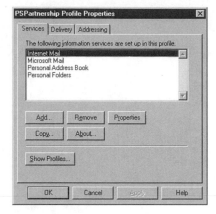

This dialog allows you to create different profiles and see the main components of a profile: Services, Delivery, and Addressing.

Complete details of configuring Microsoft Exchange, both client and server, could fill an entire book (and probably do).

Microsoft Mail Post Office

To assist users in smaller companies, Windows NT Workstation also supports a basic Microsoft Mail post office, which you can use in conjunction with the Exchange client. The Microsoft Mail Post Office applet allows you to configure or create a Microsoft Mail post office.

Modems

A modem is a small piece of electronics that enables your PC to call other systems and transfer data. It's hard to understand, at times, how such a small bit of hardware can cause such problems. I regard anything to do with modem configuration to be a black art, best left to the high priest who mumbles the magic incantations of s54=129 and so on. The good news is that after you get your modem configured, you can pretty much forget about it until you upgrade it—then the fun begins all over again.

In order to utilize the dial-up networking features of Windows NT, you need to install and configure a modem. Only a member of the Administrator's local group can add a modem. The Modems applet, shown in Figure A.42, installs and configures a modem.

Figure A.42.

Modem configuration.

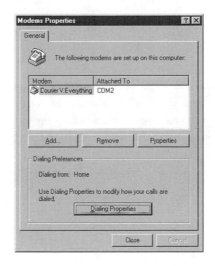

Selecting and Configuring a Modem

At the top of the dialog shown in Figure A.42, you can see the currently installed modems. The Add button brings up a modem detection wizard that can detect your modem or allow you to specify the specific model and manufacturer.

After installing the modem, you might need to configure it. Selecting the Properties button shown in Figure A.42 invokes the Modem Properties dialog, as shown in Figure A.43.

Figure A.43.

Configuring modem properties.

The modem properties include the communications port the modem is physically attached to, the modem speaker volume, and the maximum speed at which to run the modem.

Generally, your modem is attached to one of your serial ports, either COM1 or COM2, although on some systems you can use COM3 and COM4. Be careful if you use ports other than COM1 or COM2 because some hardware, particularly some graphics cards, can cause conflicts.

Some modems, notably internal modems, might not have a speaker, and as a result, the speaker volume slider might be grayed out. On some modems, the speaker might run at only two volumes: on or off. More sophisticated external modems (that is, the most expensive ones!) tend to have volume controls in the modem. The modem speaker can be highly useful during initial installation if you want to ensure that you dialed the right number and observe the progress of a call. It also can be useful if you use an ISP with less than perfect equipment. Some folks, on the other hand, find the noise quite irritating, particularly late at night!

The Maximum Speed list box refers to the maximum speed at which data is physically transferred between your modem and the computer, and not the speed that a data stream is transferred between the remote computer and yours. When transferring data between systems, most modems can compress the data being sent and decompress the data being received.

With data compression. the compressed data will travel between systems at the chosen rate (for example, 28.8Kbps), but the effective throughput is higher.

This assumes, of course, that compression of the data is possible—not all data is compressible. If you are downloading NNTP network news from the Internet, a modern 28.8KB modem can achieve effective download speeds of 5000 to 6000 characters per second (cps) or higher at times. On the other hand, binary data top an effective 3000 cps. Note that these speeds assume you're using a 28.8KB modem. If you are using a slower modem, you get correspondingly slower throughput figures. With modern PCs, you usually can also select the fastest speed supported by your modem (shown in the dialog box).

In general, run your modem as fast as you can, but check with the dial-up monitor to avoid running it too fast and generating overruns.

Dialing Preferences

Selecting the Dialing Properties from the main Modem Properties dialog displays the Dialing Properties dialog, which is a part of the Telephony facility, described in more detail later in this appendix.

A

The Dialing Properties dialog, shown in Figure A.44, allow you to specify how Windows NT should dial, including how to get an outside line, how to disable call waiting, and so on.

Figure A.44.
Dialing preferences.

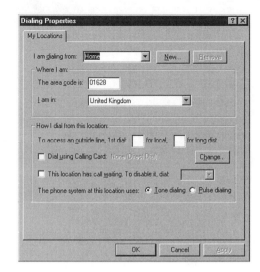

By setting up a location, you can define how Windows NT dials from one specific location. Mobile users often define a number of different locations for use on the road.

Before Windows NT dials a dial-up networking connection, it determines where in the world you are by reference to your currently selected location and where you're dialing. It can then put in the relevant country codes, international dialing access codes, and so on. This can be quite a time saver, but only if you have locations set up in advance.

Mouse

For most users, using Windows NT means using a mouse or some other pointing and selecting device such as a trackball, glide pad, and so on. NT does a good job at detecting all supported pointing devices, but you might want to configure it to your own personal tastes.

Selecting the Mouse applet from the Control Panel brings up the Mouse Properties dialog, shown in Figure A.45, from which you can configure your mouse.

Figure A.45.

Mouse properties.

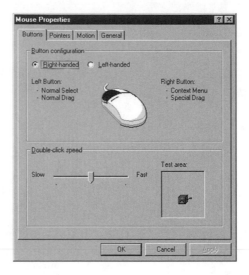

The mouse preferences are user specific and are stored in the Registry under the key HKEY_CURRENT_USER\Control Panel\Mouse.

The Button configuration enables you to configure which button is the primary button (used for selecting and dragging objects) and which is the secondary button (used to bring up context menus). Left-handed users might find this helpful, although many left-handed users I know use the right-handed settings because many books and articles (including this appendix) simply refer to right-clicking and left-clicking.

Double-clicking involves pressing one of the mouse buttons, usually the left or primary button, twice quickly in succession. Windows NT interprets a double-click differently from a single-click, and in many dialog boxes, a double-click has a specific action. For example, double- (left-) clicking a folder on your NT Workstation desktop opens the folder, whereas double-clicking a specific file in a standard File Open dialog selects that file. Double-clicks are an important power-user technique.

The Double-Click Speed option allows you to adjust how sensitive Windows NT is to double-clicking. If you click too slowly or the double-click speed is set too high, Windows NT assumes you are just single-clicking the same object twice instead of double-clicking it. In general, less experienced users tend to be more comfortable with a slower double-click speed. If you make the speed too quick, double-clicking becomes almost impossible.

The test area allows you to move the mouse pointer into the area to see the effect of changing the double-click speed. Each time a double-click is detected by NT, the jack-in-the-box animation is triggered. Children of all ages love the animation!

A

Mouse Pointers

Applications running on Windows NT, including NT itself, can use one of 14 different standard pointer types to indicate the state of the current application. When the system or an application is busy and will not accept any user input, the mouse pointer is an hourglass, whereas when NT is busy in the background, you might get the pointer and hourglass combination pointer. The pointer shape provides useful and important feedback to the user.

Selecting the Pointers tab from the Mouse Properties dialog invokes the Pointers dialog, shown in Figure A.46.

Figure A.46.

Mouse pointers.

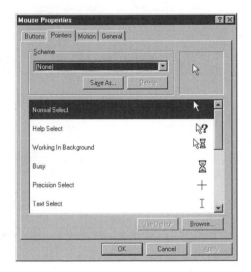

The shape of the mouse pointer is one of those desktop configuration issues that virtually no two users agree on. Some people just love the animated cursors, but others hate them. Personally, I intensely dislike the dinosaur cursors, but others feel quite different. To each his own!

Microsoft has grouped together sets of the 14 cursors into a cursor scheme, and 11 cursor schemes ship with Windows NT Workstation. Of course, you can choose different static or animated cursors for any of the 14 cursor types and save your choices as a new cursor scheme.

In addition to changing the entire cursor schemes, you also can change an individual cursor. Simply select the cursor to be changed and either double-click it or click the Browse button. This displays a common dialog to help you choose your cursor.

Cursors are stored, by default, in the SYSTEM32 directory (%SYSTEMROOT%\System32) with an extension of either CUR or ANI. The ANI cursors are animated and require more CPU power. These generally are not recommended for low-power systems.

Motion

Selecting the Motion tab from the Mouse Properties dialog invokes the dialog shown in Figure A.47. This dialog allows you to set the pointer speed as well as activate the Snap to Default feature.

Figure A.47.

Mouse properties—motion.

By moving the slider bar in the dialog, you affect the relationship between how far you move the actual mouse and how far the mouse pointer moves on the screen. Moving the slider to the right makes the mouse pointer on the screen move farther for any given movement of the actual mouse. As with the cursors settings, the setting here is a highly individual choice.

The Snap to Default feature is another thing you'll either hate or love—there seems to be no middle ground. When you select this option, any time a Windows NT message box is displayed, the mouse automatically moves over the default button (for example, OK, Cancel, and so on). For users with large screens, this can save a lot of mouse movement.

Selecting the Correct Mouse Hardware

Selecting the General tab in the Mouse Properties dialog brings up the General dialog, shown in Figure A.48, which displays the type of mouse hardware you currently have installed.

Figure A.48.

Selecting the mouse.

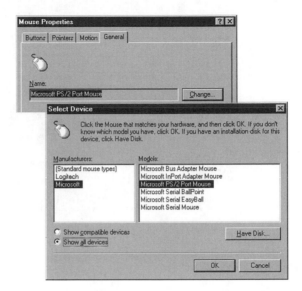

When you click the Change button, you get another dialog in which you can see all the different mice supported, out of the box, by Windows NT. If you have a mouse that is not supported as standard, you can select the Have Disk button and install the driver from a floppy disk.

Multimedia

The Multimedia capabilities of personal computers have improved dramatically over the past decade, and what once was considered highly sophisticated features are now becoming almost commonplace. Windows NT Workstation does come with a good level of Multimedia capability, but Windows 95 and the Macintosh are possibly more appropriate for more sophisticated multimedia applications.

The Multimedia Control Panel shown in Figure A.49 configures the multimedia functions and installs and configures the related hardware.

Figure A.49.

Multimedia.

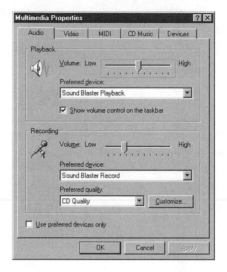

Audio Playback

The Audio tab, shown in Figure A.49, controls playback and recording. Usually, playback is via a sound card and a pair of external speakers, whereas recording is via a microphone attached to the sound card. If you have multiple sound cards, you can select which one Windows NT should use.

The volume slider in the Playback section is a master volume control controlling the overall output levels. Many sound cards have additional volume controls, as do the speakers shipped with many computer systems. Selecting the right level on all three can take some time, but after they're set, you usually don't have to change them.

If you select the Show Volume Control on the Taskbar option, Windows NT places a small icon of a speaker on the right side of the taskbar. You can then use this control to change the master output level. Double-clicking this control displays a more comprehensive volume control dialog.

The Recording settings control the microphone input levels and the sampling rate. If the recording level is too high, the resulting sound quality is poor, so you need perform some testing prior to doing any important recording.

All recording is done using digital sampling. When recording from a microphone, Windows NT samples the input port and records the result as digital data. The more samples taken,

A

the better the quality of the resulting recording—but more data is needed to represent the recorded sound. The specific dialog is sound-card dependent.

Video

Windows NT Workstation includes Video for Windows, which means you can play back video clips on your PC. One small drawback to this otherwise splendid facility is that video clips take up considerable amounts of disk space. If you start collecting useful (that is, long) video clips, be prepared to invest in large amounts of storage space.

Video clips are played by the media player accessory, MPLAYER.EXE. You can also use this accessory to play audio clips, CDs, and MIDI clips, assuming you have the necessary hardware support (that is, a suitable sound card and a CD-ROM). By default, the media player accessory plays back video clips at the size they were recorded (which is usually quite small).

The Video tab in the Multimedia control applet invokes the dialog box shown in Figure A.50.

Figure A.50.

Multimedia video configuration.

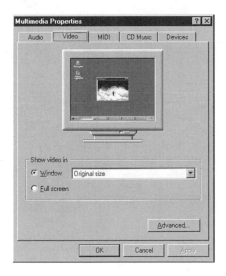

The Video dialog allows you to control the size of the video playback, which can make video files easier to see. However, by increasing the size, you experience some loss of quality.

From this dialog, you also can select the Advanced button, which allows you to configure the media player to use some older, 16-bit code. Some older video clips might not work properly on Windows NT Workstation, and this option allows you to use 16-bit code that might work better.

MIDI

MIDI (Musical Instrument Digital Interface) is an interface standard that allows you to use a large range of electronic musical instruments via a digital computer. Most modern electronic keyboards, for example, offer the capability of MIDI input and output, and many popular recording artists make significant use of this capability.

The MIDI configuration dialog, shown in Figure A.51, allows you to select the specific instrument connected to your computer.

Figure A.51.

MIDI configuration.

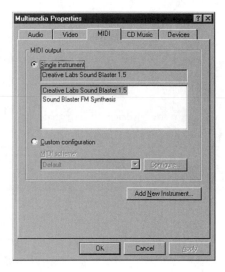

If you have multiple instruments connected, select the one you want to control. The custom settings allow you to configure additional various MIDI channels.

CD Music

By adding a CD-ROM drive to your computer, you can play normal music CDs by using the CD Player accessory (or using the media player described earlier). This makes it easy to listen while you work. If you work in a crowded office and your musical tastes are considered eclectic by co-workers, you might consider using a set of headphones (and preferably not the ones where everyone near you can hear just enough to really be annoying).

Choosing the CD Music tab brings up the dialog shown in Figure A.52.

Most CD-ROMs come with a small headphone jack on the front that allows you to listen to music CDs.

Figure A.52.

*Multimedia—CD
music.*

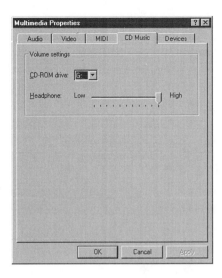

The CD Audio dialog displays the detected CD-ROMs on your system and allows you to control the headphone volume for each one. The selected CD-ROM is then used as the default for any multimedia application that uses a CD-ROM.

Devices

The Devices dialog, shown in Figure A.53, shows all the different multimedia drivers loaded on your system and allows you to specify their properties.

You must be a member of the Administrator's local group to manage multimedia devices.

Figure A.53.

*Configuring multimedia
devices.*

Network

Networking was built into Windows NT since its first release, and the networking features have steadily improved ever since. Networking is a fundamental part of the design of NT and follows a very structured and layered model. Configuring networking on Windows NT is really pretty easy once you get past the jargon.

Although networking with Windows NT Workstation is pretty easy, before installing and configuring networking, you really do need a basic understanding of what networking is and the options you need to configure for any given network situation.

The Network applet is where you do all network configuration. The Network applet is complex in that a lot of options are interrelated, and you need those options properly specified if networking is to be successful. When you understand the impact of the options and how to configure them, the dialogs are easy to use.

The Network Control Panel applet, which you can invoke by right-clicking the Network Neighborhood icon on the desktop and selecting the Properties menu, configures all networking. The applet is shown in Figure A.54. Only a member of the Administrator's local group can change the network settings.

Figure A.54.
Network configuration.

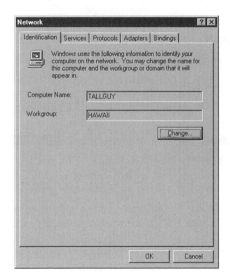

Identification

The Identification dialog, shown in Figure A.54, allows you to view and change your machine and workgroup or domain name. If you change any of these items, you must reboot your system before they take effect.

A

Services

Network services sit above the network protocols and the adapters. Network services use lower-level components to implement various network-related functions. For example, the server service allows you to share files and directories with other users, whereas the Workstation enables you to connect to the server service on another system to access the shared resources on that system.

The Services dialog, shown in Figure A.55, allows you to manage and control the network services loaded on your machine.

Figure A.55.

Network services.

The Services dialog allows you to add and delete network services. In addition, some, but not all, services can be configured from this dialog.

Protocols

The network transport protocols enable communication between two systems, possibly via other systems, using one or more of the configured network adapters. The network protocols sit below the network services and above the adapters. Examples include TCP/IP and IPX/SPX.

The network protocols loaded on your system are viewed in the Protocols dialog, as shown in Figure A.56.

Figure A.56.
Network protocols.

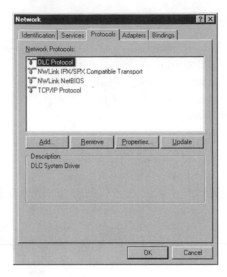

Adapters

A network adapter is a hardware component that is either built into your computer's motherboard or implemented as an add-on card, which physically connects your computer to a network. To some degree, a modem is a network adapter, although the designers of Windows NT Workstation chose to treat it separately.

With the dialog shown in Figure A.57, you can add and view the network adapters in your system.

Figure A.57.
Network adapters.

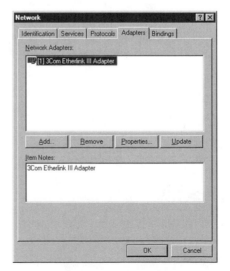

A

Bindings

A binding is a path that a given application request to the network might take from an application through the services and protocols and eventually down to the adapter layer. Although Windows NT Workstation generally configures all services bound to all protocols and adapters, the configuration might not be the best for performance because some possible bindings might not be useful. To maximize performance, you might need to remove or disable bindings.

For example, because all Novell-related traffic uses IPX and not TCP/IP, there is little point binding the client service for NetWare to TCP/IP. (In fact, the installation of the NetWare client knows this and is clever enough to set the binding.) If you have multiple cards, multiple transports, and multiple clients, adjusting your bindings can improve performance if you can eliminate unhelpful paths that can never be used in your environment. The Bindings dialog, shown in Figure A.58, allows you to modify the binding paths.

Figure A.58.

Network bindings.

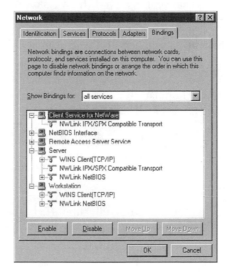

PC Card (PCMCIA)

The growth in portable computing has been matched by the growth in the add-ons available for these systems. With a specification designed by a committee (the Personal Computer Memory Card International Association, or PCMCIA), a new type of interface card, the PC card, has become very popular. These cards were initially known as PCMCIA cards, but because most end users can't pronounce or spell it, they are now called PC cards.

PC cards are small credit-card–sized hardware devices that are powered from the main system. The four physical types of PCMCIA cards are Type I, Type II, Type III, and Type IV. All these cards use the same 69-pin interface but vary in thickness and general usage.

Type I cards, which are 3.3mm thick, tend to be used for various types of memory such as RAM, Flash ROM, EEPROM, and so on. They are not very common today. Type II cards, which are 5mm thick, are very common and are used for a range of things, including network adapters. Type III cards, which are 11.5mm thick, are most often used for PCMCIA hard disks or radio communications devices that require more circuitry. Type IV cards, which have not been ratified by the PCMCIA consortium, will probably be used for higher-capacity disk drives and are expected to be 18mm thick.

Most modern laptop computers support either two simultaneous Type II cards or one Type III card. Type I cards are rarely used these days, and Type IV cards are not yet supported.

The most popular uses for PC cards are for modems and network adapters, although a wide range of alternative uses include hard disks, SCSI adapters, Global Positioning by Satellite (GPS) radio receivers, ISDN, external CD-ROM, and sound cards.

NT Workstation supports PC cards, although the list of supported cards is not all that long. As you might expect, NT supports a large number of modems and a reasonable number of network cards, but not a lot else. However, the list is increasing all the time as notebooks become more popular. In summary, be careful before you buy a PC card for a Windows NT system.

Windows NT Workstation 4 does not fully support Plug and Play, which means, sadly, you cannot just remove or insert PC cards while the system is running as you can with Windows 95. Some folks think this is an oversight by Microsoft, but Plug and Play is promised for later versions of Windows NT.

Because Plug and Play is not fully supported, you must reboot your system to change the cards you use. If you do remove a card while NT is up and running, you run the risk of locking up your system, requiring a hardware reboot.

Despite all this gloom, supported PC cards do work with great ease. For the most part, you can just treat PC cards as any other card—that is, configuring a PC card network adapter with the Network applet or a modem with the Modem applet.

Invoking the PC Card (PCMCIA) Control Panel applet brings up the dialog shown in Figure A.59. This has two subdialogs, Socket Status and Controller.

A

Figure A.59.

PC card (PCMCIA)
configuration.

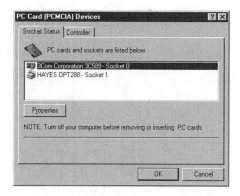

This dialog shows you the PC cards currently plugged into your computer. By selecting the Properties button, you can bring up a further dialog to enable you to configure the card, although as noted earlier, this is rarely necessary. The Configuration dialog is implemented by the card driver itself and thus will vary with the card. The Configuration dialog for a 3COM 3C589 PC Card Network adapter is shown in Figure A.60.

Figure A.60.

Properties of a 3COM
PC card.

Controller

The Controller dialog, shown in Figure A.61, enables you to view the resources currently used by the PCMCIA controller. In general, you can't change the I/O port of conventional memory range on the controller because it is assigned automatically. In the unlikely event of a conflict with another device, you need to change the other device's resources to resolve the conflict.

Figure A.61.

PC card controller status.

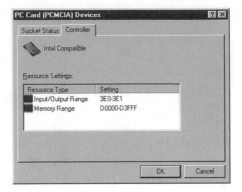

Ports

Personal computers connect with the outside world using one or more ports. A port is simply a connection between the system and an external device. Two main ports supplied on all PCs are serial, or communications, ports and parallel, or printer, ports. Serial ports, as their name implies, transfer data serially, one bit at a time, whereas parallel ports can transfer data eight bits at a time.

Most PCs usually have two serial, or communications, ports that use either 9- or 25-pin serial connectors. You can connect a number of things to these serial I/O ports such as a modem, a mouse, or a printer. Historically, all modem communication happens via the serial port.

Windows NT Workstation supports up to 256 serial ports, although some substantial hardware is required if you want to support all 256! In my experience, all software that uses the serial ports is capable of configuring the serial port, so this applet is really not all that useful except to define additional ports.

The Ports Control Panel applet is shown in Figure A.62.

Figure A.62.

The Ports applet.

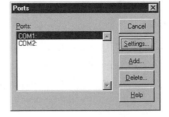

Selecting the dialog shows you the currently installed ports. Clicking the Settings button brings up a Settings dialog, shown in Figure A.63, from which you can configure the key settings for your serial port. The specific settings required are usually defined either by the

A

software connected to the serial port (for example, the modem, the printer, and so on) or by the software you use, so be sure to read the relevant manual.

Figure A.63.

Configuring serial ports.

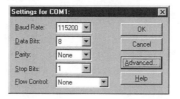

If you are installing more than the standard four serial ports, you need to configure the IRQ and I/O port. This is done using the Advanced Port Configuration dialog, shown in Figure A.64. You must be a member of the Administrator's local group to use the Advanced Port Configuration dialog.

Figure A.64.

Advanced serial port configuration.

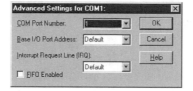

Printers

Printing in Windows NT has always been a mixture of good news and bad news. The bad news is that the internal architecture is rather complex, but the good news is that printing works. In my experience with Windows NT, virtually all the printing problems I've encountered are easy ones: the hardware isn't plugged in, connected, or turned on, or I have the wrong drivers.

Printing Basics

Before I introduce the Printer applet, it's important that you understand the basics of printing on NT and the following NT-specific definitions:

☐ The printing device is the chunk of hardware that actually puts the ik (or toner) onto the page.

☐ The printer is the software interface between the application and the printing device. That is, the application prints to a printer, and NT handles the transition to the printing device.

☐ The printer queue is simply the list of jobs waiting to print at a printer. The term *queue* has no actual significance (unlike in Novell).

☐ The print monitor is the software component that routes the final output from the printer to the printing device.

☐ The print server is the NT system on which the printer is defined and on which the print monitor runs.

☐ The port is where the print monitor sends the output. Usually, this is your system's parallel or serial port. However, this can also be a network port—for example, an HP printer with a Jet Direct card.

These definitions might be different from other systems you've used, particularly Novell NetWare, but they are the definitions used with NT, so you'll need to get used to them.

Before your application can do any printing, you first have to define a printer on your system, either by creating a printer on your machine or connecting to a printer somewhere on your network. After you have created or connected to the printer, your applications can then use the printer, although you might want to modify the printer's configuration.

The printer folder in Windows NT Workstation is the place where all printing-related configuration and management is carried out. You can access the printer folder in one of the following three ways:

☐ Opening the My Computer folder

☐ Using Start | Settings | Printers

☐ Selecting the Printers applet (or strictly speaking, shortcut) from the Control Panel

The printer folder is the same, no matter which method you choose to invoke it. The Printers folder on my system is shown in Figure A.65.

Figure A.65.

The Printers folder.

To set up a new printer on your system or connect to a printer on the network, you should use the Add Printer wizard, which is more clearly examined in Hour 7, "Setting Up Printers with NT Workstation." This is a quick, easy, and almost foolproof way to define the printer.

A

Networked Printer Drivers

As shown in Hour 7, setting up any printer is quick and easy. I hear you ask, "What about printer drivers?" You do need them, and the process of creating a printer requires you to load the printer drivers. These are typically on your Windows NT Workstation CD-ROM. Alternatively, you might get them on disk with new printers, or you can download them from the Internet or the manufacturer's electronic bulletin board.

When you create a local printer, Windows NT loads the printer drivers for local printing. For network printing, NT gets clever—when you connect to a network printer, Windows NT simply downloads the printer driver for you from the machine where the printer was initially created. That's it!

NT achieves this by sharing the `%SYSTEMROOT%\System32\Spool\Drivers` folder as `PRINT$`. When a remote system wants to get print drivers from your system, it merely connects to `\\YOURSYSTEM\PRINT$` (where *yoursystem* is the NetBIOS machine name, defined in the Network applet). Directly below this, Windows NT creates one extra folder for each hardware platform for which drivers are held.

The only real issue to resolve is which printer drivers you should hold. A printer driver is an executable program, typically a DLL, designed to run on a particular operating system and hardware. If you define a printer for use by other users on the network, it is important that you hold all the printer drivers for all the various combinations of systems that are likely to access it. If Windows NT fails to find the correct drivers on the remote machine, it simply prompts for a location to find them, and when fed the appropriate disk, CD-ROM, or network share point, it then can load the drivers for this alternative location.

With NT Workstation Version 4, you can automatically load printer drivers for other NT systems as well as for Windows 95.

If you access the printer via Windows for Workgroups, Windows 3.*x*, or DOS, you have to load the printer manually on each of the client systems. Also, if you connect from your system to a printer defined on a non-Windows NT system (for example, Windows 95), you also must load printer drivers manually.

Printing from DOS Applications

If you are using DOS applications, printing becomes slightly more difficult. First, DOS applications each require their own printer drivers; sadly, they cannot use the Windows NT drivers. DOS printer drivers are usually application-specific and must be obtained from the application vendor. This can be an issue for very old programs.

DOS applications also have no concept of networking and tend to open a configured LPT or COM port and dump their output, which is not much help when the printer is remote.

To enable DOS applications to print successfully, you need to use the NET command from the command line on the client system. Go to the command line and use the following syntax:

```
NET USE LPT2: \\server\remoteprinter
```

LPT2 is the port your DOS application uses, and *server* is the machine on which the printer shared as *remoteprinter* is located.

After you have done this, you must configure your DOS application to use the port you just used. Printing across the network now should work!

You can view the printers you are currently using by typing NET USE from the command line.

Printer Summary

Printing is extremely easy to set up and get working. Properly securing the printer takes a bit more work, but all the permissions are consistent with NT's overall security model.

Happy printing!

Regional Settings

As with earlier versions of Windows, Windows 95, and Windows NT, Windows NT 4 Workstation was designed as an international product. This means that it should be easy for anyone to customize it, taking normal national preferences into account. The Regional Settings applet configures Windows NT's international settings. Your applications, if properly programmed, can use these settings to make your version of Windows NT Workstation work properly in different geographical areas.

The Regional Settings dialog is shown in Figure A.66. This dialog allows you to select a specific region. Based on the chosen region, Windows NT can then automatically modify all the related settings, including the formats of numbers, currency, time, dates, and keyboard.

The following additional tabs in the dialog shown in Figure A.66 allow you to override the defaults based on the chosen region:

A

Figure A.66.

Regional settings.

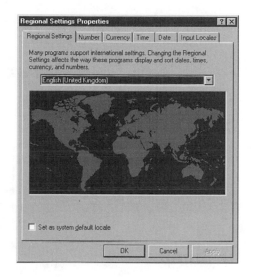

The Number dialog, shown in Figure A.67, allows you to select the ways numerical values are displayed.

Figure A.67.

Number format.

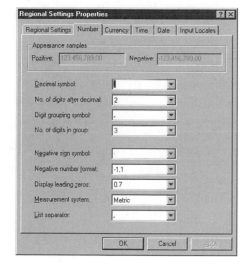

☐ The Currency dialog, shown in Figure A.68, enables you to change the way currency values are displayed.

Figure A.68.

Currency format.

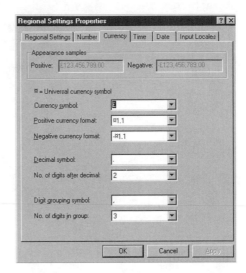

☐ Using the Time dialog, shown in Figure A.69, you can change the way time of day values are displayed.

Figure A.69.

Time format.

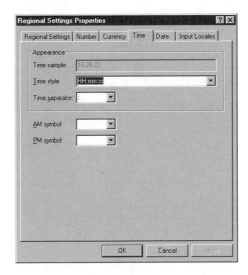

☐ With the Date dialog, shown in Figure A.70, you can change the way dates are displayed.

Figure A.70.

Date format.

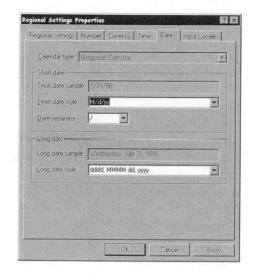

☐ The Input Locales dialog, shown in Figure A.71, enables you to change the keyboard layout. Only a member of the Administrator's local group can use this dialog.

Figure A.71.

Input locales.

Most users do not need, or want, to modify these settings because the most obvious application (Excel 95) takes no notice of them. Don't forget that choosing the region also modifies all the related settings.

Some users, however, might want to make some specific changes, including the following:

☐ Adding digits after the decimal: Choose the Number tab and select the No of Digits After Decimal. To do this for currency values, change this setting in the Currency dialog.

☐ Changing the default measurement system: (This is particularly useful in the U.K., where we use both the Imperial and Metric measurements.) Choose the Number tab and select Measurement System.

☐ Changing the thousands and decimal separators: Some countries, such as France, use the . (period) as the thousands separator and the , (comma) as the decimal, so the number 1,234,345.33 is written as 1.234.345,33. To change this, modify the Decimal Symbol and the Digit Grouping Symbol in either the Number or Currency tabs (or both!).

☐ Changing the date and time displayed: Like many settings, this is another choice that is often quite personal. Use the Time and Date tabs to select time and date displays for your personal preference.

The individual settings for numbers, currency, and so on are user specific and are stored in the Registry under HKEY_LOCAL_USER\Control_Panel\International.

SCSI Adapters

SCSI, Small Computer Systems Interface, is one of two principal ways of connecting disk drives and other peripherals to a Windows NT system.

The SCSI Adapters applet is possibly misnamed. In the initial version of Windows NT, this applet, which was then part of the Windows NT Setup program, only handled true SCSI adapters. In later versions, and now in Windows NT 4 Workstation, this applet is also used to install certain supported but non-SCSI CD-ROMs.

For the most part, this dialog is rarely used because the devices handled by this applet are automatically detected at the time the system is loaded. You will most often use this applet when you are upgrading your system, adding new hardware, or updating your SCSI disk device drivers.

Selecting the SCSI Adapter applet from the Control Panel displays the dialog shown in Figure A.72. This dialog shows all the installed SCSI controllers and the devices attached to each controller.

A

Figure A.72.
SCSI adapters.

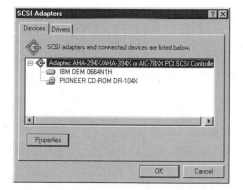

Devices

Selecting the controller, or a device, and clicking the Properties button brings up additional information about the drive or controller, as shown in Figures A.73 and A.74.

Figure A.73.
SCSI adapter properties.

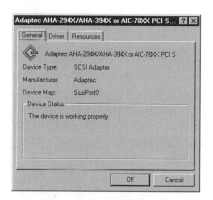

Figure A.74.
SCSI peripheral properties.

Drivers

Clicking the Drivers tab in the SCSI Adapters applet brings up the dialog box shown in Figure A.75. This dialog shows all the SCSI adapters loaded in your system and whether they have been started. In the example shown in Figure A.75, one driver was started, but the other failed to start.

Figure A.75.

SCSI driver properties.

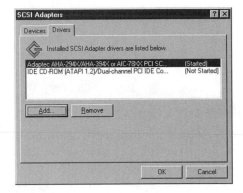

From the Drivers dialog, you can add and remove SCSI device drivers.

Because changing SCSI controllers and drivers is considered a relatively secure event, you must be a member of the Administrator's local group on your machine before you can use the Device properties.

Server

A great feature of Windows NT Workstation is the built-in peer-to-peer networking. Installing the file and printer sharing features is quick and easy.

At the core of Windows networking are two key network services: the workstation service and the server service. The workstation service redirects I/O requests from your workstation to other systems on the network, whereas the server service accepts such remote requests from other systems, subject to the security you place on your system. These two software components work in conjunction with the I/O manager to allow you to share files and printers in an easy and secure fashion.

Both services sit on top of whatever networking infrastructure you have installed. At least in theory, you can run these on any installed transport protocol and with any installed networking adapter. Essentially, these two components are transport and hardware independent (although highly reliant on the proper functioning of the lower-level modules).

The Server Control Panel applet allows you to examine and manage the behavior of the server service. This is probably more important if you are managing a larger NT Server instead of an NT Workstation system, but it can still be useful, particularly if other users on your network are accessing files on your system.

Selecting the Server applet from the Control Panel invokes the dialog shown in Figure A.76. You must be a member of the Administrator's local group to use this applet. The applet, when it is invoked, summarizes the state of the server service.

Figure A.76.

The Server dialog box.

The Server applet offers five buttons that you can use to display and manage aspects of the server service:

- ☐ Clicking Users displays the dialog shown in Figure A.77, which shows the users currently logged on to your system. By selecting a user, you can force a disconnection of that user or you can disconnect all users. This can result in data loss, so be careful.

Figure A.77.

Active user sessions.

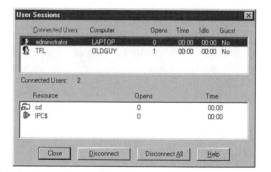

- ☐ As shown in Figure A.78, the Shared Resources dialog shows all the directories shared on your system and how many users are currently connected to that share. As with the Users option described previously, you can forcibly disconnect one specific user or all users. You cannot disconnect a single user from a single share, however.

Figure A.78.

Shared Resources.

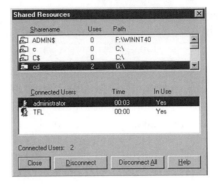

□ Selecting the In Use button invokes the dialog shown in Figure A.79. This shows the specific files currently in use by others on your network. You have the option to close a specific resource or all resources. Unlike your work with the Shares and Users dialogs, you can refresh this view to display any changes to open resources.

Figure A.79.

Open Resources.

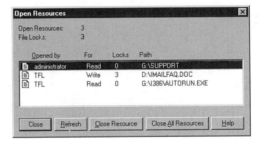

□ The Replication dialog in Figure A.80 allows you to manage the Directory Replication service. Directory Replication allows Export servers (which must be Windows NT Servers) to export directories to Import servers (which can be other NT Server or Windows NT Workstation systems). Only administrators can configure replication.

Figure A.80.

Directory Replication.

The Export server exports one or more directories to specific, named systems. On the Import server, you first choose where the root of the imported directories is located in the To Path box in the dialog in Figure A.80. Usually, the import path is %SYSTEMROOT%\SYSTEM32\REPL\IMPORT.

Using the Manage dialog, shown in Figure A.81, you can choose which systems you want to accept imports from and which of the exported directories you want to import. When Directory Replication is fully working, this dialog displays the status of the imported directories.

Figure A.81.

Managing imported directories.

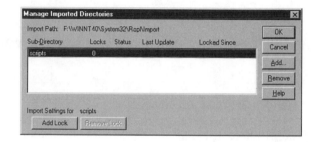

☐ When a Windows NT Workstation system discovers a problem in the environment—for example, a UPS that has just lost power—it generates an administrative alert. Generally, these alerts are local to the system. By using the Alerts dialog, shown in Figure A.82, you can redirect these alerts to other systems or users on the network. This is probably less useful on NT Workstation than on NT Server. Only administrators can manage alerts.

Figure A.82.

Administrative alerts.

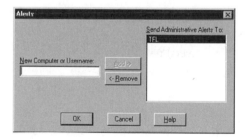

Most of these functions are straightforward, although Directory Replication can be more problematic. The error messages generated by the Directory Replicator service are often cryptic in the extreme and often can be downright mystifying.

Most problems with the replication process are caused because the Directory Replication service has not started or because of permission problems on the import directories. In the Services dialog (see the next section), you must select the Directory Replication service and ensure that you have specified a valid user for the service to log in, as shown in Figure A.83. The chosen user must have the right to log in as a service and be a member of the Replicator local group on your system. Also, the user must have access to the import directories.

Figure A.83.

Configuring the Direc-
tory Replicator service.

Another potential problem with directory replication is passwords. Make sure the directory replication user's password is set to Never Expire and make sure the User Must Change Password At Next Logon box is not checked.

Directory Replication is pretty simple, but it's also easy to get wrong, and the error messages could be improved. Have fun!

Services

A service is a Windows NT process loaded by the operating system at boot time. NT services work in the background and perform useful functions, such as the server service, which responds to requests for access to files and printers on your system.

A service is a driver in the sense that it is part of the operating system, as described in the previous section.

The Services Control Panel applet, shown in Figure A.84, shows all the currently defined services, their status, and when the service is started. You also can stop, pause, or start a service from this dialog. You must be a member of the Administrator's local group to start, stop, or configure services.

Figure A.84.

The Services dialog in the Control Panel.

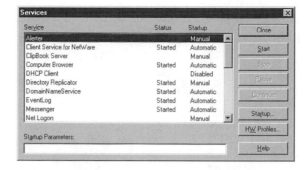

In this dialog, you see the service's common name, which is usually different from the filename of the executable file containing the service. The Windows NT service architecture enables a single executable file to contain one or more services.

In the Services Control Panel applet, you also see the network services, which are not shown in the task list (as noted in the previous tip). These are configured using the Network applet and should not need any additional configuration.

By selecting the Startup button, you bring up a subsidiary, as shown in Figure A.85, which tells Windows NT when to start the service. This dialog also allows you to enter a user name under which the service should start. This can be useful to deny access to certain sensitive data to the service, thus increasing the security on your system. With the exception of the Directory Replication service, this security is rarely necessary.

Figure A.85.

Configuring service startup.

Hardware Profiles

As with devices, you can set up hardware profiles in which services can be enabled or disabled. Selecting a service and then clicking HW Profiles brings up a dialog box, as shown in Figure A.86, which allows you to disable or enable the service in a profile. In Figure A.86, I've disabled the Directory Replicator service because there is nothing to replicate if I'm starting with no network.

Figure A.86.

Configuring a hardware profile.

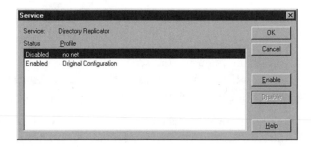

Sounds

In Windows NT, sound is a prerecorded digital representation of a sound. Sounds are usually played through the audio playback channel of a sound card and through speakers or headphones. Sounds can be recorded via your sound card and can come from a microphone or any other input media. Sounds are usually stored with the extension .WAV.

The Sounds Control Panel applet allows you to assign specific sounds to various Windows events. Whenever the event occurs, such as when you empty the Recycle Bin, start Windows, or pop up a menu, the associated sound plays through your sound system.

Sounds were originally intended to assist the visually handicapped, and children generally love this feature, whereas adults generally hate it. Judicious use of sound can be fun—but overuse it and it can become annoying to everyone!

You can program any application to use the sounds setup with the Sounds applet. The application does this by first placing in the Registry a definition of the events that result in playing a sound. Then, each time the event occurs, the application reads the Registry and determines the sound to play. The sound player application is then invoked to play the relevant sound.

The sound event definitions are held in the Registry under the key HKEY_CURRENT_USER\AppEvents\Schemes\Apps. Each application that uses sound places an additional key for the application under this key with further subkeys for each sound-related event.

The Sounds dialog is shown in Figure A.87. As you can see, you can associate each event with a sound clip. Whenever that event occurs, Windows NT plays the associated sound.

Figure A.87.

Sounds properties.

In the example shown in Figure A.87, I've associated the Exit Windows event with Humphrey Bogart's line from the *The Maltese Falcon* where he says, "Now, that'll be all. Just be sure to lock the door behind you on your way out. Good night." Personally, I love it—but other people might have different tastes.

Sound Schemes

You can collect a number of sound settings together in a single sound scheme. This is a good way to minimize the work needed to switch sound settings.

To create a sound scheme, set up the specific sounds you want to hear for each application event and then click the Save As button and enter your scheme name.

System

The System Control Panel applet is shown in Figure A.88. This applet displays general information about the system and allows you to configure a number of system-level settings. You also can invoke this dialog by right-clicking the My Computer icon on the desktop and choosing the Properties menu.

Figure A.88.
*NT Workstation system
properties.*

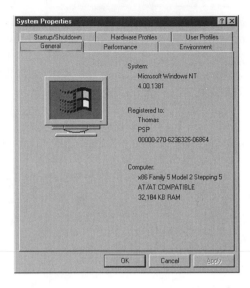

This applet has six tabs, each of which are described in the following sections in more detail.

General

The General tab, which is shown in Figure A.88, provides some basic information about the system, including the following:

☐ System shows which version of Windows NT is installed on your system, along with the internal build number.

☐ Registered to shows the registered owner and organization. Usually, this is the information entered at the time Windows NT Workstation was installed, but you can change it (see the following tip).

☐ Computer gives a summary of the type of computer and how much physical memory NT detected in your system.

You might need this information if you make any support calls to Microsoft.

Performance

The Performance dialog, shown in Figure A.89, enables you to view and modify how much of a performance boost applications in the foreground get and the details of where Windows NT should place its paging files.

Figure A.89.

Configuring system performance.

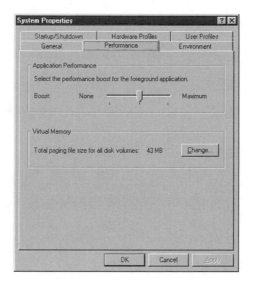

By default, applications that are running in the foreground get a scheduling boost over applications running in the background. For most Windows NT Workstation users, this is the correct behavior, but in certain circumstances, it might not be appropriate. If you are running a large FTP download or sending a large mail message, you want your FTP or mail application to get good performance, but you probably don't want to leave it in the foreground.

The application performance slider has three settings. Setting the boost to Maximum gives the foreground application the best response time. If you set the boost in the middle, the foreground application gets a "better" response time, whereas setting the boost to none means the foreground application gets no priority boost. A boost of None is probably the correct setting if you use communications programs or have multiple CPU-intensive applications running concurrently.

Windows NT achieves this better performance by increasing the internal priority of all threads belonging to the foreground application. As a result, with appropriate settings of Application Priority, the foreground applications usually get priority over the background.

The other function of the Performance dialog is to configure your virtual memory settings. Windows NT Workstation uses virtual memory extensively to enable it to swap information between the hard disk and physical memory. These settings can have a significant impact on performance.

The current amount of virtual memory defined is shown in the dialog box in Figure A.89. Clicking the Change button invokes the Virtual Memory dialog, shown in Figure A.90, which enables you to make changes to your virtual memory allocations.

Figure A.90.

Virtual memory settings.

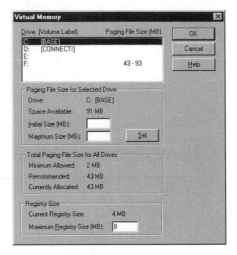

The Virtual Memory dialog lets you modify how much virtual memory is allocated on each disk partition in your system. You also use this dialog to change the maximum size of the Registry, which can be important if you load a large number of applications and other goodies onto your system. Only a member of the Administrators local group can manage page file settings.

The Virtual Memory page file is called PAGEFILE.SYS, and by using the Virtual Memory dialog, you can place a paging file on each partition of your system. You cannot put a paging file on a floppy disk or on the network.

The Virtual Memory dialog shows, at the top, each partition in your system and how big a paging file you have currently allocated on that drive. In Paging File Size for Selected Drive, you can review and modify how big your paging file is for each partition.

After making any changes to your Virtual Memory settings, you must click the Set button for your changes to be registered. Additionally, you need to reboot before these new settings can take effect.

A

Total Paging File Size for All Drives shows how much total paging file space was allocated. This section also gives a recommendation on the minimum amount of paging file space that you should allocate.

The Virtual Memory dialog also allows you to change the maximum size of your system's Registry. Most users do not need to change this. However, if you load a large number of applications, you might need to increase this size.

As noted previously, if you make any changes to the virtual memory settings, including changing the maximum size of your Registry, you need to reboot the system in order for the changes to take effect.

Unlike most of the Control Panel applets, the Virtual Memory dialog has a Help button and some good help information. If you're not a virtual memory whiz kid, you might find this information useful.

Environment

Since the very early days of MS-DOS, application programs have used variables defined in the environment for extra control information. Although environment variables have been largely superseded by .INI files and the Registry for holding key configuration information, Windows NT still uses environment variables for holding extra information.

NT makes heavy use of a few important environment variables. The variable SYSTEMROOT holds the full path of where Windows NT Workstation is installed, and USERPROFILE contains the path to the currently logged-in user's profile. You can see all the variables currently available to you by typing SET at the command prompt. You also can use these variables at the command prompt (CMD.EXE) and in batch files, although you must surround the variable name with %. At the command prompt, you can issue the command DIR %SYSTEMROOT% /S to get a full listing of all the files in the Windows NT installation directory (and all subdirectories).

Windows NT Workstation has two types of environment variables: system and user. System environment variables are set system wide, usually during the installation of an application or the operating system itself. User environment variables are set on a per-user basis. Both sets of variables are stored in the Registry. System environment variables are stored under the key HKEY_LOCAL_MACHINE\SYSTEM\CurrentControlSet\Control\Session Manager\Environment. User environment variables are stored in the key HKEY_CURRENT_USER\Environment.

Selecting the Environment tab brings up the Environment dialog, shown in Figure A.91. This dialog shows all the currently set user and system environment variables.

Figure A.91.

Setting environment variables.

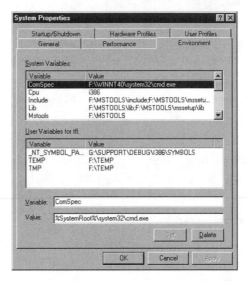

To set a user environment variable, just enter the variable name and value and click the Set button. To set a system environment variable, you first must click in the System Variables area and then enter the variable name and value. To delete any variable, just click it and then click the Delete button.

You also can set environment variables at the command prompt by using the SET command (for example, Set MYFILE=c:\myfile.dat). However, any environment variables set this way are lost when you exit the command prompt.

Startup/Shutdown

When Windows NT Workstation starts up, the NT System loader scans the file BOOT.INI, located in the root directory of your system disk, to build the boot selection menu. The BOOT.INI file contains a list of NT versions to load and where to load them from. This file is initially given the file attributes system and read-only, which makes it more difficult to accidentally erase.

My BOOT.INI file resembles the following code segment:

```
[boot loader]
timeout=30
default=multi(0)disk(0)rdisk(0)partition(2)\WINNT40
[operating systems]
```

A

A

```
multi(0)disk(0)rdisk(0)partition(2)\WINNT40="Windows NT Workstation
➥Version 4.00" /sos
multi(0)disk(0)rdisk(0)partition(2)\WINNT40="Windows NT Workstation
➥Version 4.00 [VGA mode]" /basevideo /sos
multi(0)disk(0)rdisk(0)partition(2)\WINNT35="Windows NT Workstation
➥Version 3.51"
multi(0)disk(0)rdisk(0)partition(2)\WINNT35="Windows NT Workstation
➥Version 3.51 [VGA mode]" /basevideo /sos
multi(0)disk(0)rdisk(0)partition(3)\WINNT40="Windows NT Server
➥Version 4.00" /sos
multi(0)disk(0)rdisk(0)partition(3)\WINNT40="Windows NT Server
➥Version 4.00 [VGA mode]" /basevideo /sos
multi(0)disk(0)rdisk(0)partition(3)\WINNT35="Windows NT Server Version 3.51"
multi(0)disk(0)rdisk(0)partition(3)\WINNT35="Windows NT Server
➥Version 3.51 [VGA mode]" /basevideo /sos
C:\="Microsoft DOS 6/x and Windows 95"
```

As you can see, the BOOT.INI file has two sections:

☐ Boot Loader tells the loader how long to wait for the user to make a selection before taking the default, which also is specified.

☐ Operating Systems contains all the various copies of Windows NT, plus a reference to DOS/Windows 95.

In both sections, each version of NT is shown using the ARC (Advanced RISC Computing) naming convention. This is followed by a string in quotes used to build the boot menu and some system startup options (for example, /SOS to display the details of drivers loaded during the boot process).

After parsing the BOOT.INI file, the NT Loader displays a screen that is derived on the BOOT.INI file. Based on the BOOT.INI file shown previously, it might resemble the following segment:

```
OS Loader V4.00

Please select the Operating System to Start:


    Windows NT Workstation Version 4.00
    Windows NT Workstation Version 4.00 [VGA mode]
    Windows NT Workstation Version 3.51
    Windows NT Workstation Version 3.51
    Windows NT Server Version 4.00
    Windows NT Server Version 4.00 [VGA mode]
    Windows NT Server Version 3.51
    Windows NT Server Version 3.51 [VGA mode]
    Microsoft DOS 6/x and Windows 95

Use ↑ and ↓ to move the highlight to your choice
Press Enter to Choose


Seconds until highlighted choice will be started automatically: 30
```

In this boot menu, the default, the first version of Windows NT 4 Workstation, will be highlighted. You then can use the up and down arrows to choose one of the other operating systems and select it by pressing the Enter key. Alternatively, you can wait the configured amount of time for the default to start. If you move the up and down arrows, the last line of the menu disappears, and for any system to get loaded, you must select the system and press the Enter key.

With this introduction to ARC names and the boot-up process out of the way, the Startup/Shutdown dialog is shown in Figure A.92.

Figure A.92.

Windows NT Startup/
Shutdown.

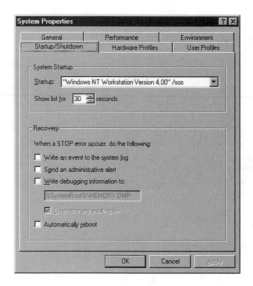

With the System Startup options, you can easily configure the [default] section of the BOOT.INI file, which is possibly the safest way for a beginner.

The Recovery options tell Windows NT what actions are taken in the unlikely event of a system crash. System crashes, which should be very rare, are also called the Blue Screen of Death because all you see is a blue screen containing details of the crash when Windows NT really crashes.

You have several options, and you can choose any or all (or none) of them:

☐ Write an Event to the System Log: When NT crashes, this option writes an event to NT's event log. You can view this later to determine the cause of the crash.

A

☐ Send an Administrative Alert: This option sends an alert to any user or system configured to get administrative alerts. A sample administrative alert is shown in Figure A.93. The information saved in the event log and the information displayed by this dialog are identical.

Figure A.93.

Alert after a system crash.

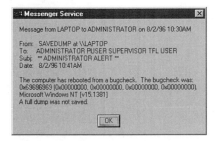

☐ Write Debugging Information: This choice determines whether you generate a full memory dump when the system crashes and where to write the memory dump.

☐ Automatically Reboot: In the event of a system crash, this option causes NT to reboot.

For most users, these options are probably not all that useful. In practice, NT is so stable that the options are rarely used. The memory dump in particular is huge (it is basically your entire swap file!) and tends to be useful only to highly trained technicians.

On my main desktop and laptop systems, I usually run with these options turned off. However, if you are a developer writing device drivers or other low-level code, these options are vital because they are often the only clue about why your code did not work as you intended.

Hardware Profiles

Hardware profiles provide a good way to create different configurations that you can choose at system startup. As noted in the sections "Devices" and "Services," you can disable almost any device or driver in a profile. This can be very useful for laptop users on the run—simply turn off all the services and drivers that are not actually needed.

By reducing services, you can reduce the system startup time and avoid running services that are not much good. Disabling the Alerter service might be quite sensible if you are using your laptop on an airplane—after all, who are you going to tell about administrative alerts when you're 35,000 feet over the North Atlantic?

The Hardware Profiles dialog, shown in Figure A.94, enables you to create, delete, and rename profiles and view and modify the property of a profile. You can also use this dialog to configure how NT should behave at startup with respect to hardware profiles.

Figure A.94.

Managing hardware profiles.

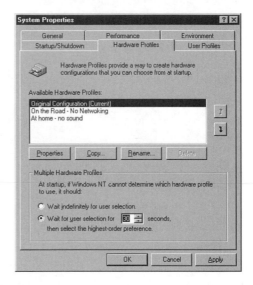

To create a new hardware profile, select an existing profile and click the Copy button. After a profile is created, you can rename it or delete it. The profile at the top of the Available Hardware Profiles list box is the default profile, and you can use the arrow buttons at the side of the dialog to adjust the order of the list.

When you define multiple hardware profiles, the section at the bottom of the Hardware Profiles dialog instructs Windows NT Workstation about its behavior at boot time. NT will either wait indefinitely for you to choose the profile or wait for some predefined time (the default is 30 seconds) and then choose the default hardware profile. Note that this menu appears in addition to the menu generated by the BOOT.INI file. You only see this menu if you have more than one hardware profile.

User Profiles

In Windows NT, all desktop and user-related settings are contained in a user profile and stored locally. These settings are set in the HKEY_CURRENT_USER tree in your system Registry. In addition, Windows NT creates a set of folders in the %SYSTEMROOT%\Profiles\userid directory, where userid is the user name you logged in with. This folder, which also is known as %USERPROFILE%, contains the contents of your desktop, your personal Start program menus, your favorite places, and your Send To menu.

If you use Windows NT Workstation on a computer that is a member of an NT Server domain, you can have a roaming profile. With roaming profiles, your profile is stored on a server and downloaded, if necessary, to your workstation each time you log in. Any changes are then uploaded back to the server when you log off.

Windows NT caches your profile locally and only downloads your profile when the locally cached profile is older than the profile on the server or when you have no profile currently cached on the system. Roaming profiles are very useful for users on the move, but they do have disadvantages.

Any file or folder stored on your desktop is automatically saved in the hidden directory %USERPROFILE%\Desktop. Dragging a couple of large files onto your desktop can dramatically increase the size of the Desktop subdirectory and the time it takes to download it from the server.

Each user who logs in to a Windows NT 4 system automatically gets a new set of profile directories created on that system. If you are the sort of user who has a lot of stuff on your desktop and you log in to a system, that desktop remains on that system until it's deleted.

The User Profiles dialog, shown in Figure A.95, shows you the profiles defined on your system, the user who created each profile, and its current size. For users in an NT Server domain, the profile can be changed from a local profile to a roaming profile—if you are not in a domain, this option is grayed out.

Figure A.95.

User profiles.

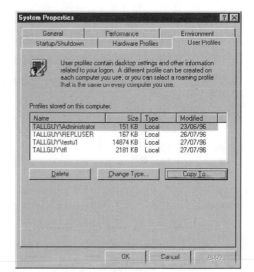

As you can see in Figure A.95, the user testu1 has a large profile, nearly 15MB on my system! If this were a roaming profile, it certainly would take some time to download. If you select the profile and click the Delete button, the profile is deleted from your system.

Tape Devices

For many users, tape backup is the main method of backup. With CDR drives becoming affordable and new devices such as Iomega's ZIP and JAZ drives appearing on the market, the primacy of tape is, if not threatened, at least under review for the Windows NT Workstation user. With disk prices falling by the week, why bother backing up?

Windows NT comes with a built-in backup utility, NTBACKUP. The important thing about this program is that it can back up, and later restore, your Registry.

NT Backup supports only a small range of tape devices, including QIC 40 and QIC 80 IDE-based devices and a wide range of 4MM DAT drives. For full details about the devices supported, you should refer to the hardware compatibility list.

To install, you first start the Tape Devices applet, shown in Figure A.96. This simple applet lets you detect and install a tape drive and load and unload tape device drivers.

Figure A.96.

Tape devices.

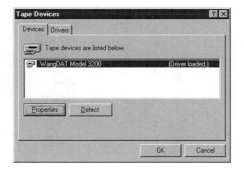

The first time you run this applet, the drive list will probably be empty. If so (and if you have a tape drive installed), simply click the Detect button, and the Tape Devices applet searches for a supported tape drive. If it finds one, it pops up a dialog box similar to the one in Figure A.97, from which you can install the necessary device driver. Be sure to have your installation CD-ROM available.

A

Figure A.97.

Installing a tape device.

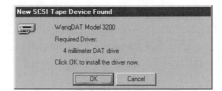

After the tape device is installed, you can use the Properties button in the Tape Devices applet to bring up the detailed properties, as shown in Figure A.98 and Figure A.99. This is probably extra information, but if you're installing the tape drive for the first time, it doesn't hurt to check that NT did pick up the right device.

Figure A.98.

Tape drive general properties.

Figure A.99.

Tape device settings.

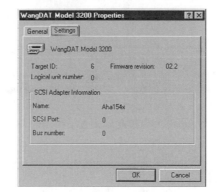

As with SCSI adapters, you can install the tape device drivers independently of the tape device itself. This might be particularly useful if you use one or more external tape devices. You can install the device driver and then configure the actual tape drive when necessary. To do this, select the Drivers tab from the Tape Device applet to display the dialog shown in Figure A.100.

Figure A.100.

Tape drivers.

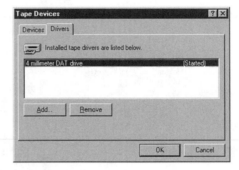

Only members of the Administrator's local group can add or remove tape device drivers.

Telephony

As noted in the section "Modems" earlier in this appendix, Windows NT comes with some powerful telephony functions, often referred to as TAPI (Telephony API). The TAPI functions are used in Windows NT Workstation's Dial-Up Networking feature to dial the modem.

Central to TAPI is the concept of a location. A TAPI location is the place you are dialing from and includes the details of how you dial your phone. In a dial-up networking connection, you specify the details of the system you are dialing, including the country it's in and its dialing code and phone number. When TAPI dials this connection, it can work out where you're dialing from and add any necessary dialing codes (for area, country, and so on).

If you're moving around from place to place, country to country, this can be a major time saver. When you get to a new location, just start the Telephony Control Panel applet and define a new location, and you can then correctly dial any of the sites in your DUN phone book. If (or when) you return to a previously defined location, you just select the location before dialing. It couldn't be simpler.

A

The Telephony applet is shown in Figure A.101. This allows you to select, remove, or modify a location or define an entirely new location. Unlike most of the other applets, the name of the applet (Telephony) is quite different from the name of dialog box (Dialing Properties). Don't let this throw you!

Figure A.101.

Telephony (Dialing Properties).

At the top of this dialog box, you can select an existing location with the pull-down combo box. If you type a new name into the combo box and click the New button, you can create a new location. If you have more than one location defined, you can select any of the locations and delete it.

To define a dialing location, you must first specify where the location is in terms of the country or area code. Note that some countries use different terms for what TAPI calls the area code. The United Kingdom, for example, uses the term dialing code or STD code instead of area code. As far as TAPI is concerned, these are the same.

The dialing codes should remain more or less constant, but they might not! TAPI country codes are stored in the Registry under the key HKEY_LOCAL_MACHINE\SOFTWARE \Microsoft\Windows\CurrentVersion\Telephony\Providers. The details of country names are stored using Unicode, so be careful when making any changes to these settings.

After defining your country and area codes, you need to define how you get an outside line. Generally, most offices use a 9 to get an outside line, regardless of whether it's local or long distance, but some offices use different codes.

TAPI assumes all calls are via an outside line and inserts the outside line code or long distance code for all calls. TAPI also uses the long distance code any time it needs to add the area code, which includes any international calls (that is, where it also has to add a country code).

The next configuration item is the Calling Card setup. You usually simply dial most calls and let the call charges fall on the owner of the phone connection you're using. If you are using a calling card or phone company credit card to pay for the call, select the Dial Using Calling Card box and then configure your calling card details by clicking the Change button. This displays the Change Calling Card dialog shown in Figure A.102.

Figure A.102.

Change calling card setup.

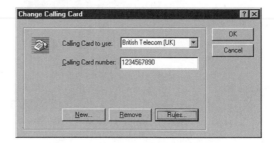

If your credit or phone calling card is not listed, you can select the New button on the Change Calling Card to define a new card. After entering the new card name, you are prompted to define the Dialing Rules, using the dialog box shown in Figure A.103. This tells TAPI what tones to dial in order to invoke the new calling card.

Figure A.103.

Calling card dialing rules.

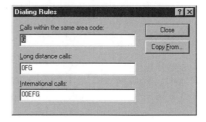

Call waiting is a feature of most modern phone systems that tells you that someone else is trying to dial you when you're talking on the phone. This is neat because the second caller is unaware that you are busy. However, the call-waiting signal neatly disrupts modem traffic, usually killing the call. If you have this feature on your phone, click the This Location Has Call Waiting checkbox and enter the sequence of digits to disable it.

Most telephones and company switchboards these days use tone dialing, but there are still a lot of places where this is not available or the PABX does not support tone dialing. In these cases, you need to select Pulse dialing from the Dialing Properties dialog.

At first sight, this seems like a lot of effort to go through just to dial up a BBS or your Internet provider, but in practice, you usually can set up a new location in a matter of seconds. The tricky thing is getting the first location right!

UPS

Electricity to power a computer is something we take for granted. Generally, you just plug in your PC, turn it on, and it works. From time to time, the power to the socket you use for the system can disappear. This loss can be caused by something as simple as someone accidentally pulling the wrong fuse or a temporary loss of all main power. In today's crowded office where four-way power extensions are almost a normal occurrence, loss of power is all too common.

One solution to this possible loss of power is an Uninterruptible Power Supply, or UPS. A UPS is nothing more than a large, expensive, rechargeable battery, possibly with some intelligence built in. It's a simple concept, but when the power goes off, a UPS can be a life-saver.

A modern UPS can also provide line filtering. This can prevent voltage spikes from damaging delicate computer equipment or prevent temporary voltage drops from affecting your system. Line spikes are all too common in older office blocks or houses that were probably not designed to handle today's modern power requirements.

The two types of UPS are intelligent and dumb. A dumb UPS just provides a simple battery capability: When main power is lost, the battery kicks in and provides the computer with power. Hopefully, the main power is restored before the battery runs down.

You can set up an intelligent UPS to communicate with Windows NT via a serial port. This allows the UPS to inform Windows NT that the power has been lost (or restored), which allows the UPS service to shut down the system gracefully. Before you can use this feature, you need to configure the UPS service using the UPS applet, shown in Figure A.104. You must be a member of the Administrator's local group to manage the UPS.

Figure A.104.

Configuring the UPS.

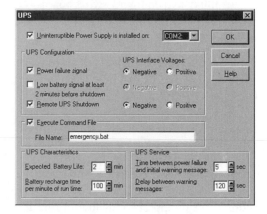

Because the UPS service can support an intelligent UPS only via a serial port, you first must tell Windows NT which port to monitor. This can be any configured serial port (as defined with the Ports applet).

Because a UPS has no automatic configuration, you must tell Windows NT the details about the UPS, including the following information (where appropriate):

☐ Power Failure Signal: If the UPS has this feature, power loss is communicated using the CTS cable signal. You need to tell the UPS service which voltage on the cable is set to indicate power loss (this information is in your UPS documentation).

☐ Low Battery Signal: If the UPS can tell Windows NT that the battery is low, you select this and define the voltage. The Low Battery condition is signaled using the DCD cable signal.

☐ Remote UPS Shutdown: If the UPS can accept a Remote Shutdown signal from the computer, this is signaled on the DTR cable signal. Even if you do not intend to use this facility, be sure to configure it.

If your UPS has a power failure signal but does not support the low battery facility, you must define the UPS characteristics in terms of Expected Battery Life and the Battery Recharge Time. You will find these figures in the documentation that accompanied your UPS.

If power is lost and NT determines that the battery is nearly exhausted because of the expected battery life or a low battery signal, it starts shutting down the system.

If you select the Execute Command File option and enter a filename, NT executes a command before shutting down the system. This command could attempt to gracefully close applications, for example, or send messages over the network indicating that shutdown is imminent. This command file must be either a batch or an executable file and must reside in the %SYSTEMROOT%\SYSTEM32 directory.

If the UPS implements a power failure signal, NT issues administrative alerts after the power failure is first detected and follows with alerts at regular intervals. You can configure the length of time the UPS service waits before issuing the first warning and the time between warnings using the two spin boxes in the UPS Service group.

Systems Management: Managing the System Using the Control Panel

The previous sections have introduced in some detail the various functions of the Control Panel. In this final section, I look at a few specific management tasks you might need to perform and which Control Panel applets would assist you.

Display

Some users tend to play around with their system settings and get their systems into a terrible state. Use the Display applet to fix display settings. If things get too bad, use the User Profiles dialog in the System applet to remove the profile altogether.

Modems

Configuring modems successfully is a bit of a black art. If you have trouble communicating with a remote site, try creating a modem log. This might assist in tracking down modem problems.

The default modem initialization strings set by Windows NT when you install the modem always enable all modems to reliably connect to all remote systems—sometimes, you must change or add specific settings. Use the Modem's Properties | Connections | Advanced to set these additional initialization settings.

Keyboard and Mouse

Use the Keyboard and Mouse applets to adjust the keyboard to your personal tastes. Remember that the Accessibility settings can override keyboard settings.

Troubleshooting Services and Devices

If devices or services fail to start during the boot process, you get a message suggesting that you look at the event viewer for more details. Sometimes, particularly if users are playing around, the system attempts to start drivers that do not exist or for which it does not have the appropriate hardware. Fix this with the Drivers applet by disabling the driver.

Although most services start with no user or password specified, some services do require that you specify a user ID. Use the Services applet to correctly specify the user name and password to start each service.

NT comes with the latest drivers for supported hardware. However, the drivers for most hardware are in a state of continuous improvement. If you have problems with a device, one possible solution is always new or updated drivers, which you usually can obtain from the hardware vendor's Internet or BBS site. Use the Control Panel to install new SCSI controllers and network and multimedia drivers.

Some motherboards do not allow Windows NT to use more than a certain amount of RAM, regardless of how many SIMM chips you add. Others might need BIOS settings changed before it can use the new RAM. If you add more RAM to your system, check the System applet to ensure that Windows NT is actually using the extra memory.

If you get regular Blue Screens of Death (that is, NT crashes), use the System applet to create a dump file. This might help the hardware vendor or Microsoft support track down the problem.

Sound

Turn sound schemes off unless you really need them.

A

INDEX

Symbols

Peter Norton's Complete Guide to Windows NT 4 Workstation

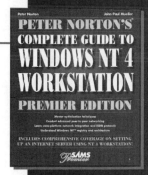

—Peter Norton and John Paul Mueller

This book explores everything from interface issues to advanced topics such as client/server networking, building your own Internet server, and OLE. Readers will master complex memory management techniques. Explores peer-to-peer networking.

$39.99 USA/$56.95 CDN   *User level: Casual — Accomplished*

ISBN: 0-672-30901-7   *936 pp.*

Windows NT 4 Server Unleashed

—Jason Garms, et al.

The Windows NT server has been gaining tremendous market share over Novell, and the new upgrade—which includes a Windows 95 interface—is sure to add momentum to its market drive. To that end, Windows NT 4.0 Server Unleashed is written for that growing market. It provides information on disk and file management, integrated networking, BackOffice integration, and TCP/IP protocols. The CD-ROM includes source code from the book and valuable utilities. Focuses on using Windows NT as an Internet server. Covers security issues and Macintosh support.

$59.99 USA/$84.95 CDN   *User level: Accomplished — Expert*

ISBN: 0-672-30933-5   *1,100 pp.*

Windows NT 4 Web Development

—Sanjaya Hettihewa

Windows NT and Microsoft's newly developed Internet Information Server are making it easier and more cost-effective to set up, manage, and administer a good Web site. Because the Windows NT environment is relatively new, there are few books on the market that adequately discusses its full potential. Windows NT 4 Web Development addresses that potential by providing information on all key aspects of server setup, maintenance, design, and implementation. The CD-ROM contains valuable source code and powerful utilities. Teaches how to incorporate new technologies into your Web site. Covers Java, JavaScript, Internet Studio, and Visual Basic Script.

$59.99 USA/$84.95 CDN   *User level: Accomplished — Expert*

ISBN: 1-57521-089-4   *744 pp.*

Programming Windows NT 4 Unleashed

—David Hamilton, Mickey Williams, and Griffith Kadnier

This book gives you a clear understanding of the modes of operation and architecture for Windows NT. Execution models, processes, threads, DLLs, memory, controls, security, and more are covered with precise detail. The CD-ROM contains source code and completed sample programs from the book. Teaches OLE, DDE, Drag and Drop, OCX development, and the component gallery. Explores Microsoft BackOffice programming.

$59.99 USA/$84.95 CDN   *User level: Accomplished – Expert*

ISBN: 0-672-30905-X   *1,200 pp.*

Designing and Implementing Microsoft Internet Information Server 2

—Arthur Knowles and Sanjaya Hettihewa

This book details the specific tasks involved in setting up and running a Microsoft Internet Information Server. Readers will learn troubleshooting, network design, security, and cross-platform integration procedures. Teaches security issues and how to maintain an efficient, secure network. Readers learn everything from planning to implementation.

$39.99 USA/$56.95 CDN   *User level: Casual – Expert*

ISBN: 1-57521-168-8   *336 pp.*

Microsoft Internet Information Server 2 Unleashed

—Arthur Knowles, et al.

The power of the Microsoft Internet Information Server 2 is meticulously detailed in this 800-page volume. Readers will learn how to create and maintain a Web server, integrate IIS with BackOffice, and create interactive databases that can be used on the Internet or a corporate intranet. Readers learn how to set up and run IIS. Teaches advanced security techniques and how to configure the server. CD-ROM includes source code from the book and powerful utilities.

$49.99 USA/$70.95 CDN   *User level: Accomplished – Expert*

ISBN: 1-57521-109-2   *800 pp.*

Microsoft Exchange Server Survival Guide

—Greg Todd, et al

Readers will learn the difference between Exchange and other groupware such as Lotus Notes. This book also covers everything about the Exchange Server, including trouble-shooting, development, and how to interact with other BackOffice components. Includes everything operators need to run an Exchange server. Teaches how to prepare, plan, and install the Exchange server. Explores ways to migrate from other mail apps such as Microsoft Mail and cc:Mail.

$49.99 USA/$70.95 CDN   *User level: New – Advanced*

ISBN: 0-672-30890-8   *800 pp.*

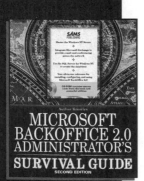

Microsoft BackOffice 2.0 Administrator's Survival Guide, Second Edition

—Arthur Knowles

This all-in-one reference describes how to make the components of BackOffice version 2.0 work best together and with other networks. BackOffice is Microsoft's complete reference for networking, database, and system management products. Contains the fundamental concepts required for daily maintenance, troubleshooting, and problem solving. The CD-ROM includes product demos, commercial and shareware utilities, and technical notes from Microsoft vendor technical support personnel. Covers Version 2.0

$59.99 USA/$84.95 CDN   *User level: Accomplished*

ISBN: 0-672-30977-7   *1,200 pp.*

Add to Your Sams Library Today with the Best Books for Programming, Operating Systems, and New Technologies

The easiest way to order is to pick up the phone and call

1-800-428-5331

between 9:00 a.m. and 5:00 p.m. EST.
For faster service please have your credit card available.

ISBN	Quantity	Description of Item	Unit Cost	Total Cost
0-672-30901-7		Peter Norton's Complete Guide to Windows NT 4 Workstation	$39.99	
0-672-30933-5		Windows NT 4 Server Unleashed (Book/CD-ROM)	$59.99	
1-57521-089-4		Windows NT 4 Web Development (Book/CD-ROM)	$59.99	
0-672-30905-X		Programming Windows NT 4 Unleashed (Book/CD-ROM)	$59.99	
1-57521-168-8		Designing and Implementing Microsoft Internet Information Server 2	$39.99	
1-57521-109-2		Microsoft Internet Information Server 2 Unleashed (Book/CD-ROM)	$49.99	
0-672-30890-8		Microsoft Exchange Server Survival Guide	$49.99	
0-672-30977-7		Microsoft BackOffice 2.0 Administrator's Survival Guide, Second Edition (Book/CD-ROM)	$59.99	
❏ 3 ½" Disk		Shipping and Handling: See information below.		
❏ 5 ¼" Disk		TOTAL		

Shipping and Handling: $4.00 for the first book, and $1.75 for each additional book. Floppy disk: add $1.75 for shipping and handling. If you need to have it NOW, we can ship product to you in 24 hours for an additional charge of approximately $18.00, and you will receive your item overnight or in two days. Overseas shipping and handling adds $2.00 per book and $8.00 for up to three disks. Prices subject to change. Call for availability and pricing information on latest editions.

201 W. 103rd Street, Indianapolis, Indiana 46290

1-800-428-5331 — Orders   1-800-835-3202 — Fax   1-800-858-7674 — Customer Service

Book ISBN 0-672-31011-2

MACMILLAN COMPUTER PUBLISHING USA
A VIACOM COMPANY

Technical Support:

If you need assistance with the information in this book or with a CD/Disk
accompanying the book, please access the Knowledge Base on our Web
site at **http://www.superlibrary.com/general/support**. Our most
Frequently Asked Questions are answered there. If you do not find the
answer to your questions on our Web site, you may contact Macmillan
Technical Support **(317) 581-3833** or e-mail us at **support@mcp.com**.

The Common Control Panel Applets

Icon	Control Panel Applet	Applet Function	System or User Setting
	Accessibility Options	Changes the accessibility options	User
	Add/Remove Programs	Installs and deinstalls certain applications and key NT components	System
	Console	Configures the console window	User
	CSNW	Configure Client Services for NetWare	User
	Date/Time	Sets the date, time, and time zone	System
	Devices	Starts/stops device drivers	System
	Dial-Up Monitor	Monitors the dial-up port(s)	System
	Display	Changes the Display settings	User/System
	Fonts	Displays, adds, or removes fonts	System
	Internet	Configures Internet Explorer settings	System
	Keyboard	Configures your keyboard	User/System
	Mail	Manages Microsoft Exchange profiles	User
	Microsoft Mail Post Office	Sets up and maintains a Microsoft Mail Workgroup Post Office	System
	Modems	Installs and configures your modem	System
	Mouse	Configures the mouse	User